# BEHAVIOURAL ANALYSIS OF CRIME

# PSYCHOLOGY, CRIME AND LAW SERIES

*Series Editor: David Canter*
*International Centre for Investigative Psychology*
*The University of Liverpool, UK*

**Other titles in the series**

Psychological Expertise in Court
Psychology in the Courtroom, Volume II
*Daniel A. Krauss and Joel D. Lieberman*

Jury Psychology: Social Aspects of Trial Processes
Psychology in the Courtroom, Volume I
*Daniel A. Krauss and Joel D. Lieberman*

Principles of Geographical Offender Profiling
*David Canter and Donna Youngs*

Applications of Geographical Offender Profiling
*David Canter and Donna Youngs*

Psychology and Law: Bridging the Gap
*David Canter and Rita Žukauskienė*

The Investigative Psychology of Serial Killing (forthcoming)
*David Canter and Donna Youngs*

Profiling Violent Crime (forthcoming)
*David Canter and Donna Youngs*

# The Behavioural Analysis of Crime:

## Studies in David Canter's Investigative Psychology

Edited by
DONNA YOUNGS
*The International Research Centre for Investigative Psychology*

Routledge
Taylor & Francis Group
LONDON AND NEW YORK

First published 2013 by Ashgate Publishing

Published 2016 by Routledge
2 Park Square, Milton Park, Abingdon, Oxon OX14 4RN
711 Third Avenue, New York, NY 10017, USA

*Routledge is an imprint of the Taylor & Francis Group, an informa business*



**British Library Cataloguing in Publication Data**
Behavioural analysis of crime : studies in David Canter's investigative psychology. – (Psychology, crime and law series)
1. Canter, David V. 2. Criminal psychology. 3. Crime forecasting.
I. Series II. Youngs, Donna.

**Library of Congress Cataloging-in-Publication Data**
Behavioural analysis of crime : studies in David Canter's investigative psychology / [edited] by Donna Youngs.
pages cm. – (Psychology, crime and law)
Includes bibliographical references and index.
ISBN 978-0-7546-2622-0 (hbk) – ISBN 978-0-7546-2628-2 (pbk)
1. Criminal psychology. 2. Criminal behavior, Prediction of. 3. Criminal investigation–Psychological aspects. 4. Canter, David V. I. Youngs, Donna, editor of compilation.
HV6080.B394 2013
364.3–dc23

2012051338

ISBN 9780754626220 (hbk)
ISBN 9780754626282 (pbk)

# Contents

**SECTION 3: IP: A PROBLEM-SOLVING DISCIPLINE**



**SECTION 4: SELECTED WORKS OF PROFESSOR CANTER**

# List of Figures

# List of Tables

# Editor's Notes

Although the studies presented in this volume represent only a very select sample of Professor Canter's research directions, developed by the elite of the young researchers who have worked with him to date, the range of Investigative Psychology topics addressed is enormous. To help the reader, I have therefore provided an introductory overview chapter that sets out some of the basic premises of the Canter-IP approach.

I also provide a brief commentary at the start of each chapter to help the reader position each individual's contribution within the overall Canter-IP framework and in particular relate it to a few of his recent key writings. The writings I cite in these commentaries are listed below for ease of reference.

Donna Youngs
Cambridge, September 2013

**Selected References**

A useful reading list for any serious scholar of Professor Canter's Investigative Psychology. Further reading on Investigative Psychology: www.davidcanter.com; www.ia-ip.org


Bennell, C. and Canter, D. (2002). Linking Commercial Burglaries by Modus Operandi: Tests using Regression and ROC Analysis. *Science and Justice*, 42, 153–164.

Canter, D.V. (1995). Psychology of Offender Profiling, in R. Bull and D. Carson (eds) *Handbook of Psychology in Legal Contexts*. Chichester: Wiley Chapter (4.5, pp. 343–335).

Canter, D. (1995a). *Criminal Shadows*. London: Harper Collins.

Canter, D. (2000). Offender Profiling and Criminal Differentiation. *Legal and Criminological Psychology*, 5, 23–46.

Canter, D.V. (2011). Resolving the Offender 'Profiling Equations' and the Emergence of an Investigative Psychology. *Current Directions in Psychological Science*, 20, 5–10.

Canter, D.V. and Alison, L.J. (2003). Converting Evidence into Data: The Use of Law Enforcement Archives as Unobtrusive Measurement. *The Qualitative Report*, 8, June.

Canter, D. and Fritzon, K. (1998). Differentiating Arsonists: A Model of Fire Setting Actions and Characteristics. *Legal and Criminological Psychology*, 3, 73–96.

Canter, D. and Heritage, R. (1990). A Multivariate Model of Sexual Offence Behaviour: Developments in 'Offender Profiling'. *The Journal of Forensic Psychiatry*, 1, 185–212.

Canter, D.V. and Youngs, D.E. (2003). Beyond 'Offender Profiling'. The Need for an Investigative Psychology, in D. Carson and R. Bull (eds) *Handbook of Psychology in Legal Contexts*. Chichester, UK: John Wiley and Sons p. 233–249.

Canter, D. and Youngs, D. (eds) (2008a). *Principles of Geographical Offender Profiling*. Aldershot: Ashgate.

Canter, D. and Youngs, D. (eds) (2008b). *Applications of Geographical Offender Profiling*. Aldershot: Ashgate.

Canter, D. and Youngs, D. (2008c). iOPS: An Interactive Offender Profiling System, in S. Chainey and I. Thompson (eds) *Crime Mapping Case Studies*. Wiley: Chichester.

Canter, D. and Youngs, D. (2009). *Investigative Psychology: Offender Profiling and the Analysis of Criminal Action*. Chichester, UK: Wiley.

Canter, D. and Youngs, D. (2012a). Narratives of Criminal Action and Forensic Psychology. *Legal and Criminological Psychology*, 00, 1–17.

Canter, D. and Youngs, D. (2012b). Victim Role Assignments of Sexual and Violent Offenders: A Generic Model for the Differentiation of Offending Style. *Journal of Forensic Psychiatry and Psychology*.

Canter, D., Youngs, D. and Hammond, L. (forthcoming). *Systemic Modelling of Criminal Acitons: Pitfalls and Potential*.

Youngs, D. and Canter, D. (2011). Narrative Roles in Criminal Action: An Integrative Framework for Differentiating Offenders. *Legal and Criminological Psychology*, p. 171–207. ISSN 1355-3259.

Youngs, D. and Canter, D. (2012). Offenders' Crime Narratives as Revealed by the Narrative Roles Questionnaire. *International Journal of Offender Therapy and Comparative Criminology*, pp. 1–23. ISSN 0306-624X.

Chapter 1

# Investigative Psychology: David Canter's Approach to Studying Criminals and Criminal Action

Donna Youngs

It is not possible to capture anything more than a flavour of Professor Canter's contributions thus far to 20th and 21st century social scientific activity in a single volume. In part this is because he is a prolific scientist, exploring everything from alternative medicine (Canter, 1995) to open plan offices, with consultancy work on biscuit and chocolate usage, and the impact of solitary confinement along the way.

The focus in this chapter is on his work in relation to crime and criminals which has dominated his activities for the last quarter of a century. It is no exaggeration to say that he masterminded and actualised the development of a whole new sub-discipline within psychology in a few short years. Working with a team of energetic PhD students, he carried out most of the studies that laid the basis of the new sub-discipline of Investigative Psychology. This early work inspired a first generation of Investigative Psychologists many of whom are now established figures themselves and have contributed to this book.

Others have taken his ideas into a practical context and as a result of what they learnt under his tutelage are now changing the way investigation systems work around the world. Professor Canter himself eschewed the lure of becoming the police's expert 'profiler', preferring instead to limit his forays into working with the police or lawyers to those cases where the science was being used in new and innovative ways. This has given rise, for example, to ways of assessing the possibility of entrapment by undercover officers both in cases of supplying drugs and those pertaining to anti-terrorist legislation. Another instance is his work exploring the veracity of rape allegations.

Perhaps one of his most significant contributions to actual cases in court grew out of his concern at the hold that the Cusum technique was starting to have in legal proceedings, purporting to be able to determine whether the claimed authorship of questioned documents or statements was trustworthy. Notably, he set about carrying out careful studies of the proposed Cusum procedure (Canter, 1992) and even managed to get the Crown Prosecution Service to fund a detailed report that resulted in Cusum no longer being allowed as evidence.

His fascination with the role of psychological analysis of linguistic claims, like Cusum, which have legal implications, that he has called Forensic Psycholinguistics (Canter, 2000), reached widespread public notice in his examination of the conviction of Eddie Gilfoyle for the murder of his wife Paula, even though a suicide note clearly written by Paula was found at the time of her death. Once again, his initial interest in the psycholinguistic challenge of determining the validity of the suicide note, which friends of Paula had claimed was dictated by Eddie, led Professor Canter to set up studies of suicide and associated notes which gave rise to a number of postgraduate dissertations and pieces he wrote directly for *The Times* (<http://hopc.bps.org.uk/hopc/hopc_home.cfm>; see Canter, 2005).

But the challenge in capturing Professor Canter's contributions to date is also a product of their eclectic nature and his refusal to follow the perhaps easier, more narrowly-defined route to personal success that is the tradition within academia. Many of those who know him in the investigative context are familiar with his related contributions to the understanding of human behaviour in emergencies from the Bradford City Football Ground fire that gave rise to his contribution to the Popplewell Enquiry and his subsequent book *Football in its Place* (Canter et al., 1989). He also contributed to the Taylor Enquiry that followed the King's Cross underground fire (Donald and Canter, 1990). More recently he has studied the evacuation of the World Trade Centre on 9/11. But they are surprised to hear that Investigative Psychology is not the first sub-discipline he has been centrally responsible for creating. Professor Canter's first specialisation in what became known as Environmental Psychology was originally known as Architectural Psychology. Indeed in his early 20's when he was a PhD student in the School of Architecture at Strathclyde University (studying the psychological effects of open plan offices, Canter 1968) he organised the first ever Architectural Psychology conference to be held outside the US (Canter, 1970). This involvement in the exploration of human activity in naturally occurring settings was very influential in leading him into his subsequent study of behaviour in emergencies, which was the launch pad for contributing to police investigations out of which Investigative Psychology grew. (He describes this in *Mapping Murder* (Canter, 2003), as well as in his bestselling *Criminal Shadows* (Canter, 1994). This intellectual pathway is also documented in Canter (1996) and at <http://hopc.bps.org.uk/hopc/hopc_home.cfm>.

## Professor Canter's Investigative Psychology

From his early work contributing to police investigations and his awareness of how scientific disciplines develop through his experience of the growth of Environmental Psychology, Canter identified Investigative Psychology as a scientific discipline waiting to happen. He saw the need to bring together the contributions that psychology can make to the investigation of all forms of criminal behaviour through the psychological and social scientific analysis of the actions of offenders as well as the investigative strategies and legal processes (for overviews, see Canter, 1993; Canter and Youngs, 2009; and Canter, 2011). From the start he was clear that this encompasses the modelling of patterns of criminal action to facilitate the identification and location of a potential perpetrator through to examinations of detective decision making and interview strategies in an investigation and on to assessments of the credibility and validity of evidence as well as the effective court presentation of the case. It also quickly became apparent that many aspects of legal and investigative processes in civil as well as criminal courts, such as psychological autopsies (Canter, 2000), hostage negotiation and the examination of criminal networks or the forensic psycholinguistics of anonymous letters, were all very appropriately within the Investigative Psychology domain.

Given its power and breadth it is perhaps not surprising, then, that Investigative Psychology represents an increasingly prominent perspective among criminal psychologists. It has reset the focus of forensic psychology over the last two decades, perhaps prompting the Telegraph's description of Professor Canter as 'the father of forensic psychology in the UK'. But it is particularly noteworthy that despite its origins deep within scientific, academic activity, Investigative Psychology has also had a significant impact on investigative practice throughout the world, underpinning the development of 'offender profiling' and 'geographical offender profiling', for example. Specialist IP units now exist in countries including Japan, Israel and South Africa. In the US recognition of his contribution to Geographical Offender Profiling has led to national debate about the most effective of these techniques (National Institute Justice: Evaluation Geographic Profiling Debate; 8th International Crime Mapping Research Conference September 2005, Savannah, USA)

But perhaps the broadest legacy of the rapid emergence of Canter's Investigative Psychology will come from his mapping out of an approach to psychological research, through the development of this discipline, which has relevance far beyond the criminal context. This is an approach to studying people and their actions in their natural context. In conversation Professor Canter has often referred to this approach as a form of anthropology or even archaeology. By this he means it is a psychological study that looks at what actually happens rather than creating artificial, laboratory situations in which to study behaviour. This is not to confuse his work with the anthropological and archaeological study of cultures past and present. His work is still firmly rooted in the study of individuals. He is also quite comfortable with standard psychological procedures such as questionnaires, provided they deal directly with aspects of people's actual lives, although he has favoured work that examines their actions rather than what they say about them. Further he has always claimed that it is most appropriate for psychologists to attempt to answer questions initially formulated by people who must act on the answers. This eschews issues that are only of interest to other academic psychologists, but does not prevent him from encouraging exploration of fundamental psychological issues that may be relevant to assisting practitioners and policy makers.

However, he has long emphasised that there is a world of difference between applicable research, applied research and consultancy. Canter sees the need to formulate research questions, methods and results that enables the work to be drawn on by practitioners. Yet he distinguishes this scientific activity from what he calls 'engineering', which is the attempt to build processes and conclusions that can be put directly into use. The overall principles (see Table 1.1) on which the approach is based are described in Canter (1993), Canter (2000) and Canter and Youngs (2009).

It is an approach that seeks to work directly with the material available within any context no matter how limited or challenging that 'data' may be. But although problem-focused it is an approach that looks for solutions in the understanding of human meaning and agency. This comes together in the approaches Canter developed to allow the advanced and complex quantitative modelling of psychologically-rich qualitative material, producing models that give rise to problem-solving tools and solutions. It is illustrated well, for instance, in his development of methods for linking crimes that draws on advanced conceptual models generated by a form of non-metric multi-dimensional scaling (see Canter and Youngs, 2009).

Investigative Psychology, both as the specific crime and investigation-focused discipline and as a style of and approach to doing psychological and social research, emerged as a result of the tension created by Canter's attempts to resolve the inherent contradictions in the particular intellectual tendencies and convictions he held. David Canter spent the first six years of his early career within a School of Architecture, where the humanist, artistic academic tradition merges with the concrete, mechanical disciplines. Within this context he developed a keen sense of the different contributions of the different forms of academic discipline to the human condition. As he describes it he saw the engineering and technology disciplines that make life comfortable and the arts and humanities that make it worthwhile. His quest to integrate these fundamentally distinct ways of thinking about human beings is an influence that can be seen throughout his work.

**Table 1.1 Canter's principles for research**

| Principle no. | Canter research principle |
|---|---|
| 1 | All research has a philosophical style |
| 2 | Data speaks theories |
| 3 | Theories should be practical |
| 4 | Context provides meaning |
| 5 | Structures explain |
| 6 | Methodologies carry substantive assumptions |
| 7 | Research strategies imply types of psychological theory |
| 8 | Research tactics imply models of human beings |

*Source*: Adapted from Canter (2000) and Canter (1993).

David Canter is on the one hand, a conventional empirical scientist yet at the same time, paradoxically, has a strong interest in those aspects of psychology and in particular the significance of human agency that has its origins in the work of William James and George Kelly. He has always argued that, what was known in the 1960's as the 'third stream'of psychology – distinguished from the first stream of psychoanalysis and behaviourist second – a constructivist, humanist approach to looking at human beings, but using what many would regard as highly positivist, empirical procedures, was particularly appropriate for a problem-solving psychology that was firmly rooted in what he refers to as 'real world issues'. Three intellectual strands can be identified, then, within the work of this distinctive psychologist.

## 'Third Stream' Perspective on Human Beings

Professor Canter's core sympathies sit with the humanist and phenomenological schools. His researches draw on ways of understanding the individual that go back to William James, being concerned with the person's way of making sense of and dealing with the world. In line with Harre (1979) amongst many others, they assign the individual the role of expert on his or her own life. This standpoint was clear in his earliest student project, a study of his correspondence with his friend, film director Mike Leigh.

This concern with understanding the meanings events and objects have for people as the basis for understanding their behaviour is writ large in his long-standing interest in George Kelly's Personal Construct Theory. He has used this approach most recently and particularly notably in studies of the radicalisation processes of terrorists; although he first started using this procedure in the school of Architecture in the mid-60s. The studies of terrorists that he supervised (for example, Sarangi, Canter, and Youngs (in press)) were some of the first to examine directly the actual psychological processes of convicted terrorists. In the most recent example of this fascinating work, conducted with a senior police officer (Canter, Sarangi, and Youngs, 2012) Personal Constructs concerning the significant figures in their lives were elicited from 49 Islamic *Jihadis* in India.

These Personal Construct analyses throw light on the psychological processes of radicalisation of Islamic terrorists and the different pathways to terrorist involvement. To take just one example as an illustration, one terrorist saw himself as very law abiding at the time he met active terrorist X who he saw as a law breaker but he also saw the Police as law breakers. Curiously, the important people in his life include his wife and both Rajeev and Indira Ghandi. Furthermore analysis of this man's Repertory Grid also shows that this individual does not see any changes in his view of himself in relation to his involvement in terrorism. He was actually convicted of helping finance terrorism and declares that he has no commitment to an armed struggle. This challenges the common belief that Jihadi terrorists are simply driven by fundamentalist religious beliefs. It also shows how Canter sees psychological explanations as part of a broader social set of explanations which he brought together in his recent book on the *Faces of Terrorism* (Canter, 2009).

Some may be surprised to learn that a third stream perspective also runs through his Geographical profiling work. For although that is concerned with analysing offender spatial behaviour, it is through understanding the sense individuals make of their environments rather than the more mechanistic, direct route learning models that other researchers have implicitly favoured that he has developed his approach. This distinction between a general understanding of the environment and an unthinking use of it he recognised as reflecting the Hull-Tolman debate within 20th century psychology (see Canter and Youngs, 2007). Canter tied offender spatial behaviour into environmental psychological concepts from those outlined in his 'Theory of Place' (Canter, 1977) as well as ideas about mental maps, environmental buffers, scale consistency, domocentricity and magnitude estimation (Canter and Larkin, 1993; Canter and Gregory, 1994; Canter and Hodge, 1998; Canter and Hammond, 2006). The much-cited Commuter–Marauder model however was always a heuristic device rather than a psychological theory of offender spatial behaviour. His most recent thinking on the processes underpinning offenders' spatial decisions, described in the popular book *Mapping Murder* as well as the Investigative Psychology text (Canter and Youngs, 2009) is opening up considerations of individual differences in this field.

## A Problem-solving Focus

Professor Canter's research has been driven by a basic desire to do something useful. The origins of this no doubt lie in his socialist perspective on the world; the belief that everybody's challenges have merit and that the focus should be not on any value judgements but on overcoming those challenges. Canter wants to move away from what he saw as the default academic position whereby problems are defined in terms relevant to moving on a given discipline, meaning that academics end up talking only to each other. He sees such a focus as particularly inappropriate for a psychologist because psychology is fundamentally about how people deal with their world and interact with others. Moreover because human beings are enormously adaptable and responsive to their external environments any research that ignores the context of human activity is doomed to be superficial. Consequently, he remains deeply sceptical of the controlled laboratory experiment, with its reductionist, atomising of dependent and independent variables. He sees that methodological emphasis as destroying the possibility of considering the whole person.

Rather than attempting to control out the real world, Canter's argument is that research should find ways of exploring what people actually do and the processes that underlie those actions. This also allows research to be sufficiently grounded in the concerns of the real world and its results can be integrated directly with action strategies. In this way research is 'investigative' rather than simply 'applied' after the fact. It was his commitment to this framework for psychological contributions to police investigations that has encouraged the development of a new branch of science rather than this potential being used only to give rise to a small number of 'expert profilers'.

In many of his writings, Professor Canter makes the point that for theoretical as well as ideological reasons, researchers should focus on phenomena of interest to non-psychologists producing work of social value that respects the people it studies. As a result, his research has increasingly reflected a willingness to take the next step, to develop ideas of the implications of the work and convert these into procedures that would support decision makers. In private he mentions wryly his early applied research that produced massive documents with plenty of complex statistics that was just shelved by the policy makers who commissioned it, and how he learnt from that the importance of drawing out the implications of the work as simply and directly as possible, if anyone is to take any notice of it.

Two particularly important software tools have emerged as a result. One, Dragnet, a geographical offender profiling tool, that studies have shown can effectively predict the likely home base of a perpetrator from the location of his/her crimes (see Canter, 2005; Canter, Coffey, Missen, and Huntley, 2005). His most recent work in this area is revealing an exciting step-change in the precision of these predictions (Canter, 2011).

The second software tool is a decision support system for prioritising the likely perpetrator of a given crime and for linking offence series to a common offender. The IOPS version of this tool (see Figure 1.2), developed for the London Metropolitan police, drew on the 20 years of empirical findings from Canter's research team, to offer investigators the potential to improve their detection rates by very significant margins (see Canter and Youngs, 2008).

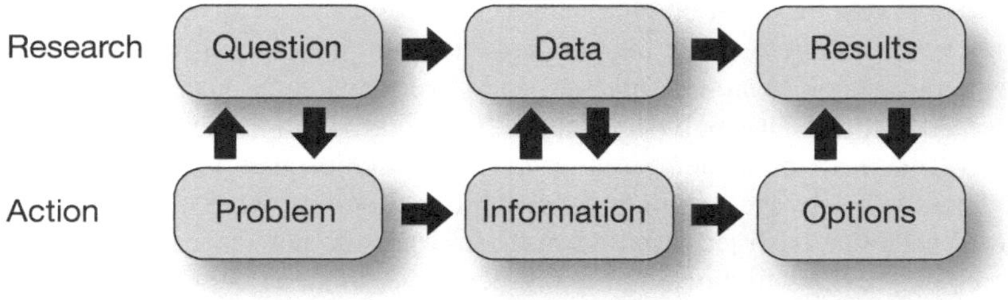


**Figure 1.1 Research that is 'investigative': Canter's framework for integrating research and action (adapted from Canter, 1993)**

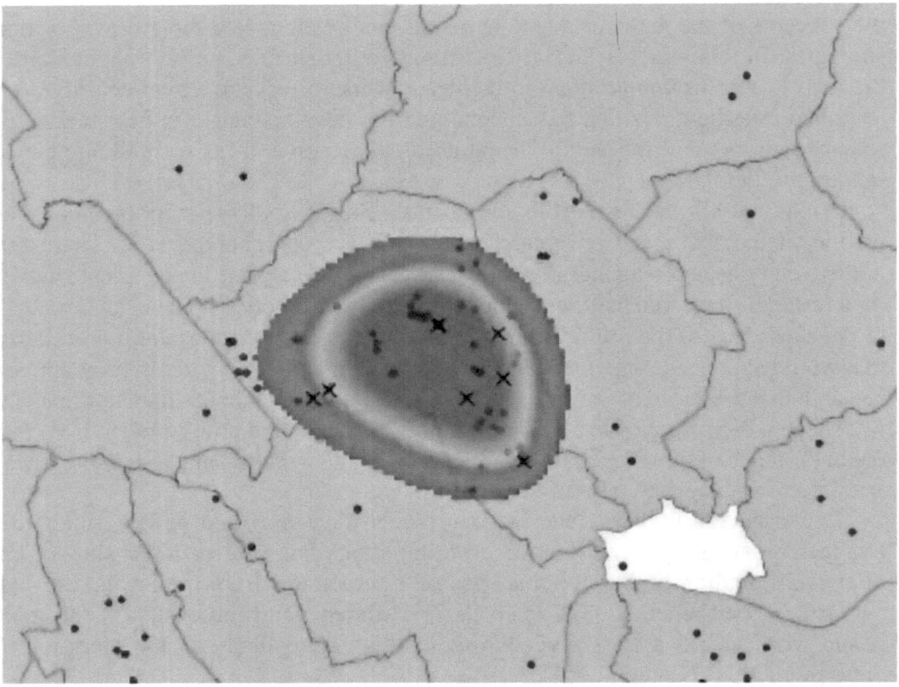

**Figure 1.2 A geographical profile of an offending series (the cross symbols), shown with possible suspects (the dot symbols)**

## An Empirical Emphasis

Professor Canter has always been an empirical scientist, schooled in the deep traditions of British psychology that emphasise data collection and analysis. For although he has always been interested in the humanist tradition it is only in the last few years in his popular book *Criminal Shadows*, and in very recent publications (Youngs and Canter, 2011) that he has published intensely qualitative studies exploring individual cases. Most of his published research has been highly quantitative often working with large data sets. He willingly follows the tradition of being genuinely directed by the results that emerged, even when those results do not accord with established theories or previous findings. On many occasions this has demanded recognising the limitations of existing complex psychological theories. Canter has always been ready to accept the significance of more prosaic concerns such as context and show how these concerns allowed a richer understanding of human behaviour.

This ability to draw more from the data than many of his contemporaries is facilitated by a remarkable proficiency with multivariate statistical approaches, particularly the integration of visual outputs from multi-dimensional scaling technique and the conceptual clarity of the facet theory approach (Canter, 1985). Students often despair at his ability to understand in a brief glance the meaning of a computer output that they have spent hours trying to make sense of. Yet they quickly embrace his excitement at the power of multi-dimensional procedures as the contributions to this volume illustrate.

He will argue forcefully whenever given the chance that the facet approach fuses qualitative and quantitative methodologies, allowing individuals and individual variables to be considered directly, as in the best qualitative traditions, whilst still seeing their role in the total picture. Canter also tells every student not to look for the precision of the sort of replicable results that are expected in laboratory studies, such as those exploring visual illusions or reaction times. Rather they should be aware of the huge variations in people and contexts that will make any general consistency from one sample to the next a real discovery. Indeed, over the years he has caught out a couple of fraudulent students by spotting that their results could not have been so tidy if they had not invented the data themselves.

## A Style of Research

Perhaps one of Canter's most iconoclastic comments is that researchers each have a preferred style of doing research. His recognition of this undoubtedly has its roots in his experience of architecture; in which 'style' is seen as the essence of great design and differences between styles are a valid source of study. In scientific circles the unwritten assumption is that each study uses the most appropriate methodology for the task at hand. Any individual preferences are supposed to be totally subservient to scientific purity. Canter challenges this: claiming that there can be a number of appropriate ways of studying psychological phenomena and the one chosen is partly a preference of the particular researcher, probably rooted in his education, experience and resources. Canter has therefore quite openly offered an approach to doing real-world research that he is comfortable with because it works for him. Hundreds of people who have studied with him have found the approach of value too, so that it has now become an accepted meta-methodology.

Anyone who has worked with 'real-world' data will recognise the challenge of making sense of it and studying it systematically to address those existing problems that are Canter's academic priority. Material from police investigations and court cases or crime scenes, or indeed many of the reviews of emergencies such as the King's Cross fire or 9/11, to which he contributed, does not exist in a form amenable to the average researcher. The now widely used 'Investigative Psychology' meta-method that Canter pioneered sets out an approach to overcoming the challenges at three key stages of the real-world research process. Different aspects and stages of his approach are described by Giles, Lee and Salfati in this volume.

*Data Harvesting*

As a first stage, it advances an approach to harvesting as data material from contexts that were not only not set up as 'experiments' for research but where the material was generated for alternative and often directly conflicting objectives, such as preparing the case for the defence, or personal letters that were never thought to be examined objectively. In his paper on 'Unobtrusive Measures' (Canter and Alison, 2003), he argues that the excitement over data sources in psychology that were not influenced by the processes of collecting the data, first articulated by Webb et al., (1966) is especially pertinent for the data that is at the heart of investigative psychology, such as crime scene reports, offence and offender locations and offensive letters. Of course these sources have their own biases that need to be taken into account, but they are naturally occurring biases, not distortions introduced by the researcher, as happens when people are given a task to perform.

The value of Canter's approach to research methodology is epitomised in the capability he developed to draw psychological patterns from crimes even though these are activities underpinned by the intent to conceal. This was first set out in the seminal paper with Rupert Heritage on modelling sexual assault (Canter and Heritage, 1990).

*Data-driven Content Analysis*

As a second stage, the Investigative Psychology meta-method advances an approach to the content analysis of naturally occurring data that has many parallels in other qualitative methodologies, but is perhaps closest to the 'grounded-theory' approach. David points out that it took about two years to find the appropriate level of analysis for the first paper he published on rape-statements (Canter and Heritage, 1990). Working with the police officer assigned to him for this work, Rupert Heritage, they had started with very detailed content categories, such as the arm being grabbed, or a cloth gag being fastened round the victim's mouth. But this generated a very sparse data matrix with very few examples of each behaviour across the sample of cases. Much broader categories, such as 'general aggression' or 'untidy search' could not be utilised with any inter-rater reliability, so they ended up with the mid-level categories that are now illustrated in many publications (for example, Canter, Kaouri, and Ioannou, 2003) and in chapters in this book.

It is apparent that Canter's approach to content analysis of crime scene material and witness statements was influenced by what he had found to be valuable in his earlier work, modelling human actions in buildings on fire (Canter, Donald, and Chalk, 1992). This distinguished it from the very detailed, highly quantitative approach to content analysis that computerised linguists have favoured. It was also compatible with the pointers that FBI agents, notably Hazelwood (1987) were giving at the time as part of their framework for creating typologies for use in profiling. However, unlike the FBI Canter followed the careful procedures of creating content dictionaries that were checked for reliability.

*Qualitative Structural Analysis*

The third stage in working with material derived from records and other existing sources is perhaps the most novel aspect of Canter's meta-method. Rather than staying with frequencies or gross group comparisons, he set about looking for empirical structures across co-occurrences within the data. This was derived from his early interest in factor analysis, as well as George Kelly's ideas about ways of representing cognitive structures. When studying peoples' satisfactions with the schools or offices in which they worked, or the prisons in which they were incarcerated, he had carried out multivariate analysis of questionnaires. He had been uncomfortable with the assumptions underlying the ubiquitous principal component analysis and its factor analysis derivatives, so there was something of an epiphany when he met Louis Guttman in Tokyo and learned of Smallest Space Analysis and its related non-metric multi-dimensional scaling (MDS) procedures.

Up until that point in the mid-1970s, MDS had almost entirely been applied to data created for research purposes, usually questionnaires. It was Canter's breakthrough to see the possibility for using this with the qualitative content analysis material derived from police documents. This is such a widespread practice now within Investigative Psychology that it is easy to forget how novel Canter's use of this methodology was when he first applied it.

There was no simple and immediate success in the application, but by trial and error he developed a procedure which incorporated such technical innovations at using Jaccard's coefficient that it began to reveal interesting and consistent results. The novelty of this approach is still not appreciated by many people, nor are the details for using the approach effectively fully understood by all who publish using it. This has given rise to some very confused challenges to the consistent results found by Canter, his colleagues and others around the world, following his approach but without any direct contact with him. It is thus a sad reflection on research in this area that people have published papers which have elementary technical mistakes in them, yet make the implicitly libellous, and erroneous claim that only Canter and his close associates can obtain the consistent results that have been widely reported. Sean Hammond's recent study (Chapter 7) is an important clarification on this point.

*Models of Human Action and Experience*

The fourth stage of Canter's meta-methodology is the representation of the structures that emerge from MDS as models of human action and experiences. The lack of understanding of these models and their derivation is the basis of confused challenges to this work. Some of the criticisms expressed ignorance of the how Facet Theory informs Canter's use of MDS. This is a 'theory' about how research is most effectively carried out, developed by Guttman (Gratch, 1973) 50 years ago, but still not widely studied although now clearly articulated in many books (Canter, 1985;

Borg and Shye, 1995). Those who have used this approach have found it to be very powerful as demonstrated by the hundreds of papers that have been published utilising this framework.

Canter himself prefers to call what he uses the 'Facet Approach' because it is a way of conceptualising research questions and carrying out data analysis and the interpretation of the results. This seeks consistencies in the relationships between sets of variables. Such consistencies are interpreted as revealing components of structures that contribute to an understanding of the actions and experiences being considered. This approach has given rise to reliable ways of characterising criminal actions, which have formed the basis for theory development and practical applications.

## Emergent Intellectual Principles

A number of core Investigative Psychology principles have emerged as manifestations of Canter's attempts to resolve the paradoxical perspectives that characterise his approach to human beings and how they should be studied. These are set out in detail in the recent major textbook, the first to provide a thorough overview of Investigative Psychology, (Canter and Youngs, 2009). Three interesting examples drawn from that book illustrate Canter's readiness to challenge pervasive 'psychological' concepts.

### *A Challenge to the Concept of Motivation*

Although ubiquitous, particularly in the criminal context, the notion of the motive as a simple and direct reason for a given human action is not accepted within Canter's Investigative Psychology. This challenge to the concept of motivation has its roots in the arguments of George Kelly. Kelly's insight was that explaining what *moves* people is unnecessary because people are naturally in motion. Rather, he argued, it is the direction of motion that requires explanation. Professor Canter has caricatured this as the psychological equivalent of Newton's First Law of Motion; the principle that a human being will continue in their normal activity unless and until acted on by some external process.

Canter eschews explorations of specific motives in favour of a narrative perspective that positioned the criminal action within a broader, unfolding storyline that the offender is already pursuing. Canter's argument is that 'as part of a story or narrative form, motivation and meaning necessarily become the intention to act; the dynamic process that is required to move the drama forward' (Youngs and Canter, 2011). His view is that by understanding the narrative we get closer to understanding the action.

The first to apply narrative ideas to criminal action in his semi-autobiographical book, *Criminal Shadows*, (Canter, 1994), he emphasises the unfolding continuity of the narrative in shaping human action 'we construct life stories for ourselves. We invent autobiographical narratives in which the central character has some semblance of continuity. The stories we tell have great power in giving shape and meaning to our lives. Thus narrative encapsulates both the dynamic and the episodic nature of human existence' (1994, pp. 226–228). In *Criminal Shadows*, Canter draws attention to the destructive and multiple, yet limited, versions of the narratives available within our culture that criminals live by. He expands, 'ill-formed narratives ... may be changed dramatically by episodes in which the central character experiences relatively minor mishaps. Perhaps here is the clue to the hidden nature of the narratives that violent offenders live: their dominant narratives are confused and sensitive to episodes that most people would ignore; their plots can be set off course by experiences that their friends and relatives might never notice' (p. 230). For Canter, it is understanding these narratives that is the key to understanding the patterns of criminal action.

A corollary of this is the consistency hypothesis central to Investigative Psychology. Criminal action is understood not as some displacement activity or cathartic expression but as a continuation of the offender's non-criminal activity. This can be understood as a psychological development of 'Routine Activity Theory'. Instead of focusing only on location and actions in a rather generic sense, he points to consistencies in how offenders deal with others and the world around them. In this way, Canter has always argued that theories of normal, non-criminal behaviour and explanatory frameworks can be applied to the interpretation of offending action.

In his earliest commentaries on the emerging field, he conceptualised offending behaviour as a form of interpersonal interaction between the offender and victim, whether that victim was explicit as in most violent crime or implicit as in most property crime (Canter, 1989). He was clear that the Investigative Psychology perspective had to be distinct from the clinical perspective that would see offending as an abnormality in some way and from the sociological perspective that neglected individual agency and variation (Canter, 1989). This standpoint laid the groundwork for the many subsequent models of offending style based on the assumption of an interpersonal transaction that could be interpreted in 'normal' terms and applied to all forms of offending rather than being limited to the most extreme sexually violent variants. This indeed was the earliest hallmark of his difference from FBI views on profiling. They claimed that profiling was only relevant to bizarre, unusual crimes. From the beginning of Investigative Psychology Canter argued this was nonsense.

One particularly inventive intellectual direction that emerged out of this conceptualisation of offending activity in terms of normal processes was Canter's perspective on organised crime. In 1999, he put forward his theory of Destructive Organisational Psychology. This was based on the idea that the criminal networks responsible for organised crime could be assessed in terms of the same organisational effectiveness criteria as legal business organisations. As he noted, this opens up the possibility of weakening criminal organisations by targeting the very factors that organisational psychologists in the legal environment seek to improve. He explained how illegal organisations could be dealt with by damaging those aspects that psychologists usually help to strengthen including organisational structure, communication networks, employee retention and effective leadership (Canter, 1999). This has been seen as such a powerful way of thinking about the investigation and reduction of organised crime that it formed the basis of a major EU-funded research project involving police forces from many northern European countries.

### *Differentiation as a Route to Understanding*

An important emphasis within the development of Investigative Psychology has been the model of the variations within phenomena. Canter saw that it was through determining the basis for the differences in people's styles of conducting an activity or approaching a phenomenon that we can understand what that activity or phenomenon is. Yokota provides an interesting illustration of this process in Chapter 4. Canter traces his interest in distinguishing between people and their activities, instead of the dominant cognitive psychology trend of looking for consistencies across people, to his early studies in school of the development of Darwin's theory of evolution.

Canter was struck by how the five years Darwin spent in his voyage on The Beagle, collecting specimens and puzzling over the differences between species, was crucial to the emergence of the theory of evolution. There is a tradition in psychology that undervalues descriptive studies of what happens and seeks the causal explanations that can emerge from controlled laboratory explanations. But Canter points out that the major scientific theories have all grown out of careful description and categorisation. It is only when the variations between apparently similar phenomena are established that effective explanations and powerful theories about those phenomena can be developed, whether the phenomenon is cancer, cuisine or criminal behaviour.

This focus on differentiation as a route to understanding phenomena was greatly influenced by Guttman's first and second laws for the social sciences (Gratch, 1973). The first laws can be expressed informally as stipulating that if entities that have a common focus are evaluated on a representative sample they will not be negatively correlated. The two most well established first laws that illustrate this principle are those of intelligence and attitudes.

The first law of intelligence declares that any test item that can have a correct or incorrect answer will not be negatively correlated with any other item that has a correct or incorrect possible answer, provided the population as a whole is representatively sampled for the test. So, for example, across a population intelligence test items that measure ability in maths will be correlated at zero or above with items that measure spatial ability. Guttman claimed that this can be regarded as a law because it has found support in virtually all the studies that have tested it.

A possibly more controversial first law that Guttman promulgated (Levy, 1985) relates to attitudes. This states that indications of positive valence towards a common object will never be negative, so that a question about belief in God and another about support for religious beliefs would not be negatively correlated. However, this becomes more controversial when actions are included in the indications of positive valence. This would be reflected in the lack of a negative correlation between belief in God and visiting a place of religious worship.

Guttman's second laws identify differentiation within the general relationships that are at the heart of the first laws. So although all intelligence test items will correlate at zero or above, there are expected to be higher correlations between those items that have similar content. Thus, mathematics items will correlate more highly with each other than they do with purely verbal items. The power of these second laws comes from the identification of the components that distinguish the content domains. This is especially fruitful in the area of attitudes. Many studies have demonstrated that attitudes can take on one of three modes: Thoughts (Cognitions), Feelings and Actions. This would be illustrated in beliefs about God being more highly correlated with each other (Cognitions) than they are with frequency of church visits (Actions).

Following these ideas central to Guttman's Facet Theory, Canter argued that there will be a coherence to an individual's offending actions, across his mode of planning actions and mode of thinking about the crime, his mode of dealing with the victim and related activity, and the mode he adopts in actually executing the offence.

Building on these ideas, Canter proposed that there will be themes underlying all the different aspects of an individual's actions, which will be the basis for the differentiation of offending style within criminal behaviour. Out of this he showed the power of one particular structure for understanding the variations in criminal action: the radex (Canter, 2000).

The hypothesis of the radex is that the variations among any set of criminal actions will have two facets. One, a facet of specificity, moving from the general, shared by all offences and therefore conceptually central, with the specific variants of the actions at the periphery. This really reflects a first law of criminal activity that all criminal actions will have some potential of co-occurring. Or as Canter has expressed it, 'a person who breaks the law in one domain is likely to do so in another domain'. The second facet is a thematic facet that distinguishes between the different qualities of the offences, conceptually radiating around the 'core'. This reflects the second law as Canter expresses it. The more similar the domains the more likely is an offender to commit crimes in those domains'. This two facet model combining a quantitative variation in specificity with a qualitative variation in content was called a 'radex' by Guttman (1954) in his first paper on the topic where he argued it was a new form of factor analysis. Since that time, it has been found to be a powerful framework for considering such a range of issues as intelligence, attitudes, organisational behaviour, satisfaction with the design of hospital wards (Canter and Kenny, 1983) and many other areas of human activity and experience.

The radex structure that has been supported from empirical examination in a wide range of crime types (see Canter and Youngs, 2009). Support for this conceptual structure is also found in more general aspects of a crime, equally typical of all criminals are hypothesised to be at the centre of the radex, while actions that are more conceptually-specific to the activity form are at the periphery as shown in Figure 1.3. The first published study to demonstrate the existence of such a radial structure for crime was Canter and Heritage's (1990) study of rape. Canter and those

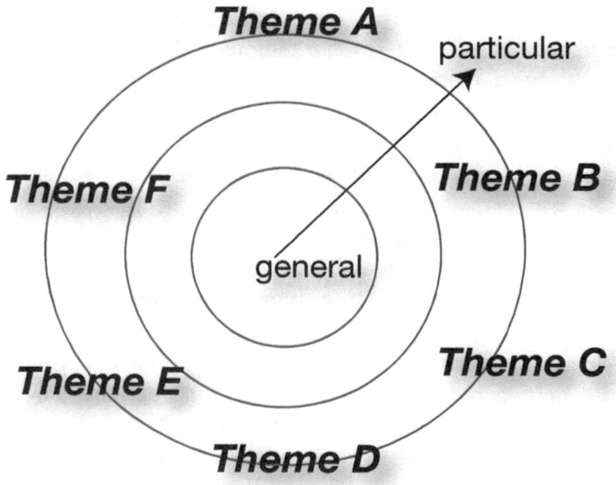


**Figure 1.3 A general model for a radex as applied to the actions of criminals. Adapted from Canter (2000)**

who have followed his lead have demonstrated the radex structure in many areas of criminal activity (see Canter, 2000) giving rise to the general radex model of criminality illustrated in Figure 1.3

The radex model is a refutable hypothesis because it is possible that distinct sub-groups of actions could occur in any class of crime which, whilst frequent, were typically associated with distinct sets of rarer actions. In such a case, the concentric circles that make up the radex would not be found. Canter (2000) discusses the usefulness of the radex in relation to his 1998 study of paedophilia: '… the radex model … indicate(s) the salient aspects … For although the three activities of "initial force used by offender", "the offender was recorded to have carried out the offence only once" and "the offender tried to desensitise the victim to the offence" all occurred in about 40% of the 97 cases they studied, the distribution in the MDS plot shows that they tended to occur in very different crimes'.

As with the SSA methodology there have been confused challenges to the ubiquity of the radex model (Taylor, Donald, Jacques, and Conchie, 2012). These challenges claim that it is an artefact of the use of Jaccard's coefficient. However, as Canter, Youngs, and Hammond (2012) show this view is based on a number of errors. Perhaps the most fundamental is shown by Sean Hammond (Chapter 7) where he deliberately creates a coefficient (that he names after Canter) that avoids the putative distortions of Jaccard's, yet shows that when applying this coefficient the radex is still found. Another demonstration of the confusion in the criticism of the radex is that, unlike in the random numbers approach used in the critique when real data is used, the radex is not always found if there is something in the data that does not fit the first law requirement that it is not being tested on a biased sample. Eccentric radexes are found from time to time, which make theoretical sense, although being at variance with the claims that the radex is an artificial creation.

This debate on the technicalities of the research carried out in Investigative Psychology does demonstrate how rapidly the field has matured. There are now schools of thought within the field and a level of methodological development that can leave behind those who have come to it recently without a full understanding of what is involved.

**Psychological Bases of Differentiation**

While developing these advances to our understanding of the structure of criminal differentiation, Professor Canter has also driven thinking on the psychological basis of the variations in offending style that have now emerged in the large number of studies. Recently, he has developed an advanced psychological framework for differentiation, the Narrative Action System model, that he has shown can be applied not only to the full range of interpersonal crimes, from stalking, rape to murder but also to property-focused crimes from robbery and burglary to arson (Canter and Youngs, 2009). This model is a particularly rich one; integrating three of the different frameworks that have found support during the development of IP.

The first psychological framework for differentiation was advanced in relation to violent interpersonal crime as part of the general narrative perspective offered by Canter in *Criminal Shadows* (1994) and Canter and Youngs (2012). The Victim Role model described three proposed roles assigned within the narratives of the offenders to their victim: The Victim as Object Role, the Victim as Vehicle Role and the Victim as Person Role. Canter proposed that the roles assigned to victims were a product of variations in the empathy felt by the offender for his victim and the degree of control maintained over the victim.

The first, Object role, Canter describes in the following terms: the 'victims are little more than animate objects … In the assault the victims were not expected to play any active part at all'. (p. 255). In the second, Vehicle role, he notes 'these rapists and murderers assign their victim a more active and sometimes more brutal role in the violent drama'. As Canter explains, these offenders are 'forcing their victims to carry some of the meanings the men had derived from their contact with other women'. The third, Person role, is one where the 'role given to the victim is closest to normal relationships in which the woman is a person who has thoughts and feelings' but this 'normality' provides the context for coercion, manipulation and abuse. The Victim Role framework has been applied to the patterns derived in studies of rape, stalking, serial murder and sexual abuse (Canter, 1994; Canter and Youngs, 2012; Hodge, 1999; Almond, this volume) as well as other studies in press.

A second framework that has also proved useful in interpreting the empirical patterns emerging in many of the studies was an Action Systems framework. The Action System model is derived from Parson's (cf. Parsons and Shills, 1951) exploration of socio-psychological systems. From this, Shye (1985) developed a more straightforward conceptualisation of behavioural actions systems that was directly open to empirical test. The model posited four modes of operation that were possible for any 'system', as Fritzon and Yokota both illustrate in their studies in this volume. Canter and Fritzon (1998) describe these in relation to arson:

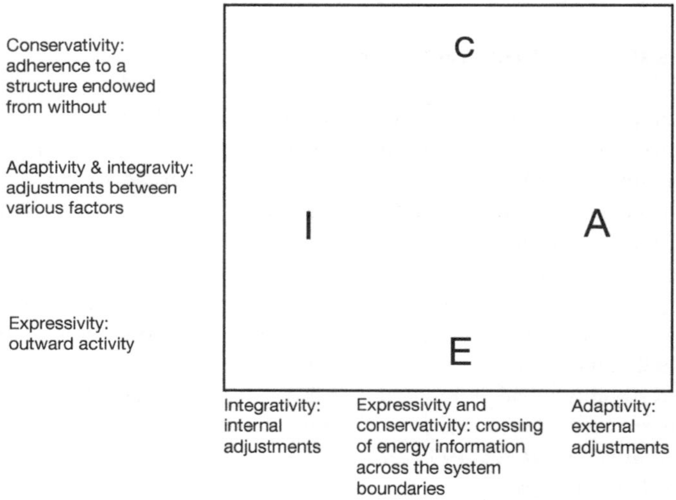


**Figure 1.4** **The conceptual interrelationships among the functioning modes of an action system, represented by means of geometric–spatial proximities. Reproduced from Fritzon, Canter and Wilton (2001)**

**Table 1.2** **Summary of action system modes of functioning**

| Source of action in relation to agent | Locus of effect in relation to agent | Mode |
|---|---|---|
| External | External | Adaptive |
| Internal | External | Expressive |
| Internal | Internal | Integrative |
| External | Internal | Conservative |

Canter's third psychological framework for differentiation drew on narrative themes that he advanced as the destructive variants of the archetypal stories identified in literary criticism and most notably the work of Norbert Frye (Canter, Kaouri, and Ioannou, 2003; Canter and Youngs, 2009, 2012; Youngs and Canter, 2011, 2012). Showing support for these themes in interviews with offenders, Youngs and Canter (2011) summarise the four narrative styles of offending in the following way:

> *The Romantic Quest Narrative* The person who sees himself as powerful and for whom one or more other people and their reactions are a significant part of his narrative, may be thought of as acting out a Revengeful Mission role.
>
> *The Tragedy Narrative* By contrast the criminal who feels he is being pushed by the fates, having little control over his actions and little concern for others plays the role of the Tragic Hero, within a general narrative of Tragedy.
>
> *The Adventure Narrative* The offender who lives out a narrative in which he is in control, enjoying his power and for whom others are irrelevant, acts the role of Professional, as part of an Adventure narrative.
>
> *The Irony Narrative* Here the offender sees himself as having no power and being alienated from others who are nonetheless significant to him, so seeing himself as a Victim within this Irony narrative.

The integration of these three theories of differentiation: the Victim Role, Action System and Narrative perspectives, has allowed the development of a generic framework for the differentiation of criminality (see Canter and Youngs, 2009). To date, this Narrative Action System (NAS) model appears to offer a basis for understanding offending styles across all forms of criminality.

## The Development of a Discipline: David Canter's Investigative Psychology

This eclectic combination of particular intellectual stands, research preferences and scientific tastes has proved remarkably fruitful and has inspired a generation of research and researchers. Under this vision, a thriving area of psychological activity has developed with remarkable rapidity. There is now vast literature on geographical offender profiling, linking crimes, investigative interviewing, determining the veracity of all sorts of investigation information, on criminal differentiation and offence modelling and, of course, on drawing inferences about offender characteristics from their offending style.

Indeed the ideas that began in Professor Canter's office at Surrey University some 25 years ago have now become so widespread that many people do not realise that what they are doing in their research is Investigative Psychology. Yet just a few short years ago such studies would not have been thought of. Certainly, few would have had any notion of how to conduct such studies, how to move, for example, from crime scene photographs to psychological models of offence behaviour and offenders, or how to consider the detailed case characteristics to distinguish false and genuine allegations, or linked and unlinked offences.

Of course, it has not taken police and other investigative bodies long to recognise and seek to harness the applied potential of the growing body of IP knowledge. This science is now put into direct operational use around the world, underpinned by the professional academy (IA-IP) he founded to support operational application as well as IP research. From the military to commercial bodies and the courts, as well as the police and crime analysis communities, IP is put into practice every day. The discipline Professor Canter conceived and has driven has unquestionably saved lives and brought justice in thousands and thousands of cases across the globe.

Clearly, this all raises the question as to the personal attributes and character of the man without whom none of this would have happened. To conceptualise a new strand of academic thinking clearly requires someone of unusual intellectual capacity. Few who have met David Canter are left in any doubt about the incisiveness and clarity of his thinking. The subtlety and sophistication are perhaps inevitably less obvious but underpin an ability to understand the reality of human nature that distinguishes him from many scientists. And an instinct for research that cannot be explained by reference to an unusual methodological and analytical prowess. He can just see what the issue is and how to study it.

The personal qualities that have facilitated this remarkable contribution to academic thought, as well as to society more generally, include a liveliness, endless curiosity and wit that attenuate (mostly!) the uncompromisingly high standards he insists upon. As students down the years frequently attest, Professor Canter is nothing if not entertaining! Importantly, perhaps, he has an inability to understand the role pettiness or jealousies can play in professional life and an absolute intolerance of pomposity in any of its forms. Early in his exposure to it, David Canter developed a distaste for the sensationalist aspects of the field that has been central in focusing him on developing the science.

To the alarm of some (but amusement of those who know him better), David Canter doesn't just have the courage to be controversial, he relishes it. He has a willingness to stand alone if necessary, yet a genuine desire to share that has allowed many of his former students to carve out successful careers. Indeed the chapters in this book are all written by people who have benefited from David Canter's tutelage and generous support. This continues to this day and indeed his current research team is probably the largest and most energetic yet. Many of us look forward to the next advances in this remarkable career.

**References**

Borg, I. and Shye, S. (1995). *Facet Theory: Form and Content*. London: Sage.

Hazelwood, R.R., Ressler, R.K., Depue, R.L., and Douglas, J.E. (1987). Criminal personality profiling: an overview, in *Practical Aspects of Rape Investigation: A Multidisciplinary Approach*, edited by R.R. Hazelwood and A.W. Burgess (pp. 137–149). New York: Elsevier.

Canter, D.V. (1968). *The Study of Meaning in Architecture*. Publisher: D.V. Canter.

Canter, D. (1970). *The Architectural Psychology Conference*. Kingston Polytechnic.

Canter, D. (1977). *The Psychology of Place*. London: The Architectural Press.

Canter, D. (ed.) (1985). *Facet Theory: Approaches to Social Research*. New York: Springer Verlag.

Canter, D. (1989). Offender profiles. *The Psychologist*, 2, pp. 12–16.

Canter, D. (1992). An evaluation of the 'cusum' stylistic analysis of confessions. *Expert Evidence*, 1, 93–99.

Canter, D. (1994). *Criminal Shadows*. London: Harper Collins.

Canter, D. (1994). Psychology of offender profiling, in *Handbook of Psychology in Legal Contexts*, edited by R. Bull and D. Carson. Chichester: John Wiley and Sons, 3, 43–355.

Canter, D. (1995). The psychology of offender profiling, in *Handbook of Psychology in Legal Contexts*, edited by R. Bull and D. Carson. Chichester: Wiley.

Canter, D. (1996). The wholistic, organic researcher: central issues in clinical research methodology, in *Psychology in Action*, edited by D. Canter. Aldershot: Dartmouth, pp. 23–38.

Canter, D. (1996). In search of objectives: an intellectual autobiography, in *Psychology in Action*. Aldershot: Dartmouth Publishing Company, pp. 3–22.

Canter, D.V. (1999). Investigating equivocal deaths, in *Profiling in Policy and Practice, Networks. Offender Profiling Series*, Vol II, edited by D.V. Canter and L.J. Alison. Aldershot: Dartmouth.

Canter, D. (2000). Offender profiling and criminal differentiation. *Journal of Legal and Criminological Psychology*, 5, pp. 23–46.

Canter, D. (2000). Psycholinguistics, in *Encyclopaedia of Forensic Science*. London: Academic Press.

Canter, D. (2003). *Mapping Murder: The Secrets of Geographical Profiling*. London: Virgin Books.

Canter, D. (2005). Confusing operational predicaments and cognitive explorations: comments on Rossmo and Snook et al. *Applied Cognitive Psychology*, 19, 663–668.

Canter, D. (2005). Suicide or murder: implicit narratives in the Eddie Gilfoyle case, in *The Forensic Psychologist's Casebook*, edited by L. Alison. Cullumpton: Willan.

Canter, D.V. (2005, September). National institute justice: evaluation geographic profiling debate. 8th International Crime Mapping Research Conference. Savannah, USA.

Canter, D. (2009). *The Faces of Terrorism: Multidiscipline Perspectives*. Singapore: Wiley-Blackwell.

Canter, D.V. (2011). Resolving the offender 'profiling equations' and the emergence of investigative psychology. *Current Directions in Psychological Science*, 20, 5–10.

Canter, D. and Alison, L. (2003). Converting evidence into data: the use of law enforcement at archives as unobtrusive. *The Qualitative Report*, 8, 151–176.

Canter, D.V., Coffey, T., Huntley, M., and Missen, C. (2000). Predicting sexual killers' home base using a decision support system. *Quantitative Criminology*, 16, 457–478.

Canter, D., Comber, M., Uzzell, D., and Popplewell, O. (1989). *Football in its Place: An Environmental Psychology of Football Grounds*. Routledge.

Canter, D., Donald, I., and Chalk, J. (1992). Pedestrian behaviour during emergencies underground: the psychology of crowd control under life threatening circumstances, in *Safety in Road and Rail Tunnels*, edited by A. Vardy. Bedford: Independent Technical Conferences Ltd., pp. 135–150.

Canter, D. and Fritzon, K. (1998). Differentiating arsonists: a model of firesetting actions and characteristics. *Journal of Legal and Criminological Psychology*, 3, 73–96.

Canter, D.V. and Gregory, A. (1993). Identifying the residential location of rapists. *Journal of Forensic Science Society*, 34, 169–175.

Canter, D. and Hammond, L. (2006). A comparison of the efficacy of different decay functions in geographical profiling for a sample of US serial killers. *Journal of Investigative Psychology and Offender Profiling*, 3, 91–103.

Canter, D., Hammond, L., Youngs, D., and Juszczak, P. (2012). The efficacy of ideographic models for geographical offender profiling. *Submitted to the Journal of Quantatative Crime*.

Canter, D. Hughes, D., and Kirby, S. (1998). Paedophilia: pathology, criminality, or both? The development of a multivariate model of offence behaviour in child sexual abuse. *The Journal of Forensic Psychiatry*, 9, 532–555.

Canter, D., Kaouri, C., and Ioannou, M. (2003). The facet structure of criminal narratives. Paper presented at the 9th International Facet Theory Conference.

Canter, D. and Kenny, C. (1983). *A Multivariate Model of Hospital Ward.* University of Surrey: Guildford (UK).

Canter, D. and Larkin, P. (1993). The environmental range of serial rapists. *Journal of Environmental Psychology*, 13, 63–39.

Canter, D., Sarangi, S., and Youngs, D. (in press). Personal construct systems and terrorists' roles: a comparison of three Jihadi terrorists. *Legal and Criminological Psychology*.

Canter, D. and Youngs, D. (2008). iOPS: an interactive offender profiling system, in *Crime Mapping Case Studies*, edited by S. Chainey and I. Thompson. Chichester: Wiley.

Canter, D. and Youngs, D. (2009). *Investigative Psychology: Offender Profiling and the Analysis of Criminal Action.* London: John Wiley & Sons.

Canter, D. (2011). Resolving the offender 'profiling equations' and the emergence of an investigative psychology. *Current Directions in Psychological Science*, 20, 5–10.

Canter, D. and Youngs, D. (2007a). *Principles of Geographical Offender Profiling*. Aldershot: Ashgate.

Canter, D. and Youngs, D. (2012). Violent and sexual offenders' victim role assignments: a general model of offending style. *Journal of Forenisc Psychiatry and Psychology*.

Donald, I.J. and Canter, D.V. (1990). Behavioural aspects of the King's Cross disaster, in *Fires and Human Behaviour*, 2nd ed., edited by D.V. Canter. London: David Fulton Publishers.

Fritzon, K., Canter, D., and Wilton, Z. (2001). The application of an action systems model to destructive behaviour: the examples of arson and terrorism. *Behavioral Science and the Law*, 19, 657–690.

Gratch, H. (1973). *Twenty-five Years of Social Research in Israel*. Jerusalem: Jerusalem Academic Press.

Guttman, L. (1954). A new approach to factor analysis: the radex, in *Mathematical Thinking in the Social Sciences*, edited by P.F. Lazarsfeld. New York: Free Press (pp. 258–348).

Levy, S. (1985). Lawful roles of facets in social theories, in *Facet Theory: Approaches to Social Research*, edited by D.V. Canter. New York: Springer (pp. 59–96).

Harre, R. (1979). *Social Being*. Oxford: Blackwell.

Hodge, S. (1999). Canter's victim role model of serial murder. Unpublished internal report to the International Research Centre for Investigative Psychology (IRCIP).

Hodge, S. and Canter, D. (1998). Victims and perpetrators of male sexual assault. *Journal of Interpersonal Violence*, 1, 222–239.

Parsons, T. and Shils, E. (1951). *Toward a General Theory of Action*. New York: Harper.

Sarangi, S., Canter, D., and Youngs, D. (in press) Themes of radicalisation revealed through the personal constructs of jihadi terrorists.

Taylor, P., Donald, I., Jacques, K., and Conchie, S. (2012). Jaccard's heel: radex models of criminal behaviour are rarely falsifiable when derived using Jaccard coefficient. *Legal and Criminology Psychology*, 17, 41–58.

Webb, E.J., Campbell, D.T., Schwartz, R.D., and Sechrest, L. (1966). *Unobtrusive Measures: Non-reactive Research in Social Sciences*. Chicago: Rand McNally.

Youngs, D. and Canter, D. (2011). Narrative roles in criminal action: an integrated framework for differentiating offenders. *Legal and Criminal Psychology*, 00, 1–17.

Youngs, D. and Canter, D. (2012). Offenders' crime narratives as revealed by the narrative roles questionnaire (NRQ). *International Journal of Comparative Criminology and Offender Therapy*.

# SECTION 1
# On David Canter's IP Theories and Models

# Chapter 2
# Violent Self-narratives and the Hostile Attribution Bias

Shadd Maruna and Michelle Butler

## Editor's Introduction

In this chapter Shadd Maruna and Michelle Butler explore the innovative use of narrative psychology in relation to crime and criminals that David first developed in the award-winning popular book Criminal Shadows. David's thesis was that it would be through the offender's narrative that we would really understand the underlying meaning of the criminal action. He argued that as narratives or stories, meaning and motivation takes a dynamic form becoming the direct and detailed intention to act that drives the drama. In this way, he opened up a perspective on crime that in contrast to general ideas about offenders' personality or general background criminogenic factors, offers immediate and specific explanatory processes and an approach to interpreting particular patterns of criminal actions (Canter and Youngs, 2012a; Youngs and Canter, 2012).

## Introduction

As is evident in the various contributions to this volume, Professor Canter has made numerous contributions to the field of psychology and to criminological or forensic psychology in particular. He is widely recognised as a pioneering thinker in environmental psychology, quantitative methodology and of course in the research speciality he helped to establish himself, investigative psychology. One legacy that is sometimes overlooked, however, is his work on the self-narratives behind patterns of violent offending. Writing in the early 1990s, Canter and his students (e.g., Alison and Parkinson, 1995; Canter, 1994) were among the first in forensic psychology to show an interest in the personological study of identity narratives. In his classic book *Criminal Shadows* – later versions of which were even subtitled "Inner Narratives of Evil"[1] – Canter argues that the analysis of self-narratives should be "at the heart of offender profiling" (1994: p. 119). In doing so, he introduced the personality

1 This replaced the more commercial "Inside the Mind of the Serial Killer" subtitle from earlier versions.

psychology of Dan P. McAdams (1985) to an entirely new audience of policing experts, criminologists, and forensic psychologists.[2]

Canter and his students argued that violence should be seen as an interpersonal transaction involving characteristic and psychologically entrenched ways of dealing with other people. This, of course, was not a new idea. Every detective knows that a serial offender is likely to have a modus operandi or a vague pattern to his or her behaviour that can link various crimes in a sequence. Canter's contribution, however, was to try to make sense out of these behaviours by connecting them to a person's internal dialogue or self-narrative. By understanding the "stories offenders live by", Canter and his students argued that investigators can better predict and understand offending behaviour. Alison and Parkinson write:

> The advantage that the narrative approach has over "modus operandi" is that in the latter the investigator can only make limited and static inferences about the offender's background. [...] In the former the investigator may gain insight into the whole psychological pattern that identifies that individual (1995: p. 21).

Although Canter (1994) traced the idea that offenders are often driven by personal "myths" back as far as Bolitho (1926), his real contribution was to situate this idea in the developing work on self-narratives and identity in contemporary personality psychology, in particular the work of McAdams at Northwestern University. In his ground-breaking theoretical work in identity psychology, McAdams (1985, 1993) argues that if you want to know the answer to the question "who am I?" (in other words, if you want to know my identity), you first have to know my "story". The construction and reconstruction of one's life story narrative (or "personal myth"), integrating one's perceived past, present, and anticipated future, is the process through which modern adults imbue our lives with unity, purpose, and meaning. Overwhelmed with the choices and possibilities of modern society (Fromm, 1941), modern individuals internalise this autobiographical narrative in order to provide a sense of coherence and predictability to the chaos of their lives.

In making this link between personality psychology and forensic sciences, Canter and his associates caught a very important intellectual wave, sometimes referred to as the "narrative turn" in the social sciences (Brown, Nolan, Crawford and Lewis, 1994). Over the last two decades, the idea that identity is an internal narrative has achieved a privileged place in the social sciences and humanities, with adherents like Paul Ricoeur, Roger Schank, and Charles Taylor. The distinguished Harvard psychologist Jerome Bruner argues:

2 Indeed, McAdams – who has never done any research involving criminal offenders – was invited to present a series of seminars at the University of Liverpool's Centre for Investigative Psychology in 1994–1995.

> Eventually the culturally shaped cognitive and linguistic processes that guide the self-telling of life narratives achieve the power to structure perceptual experience, to organise memory, to segment and purpose-build the very "events" of a life. In the end, we become the autobiographical narratives by which we "tell about" our lives (1987: p. 15).

The equally distinguished London School of Economics sociologist Anthony Giddens agrees, arguing that in modernity, "A person's identity is not to be found in behavior, nor – important though this is – in the reactions of others, but in the capacity to keep a particular narrative going" (1991: p. 54). Theodore Sarbin has even suggested that the narrative should be seen as the "root metaphor" (1986: p. *vii*) for the entire field of psychology and indeed many within the growing field of "narrative psychology" largely accept Jean-Paul Sartre's famous claim that the human being "is always a teller of stories, (s)he lives surrounded by his (or her) own stories and those of other people, (s)he sees everything that happens to him(her) terms of stories and (s)he tries to live his(her) life as if (s)he were recounting it" (cited in Bruner, 1987: p. 21).

In the 18 years since Canter's initial contribution, the role of self-narratives in the aetiology of violent or abusive behaviour has been the subject of some fascinating studies in criminology and criminological psychology (for a review, see Presser, 2009).[3] Some of the most important recent contributions to narrative criminology, in fact, has been produced by Canter and his colleagues themselves. For instance, in a highly creative recent essay (drawing on musical notation among other sources), Canter (2008) utilises the idea of narrative to try to bridge the seemingly impossible gap between psychological thought and legal thought. More recently, Youngs and Canter (2009, 2011, forthcoming) have embarked on a fascinating project to identify a typology of archetypal themes in the self-narratives of violent offenders drawing on Northrop Frye's literary criticism, among others. Indeed, much of the important work developed by graduates of Canter's Investigative Psychology Unit has been strongly influenced by narrative theory (see Alison and Stein, 2001; Canter, Grieve, Nicol and Benneworth, 2003; Canter and Ioannou, 2004; Fritzon, Lewis and Doley, 2011; Porter and Alison, 2004; Salfati, 2000; Sarangi and Alison, 2005).[4]

---

3 See also Day and Bryan, (2007), Green, South and Smith (2006), McKendy (2006), O'Connor (2000), Pulkkinen and Aaltonen (2003), Snow and Powell (2005) and Stefanakis (1999). Among the most innovative research in this regard has been in the literature on desistance from crime (Culley, 2004; Gadd and Farrall, 2004; Vaughan, 2007) and offender rehabilitation (e.g., Kleckar and Ting, 2004; Ward and Marshall, 2007).

4 Not all of this work focused on profiling or even the self-narratives of violent offenders. Indeed, in one of the most theoretically innovative contributions, Alison and Stein (2001) analyse victims' accounts of sexual assault, as reported to the police, and found that these narratives reflect abusive variants of more conventional interactional processes.

Nonetheless, it has to be said that, outside of these few examples, the study of self-narratives of violence has not occupied anything like centre stage in either forensic or investigative psychology as advocated in *Criminal Shadows* in 1994. The purpose of this chapter is to seek to reinvigorate this interest by situating the study of self-narratives within the better known and better developed tradition of cognitive information processing, in particular drawing on research on the "hostile attribution bias" as a "missing link" in forensic narrative psychology. In what follows, we briefly outline narrative identity theory, and then do the same for the role of the hostile attribution bias in the aetiology of violent or aggressive behaviour. Finally, we attempt to synthesise these two literatures in the hopes that doing so will better demonstrate the value of understanding self-narratives in the study of violent behaviour, as originally argued by Canter and his associates over a decade ago.

## Identity as a Story

> Life must be understood backwards. But ... it must be lived forwards. And if one thinks over that proposition it becomes more and more evident that life can never really be understood in time simply because at no particular moment can I find the necessary resting place from which to understand it – backwards (Kierkegaard, 1843).

According to McAdams, people solve the problem of identity by constructing a self-narrative. A self-narrative is a story that a person forms to explain their behaviour, motivations, feelings and desires within a meaningful, sequential framework. In other words, the self-narrative is the person's response to the question "Who am I and how do I fit into the wider world?" In this way, narratives have an "internal logic" (Canter, 1994) and are used to make life understandable and predictable. They are also believed to keep the human experience of meaninglessness and existential void at bay (McAdams, 2006). Consequently, the problem of identity is "the problem of arriving at a life story that makes sense – provides unity and purpose – within a sociohistorical matrix that embodies a much larger story" (McAdams, 1985: p. 18).

These stories or self-narratives represent personal outlooks and *theories* of reality, not reality itself. While based on historical fact, the self-narrative is thought to be an imaginative rendering, a sort of myth-making through which the past is reconstructed, edited and embellished in order to create a coherent plot and themes. Like the symbolic interactionist mantra "If (persons) define situations as real, they are real in their consequences" (Thomas and Thomas, 1928: p. 572), narrative psychology is premised on the idea that "stories hold psychological truth" (McAdams, 1999: p. 496) even if they are not precise or objective recalling of fact. Their value is not so much in what they tell us about the past (which will by definition be biased, incomplete and imprecise), but what they say about the person's future. Giddens writes, "Each of us not only 'has', but lives a biography" (1991: p. 14). These narratives explain actions in a sequence of events that connect up to explanatory goals, motivations, and feelings. They then act to shape and guide future behaviour, as persons act in ways that accord to the stories they have created about themselves (McAdams, 1985).

Moreover, self-narratives can also provide a framework within which to incorporate the various roles and conflicting events within a person's life (McAdams, 2006). Bruner (1986) states that it is our ability to reflect on our actions and create stories sensitive to context which allows us to explain and give meaning to behaviours which violate perceived core characteristics. In this way, we use stories to make sense of, rationalise and account for our experiences, be they successes or tragedies. Not every aspect of a person's life requires such internal explanation. Brushing one's teeth at night or saving part of one's salary in a bank are rarely central features in an identity story, because these behaviours are so common that they require little justification. Generally, narratives focus on deviations from normative behaviours or the experiences in a person's life that, when taken in totality, make them unique as an individual: achievements, predicaments, failings and aberrations. Therefore, self-narratives are:

> Based on biographical facts, but [...] go considerably beyond these facts as people selectively appropriate aspects of their experience and imaginatively construe both past and future to construct stories that make sense to them and to their audiences, that vivify and integrate life and make it more or less meaningful (McAdams, 2001: p. 101).

Unlike personality traits, which tend to be largely stable over time, the narrative identity can and does change throughout life. In fact, our stories have to be "routinely created and sustained in the reflexive activities of the individual" (Giddens, 1991: p. 52). Erikson (1959) and Elkind (1968) argue that people first begin to shape individual identities during adolescence. Teenagers therefore go through a "psychosocial moratorium" where they "try on" various possible selves "for size". As such, numerous therapeutic efforts have been directed to the possibility of re-creating one's self-narrative in more socially adaptive directions (e.g., White and Epston, 1990).

Moreover, these dynamic narratives are not created in a vacuum (Kohli, 1981). Identity theorists argue that identity is very much shaped within the constraints and opportunity structure of the social world in which people live. In this way, self-narratives are constructed by drawing from the available narratives within society:

> Societies provide occupational, ideological, and relational resources upon which the individual can draw in formulating his or her own identity. The resources are shaped into a personalised life product which ideally confers upon the individual a sense of unity and purpose – a feeling/belief that the person is whole and that his or her life is justified by a reason, mission or goal (McAdams, 1985: p. 4).

Rather than stripping individuals of community and macro-historical context, narrative analysis can inform our understandings by illustrating how the person sees and experiences the world around them. Narratives are therefore excellent data for the analysis of the underlying sociostructural relations of a population (Bertaux, 1981).

## Self-narratives and Crime

Self-stories may be especially crucial in understanding offending behaviour. Personal "myths" are thought to be the primary mechanism through which individuals are able to maintain a sense of self-worth in the face of moral, social and personal failings and stigmatisation. Epstein and Erskine use this "need to maintain a coherent, integrated conceptual system" or "theory of reality" to explain "behaviour that either is manifestly self-destructive or is maintained in the absence of reinforcement" (1983: p. 135). Most critically, narrative reconstruction becomes necessary when a person experiences some threat to his or her identity (see Maruna and Ramsden, 2004). Scott and Lyman argue: "Since it is with respect to deviant behaviour that we call for accounts, the study of deviance and the study of accounts are intrinsically related, and a clarification of accounts will constitute a clarification of deviant phenomena". (1968: p. 62).

Indeed, the question of "why did they do it?" is central to the criminologist's quest, and posing the same question to offenders themselves has been a part of criminology since the origins of the discipline (see Bennett's 1981 history in *Oral History and Delinquency*). Perhaps the best known response to this line of inquiry is the account that makes up Clifford Shaw's (1930) *The Jack-Roller: A Delinquent Boy's Own Story*. Traditionally, life stories such as these were interpreted somewhat literally by criminologists in the Chicago School as indications of the social processes that might lead to criminal behaviour (see Hollway and Jefferson, 2000). For instance, Shaw "made no attempt to pursue the implications of the Jack-Roller's idiosyncratic point of view for an understanding of his involvement in delinquent conduct" (Finestone, 1976: p. 101). Instead, these life histories were collected in order to provide "concrete and vivid" illustrations of the lives of young people in disadvantaged areas (Shaw, 1929: p. 124) or to focus attention on the social factors involved in criminal aetiology (Shaw and McKay, 1931). To some extent, this literalist tradition continues today in oral history research in criminology (see Laub and Sampson, 2003).

Yet, this is not the only way to interpret the accounts people give for their actions (see esp. Gadd and Jefferson, 2007; Koesling and Koesling, 2007; Maruna and Roy, 2007). As C. Wright Mills suggested, "The differing reasons men give for their actions are not themselves without reasons" (1940: p. 904). The interest in life narratives among many contemporary social scientists is not so much in the substantive events these stories depict (what happened in their lives), but more the meanings individuals attach to such facts. How people choose to frame the events of their lives says as much about the psychology of the individual – their personality, identity or self – as it does the actual events and structural conditions experienced (Bruner, 2004; McAdams, 1985, 1993). In his interview with John Laub, Donald Cressey put the argument this way: "Listening to people tell you why they did it *does not* give you explanations of why they did it. When you ask people why they commit crime, they make sounds. I call them verbalizations. These are data. You study them" (Laub, 1983: p. 139, emphasis added).

The study of offender verbalisations as "data" in criminology might have originated with Cressey's (1953) study of embezzlers' excuses, but it has since become associated primarily with Gresham Sykes and David Matza's (1957) article "Techniques of Neutralization: A Theory of Delinquency". The important idea at the heart of this argument (hereafter, "neutralization theory") was that the excuses and justifications that deviants use to rationalize their behaviours might *themselves* be implicated in the aetiology of deviant behaviour. As Sykes and Matza note "It is by learning these techniques that the juvenile becomes delinquent" (1957: p. 667).

Nonetheless, identity is an on-going process, not a tangible or permanent quality of an individual. Any narrative typology needs to be based on the understanding that individuals develop and adapt their stories constantly over time (Giddens, 1991). Though various categories of self-*stories* may be identified, narrative psychology does not seek to divide *persons* into "types" in the way that offender categories based on trait scores might (Megargee and Bohn, 1979). Canter characterises such a misuse of narrative psychology as being based on a "cafeteria view" of life stories, whereby a narrative identity is understood as a permanent "thing" that can be quickly identified and labelled:

> The cafeteria view of life stories pulls the framework back into the realms of static characteristics. Instead of having distinguishing ear lobes, criminals can be recognised by the particular heroes they endorse. Life is not that simple. Narratives are moving targets that change their shape in response to life circumstances (1994: p. 312).

Trait psychology implies that the "criminal personality" is something stable and permanent. Yet, considerable longitudinal and ethnographic research on crime over the life course indicates that so-called "criminal careers" are sporadic, short-lived and largely shaped by social and developmental context (Canter, 1994; Currie, 1991; Graham and Bowling, 1995; Katz, 1988; Sampson and Laub, 1992, 1993; Sullivan, 1989). Narrative psychology offers a dynamic, developmental perspective that can be seen as a viable alternative to the positivist paradigm in criminology (Sarbin, 1986). By going beyond traits or simple "modus operandi" and trying to understand aspects of the whole person, criminologists and psychologists can better understand the change and development in criminal behaviour over time.

Increasingly, researchers are beginning to use narrative psychology to understand changes in criminal behaviour and the conscious, and unconscious, processes involved in the construction and maintenance of identities. This is particularly true in research on the topic of desistance from crime (see Maruna, 2004; Culley, 2004; Gadd and Farrall, 2004; Vaughan, 2007). For example, Maruna (2001) investigated the process through which offenders are able to desist from criminal activity by comparing the self-narratives of active and desisting offenders as well as their scores on a variety of psychometric questionnaires. Whereas few significant differences were observed between the two groups on their basic personality tests, the two groups did differ in terms of the patterns in their self-narratives. Those continuing to engage in criminal activity were characterised as ascribing to a "condemnation script" in which they attributed a distinct lack of hope for the future to the lessons they had learned in a contaminated past. In contrast, the desisting group typically ascribed to a self-narrative that Maruna labels a "redemption script" emphasising their inherent goodness and characterising their involvement in criminal activity as a temporary attempt to obtain power in bleak circumstances. This and similar studies of desistance complements the applied research and theory around offender rehabilitation that links offending to patterns of thought and social cognitions (e.g., Bosch and Monshouwer, 2002; Bush, 1995; de Castro, Veerman, Koops, Dodge, 2003).

## Biased Cognitions

In recent years, the role of social-information processing has taken a central place in the psychological understanding of violence. Theories of social-information processing provide a framework for understanding how aggression is mediated by cognition (Barlett and Anderson, 2011; Dodge, 2003; Reijntjes, Thomaes, Kamphuis, Bushman, de Castro and Telch, 2011). These theories suggest that individuals develop routinised patterns of processing social cues that help to shape behavioural outcomes (Dodge, 2003; Huesmann, 1988; Newell and Simon, 1972). Crick and Dodge (1994) propose a social-information processing theory involving six steps: the encoding of social cues; the interpretation of social cues; the clarification of goals; response access and construction; response decision; and behavioural enactment. Numerous researchers have examined the social-information processing of habitually violent individuals to determine whether they have "biases" or "errors" in their cognitions that might contribute to their aggressive behaviours (see Dodge and Newman, 1981; Huesmann, 1988).

The most robust finding in this regard is the hostile attribution bias (see esp. the meta-analysis by de Castro, et al. 2002). Hostile attribution bias involves the tendency of some individuals to routinely make attributions of hostile intent to the actions of others (Nasby, et al. 1979). In particular, hostile attribution bias has been found to be strongly associated with reactive aggression whereas instrumental forms of aggression are typically linked to positive outcome expectancies for violence (de Castro et al. 2002; Walters, 2007; Reijntjes et al. 2011). Longitudinal studies of children, such as those by Weiss, Dodge, Bates and Pettit (1992), Dodge, Pettit, Bates and Valente (1995), Egan, Monson and Perry (1998), and Dodge, Crozier and Lansford (2001), find a relationship between measures of the hostile attribution bias and aggressive behaviour, even when controlling for prior levels of aggressive behaviour and intelligence. This effect has also been found among adolescents and samples of adults convicted of serious violent crimes (see Dodge, et al. 2001). Individuals who engage in aggressive behaviour are therefore believed to selectively focus upon and perceive more hostile cues over and above other cues within a social setting, form more hostile interpretations of ambiguous situations and generate more violent responses to these situations (Dodge, 2003; Dodge and Newman, 1981).

A related cognitive bias is the denial of responsibility for one's aggressive actions. For instance, neutralisation theory in criminology suggests that "much delinquency is based on what is essentially an unrecognized extension of defenses to crimes, in the form of justifications for deviance" (Sykes and Matza, 1957: p. 666). Sykes and Matza identify five "neutralization techniques" that allow offenders to engage in wrongdoing without suffering from pangs of guilt: denial of responsibility, denial of injury, denial of the victim, condemnation of condemners, and the appeal to higher loyalties. They argue that it is by learning these techniques that juveniles become delinquent. More recently, Bandura (1990) developed a similar theory of "moral disengagement" involving the following "techniques" for avoiding self-sanction: displacement of responsibility, diffusion of responsibility, distorting the consequences of an action, dehumanising the victim, and assuming the role of victim for one's self (see also Barriga, Landau, Stinson, Liau, and Gibbs, 2000; Gibbs, Potter and Goldstein, 1995; Slaby and Guerra, 1988).

This theoretical focus on the role of excuse-making in the psychology of crime and violence has had a profound influence on the applied world of offender treatment, where excuses and justifications are often assigned the specialist label of "cognitive distortion" (see Abel, Gore, Holland, Camp, Becker and Rathner, 1989; Blumenthal, Gudjonsson and Burns, 1999). Murphy defines "cognitive distortions" as "Self-statements made by offenders that allow them to deny, minimize, rationalize and justify their behaviour" (1990: p. 332). A primary purpose of treatment interventions is "to identify and confront [these] cognitive distortions, rationalisations and excuses for offending" (Salter, 1988: p. 114), although this is controversial (see esp. Maruna and Mann, 2006)

Considerable questions remain, moreover, about how and why these cognitive patterns emerge in the first place. Dodge (2003) theorises that environmental stimuli, emotions and life scripts influence an individual's social-information processing. Additionally, he states that an individual's biased cognitions "may emerge at least partially as an adaptive response to past life experiences of actual threat, such as physical abuse and peer victimization" (Dodge, 2003: p. 256).

## Self-narratives and Social Information Processing

We suggest that hostile interpretation biases and other habitual cognitions might usefully be understood as emerging out of a person's self-narrative. Indeed, the storied identity itself can be seen as an active "information-processing structure", a "cognitive schema" (Blackburn, 1994) or a "construct system" (Tagg, 1985) that is both shaped by and later mediates social interaction. Caspi and Moffitt (1995) argue that a person's self-narrative may act as a filter for the encoding and processing of social information as different people exposed to the same situation will react differently as they interpret events in a manner consistent with their understanding of self (self-narrative), their understanding of others and their previous experience. Self-narratives may also act as a filter in the clarification of goals by filtering out goals that are inconsistent with an individual's self-narrative.

Lonnie Athens (1997) takes something like this perspective in his study of violent men. In his analysis, he suggests that there are four interpretations of situations which can result in aggressive behaviour: physically defensive, frustrative, frustrative-malefic and malefic. According to Athens, physically defensive interpretations are formed when individuals believe they will soon be physically attacked and/or that someone close to them is in danger of being physically attacked. Frustrative interpretations are formed when an individual assumes that their wishes are being resisted and/or when they feel they are being forced to carry out a specific action against his or her will. Frustrative-malefic interpretations are formed when an individual assumes that he/she is being resisted, disrespected or forced to engage in behaviour against their will. Finally, malefic interpretations refer to an individual's assumption that the actions of another are deliberately attempting to belittle or disrespect them. Athens suggests that people with violent self-images tend to engage in more confrontations as they tend to form more frustrative, frustrative-malefic and malefic interpretations. He argues that individuals with non-violent self-images typically only behave aggressively when they form physically defensive interpretations.

Beck (1999) also suggests that individuals tend to engage in confrontations when they form hostile interpretations. However, Beck expands upon this to propose that individuals with a vulnerable or insecure sense of self will be extra sensitive to certain social situations and perceive insults where none were intended. A vulnerable or insecure sense of self is thought to be one which is steeped in feelings of shame and humiliation (Beck, 1999; Butler, 2008; Gilligan, 1996, 2001; Scheff and Retzinger, 1991; Young, 1999, 2003). Beck (1999) argues that a shame based sense of self leads an individual to react to perceived assaults by fighting back or attacking someone weaker than him/herself. In addition, such individuals are assumed to believe that the only way available to them to maintain their identity, reputation and claim to respectability is through the use of aggression. More specifically, he suggests that an insecure sense of self may increase an individual's biased cognitions, such as their overgeneralisations of hostility, hostile attributional bias and denial of responsibility for aggressive behaviour.

**Narratives of Shame and Over-sensitivity to Disrespect**

However, recent research has failed to confirm this theoretical relationship. Butler (2007, forthcoming) did not find a significant association between themes present in the men's self-narratives and the extent to which they engaged in a hostile attributional bias, overgeneralised feelings of hostility, generated hostile responses to social situations and denied responsibility for their aggressive behaviour. The extent to which the men demonstrated these "biased" cognitions was also not predictive of their self-reported involvement in prisoner confrontations during a one-month follow-up period. Interestingly, however, Butler (2007, forthcoming) found that themes of personal shame within the men's self-narratives were predictive of future involvement in prisoner confrontations, even controlling for a measure of previous violent behaviour and other possible confounding variables.

Numerous researchers theorise that the emotion of shame can lead to aggressive behaviour as people attempt to transform and/or deflect feelings of shame into feelings of anger (see Braithwaite, 1989; Katz, 1988; Gilligan, 1996; Lewis, 1971; Scheff, 2000; Scheff and Retzinger, 1991; Young, 1999). Gilligan (1996; 2001), for instance, suggests that shame based self-narratives may lead men to engage in confrontations as they attempt to replace feelings of shame with feelings of pride achieved through an aggressive display of "manly" behaviour. Individuals with an insecure self tend to hold less positive views about themselves and seek to enhance their self-worth by obtaining positive interpersonal feedback from others (see also Brown, Collins and Schmidt, 1988; Baumeister, Tice and Hutton, 1989; Vohs and Heatherton, 2001). As a result, they may be especially prone to engaging in confrontations out of a psychological need to protect the self and/or demand respect from others (see Butler, 2008; Butler and Maruna, 2009; Crocker, Park and Lee, 2006; Toch, 1992).

Indeed, considerable research indicates that violence tends to be used in situations in which individuals feel their identity, status and/or social honour is being threatened (Katz, 1988; Staub, 2006; Wolfgang, 1958). This process is illustrated clearly in a recent study of prisoner-on-prisoner violence conducted by the authors. In interviews with 89 male, Category C prisoners at an English prison, Butler and Maruna (2009) found that the men generally engage in an uneasy truce with one another that appears to be broken only "when there are triggers from the social environment which act on a personality that has been sensitised to shame" (Gilligan, 1996: p. 223). One interviewee described the causes of violence within the prison as such:

> I don't know, I think, I don't know, disrespect is like, I think people think they are made to look little in front of other people, it is insecurity isn't it, do you get me? Insecure in themselves so they react because they want to show the person that they can't do that to them because they will do this and then that will send a

> message to anybody else who is thinking of dissing[5] you, do you get me? (Int. #78, aged 26 – All quotes from Butler and Maruna, 2009).

When challenged or insulted, individuals with an insecure sense of self may feel that they must react to this challenge to reaffirm their sense of self and status:

> Definitely, yeah, definitely, you get a lot of people who while they are in jail, a lot of people, like their mentality, a lot of people think that they have got something to prove, especially a lot of people trying to talk down to people, like disrespecting them (Int. #40, aged 32).

Somewhat ironically, then, the use of confrontational behaviour between prisoners might be seen as an expressive demand to be treated with respect among those who feel they have none:

> I have a lot of expectations about what I want to be. I want to be a somebody, I don't want to be a nobody (Int. #85, aged 26).

Interviewed prisoners consistently described incidences of disrespect as being the most important immediate trigger for episodes of violence within the prison. Some used the term "disrespect" directly, which allowed interviewers to probe what they meant by this phrase. The most consistently used synonym for disrespect was the experience of being "made to feel small" or feelings of "invisibility":

> I was just queuing up and some person cut in in-front of me. I said something like "What is wrong with the rest of the queue?" and he just turned round and started sort of squaring up to me and giving it this and that, and I just sort of explained to him that it wouldn't look very good for him to be laid out on the floor [...] with his little plate trying to get his dinner, you know, it might get a bit messy for him. [...] I think it was more "Hang on, what am I invisible" you know? [...] Yeah, you know "You're nothing and I'm better than you and I'm going to cut in in-front of you" (Int. #38, age 41).

Participants were clear that the issue was one of both internal pride, but also external reputation. The self being shamed by acts of disrespect was a "looking-glass self" (Gecas and Schwalbe, 1983) involving the eyes of significant others:

> He was queue jumping [i.e. *cutting in line*] and it is the same here as it is on any [prison] wing. It is sort of a respect issue, if you let someone push in in-front of you in a queue or whatever, people's opinion of you goes down slightly (Int. #68, aged 36).

5 "Dissing" was a term used by participants to refer to the process of being disrespected.

> [He] went around and told everybody on the wing that I was an idiot. Yeah, calling me an idiot because I couldn't pay him back [for a borrowed phone card]. I thought [...] "Yeah, going to sort this out". So I went up to him and I said "What's all this I hear about me being an idiot?" [...] Before he said anything, I like punched him in the nose. [...] I'm the sort of geezer that is a nice fellow but if someone is going around taking the piss[6] out of me, things going round, people saying stuff about me, then I'll do something about it (Int. #74, age 35).

As a result of perceived challenges to their identity, the participants generally felt compelled to "defend their honour" in a similar manner as discussed by Gilligan (1996). Sometimes this sense of dignity was ascribed to one's upbringing:

> I don't take disrespect, I'm from somewhere where we don't take disrespect. If you disrespect me I'll honour myself (Int. #60, aged 29).

For many prisoners, the easiest way available to them to defend their honour, and replace their feelings of shame with feelings of pride, was through aggressive means.

## Conclusions and Implications for Policy

Theories of social-information processing suggest that violence is linked to an over-sensitivity to perceived disrespect. Narrative research suggests this over-sensitivity may be related to personal feelings of low self-worth and shame. Numerous interventions have been developed in an attempt to help offenders reinterpret their self-narratives so as to reduce the psychological need they feel to engage in aggression. Indeed, interventions have been developed specifically focusing on the relationship between feelings of shame, masculinity and aggression (see Asser, 2002, 2004; Dobash, Dobash, Cavanangh and Lewis, 2000; Gilligan, 2001). In the Resolve to Stop the Violence Programme, for instance, men deconstruct their concept of masculinity and discuss how societal ideas of masculinity can pressurise them to engage in violence (Gilligan, 2001). The Shame Violence Intervention attempts to reduce violence by teaching men to replace feelings of shame with feelings of confidence and self-assurance obtained through non-aggressive means (Asser, 2002, 2004). Further, Maruna and LeBel (2003) argue that strengths based interventions that "ask not what a person's deficits are, but rather what positive contribution the person can make" (Maruna and LeBel, 2003: p. 97) can help individuals reconstruct shame-based self-narratives and reclaim a sense of personal dignity.

---

6 "Taking the piss" is a colloquially term used by the participants to refer to an individual or group of individuals attempting to disrespect or belittle another.

Unfortunately, however, such interventions are few in number and some of the more common treatment interventions available inside prison can tend to further pathologise prisoners by attributing violent behaviour to "errors" or biases within their cognitions (see Gadd, 2004; Henriques, Hollway, Urwin, Venn and Walkerdine, 1984; Maruna and Mann, 2006). Moreover, even the best designed treatment interventions are easily overwhelmed by the wider climate of hostility (inside and outside penal establishments) faced by prisoners and ex-prisoners. For example, Butler (2008) notes that prisoners with an insecure self-tended to express more themes of stigmatisation, discrimination and exclusion in their self-narratives than those secure in their identity. She notes that these narrative themes appeared to reflect broader societal and political narratives of prisoners and their behaviour. This implies that while cognitive-based interventions may be somewhat effective at reducing aggressive behaviour, their effectiveness will remain limited until attempts are also made to understand the wider processes involved in the construction and maintenance of an individual's identity as well as the meaning aggressive behaviour holds for their sense of self.

In particular, future research on self-narratives and violence might seek to situate these narratives within a gender and developmental context. As Professor Canter argued in *Criminal Shadows*, "Many acts of violence seem to erupt at a time when the perpetrator is searching for identity and personal meaning" (1994: p. 326). Research by Canter and others has been instrumental in drawing attention to the potential of self-narratives to drive individuals toward pathological behaviours. The next generation of research might usefully explore what factors lead to the development of these self-myths and what meta-narratives in the public domain (e.g., the media, popular culture, national myths about masculinity and power) work to sustain them (e.g., Matza and Sykes, 1961).

## References

Abel, G.G., Gore, D., Holland, C., Camp, N., Becker, J. and Rathner, B. (1989). The measurement of the cognitive distortions of child molesters. *Annals of Sex Research*, 2, 135–153.

Alison, L.J. and Parkinson, M. (1995). *Criminal Autobiographies: Generating and Extracting the Destructive Life Stories of Adult and Juvenile Offender*. University of Liverpool, internal report.

Alison, L. and Stein, K.L. (2001). Vicious circles: accounts of stranger sexual assault reflect abusive variants of conventional interactions. *Journal of Forensic Psychiatry & Psychology*, 12, 515–538.

Asser, J. (2004). Working with the dynamics of shame and violence. *Organisational and Social Dynamics*, 4, 88–106.

Asser, J. (2002). Working with prisoners in a transitional space. *Psychodynamic Practice*, 8, 7–19.

Athens, L. (1997). *Violent Criminal Acts and Actors Revisited.* Chicago: University of Illinois Press.

Bandura, A. (1989). Human agency in social cognitive theory. *American Psychologist*, 44, 75–184.

Barlett, C.P. and Anderson, C.A. (2011). Reappraising the situation and its impact on aggressive behavior. *Personality and Social Psychology Bulletin*, 37(12), 1564–1573.

Barriga, A.Q., Landau, J.R., Stinson, B.L., Liau, A.K. and Gibbs, J.C. (2000). Cognitive distortion and problem behaviors in adolescents. *Criminal Justice & Behavior*, 27, 36–56.

Baumeister, R.F., Tice, D.M. and Hutton, D.G. (1989). Self-presentational motivations and personality differences in self-esteem. *Journal of Personality and Social Psychology*, 74, 606–621.

Beck, A.T. (1999). *Prisoners of Hate: The Cognitive Basis of Anger, Hostility and Violence*. New York: Harper Collins Publishers.

Bennett, J. (1981). *Oral History and Delinquency*. Chicago: University of Chicago Press.

Bertaux, D. (1981). From the life-history approach to the transformation of sociological practice. *Biography and Society: The Life History Approach in the Social Sciences*, edited by D. Bertaux. London: Sage.

Blackburn, R. (1994). *The Psychology of Criminal Conduct: Theory, Research and Practice*. New York: John Wiley and Sons.

Bolitho, W. (1926). *Murder for Profit*. London: Jonathan Cape.

Blumenthal, S., Gudjonsson, G. and Burns, J. (1999). Cognitive distortions and blame attribution in sex offenders against adults and children. *Child Abuse & Neglect*, 23, 129–143.

Braithwaite, L. (1989). *Crime, Shame and Reintegration*. Cambridge: Cambridge University Press.

Brown, B., Nolan, P., Crawford, P. and Lewis, A. (1994). Interaction, language and the "narrative turn" in psychotherapy and psychiatry. *Social Science and Medicine*, 43, 1569–1578.

Brown, J.D., Collins, R.L. and Schmidt, G.W. (1988). Self-esteem and direct versus indirect forms of self-enhancement. *Journal of Personality and Social Psychology*, 55, 445–453.

Bruner, J.S. (1987). Life as narrative. *Social Research*, 54, 11–32.

Bruner, J.S. (2004). Life as narrative. *Social Research*, 71, 691–710.

Bush, J. (1995). Teaching self-risk management of violent offenders, in *What Works: Reducing Reoffending. Guidelines from Research and Practice*, edited by J. McGuire. Chichester: Wiley.

Butler, M. (forthcoming). Prisoner interpersonal violence – shamed into it? *The Prison Journal*.

Butler, M. (2008). What are you looking at? Prisoner confrontations and the search for respect. *British Journal of Criminology*, 48(6), 856–873.

Butler, M. (2007). *Prisoner Confrontations: The Role of Shame, Masculinity and Respect*. Cambridge: Unpublished PhD Thesis.

Bulter, M. and Maruna, S. (2009). The impact of disrespect on prisoners' aggression: outcomes of experimentally inducing violence-supportive cognitions. *Psychology, Crime & Law*, 15(2 and 3), 235–250.

Canter, D.V. (1994). *Criminal Shadows*. London: Harper Collins.

Canter, D.V. (2008). In the kingdom of the blind (pp. 1–21), in *Psychology and Law: Bridging the Gap*, edited by Canter, D.V. and R. Zukauskiene. Aldershot: Ashgate.

Canter, D.V., Grieve, N., Nicol, C. and Benneworth, K. (2003). Narrative plausibility: the impact of sequence and anchoring. *Behavioral Sciences & the Law*, 21, 251–267.

Canter, D.V. and Ioannou, M. (2004). Criminals' emotional experiences during crimes. *International Journal of Forensic Psychology*, 1, 71–81.

Caspi, A. and Moffitt, T.E. (1995). The continuity of maladaptive behaviour: from description to understanding in the study of antisocial behaviour, in *Manual of Developmental Psychopathology*, edited by D. Cicchetti and D. Cohenen. New York: Wiley & Sons.

Cressey, D.R. (1953). *Other People's Money: A Study in the Social Psychology of Embezzlement*. Glencoe: The Free Press.

Crick, N.R. and Dodge, K.A. (1994). A review and reformation of social information processing mechanisms in children's social adjustment. *Psychological Bulletin*, 115, 74–101.

Crocker, J., Lee, S.J. and Park, L.E. (2004). The pursuit of self-esteem: implications for good and evil, in *The Social Psychology of Good and Evil*, edited by A.G. Miller. London: Guilford Press.

Culley, W.G. (2004). *Desistance from Crime a Study of Ex-inmates' Desistance Narratives*. Unpublished Ph.D. Dissertation, Duquesne University.

Currie, E. (1991). *Dope and Trouble: Portraits of Delinquent Youth*. New York: Pantheon Books.

Day, A. and Bryan, J. (2007). Personality change and personality disorder: some initial thoughts on the application of McAdams' triarchic model to the treatment of personality disorder. *Psychology, Crime & Law*, 13, 19–26.

de Castro, B.O., Veerman, J.W., Koops, W., Bosch, J.D. and Manshouwer, H.J. (2002). Hostile attribution of intent and aggressive behavior: a meta-analysis. *Child Development*, 73, 916–934.

Dobash, R.E., Dobash, R.P., Cavanagh, K. and Lewis, R. (2000). *Changing Violent Men*. Thousand Oaks: Sage.

Dodge, K.A. (2003). Do social information-processing patterns mediate aggressive behavior? in *Causes of Conduct Disorder and Juvenile Delinquency*, edited by B.B. Lahey, T.E. Moffitt and A. Caspi. London: The Guildford Press.

Dodge, K.A., Cozier, J. and Lansford, J.E. (2001). *Social Information Processing Mediators of the Effect of Early Maltreatment on the Development of Aggressive Behavior*. Paper Presented at the Biennial Meeting of the Society for the Research in Child Development, Minneapolis, MN.

Dodge, K.A. and Newman, J.P. (1981). Biased decision-making process in aggressive boys. *Journal of Abnormal Psychology*, 90, 375–379.

Dodge, K.A., Pettit, G.S., Bates, J.E. and Valente, E. (1995). Social information-processing patterns partially mediate the effect of early physical abuse on later conduct problems. *Journal of Abnormal Psychology*, 104, 632–643.

Egan, S., Monson, T. and Perry, D. (1998). Social-cognitive influences on change in aggression over time. *Developmental Psychology*, 34, 996–1006.

Elkind, D. (1968). *Children and Adolescents: Interpretive Essays on Jean Piaget*. New York: Oxford Press.

Epstein, S. and Erskine, N. (1983). The development of personal theories of reality from an interactional perspective, in *Human Development: An Interactional Perspective*, edited by D. Magnusson and V.L. Allen. New York: Academic Press.

Erikson, E. (1959). *Identity and the Life Cycle*. New York: W.W. Norton & Company.

Finestone, H. (1976). *Victims of Change: Juvenile Delinquents in American Society*. Westport: Greenwood Press.

Fritzon, K., Lewis, H. and Doley, R. (2011). Looking at the characteristics of adult arsonists from a narrative perspective. *Psychiatry, Psychology and Law*, 18(30), 424–438.

Fromm, E. (1941). *Escape from Freedom*. New York: Henry Holt.

Gadd, D. (2000). Masculinities, violence and defended psychosocial subjects. *Theoretical Criminology*, 4, 429–449.

Gadd, D. (2004). Evidence-led policy or policy-led evidence? Cognitive behavioural programmes for men who are violent towards women. *Criminal Justice*, 4, 173–197.

Gadd, D. and Farrall, S. (2004). Criminal careers, desistance and subjectivity: interpreting men's narratives of change. *Theoretical Criminology*, 8, 123–155.

Gadd, D. and Jefferson, T. (2007). *Psychosocial Criminology: An Introduction*. London: Sage Publications.

Gecas, V. and Schwalbe, M.L. (1983). Beyond the looking-glass self: social structure and efficacy-based self-esteem. *Social Psychology Quarterly*, 46, 77–88.

Gibbs, J., Potter, G. and Goldstein, A.P. (1995). *The EQUIP Program: Teaching Youth to Think and Act Responsibly through a Peer Helping Approach*. Champaign, IL: Research Press.

Giddens, A. (1991). *Modernity and Self-Identity: Self and Society in the Late Modern Age*. Stanford, CA: Stanford University Press.

Gilligan, J. (2001). *Violence and the Sacred*. Baltimore, MD: Johns Hopkins University Press.

Gilligan, J. (1996). *Violence: Our Deadly Epidemic and Its Causes*. New York: Grosset/ Putnam.

Graham, J. and Bowling, B. (1995). *Young People and Crime*. London: Home Office.

Green, G., South, N. and Smith, R. (2006). They say that you are a danger but you are not: representations and construction of the moral self. *Deviant Behavior*, 27, 299–328.

Henriques, J., Hollway, W., Urwin, C., Venn, C. and Walkerdine, V. (1984). *Changing the Subject: Psychology, Social Regulation and Subjectivity*. London: Routledge.

Holloway, W. and Jefferson, T. (2000). *Doing Qualitative Research Differently*. London: Sage Publications.

Huesmann, L.R. (1988). An information-processing model for the development of aggression. *Aggressive Behavior*, 14, 13–24.

Katz, J. (1988). *Seductions of Crime: The Moral and Sensual Attractions of Doing Evil*. New York: Basic Books.

Kierkegaard, S. (1941). *The Sickness unto Death* (W. Lowrie, Trans.). Princeton, NJ: Princeton University Press (Original work published 1843).

Kleckar, R.F. and Ting, I.D. (2004). Using a collaborative approach with criminal justice clients: a promising narrative in rehabilitation. *Journal of Systemic Therapies*, 23, 64–77.

Koesling, A. and Neuber, A. (2007). The "home-sickness" of the jack-roller. *Theoretical Criminology*, 11, 501–13.

Kohli, M. (1981). Biography: account, text, method, in *Biography and Society*, edited by D. Bertaux. London: Sage.

Laub, J. (1983). Interview with Edwin M. Lemert, in *Criminology in the Making: An Oral History*, edited by J. Laub. Boston: Northeastern.

Laub, J. and Sampson, R. (2003). *Shared Beginnings, Divergent Lives: Delinquent Boys to Age 70*. Cambridge, MA: Harvard University Press.

Lewis, H. (1971). *Shame and Guilt in Neurosis*. New York: International Universities Press.

Luckenbill, D.F. (1977). Criminal homicide as a situated transaction. *Social Problems*, 25, 176–186.

Maruna, S. (2004). Desistance and explanatory style: a new direction in the psychology of reform. *Journal of Contemporary Criminal Justice*, 20, 184–200.

Maruna, S. (2001). *Making Good: How Ex-Convicts Reform and Rebuild their Lives*. Washington: American Psychological Association.

Maruna, S. and LeBel, T.P. (2003). Welcome home? Examining the "rentry court" concept from a strength based perspective. *Western Criminology Review*, 4, 91–107.

Maruna, S. and Mann, R. (2006). A fundamental attributional error? Rethinking cognitive distortions. *Legal and Criminological Psychology*, 11, 155–177.

Maruna, S. and Ramsden, D. (2004). Living to tell the tale: redemption narratives, shame management and offender rehabilitation, in *Healing Plots: The Narrative Basis of Psychotherapy* (pp. 129–151), edited by A. Lieblich, D.P. McAdams and J. Josselson. Washington, DC: American Psychological Association.

Maruna, S. and Roy, K. (2007). Amputation or reconstruction: notes on "knifing off" and desistance from crime. *Journal of Contemporary Criminal Justice*, 23, 104–124.

Matza, D. and Sykes, G. (1961). Juvenile delinquency and subterranean values. *American Sociological Review*, 26, 712–719.

McAdams, D.P. (1985). *Power, Intimacy and the Life Story: Personological Inquiries into Identity*. New York: The Guilford Press.

McAdams, D.P. (1993). *The Stories We Live By: Personal Myths and the Making of the Self.* New York: Willam Morrow & Company.

McAdams, D.P. (1999). Personal narratives and the life story, in *Handbook of personality: Theory and research* (2nd ed., pp. 478–500), edited by L. Pervin and O. John. New York: Guildford Press.

McAdams, D.P. (2001). The psychology of life stories. *Review of General Psychology*, 5, 100–122.

McAdams, D.P. (2006). *The Redemptive Self: Stories Americans Live By*. New York: Oxford University Press.

McKendy, J.P. (2006). I'm very careful about that: narrative and agency of men in prison. *Discourse & Society*, 17, 473–502.

Megargee, E.I. and Bohn, M. (1979). *Classifying Criminal Offenders: A New System Based on the MMPI*. Beverly Hills, CA: Sage.

Mills, C.W. (1940). Situated actions and vocabularies of motive. *American Sociological Review*, 5, 904–13.

Murphy, W.D. (1990). Assessment and modification of cognitive distortions in sex offenders, in *Handbook of Sexual Assault* (pp. 331–342), edited by W.L. Marshall, D.R. Laws and H.E. Barbaree. New York: Plenum Press.

Nasby, W., Hayden, B. and DePaulo, B.M. (1979). Attributional bias among aggressive boys to interpret unambiguous social stimuli as displays of hostility. *Journal of Abnormal Psychology*, 89, 459–468.

Newell, A. and Simon, H.A. (1972). *Human Problem Solving*. New York: Prentice-Hall.

O'Connor, P.E. (2000). *Speaking of Crime: Narratives of Prisoners*. Lincoln, NE: University of Nebraska Press.

Presser, L. (2008). *Been a Heavy Life: Stories of Violent Men*. Urbana, IL: Illinois.

Reijntjes, A., Thomaes, S., Kamphuis, J.H., Bushman, B.J., de Castro, B.O. and Telch, M.J. (2011). Explaining the paradoxical rejection-aggression link: the mediating effects of hostile intent attributions, anger, and decreases in state self-esteem on peer rejection-induced aggression in youth. *Personality and Social Psychology Bulletin*, 37(7), 955–963.

Pulkkinen, M.L. and Aaltonen, J. (2003). Sense of agency in narrative processes of repeatedly convicted drunk drivers. *Counselling Psychology Quarterly*, 16, 145–159.

Salfati, C.G. (2000). The nature of expressiveness and instrumentality in homicide. *Homicide Studies*, 4, 265–293.

Salter, A.C. (1988). *Treating Child Sex Offenders and their Victims: A Practical Guide*. Newbury Park, CA: Sage Publications.

Sampson, R.J. and Laub, J. (1992). Crime and deviance in the life course. *Annual Review of Sociology*, 18, 63–84.

Sampson, R.J. and Laub, J. (1993). *Crime in the Making: Pathways and Turning Points through Life*. Cambridge, MA: Harvard University Press.

Sarangi, S. and Alison, L. (2005). Life story accounts of left wing terrorists in India. *Journal of Investigative Psychology and Offender Profiling*, 2, 69–86.

Sarbin, T.R. (1986). *Narrative Psychology: The Storied Nature of Human Conduct*. New York: Praeger.

Scott, M.B. and Lyman, S.M. (1968). Accounts. *American Sociological Review*, 33, 46–61.

Scheff, T.J. (2000). Shame and the social bond: a sociological theory. *Sociological Theory*, 18, 84–99.

Scheff, T.J. and Retzinger, S.M. (1991). *Emotions and Violence: Shame and Rage in Destructive Conflicts*. MA: Lexington Books.

Shaw, C.R. (1930). *The Jack-Roller: A Delinquent Boy's Own Story*. Chicago: University of Chicago Press.

Shaw, C. (1929). *Delinquency Areas*. Chicago: University of Chicago Press.

Shaw, C.R. and McKay, H.D. (1931). *Juvenile Delinquency in Urban Areas*. Chicago: University of Chicago Press.

Slaby, R.G. and Guerra, N.G. (1988). Cognitive mediators of aggression in adolescent offenders: 1 Assessment. *Developmental Psychology*, 27, 159–171.

Snow, P.C. and Powell, M.B. (2005). An exploration of narrative language abilities in male juvenile offenders. *Psychology, Crime and Law*, 11, 239–253.

Staub, E. (2006). Basic human needs, altruism, and aggression, in *The Social Psychology of Good and Evil*, edited by A.G. Miller. London: Guilford Press.

Sullivan, M. (1989). *Getting Paid: Youth Crime and Work in the Inner City*. Ithaca: Cornell University Press.

Sykes, G.M. and Matza, D. (1957). Techniques of neutralization: a theory of delinquency. *American Sociological Review*, 22, 664–673.

Tagg, S.K. (1985). Life story interviews and their interpretation, in *The Research Interview*, edited by M. Brenner, J. Brown and D.V. Canter. London: Academic Press.

Toch, H. (1992). *Violent Men: An Inquiry into the Psychology of Violence*, revised edition. Washington: American Psychological Association.

Thomas, W.I. and Thomas, D. (1928). *The Child in America*. New York: Knopf.

Vaughan, B. (2007). The internal narrative of desistance. *British Journal of Criminology*, 47, 390–404.

Vohs, K.D. and Heatherton, T.F. (2001). Self-esteem and threats to self: implications for self-construals and interpersonal perceptions. *Journal of Personality and Social Psychology*, 81, 1103–1118.

Ward, T. and Marshall, B. (2007). Narrative identity and offender rehabilitation. *International Journal of Offender Therapy and Comparative Criminology*, 53, 279–297.

Watlers, G.D. (2007). Measuring proactive and reactive criminal thinking with the PICTS. *Journal of Interpersonal Violence*, 22, 371–185.

Weiss, B., Dodge, K.A., Bates, J.A. and Pettit, G.S. (1992). Some consequences of early harsh discipline: child aggression and a maladaptive social information processing style. *Child Development*, 63, 1321–1335.

White, M. and Epston, D. (1990). *Narrative Means to Therapeutic End.* New York: Norton.

Wolfgang, M. (1958). *Patterns in Criminal Homicide.* New York: John Wiley & Sons.

Young, J. (1999). *The Exclusive Society: Social Exclusion, Crime and Difference in Late Modernity.* London: Sage.

Young, J. (2003). Merton with energy, Katz with structure: the sociology of vindictiveness and the criminology of transgression. *Theoretical Criminology,* 7, 389–414.

Youngs, D. (2004). Personality correlates of offence style. *Journal of Investigative Psychology and Offender Profiling,* 1, 99–119.

Youngs, D. and Canter, D. (2009). An emerging research agenda for investigative interviewing: hypotheses from the narrative action system. *Journal of Investigative Psychology and Offender Profiling.* 6: 91–99. doi: 10.1002/jip.105.

Youngs, D. and Canter, D.V. (2011). Narrative roles in criminal action: an integrative framework for differentiating offenders. *Legal and Criminological Psychology.* doi: 10.1111/j.2044-8333.2011.02011.x

Youngs, D. and Canter, D.V. (2012). Offenders' crime narratives as revealed by the narrative roles questionnaire. *International Journal of Offender Therapy and Comparative Criminology.*

# Chapter 3
# Action Sytems Models of Criminal Differentiation

Katarina Fritzon

**Editor's Introduction**

In this chapter, Kate Fritzon describes one of the theoretical frameworks used in Investigative Psychology to interpret the patterns of offence actions revealed in empirical study. Note that the Action Systems model, like the Narrative framework, was developed for 'well-functioning' systems and had not been considered in relation to criminal behaviour before the original Canter and Fritzon (1998) study showed how it could be adjusted for and applied to arson. This framework has proved particularly useful for understanding certain components of offending, although it lacks 'inferential fluency' (Youngs, 2008) until integrated with the both the Narrative and Victim Role perspectives within the overall Narrative Action System (NAS) model of offending style (Canter and Youngs, 2009).

**Introduction**

One of the central and most pervasive ideas within Investigative Psychology is that of criminal differentiation (for example Canter, 1995a, 1995b, 2000). Emphasising the need for robust models to effectively describe the nuances of criminal behaviour, Canter (2000) draws attention to the multivariate hierarchy of criminal actions and the importance of distinguishing the most psychologically relevant, in order to make meaningful inferences about the characteristics of the offenders responsible.

Crime has been described a complex interaction between personal factors, such as disposition, motivation and beliefs, as well as situational factors, such as availability of targets or victims, opportunity and absence of preventative measures (for example Cohen and Felson, 1986; Clarke, 1997). Several theories have attempted to account for one or more of these individual factors, however, what is proposed here is a unified framework for understanding the process of decision making that occurs at a socio-cognitive level, and dictates actions that will be undertaken during the commission of an offence. As will be shown, the model has implications for understanding variations and functions of behaviour and can be used to account for consistency and change in behaviour across different modalities and settings. The practical and theoretical implications of the Faceted Action Systems Theory model (FAST) will be discussed in this chapter.

## The Action Systems Framework

Systems theories of criminology arose from the work of von Bertalanffy (1947) and Talcott Parsons (1953) and have been applied to a diverse range of criminal activities, systems and networks. In a recent example, following the September 11 attacks in the US, ideas derived from systems theory were used to describe the actions and networks of al-Qaeda terrorists (Lutes, 2001). The most common application of general systems theory today, however, is within family systems therapy, particularly around the theoretical orientation developed by Murray Bowen and colleagues (for example Kerr and Bowen, 1988).

According to von Bertalanffy's original systemic theory, normal motivation implies autonomous activity, integration of behaviour, adaptability to changing situations, free use of symbolic anticipation, decision, and so forth. Psychiatric disturbances can be defined in terms of disruptions to these system functions. Thus, psychotherapy aims to evoke creative potentialities, attempts to reintegrate the individual back into society, and orientate them toward goals and the future. This position sees psychopathology, specifically neurosis, as stemming from the experience of meaninglessness, or existentialism; 'the answer whether an individual is mentally sound or not is ultimately determined by whether he has an integrated universe consistent with the given cultural framework' (von Bertalanffy, 1960).

Applying these ideas to criminal behaviour, readers may be reminded of classic criminological theories, for example Durkheim's concept of *anomie* wherein criminality can be viewed as a disturbance of symbolic functions, where the symbols are the rules and conventions of society, the social order, and moral values incorporating culture. Critics of Parson's application of systemic models to criminology have pointed to the lack of acknowledgement of the role of human emotion, and have called for perspectives that take into account both the rational and non-rational elements of human decision making (Fish, 2004). Originally developed as a model for understanding behaviour of individuals within well-functioning systems, Sam Shye's (1985) Behavioural Action Systems framework has recently been applied to criminal as well as other 'dysfunctional' behaviour, including behaviour with high levels of expressed emotions such as self-harm. Within the more recent applications of this framework, such as the self-harm example (Miller and Fritzon, 2007), the role of human emotion, as both an internal driver for behaviour, as well as a target for behavioural change is acknowledged, thus overcoming some of the criticisms of some of the original systems theories.

This framework integrates theory with methodology, utilising multidimensional scaling procedures to show that across various behavioural, social and cultural settings, four modes of functioning can be found to describe interactions that occur between the 'system' and the environment. Incorporating elements of Facet Theory (Canter, 1985), it has been labelled Faceted Action Systems Theory by Canter, Fritzon and colleagues (for example Fritzon and Brun, 2005). Shye (1985) defines a system as a collection of members that maintain interrelationships among themselves. To the extent that such a system is *active, open, organised and stable*, it can be regarded as an action system.

In general, Shye's work has been concerned with effective system functioning, or 'well designed' action systems. The challenge of applying Shye's model to criminal behaviour was in the question of whether the same essentially ordered patterns would be observed within systems that could be described as chaotic, poorly functioning and disintegrated; or whether in breaking the laws of social order, criminals also contravene the laws of systemic order.

Shye (1985) points out that in order to model all action systems which are open it is necessary to consider a) the sources of the action and b) the effect or desired target of the action. Both these aspects of the action system can be located internally or externally. Thus the source can be within or outside the acting agent, in this case the criminal. The impact or target can be within the environment or the individual. In the case of criminal behaviour, for example, this leads to the proposal that the dominant goal is either to change the state of feeling and experience of the criminal him/herself or to modify some external state of the world.

Shye (1985) has illustrated in a number of studies that the combination of a) the internal and external sources of action with b) agent or environment as the targets of the action gives rise to four basic modes of functioning of action systems labelled *Adaptive*, *Expressive*, *Integrative* and *Conservative*. The four modes of acting, derived from their two primary facets can be summarised as follows:

### *a) Integrative Mode*

This is the mode which describes adjustments that take place within the system itself. This is distinct from the expressive mode in that the impact of the action is primarily internal, rather than necessarily having an observable external effect. It is possible to see how this type of psychological integrativity might become more pathological in individuals with some level of emotional disturbance. Such individuals might, for example, engage in attention-seeking activities that could endanger both their own lives and the lives of others.

### *b) Adaptive Mode*

Functioning in this mode, the action system responds to external events in the environment by making adjustments to that environment. This involves manipulation and exploitation, and so there is some overt purpose or instrumental gain sought in the action that is, in effect, a reaction to an aspect of the context the individual is in. Crimes committed within this mode of action are expected to be opportunistic with the selection of actual target being less important than the desire to modify or gain from it.

*c) Expressive Mode*

The dominant style of operation here is the demonstration of internal psychological aspects of the agent on the external world. According to Shye (1985) this is the way in which the system 'exercises its power and influence on its surroundings [by trying to create] a reality which reflects in one way or another the system's own characteristics' (p. 102). In the context of criminal behaviour, this mode of functioning would be expected to describe the behaviour of, for example, certain sorts of sadistic sexual killers in which elaborate pre-offence fantasies are regarded as playing a dominant role in the way that victims are killed (Ressler et al, 1986).

*d) Conservative Mode*

Shye describes this as 'events [that] constitute a fundamental aspect of [the system's] identity' and gives as examples the adoption of a constitution by an American state, or perpetuation of religious beliefs. Broadly, these involve events that originate externally and are internally assimilated by the system. In the context of criminal behaviour, however, it may be more appropriate to adopt a slightly broader definition of acts that involve the conservative mode of functioning. For example, criminal acts perpetrated out of a desire for personal revenge may be seen as the individual responding to an external source of frustration that s/he wishes to hurt or remove. This would be seen as conservative particularly where the retaliation was directed at someone with whom there was a close personal relationship, so that the act would be directed at redressing the individual's own state of emotional well-being.

These modes, then, provide a hypothesis of the major variations that will distinguish between different action systems. Any system under study – in the following section various examples of criminal or deviant activity – will thus be expected to operate in a way that indicates a dominant theme to their activities which accords with one of the hypothesised modes.

In considering the four modes of acting Shye (1985) argues that they have logical similarities and differences from each other. Thus adaptivity with its emphasis on adjustments outside of the system is most distinct from integrativity with its focus on internal adjustments. Conservativity is distinct from expressivity in terms of the direction of actions, the former being an internalisation of external factors and the latter being an acting out of internal processes. These considerations of the logical relationships between the modes of action can be represented geometrically as shown in Figure 3.1.

In summary, Figure 3.1 proposes that because the conservativity and expressivity modes constitute two polar ends in the functioning of an action system, they are expected to be at opposite ends of the diagrammatic representation. Adaptivity is derivable from these two extremities and therefore maintains an affinity with both of them, and the same is true of integrativity. Although these are also distinct from

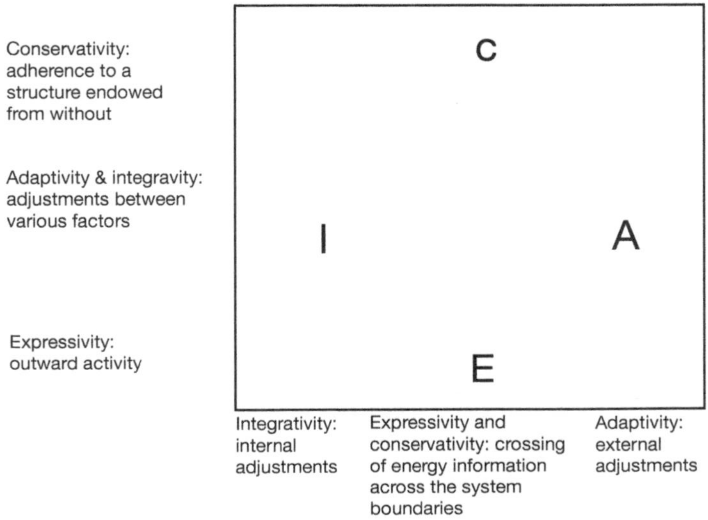


**Figure 3.1 The conceptual interrelationships among the functioning modes of an action system, represented by means of geometric-spatial proximities**

each other (the former concerning external adjustments and the latter internal adjustments) they are not as distant from each other as are the poles of conservativity and expressivity.

Faceted Action Systems Theory therefore provides a number of specific hypotheses for the consideration of criminal behaviour. One set of hypotheses is that the four modes of acting will be distinguishable in an analysis of criminal activities. A second hypothesis is that the relative similarities and differences between these modes will take the form illustrated in Figure 3.1. These are the fundamental criteria that must be fulfilled if the argument that criminal activity can be described by this framework is to be supported.

## Application of Action Systems Model to Criminal Behaviour

What is presented here as an adaptation of Shye's model, can be thought of as a systemic theory of criminal personality, incorporating both behavioural decision making and socio-cognitive processing (Fontaine, 2006). In a series of studies, Fritzon, Canter and colleagues have found support for the two main hypotheses – functional and structural – as outlined in the previous section. These studies have all utilised multidimensional scaling to test the structural hypotheses, that is variables representing the adaptive mode will be positioned on the opposite side of the MDS configuration from those representing the integrative mode, and that expressive variables will be opposite conservative. Table 3.1 summarises the variables found to represent the four functioning modes for each of the domains that have been studied. Following this is a combined discussion which gives further illustration, using the examples from criminal behaviour, to the functional definitions in the previous section.

**Table 3.1 Summary of variables representing the four modes of action systems functioning**

| Action system mode | Integrative | Adaptive | Expressive | Conservative |
|---|---|---|---|---|
| Fire setting (Fritzon, Canter and Wilton, 2001). | Own home, self, residential, suicide note, multiple items, remained, lives endangered by location, lives endangered deliberately (α =.72). | Business, car, finance, illegal entry, material brought, miscellaneous property, multiple offenders, not alert, other crime, outside, public view, school, spree, and theft (α = .62). | Public building, prior arson, remained, serial, crusade, drug use, institution, non-specific trigger (α = .62). | Partner, outburst, threat of arson, threats, accelerant, trigger specific, multiple seats, alcohol, argument, planned, targeted, victim known, witness (α = .83). |
| Fire setting (Almond, Duggan, Shine and Canter, 2005). | Own home, self, residential, lives endangered by location, hospital, trigger (α = .57). | Business, car, illegal entry, miscellaneous property, multiple offenders, theft (α = .25). | Public building, prior arson, remained, serial, multiple items, multiple seats (α = .56). | Threat of arson, threat of violence, argument, materials brought, trigger specific to victim, victim known (α = .81). |
| Fire setting (Miller and Fritzon, 2006). | Suicide attempt, person-private (own home), anxiety, negative event, depression (α = .52). | Protest, residential change, alert, serial, object-public (car, business) (α =.42). | Remain/return to scene, drug (and/or) alcohol misuse, object-private, physical aggression, verbal aggression, threat, excitement, emotional trigger, significant date (α =.53). | Psychosis, planned, previous arson, lives endangered, targeted, person-public, violence/ argument, victim known, victim partner, spree (α =.64). |
| Self-harm (Miller and Fritzon, 2006). | Varying forms, insert, hit self, self-anger, serial, genital location, planned (α = .70). | Residential change, frustration and other anger (α =.46). | Report, physical aggression, verbal aggression, threat, significant dates (α = .52). | Depression, distance, tense, burns, headbang, argument other and anxiety (α =.60). |

| Action system mode | Integrative | Adaptive | Expressive | Conservative |
|---|---|---|---|---|
| Hostage taking (Fritzon, Canter and Wilton, 2001). | Hostages injured by terrorists, hostages killed, authorities killed, terrorists escape, authorities wounded, hostages wounded. | Six+ days, alternative offer, terrorist change, media, allow to leave, bomb, concede, hostage released, authorities discuss, direct threat, prisoner, explosive, release, guns, 11+ hostages, escape, 2–5 days, group, negotiate, hostages targeted, 0–10 hostages, political, failed storm. | Authorities disagree, action demanded, deadline, surrender, hostage escape, money, kill entry. | One day, public place, terrorists captured, hostages and terrorists talk, terrorists killed, shoot-out, storm. |
| Intra-familial homicide (Fritzon, 2000). | Remain, own home, suicide, victim belief, altruistic motive, delusion, victim sleeping, nonviolent method, manual, multiple victim. | Stage, cover victim, destroy evidence, normal activity, weapon brought, post-mortem activity, multiple mode, sexual, time with victim, face. | Command, destroy property, victim escape, non-relative killed, other person trigger, other attack, planned. | Alcohol/drugs, limbs, blunt wounds, stab, torso, multiple wounds, self-alert, head/neck, weapon from scene, victim trigger, victim conflict, other threat, threat to kill, witness, ambush. |
| School homicide (Fritzon and Brun, 2005). | Shoot, head, suicide, victim female, classroom, bathroom. | Gang, monetary, location external to school, stab, personal, targeting, common area. | Outside, fight, manual injury. | Multiple wounding, injury to body, offender male, witness, plan, multiple victim, additional crime, teacher, random gunfire, dress, multiple weapon, multiple offender. |

Considering the range of behaviours described above, a number of observations that give detail to the generic descriptions of modes of functioning can be made.

## Integrative

Within all of the behavioural examples, this mode is characterised by suicidality, which is the extreme manifestation of emotional disturbance turned inward. In the case of the two homicide examples, the individual also directs their distress outward, resulting in the death of at least one other person. This has also been referred to as 'extended suicide' (Ewing, 1997). Interestingly, in the hostage taking example, the only group *not* killed during the integrative form are the terrorists themselves, therefore one can hypothesise that it is the system encompassing the authorities, terrorists and hostages, that is acting integratively here, with the resulting casualties ensuing from a chaotic intervention during which the terrorists are able to get away. In the self-harm example, this mode is arguably the most likely to eventuate in the individual's successfully completed suicide due to the serial and escalating nature of the seriousness of injuries.

## Adaptive

According to Shye's definitions, the adaptive mode of functioning is the opposite of integrative, involving the system making adjustments to external circumstances. As hypothesised, this form of behaviour is typical of general criminality, for example with arson and school homicide the context is peer group delinquency involving theft and other criminal activity. The manipulation of that which is external to the acting agent in intrafamilial homicide involves the perpetrator spending extended time at the crime scene, covering the victim, and attempting to disguise the scene.

Within the hostage taking example, the interpretation of adaptive is again somewhat different, taking a broader perspective of the system of the three interacting bodies; terrorists, authorities and hostages. Here, the adaptive form of functioning is most likely to lead to a successful resolution, in that the system remains open to its constituent parts, enabling negotiations and concessions to take place.

## Expressive

The expressive mode of functioning involves behavioural acting out of internal states. In the case of arson, there are several indicators of a fascination for fire, for example prior arson, serial, targeting of large buildings and remaining at the scene. In the Miller and Fritzon (2006) study which had an all-female sample, there are also other examples of behavioural acting-out within this mode, that is verbal and physical aggression. Additionally, the occurrence of significant dates within this sample for both fire-setting and self-harm is evidence for a ruminative internal source for the behaviour.

Within the two forms of homicide, it is a case of 'being in the wrong place at the wrong time' with both groups of perpetrators targeting victims apparently at random (in addition to the intrafamilial victim in the Fritzon, 2000 example). Although there may in some cases be some evidence of planning, this is mainly in relation to finding the location of the familial victim, and does not extend to the carrying of weapons or the risk of apprehension inherent in approaching the victim in public.

In the hostage taking example, the expressive variables indicate that the interaction between terrorists and authorities consists mainly of actions performed by the former party. However, failing to establish control, and with hostages escaping and authorities disagreeing on what course of action to take, the terrorists eventually surrender.

## Conservative

This is the mode of functioning in which external events are assimilated by the acting agent who experiences an internal locus of change. Within all forms of behaviour, the importance of the 'other' in this mode of action is apparent. Victims are known to the perpetrator, and matters are precipitated by arguments or events that have an effect of triggering an emotional response. The internal locus of change is evidenced by the planning, rumination and psychological distress experienced in the build-up to the crime, with perpetrators presumably experiencing a cathartic effect in its aftermath. This conceptualisation resembles the description of catathymic homicide (Meloy, 1997) in which, '… the violent act … is an expression of the fight on the part of the patient for the safeguarding of his personality' (Wertham, 1937 p. 978).

Again, a somewhat broader understanding within the hostage taking study (Fritzon, Canter and Wilton, 2001) is necessary. Within this 'system' the external agents of the authorities appear to have control over the interaction; the terrorists do not indicate any demands and are eventually killed or captured during the intervention.

Together, these studies give greater depth to the interpretation of the action systems model, and it is interesting to note the similarities in behaviours exhibited during very different crime types. The possibility of consistency across modes of behaviour within the same individual is examined directly in the next study. This provides the most direct proposition of the action systems model as a form of personality theory by arguing that whilst some contextual variations may occur, an individual possesses a tendency to act predominantly within one mode of functioning when engaging in behaviours of varying forms.

## Consistency in Action Systems Functioning within the Individual across Behaviour

Miller and Fritzon (2006) investigated the hypothesis that the high correlation observed between self-harming and fire setting behaviours in female patients may reflect a common functional pathway (Coid, Kahtan, Gault and Jarman, 2000). The importance of both intrapsychic and interpersonal aspects of both behaviours draws attention to the dynamic interplay between the person and their psycho-social environment, and thus the appropriateness of adopting a systemic framework to model the different forms and functions of the behaviours (Coid, Wilkins, Chitkara and Everitt, 1992; Geller, 1992; Gardner and Cowdry, 1985).

The sample for this study was 50 female special hospital patients with evidence of fire-setting and self-harm behaviour. Their mean age was 34 years, and the majority of women were diagnosed with a psychotic illness (n = 34) with comorbid Borderline personality disorder (n = 32).

The first set of analyses established the structural properties of the two behaviours and the of the 29 fire setting and 22 self-harm behaviours is reported in Table 3.1 previously. Following this, eight new variables were created from the sum of the individual variables present for each case. These variables were then correlated, with significant results for the two adaptive and integrative scores. Additionally, within the expressive mode, a number of individual variables correlated, suggesting that the lack of correlations among the scale scores for conservative and expressive self-harm/fire setting could be accounted for by considering the different psychosocial contexts and triggers for these behaviours, for example community versus hospital settings.

Secondly, a series of chi squares revealed that classifications across the two modalities were consistent across all four modes of functioning, in other words for example, that women whose fire setting was classified as adaptive (containing a majority of variables from this region of the MDS plot) were also classified as adaptive in their self-harming, etcetera.

Whilst the implications of the previous group of studies were primarily investigative, allowing for hypotheses to be generated about the personal characteristics of perpetrators according to the modal classification of their offending behaviour, the results of the Miller and Fritzon (2006) study have a clinical focus. Clearly, the high rate of self-harm among female (and male) fire-setters, suggests that treatment ought to target both behaviours, and specifically identify the common functional pathways as well as facilitating alternative modes of expression. The identification of treatment considerations gave rise to the final study discussed in this chapter, which sought to investigate whether the action systems framework could be applied to model the process of change occurring over the course of a therapeutic intervention.

## Change in Action Systems Functioning within the Individual across Time as a Result of Therapeutic Intervention

The study discussed in this section sought to analyse behaviours occurring within therapeutic interactions, in order to determine whether these behaviours themselves could be understood as representing the four modes of action system functioning. Additionally, a further aim of the study was to investigate whether action system functioning modality changes over the course of therapy, in other words whether the observable changes that occur as a result of therapy are within-mode fluctuations, rather than across-mode shifts.

Neville, Miller and Fritzon (2007) studied 68 male residents at HMP Dovegate TC having completed at least one year of therapy. The mean age of the sample was 34 years, and the mean number of previous convictions was 13.44. The most common index offences were robbery and murder, with 80% of residents having committed previous acts of violence; these occurring both inside and outside of prison.

A checklist was created to define the behaviours occurring during the therapy sessions, including both verbal and nonverbal items, and these were recorded as either present (1) or absent (0) for each therapy session attended, and as with the previous methodology, MDS was employed to test the hypothesis that the behaviours would relate to each of the four modes of action system functioning. See Neville, Miller and Fritzon (2007) for full discussion of the variables, and the original MDS configuration. Following this a series of paired-sample t-tests revealed changes in individual behaviours that were significant across six two-monthly time periods.

What this analysis showed was that over time, the behavioural changes that occurred were consistent within the original action system mode that the individual had held upon entering therapy. Changes in the emphases within modes are summarised below.

*Integrative*

An internalisation of a positive self-image held by others was achieved through providing support to other group members, instilling hope, giving advice and contributing actively to discussion. The t-tests revealed that advice giving increased over time, whilst 'grandiose' and 'contribute' decreased. The combination of the latter two variables indicated that the individual's capacity for listening to others' perspectives had increased.

*Adaptive Mode*

Of note here is Shye's (1985) discussion of the adaptive mode as involving a desire to free oneself from threats, by bringing about compatibility between the goals of the agent and the environment. It is interesting that this region of the MDS contained predominantly physical actions such as fidgeting, pulling a chair out of the circle, or physically leaving the group. These, together with disrupting the discussions and avoiding disclosure were all ways in which the individual manipulated the environment of the therapy session in order to reduce or manage the tension caused by participating, and as such these behaviours were found by the t-tests to significantly decrease over time.

*Expressive*

This mode of action manifested itself in outbursts of communicative behaviour, such as dramatic outbursts, gesticulation and crying. In addition a desire to modify the external environment was demonstrated by the variables 'argue' and 'disagree (with feedback)'. This region of the SSA also included the variable 'accept (feedback), which was found to increase over time as the variable 'disagree' decreased. Other changes occurring over time within this region included decreases in 'tension', as well as increases in assertive behaviour.

*Conservative Mode*

Readers are reminded that behaviours in this mode can be seen as ways in which the individual internalises and processes external information. Expressing anti-staff attitudes, as well as 'peace keeping' and 'asking for help' were all ways in which the individual at the start of therapy responded to others in the therapeutic environment. Other variables found in this regions of the MDS represented the way that individuals used their own frame of reference to make sense of what others brought to the group (for example asking self-referential questions, blaming, inappropriate feedback). Changes over time revealed by the t-test include decreases in criminogenic behaviours such as expressing 'anti-staff' attitudes, dominating discussions and blaming others for their own problems.

## General Discussion of the Action Systems Models of Criminal Behaviour

Collectively, the findings from the studies summarised in this chapter deliver a range of theoretical and practical implications. The FAST framework provides a way for the individual actions of criminals to be understood as representations of a consistent way of dealing with the world. Within other literature, this has been referred to as 'offence paralleling behaviour' (for example Jones, 2000). Most directly, the Neville et al (2007) paper provides support for the suggestion that future research could use the FAST framework as a way of testing empirical hypotheses about offence-paralleling behaviour (Jones, 2004).

Within the first set of papers, the theoretical and practical implications relate to ways of understanding criminal behaviour within the context of a broader set of characteristics that are likely to be drawn from the same mode of Action Systems functioning. Whilst it is suggested that individuals may have a predisposition to interact with the environment within a predominant mode of action (Expressive, Integrative, Conservative, or Adaptive), the specific form and expression of behaviours will vary across situations. For example, an individual may have a tendency to express distressing emotions either by displaying verbal aggression, physical aggression (towards others), physical aggression directed at themselves, or by setting a fire. These behaviours can all be seen as 'Expressive' within the action systems framework, but the specific choices may vary depending on the situational context.

Such expressions may have been seen as 'cries for help' and the individual is likely to have come to the notice of various agencies, including mental health services.

If there has been an emphasis toward physical aggression, the individual may have attracted a label of conduct disorder as a child, and to have a poor academic record. It is clear, therefore, that individuals with a tendency towards expressive acts will have personal records aligned with this mode of acting and interacting with the world.

Following this example through, in therapy this individual may be helped to communicate more assertively, and to channel their emotions through other expressive outlets such as diary writing, or art.

The FAST is consistent with the view that offending behaviour has a number of very different psychological origins. Adaptive criminal events may tend to be opportunistic and used by people as part of a general criminal lifestyle, who lack intellectual or psychological resources and therefore rely on manipulating the environment to achieve their goals. On the other hand, crime that originates from Integrative actions may not be viewed primarily as a crime at all, but rather as a cry for help and product of self-destructive tendencies. Persons who commit expressive acts, as previously described, are likely to use these as characteristic ways of communicating, and may be serial offenders. Finally, conservative crimes are often a way of redressing a personal slight caused by external agents and can be conceptualised as revengeful. These theoretical findings also have practical implications in terms of police investigations of crime, with specific personality and personal characteristics being found to be associated with each of the four forms of criminal behaviour. For example, the integrative mode of behaviour is most often associated with a psychiatric history, whereas those who commit adaptive crimes have usually established criminal lifestyles. Moreover persons committing conservative forms of crime are likely to have specific criminal histories including other forms of person-related offending such as assault, public disorder and weapon offences.

The specific implications for clinical work with offenders include highlighting the importance of the principle of responsivity (Andrews and Bonta, 2003) by providing a specific framework for understanding how offenders' therapeutic needs are likely to differ, and that topographical (offence) similarity does not imply functional similarity. Individuals operating within each of the four modes of the FAST are likely to respond to different modes of therapeutic interactions and even require different theoretical orientations towards therapy.

Persons operating within an integrative mode of functioning are likely to have a tendency to direct the expression of emotions inward, and to dissociate and distance themselves from others. Perhaps they may perceive verbal communication as inadequate or difficult. Therapeutic work therefore should concentrate on the individuals' difficulty in verbalising emotions and needs. An approach such as Dialectical Behaviour Therapy (Linehan, 1993) teaches clients to become more aware of their emotional responses through techniques such as 'backward chaining'.

As discussed previously, with individuals who communicate expressively, there is a need to modify the valence of this expression, and to find alternative outlets. Treatment may also address the secondary gains of the behaviour through changing environmental reinforcers. Group therapy may be help maintaining a milieu where destructive behaviour is not valued but positive change is. Participation in Therapeutic Communities (Dolan, 1988) may be an effective treatment choice in such cases.

For individuals with a tendency towards Conservative acts, there may be a heightened interpersonal sensitivity, and the objective of treatment would be to explore alternative ways of managing these emotions. A form of anger management, in which anger is first identified and clarified as such, could be used. Specifically, Schema focused therapy (Young, 1994) might challenge the beliefs that others actions and intentions are harmful and must be avenged.

Finally, treatment oriented within the adaptive mode could concentrate on acknowledging the impact that external circumstances have and reducing the desirability of manipulating the environment and others. It has been found that adaptive crime is associated with juvenile offenders (for example Canter and Fritzon, 1998) and therefore early intervention programmes are likely to be most effective here, coupled with environmental crime prevention strategies.

One of the primary advantages of the action system framework is the way in which it can facilitate an understanding of the underlying processes that give rise to behaviours. Individuals working with clients whose dysfunctional behaviour can be identified as representations of the FAST, need to recognise and label shifts towards more productive ways of living (Wanigarante et al, 1990; Ward, 2002). Therapy should aim to identify an individual's mode of functioning, and then specifically attempt to encourage the individual to deal with interpersonal situations in a more positive manner. The identification of the source and target of an individuals' behaviour means that this encouragement can be specifically tailored to meet the interpersonal style of the individual, rather than the employment of generic therapeutic interventions.

## Conclusions

The current chapter summarised a number of empirical papers testing various hypotheses derived from Shye's (1994) Action Systems Framework. The combination of this framework with methodologies and concepts associated with Canter's (1994) Facet Theory led to the creation of a new theoretical framework terms Faceted Action Systems Theory (FAST). This framework has a number of applications, including understanding the associations between the actions and characteristics of offenders (the A-C equation, Canter, 1988) as well as ways of working with offenders clinically (for example Jones, 2004). Within the field of Investigative Psychology, the use of a theoretical framework to guide hypotheses around the A-C equation is a significant contribution to this growing body of research. Within clinical psychology, further investigation is needed in order to establish whether FAST might provide a useful framework for clinician decision making when formulating cases, and structuring treatment plans. Given the alignment with personality theory also, it would be interesting to examine the associations between each of the four FAST modes, and established personality traits using inventories such as the NEO-FFI, MMPI or PAI.

**References**

Allport, G.W. (1960). The open system in personality theory. *Journal of Abnormal and Social Psychology*, 61, 301–310.

Almond, L., Duggan, L., Shine, J. and Canter, D. (2005). Test of the action system model in an incarcerated population. *Psychology, Crime & Law*, 11, 1–15.

Andrews, D. and Bonta, J. (1994). *The Psychology of Criminal Conduct*. Cincinnati: Anderson.

Andrews, D. (1995). The psychology of criminal conduct and effective treatment, in *What Works: Reducing Re-offending*, edited by J. McGuire. Chichester: Wiley.

Barkham, M., Shapiro, D.A. and Firth-Cozens, J. (1989). Personal questionnaire changes in perspective vs. exploratory psychotherapy. *British Journal of Clinical Psychology*, 28, 97–107.

Blackburn, R. (1998). Relationship of personality disorders to observer ratings of interpersonal style in forensic psychiatric patients. *Journal of Personality Disorders*, 12, 77–85.

Borg, I. and Lingoes, J. (1987). *Multidimensional Similarity Analysis*. New York: Springer.

Buckley, W. (1967). *Sociology and Modern Systems Theory*. Oxford: Prentice-Hall.

Canter, D. (1995a). *Criminal Shadows*. London: Harper Collins.

Canter, D. (2000). Offender profiling and criminal differentiation. *Legal and Criminological Psychology*, 5, 23–46.

Canter, D. and Fritzon, K. (1998). Differentiating arsonists: a model of fire setting actions and characteristics. *Legal and Criminological Psychology*, 3, 73–96.

Carver, C.S. and Scheier, M.F. (1998). *On the Self-Regulation of Behaviour*. Cambridge: CUP.

Clarke, R.R. (ed.) (1997). *Situational Crime Prevention: Successful Case Studies Second Edition*. New York: Harrow and Heston.

Clark, D.A., Fisher, M.J. and McDougall, C. (1993). A new methodology for assessing the level of risk in incarcerated offenders. *British Journal of Criminology*, 33, 436–448.

Cullen, E. (1994). Grendon: the therapeutic prison that works. *Therapeutic Communities*, 15, 301–311.

Donald, I. (1995). Facet theory: defining research domain, in *Research Methods in Psychology*, edited by G. Breakwell, S. Hammond and C. Fife-Schaw. London: Sage Publications.

Dunstan, F. and Birch, S. (2004). What makes a therapeutic community? A comparative study of ideal values, in *A Culture of Enquiry: Research Evidence and the Therapeutic Community*, edited by J. Lees, N. Manning, D. Menzies and N. Morant. New York: Jessica Kingsley.

Emery, N.W. (1969). The relationship between certain student personality characteristics and choice of college and related curricula. *Dissertations Abstracts International*, 30, 934–935.

Fritzon, K. and Brun, A. (2005). Beyond Columbine: a faceted model of school-associated homicide. *Psychology, Crime & Law*, 11, 53–71.

Fritzon, K., Canter, D. and Wilton, Z. (2001). The application of an action systems model to destructive behaviour: the examples of arson and terrorism. *Behavioural Science and the Law*, 19, 657–690.

Frost, A. and Connolly, M. (2004). Reflexivity, reflection and the change process in offender work. *Sexual Abuse: Journal of Research and Treatment*, 16, 365–380.

Genders, E. and Player, E. (1995). *Grendon: A Study of a Therapeutic Prison*. Oxford: Clarendon Press.

Greenall, P. (2004). Life in a prison-based therapeutic community: one man's experience. *The British Journal of Forensic Practice*, 6, 33–38.

Gunn, J., Robertson, G. and Dell, S. (1978). *Psychiatric Aspects of Imprisonment*. London: Academic Press.

Guttman, L. (1968). A general nonmetric technique for finding the smallest co-ordinate space for a configuration of points. *Psychometrika*, 33, 469–506.

Hobson, J., Shine, J. and Roberts, R. (2000). How do psychopaths behave in a therapeutic community? *Psychology, Crime and the Law*, 6, 139–154.

Jones, L. (1989). *The Use of the Reperetory Gird as a Tool for the Evaluation of a Therapeutic Community*. M.Sc. Thesis, Birkbeck College London.

Jones, L. (1997). Developing models for managing treatment integrity and efficacy in a prison-based TC: The Max Glatt Centre, in *Therapeutic Communities for Offenders*, edited by E. Cullen, L. Jones and R. Woodward. London: Wiley.

Jones, L. (2000). *Identifying and Working with Clinically Relevant Offence-paralleling Behaviour*. Paper presented at Division of Clinical Psychology, Forensic Special Interest Group, Nottinghamshire.

Jones, M. (1976). *Maturation of the Therpaeutic Community*. New York: Human Sciences Press.

Jones, M. (1982). *The Process of Change*. Boston: Routledge and Kegan Paul.

Kennard, D. (2004). The therapeutic community as an adaptable treatment modality across different settings. *Psychiatric Quarterly*, 75, 295–307.

Krippemdorf, K. (1980). *Content Analysis: An Introduction to its Methodology*. London: Sage Publications.

Land, G. and Kenneally, C. (1977). Creativity, reality and general systems: a personal viewpoint. *Journal of Creative Behaviour*, 11, 12–35.

Leary, T. (1957). *Interpersonal Diagnosis of Personality*. New York: Ronald Press.

Lees, J., Manning, N. and Rawlings, B. (2004). A culture of enquiry: research evidence and the therapeutic community. *Psychiatric Quarterly*, 75, 279–294.

Levy, S. (1994). *Louis Guttman on Theory and Methodology: Selected Writings*. Aldershot: Dartmouth.

Lewis, P.S. (1978). *The Prisoner's Perception of Himself and his World*. PhD Thesis, University of Leeds.

Lewis, P.S. (1997). Context for change (whilst consigned and confined): a challenge for systematic thinking, in *Therapeutic Communities for Offenders*, edited by E. Cullen, L. Jones and R. Woodward. London: Wiley.

Lingoes, J.C. (1973). *The Guttman Lingoes Nonmetric Programme Series*. Ann Arbor: Mathesis Press.

Loonis, E., Apter, M.J. and Sztulman, H. (2000). Addiction as a function of action system properties. *Addictive Behaviours*, 25, 477–481.

Losel, F. (1995). The efficacy of correctional treatment: a review and synthesis of meta-evaluations, in *What Works: Reducing Re-offending*, edited by J McGuire. Chichester: Wiley.

Manning, N. (1976). Values and practice in the therapeutic community. *Human Relations*, 29, 125–138.

Manning, N. (1989). *The Therapeutic Community Movement: Charisma and Routinization*. Florence: Taylor and Frances.

Marshall, P. (1997). *A Reconviction Study of HMP Grendon Therapeutic Community*. Home Office Research and Statistics Research Findings, No. 53.

Matthews, G. and Deary, J. (1998). *Personality Traits*. London: Routledge.

McConnaughy, E.A., Prochaska J.O. and Velicer, W.F. (1983). Stages of change in psychotherapy: measurement and sample profiles. *Psychotherapy: Theory, Research and Practice*, 20, 368–375.

McGuire, J. and Priestly, P. (1985). *Offending Behaviour: Skills and Stratagems for Going Straight*. London: Batsford.

Miller, E.J. and Gwynne, G.V. (1972). *A Life Apart*. London: Tavistock.

Miller, J. (1978). Attaining freedom in existential group therapy. *American Journal of Psychoanalysis*, 38, 179–183.

Moos, R.H. (1975). *Evaluating Correctional and Community Settings*. New York: Wiley & Sons.

Morrice, J.K.W. (1979). Basic concepts: a critical review, in *Therapeutic Communities: Reflections and Progress*, edited by R.D. Hinshelwood and N. Manning. London: Routledge & Kegan Paul.

Murray, H. (1938). *Explorations in Personality*. New York: Oxford University Press.

Newton, M. (1973). *Reconviction after Treatment at Grendon*. CP Report Series B No. 1 Prison Service, Home Office.

Newton, M. (1998). Changes in measures of personality, hostility and locus of control during residence in a prison therapeutic community. *Legal and Criminological Psychology*, 3, 209–223.

Newton, M. (2000). Psychological variables as dynamic risk factors for reconviction among residents in a prison therapeutic community, in *A Compilation of Grendon Research*, edited by J. Shine. Bucks: Leyhill Press.

Owens, W.A. and Schoenfelt, L.F. (1979). Toward a classification of persons. *Journal of Applied Psychology*, 64, 569–607.

Parsons, T. (1953). Some comments on the state of the general theory of action. *American Sociological Review*, 18, 618–631.

Prochaska, J.O., DiClemente, C.C. and Norcross, J.C. (1992). In search of how people change: applications to addictive behaviours. *American Psychologist*, 47, 1102–1114.

Rawlings, B. (1999). The therapeutic community in prison: problems in maintaining therapeutic integrity. *Therapeutic Communities*, 19, 281–194.

Richards, P.S. and Lonborg, S.D. (1996). Development of a method for studying thematic content of psychotherapy sessions. *Journal of Counselling and Clinical Psychology*, 64, 701–711.

Salfati, C.G. (2000). The nature of expressiveness and instrumentality in homicide: implications for offender profiling. *Homicide Studies*, 4, 265–293.

Salfati, G.C. and Bateman, A.L. (2005). Serial homicide: an investigation of behavioural consistency. *Journal of Investigative Psychology and Offender Profiling*, 2, 121–144.

Shine, J. and Morris, M. (2000). Addressing criminogenic needs in a prison therapeutic community. *Therapeutic Communities*, 21, 197–219.

Shye, S. (1985). Nonmetric multivariate models for behavioural action systems, in *Facet Theory Approaches to Social Research*, edited by D. Canter. New York: Springer Verlag.

Shye, S. (1999). Facet theory, in *Encyclopaedia of Statistical Sciences*, updated, vol 3, edited by S. Kotz, C. Read and D. Banks. Chichester: J Wiley & Sons.

Shye, S., Elozur, D. and Hoffman, M. (1994). *Introduction to Facet Theory – Content Design and Intrinsic Data Analysis in Behavioural Research*. London: Sage Publications.

Sommerhoff, G. (1969). The abstract characteristics of living systems, in *Systems Thinking*, edited by F.E. Emery. Harmondsworth: Penguin.

Thornton, D. (1987). Correctional evaluation of custodial regimes, in *Applying Psychology to Imprisonment: Theory and Practice*, edited by B.J. McGurk, D.M. Thornton and M. Williams. London: HMSO.

Wagner, J.R. (2003). Evaluating a core battery: a comparison of standardized, individualized and qualitative approaches to therapy outcome assessment. *Dissertation Abstracts International: Section B: The Sciences and Engineering*, 63(11-B), 5541.

Wanigarante, S., Wallace, W., Pullin, J., Keaney, F. and Farmer, R. (1990). *Relapse Prevention for Addictive Behaviours: A Manual for Therapists*. Oxford: Blackwell.

Ward, T. (2002). *Good lives*. Paper presented at Division of Forensic Psychology Annual Conference, Manchester.

Wilkinson, J. (2000). Direct observation, in *Research Methods in Psychology*, edited by G. Breakwell, S. Hammond and C. Fife-Schaw. London: Sage Publications.

Wilson, M. and Hammond, S. (2000). Structured qualitative data using a scaling procedure, in *Research Methods in Psychology*, edited by G. Breakwell, S. Hammond and C. Fife-Schaw. London: Sage Publications.

Woods, P. (1979). *The Divided School*. London: Routledge & Kegan Paul.

Woodward, R. (1999). The prison communities: therapy within a custodial setting, in *Therapeutic Communities: Past, Present and Future*, edited by P. Campling and R. Haigh. New York: Jessica Kingsley.

Yalom, I.D. (1975). *The Theory and Practice of Group Psychotherapy*. New York: Basic Books.

Zamble, R. and Porporino, F. (1990). Coping, imprisonment and rehabilitation. *Criminal Justice and Behaviour*, 17, 53–69.

Chapter 4

# Differentiation of Hostage Barricade Incidents: Through the Application of the Action Systems Model

Kaeko Yokota

## Editor's Introduction

Kaeko Yokota's application of the Action Systems framework to this dynamic form of criminal activity (hostage incidents) is a particularly interesting example of the applied potential of the academic models generated within Professor Canter's IP approach. Illustrating one of his central postulates, that structures explain (see Chapter 1), Kaeko shows how by modelling the variations in hostage actions we are able to understand what hostage-taking is about and characterise distinct forms of incident. Her use of this structure to develop an operational decision tool for rapidly identifying coherent incident types and on the basis of this make predictions about the offenders' likely response to police actions, is a nice example of the investigative approach (with a small i). The problem-solving emphasis is typical of David's research style; it integrates directly with the problems of the practitioners to provide frameworks that can be used directly in their decision-making.

## Introduction

Hostage barricade incidents are defined as incidents in which the police surround the place where the victims are being detained against their will. They are distinct from kidnapping situations where the hostage's location is unknown to the police. In incidents of this kind, the communication between hostage takers and the authorities tends to be intermittent and indirect, and is controlled almost entirely by the hostage takers (Yokota, Iwami, Watanabe, Fujita and Wanabe, 2004).

A few studies have attempted to classify hostage incidents or hostage takers in several ways, with the aim of aiding the police in dealing effectively with these crises. A variety of perspectives in past studies support the possibility that several aspects of hostage events differentiate criminals' behavioural styles in such incidents.

One of the most traditional classifications of hostage incidents is based almost entirely on a simple typology; 'instrumental' and 'expressive' (cf. Miron and Goldstein, 1979). In instrumental hostage incidents, the perpetrators have some recognisable goals, which they seek to fulfil for their benefit. In these cases, the perpetrators' primary motivation is likely to be goal attainment, and not harming the hostages (Webster, 1997). On the other hand, in expressive incidents, the perpetrators' behaviour serves only as a means of displaying their power or significance (Hammer and Rogan, 1997). In these cases, demands are less tangible and are often not expressed openly. At the same time, perpetrators may have emotional goals that they hope to attain during the incident.

Canter and Fritzon (1998) observe that the differences among previous perspectives on arson lie in the emphases that are placed on the ways in which an individual acts on the world around him/her while perpetrating the acts of arson. This depends on whether the source of the actions is internal (i.e., expressive) or external (i.e., instrumental) to the offender. The distinction between instrumentality and expressivity in hostage barricade incidents is also likely to be reflected in the cause of activities. While in an expressive hostage taking incident, the offender is likely to be aroused by an emotional need, in an instrumental hostage taking incident, the offender may take a hostage in response to an external agent. The instrumental offender is likely to make a substantive demand to the external agent; most often this demand is addressed to the police.

Nonetheless, recent findings suggest that this classification scheme may be too broad, making it difficult to differentiate among hostage incidents. Recently, some studies imply that the target of criminal actions could be another facet for differentiating hostage incidents. When the target of the perpetrators' actions is external, they seek an observable reward from the external agents. They may try to exploit any instrumental gain or they may try to influence the police or victims. One example of such incidents is an instance in which a 'trapped criminal' takes hostages after the failure of other crimes, such as bank robbery (Fuselier, 1986; Marth, 2003). In an incident of this type, the perpetrators make instrumental demands, often aiming to obtain money and immediate escape from external agents, usually the police.

Another example of incidents in which the target of perpetrators' actions is external is domestic situations, in which a perpetrator may be in a situation of conflict, may have, e.g., differences with his/her former or current partner, is substantially dissatisfied with his/her life and may have had arguments or other pressure building experiences before the hostage taking (Marth, 2003). Although incidents of this type are interpreted as expressive, in that the incidents arise from the individuals' emotional needs or frustration, the perpetrators of this type express their anger or frustration on the external world, i.e. the victims.

On the other hand, when the target of actions is internal, the desired effect of the act is internal within individuals. The perpetrators may seek to redress their own emotional state, rather than seeking a reward from outside. The act of taking a hostage may, by itself, be of significance. The study of Marth (2003) suggests that hostage incidents can be differentiated by the presence or absence of planning. The aim of planned incidents, such as hostage taking by a member of some political groups, may be self-satisfaction. For instance, a person with a certain political ideology may hold people hostages, precipitated by a major case of political corruption. The perpetrator may instrumentally demand a meeting with a significant political personality, such as a mayor, anticipating the impact on the society, even if he/she does not expect this demand to be met.

Another type of incidents in which the target of actions is internal is one committed by the mentally ill. Several previous studies have supported the argument that hostage taking incidents committed by the mentally ill are likely to form a distinct criminal style from others, revealing self-destructive behaviour. Fuselier (1986) indicated that hostage takers with mental illnesses are likely to be 'paranoid' or 'depressed'. Internal mental events of the schizophrenic are confused with external world happenings, resulting in faulty perceptions and disturbed logic (Strentz, 1986), while depressed people think and respond slowly and may act suicidal (Greenstone, Kosson and Gacono, 2000). These individuals may not seek any observable rewards from the outside.

In summary, a review of past literature suggests that two facets may exist to differentiate among hostage barricade incidents. The first facet is the source of criminal actions. When the source is external, the acts of the perpetrators are likely to be instrumental, triggered by external agents or environments. When the source is internal, the acts of the perpetrators are likely to be expressive and emotional. The second facet is the target of actions. When the target is external, the perpetrators seek an observable reward from the external agents. When it is internal, the perpetrators may seek to redress their own emotional state, rather than seeking a reward from outside.

## Action Systems Model of Hostage Barricade Incidents

Shye (1985) developed his action systems model, deriving perspectives from a series of Talcott Parsons' works (cf. Parsons, 1978). The action systems model developed by Shye assumes the source and target of actions to be two dominant modes. This model has been applied to explain various aspects of non-criminal behaviours (Shye, 1985). This model has been adopted to explain various types of criminal behaviours, such as arson (Canter and Fritzon, 1998), terrorist hostage incidents (Fritzon, Canter and Wilton, 2001; Wilton, 2000), intrafamilial homicide (Fritzon, 2000b), burglary (Thompson, 2000) and school-associated violent deaths (Brun, 2000).

In the study of criminal behaviours, one of the first suppositions is that these incidents either emerge from within the individual or from some external environmental cue. The second supposition is that the targets of the incidents can be differentiated based on whether the desired effect of the act is internal or external. Based on the combination of the source and the target of actions, the action systems model identified four basic modes of functioning: 'adaptive', 'expressive', 'integrative' and 'conservative'.

**Table 4.1 Action systems modes of functioning**

| | | Source of actions | |
|---|---|---|---|
| | | **External** | **Internal** |
| **Locus of effect** | **External** | *Adaptive* | *Expressive* |
| | **Internal** | *Conservative* | *Integrative* |

In keeping with this argument, the review of past literature on hostage incidents led to the hypothesis that the combination of an individual's behavioural orientation in the source and the target of actions could differentiate hostage barricade incidents. In hostage barricade incidents, the four modes of action systems are assumed to be as follows:

*Integrative Mode*

In the integrative mode, adjustments are made within the system itself, revealing the most disturbed styles in relation to destructive and interpersonal forms of criminal activity (Fritzon, Canter and Wilton, 2001). The criminals' behaviour is expected to be highly emotional or erratic in this mode. Criminals attempt to alleviate their distress by taking hostages. The target of their actions is internal and they do not seek an observable external effect. Arsonists who set themselves on fire are considered to be integrative since the target of their actions is focused on both internal processes and emotional disturbance (Canter and Fritzon, 1998). In the context of hostage situations, individuals who exhibit this mode of behaviour might be mentally ill.

*Adaptive Mode*

An agent functioning in this mode responds to external sources in the environment by adjusting to that environment; this involves adaptation and exploitation with some overt purpose or instrumental gain (Fritzon, Canter and Wilton, 2001). In the case of arson, fire-setting is used as a means of concealing other crimes that have been committed (Canter and Fritzon, 1998). In the case of hostage situations, crimes committed within this mode of action are opportunistically precipitated by the perpetrator's external context or environment. In addition, perpetrators are expected to be highly interactive with the authority, and seek instrumental gain. Hostage taking is a means of achieving their goal; therefore, the victims may be unknown or insignificant. Hostage taking during a robbery may represent an adaptive mode of hostage barricade incidents.

*Expressive Mode*

This mode reflects an emotional enactment, i.e. the demonstration of the internal psychological aspects of the agent in the external world is predominant. The perpetrator enacts internal forces and pressures, while he/she seeks an observable reward from the external agents. In the case of arson, 'multi-firesetters' are considered to be an extreme form of the expressive mode since emotional relief is obtained from setting fires (Canter and Fritzon, 1998). Domestic hostage situations in which a jilted husband holds his wife hostage may be included in the description of an expressive hostage incident. Hostage taking of this type arises from the personal need of the perpetrator, and he/she is likely to have a desire to influence on the external agent – the victim.

*Conservative Mode*

In crimes representing the conservative mode, the perpetrators respond to external sources, but seek to redress their own emotional state. In the case of arson, arsonists who seek revenge by setting fires can be said to represent the conservative mode of functioning; these individuals react to external frustrations by lighting fires rather than by addressing their frustrations in a more direct manner (Canter and Fritzon, 1998). In the case of hostage incidents, the perpetrators may plan hostage barricade incidents in advance, anticipating the expected impact on the external environment. At the same time, they seek internal relief or self-satisfaction.

As outlined above, the action systems model provides the framework for a clear distinction among incidents. This model is in keeping with a hypothetical framework that is derived from the literature review. Shye (1985) empirically tested the action systems model by using the facet approach. When a large number of variables are processed by Smallest Space Analysis (SSA), it is hypothesised that the resulting plot will be partitionable into four regions, each of which contains variables that reflect only one functioning mode. Furthermore, Shye (1985) predicted the partition pattern, such that the expressive variables would be located opposite the conservative variables, whereas the adaptive variables would be located opposite the integrative variables.

The primary aim of this study is to provide a unitary framework for the differentiation of hostage barricade incidents. In addition, the examination of hostage barricade incidents using the action systems model will extend the application of this model to contexts other than those in which it has been used thus far. Hence, the current research aims to examine the following hypotheses:

All hostage barricade incidents can be explained within the framework provided by the action systems model, as an interaction between the source of the action and the locus of its impact.

All hostage barricade incidents can be differentiated from each other on the basis of the four modes of functioning: 'adaptive', 'expressive', 'integrative' and 'conservative'.

## Method

The sample used in the current research was composed of 116 hostage barricade incidents that occurred in Japan from 1970 to 2002. The information was obtained from internal police documents and interviews with police officers who were involved in incidents either as negotiators or interviewers with offenders. Interviews could not be arranged in cases where several years had passed since the incidents had occurred. Two persons reviewed the content before inputting the data into the database.

Analysis of the sample focused on just 34 offence variables in order to uncover the underlying processes during the hostage situations. These variables were selected to characterise each hostage situation after an extensive reading of the available literature on hostage incidents. The variables included types of locations, weapons, demands, prior relations between hostages and offenders, the number of hostages and offenders and other issues related to planning and communication. The list of all variables is shown in the Appendix. For the current analysis, a data matrix was produced by coding the offences in terms of the presence or absence of each variable.

In order to represent the relationships among variables, the data was subjected to non-metric multi-dimensional scaling (MDS). Smallest Space Analysis (SSA-I) is one method of MDS to determine the relationship between variables. The computing algorithm of the SSA-I rank-orders the correlations between items. It then generates a spatial representation of those items, and rank-orders the distances between points. In the SSA-I configuration, the more highly correlated two variables are, the closer the points representing those variables will be in the space.

To measure similarity in the SSA procedure, the Jaccard coefficient was utilised. It operates only on the joint co-occurrences of variables and ignores non-occurrences. This allows for the fact that the non-recording of a variable does not mean that it did not occur. This was deemed the appropriate measure of association for data drawn from police records because it can never be certain that absent information was simply not recorded.

## Results

### *Focal Aspects of Hostage Barricade Incidents*

The three-dimensional solution had a Guttman-Lingoes' coefficient of alienation equal to 0.22 with 19 iterations, indicating a reasonable fit for this type of data. Figure 4.1 shows the projection of the second and third vectors of the three-dimensional space.

The percentages of occurrence of variables were calculated as a first step in the interpretation of the results of the SSA. The SSA space of Figure 4.1 was partitioned into four regions, according to the percentages of occurrence of each variable, including 0–9%, 10–29%, 30–49% and 50% or more. It should be noted that variable 30 'multiple offenders', was plotted in the '30–49%' region, although

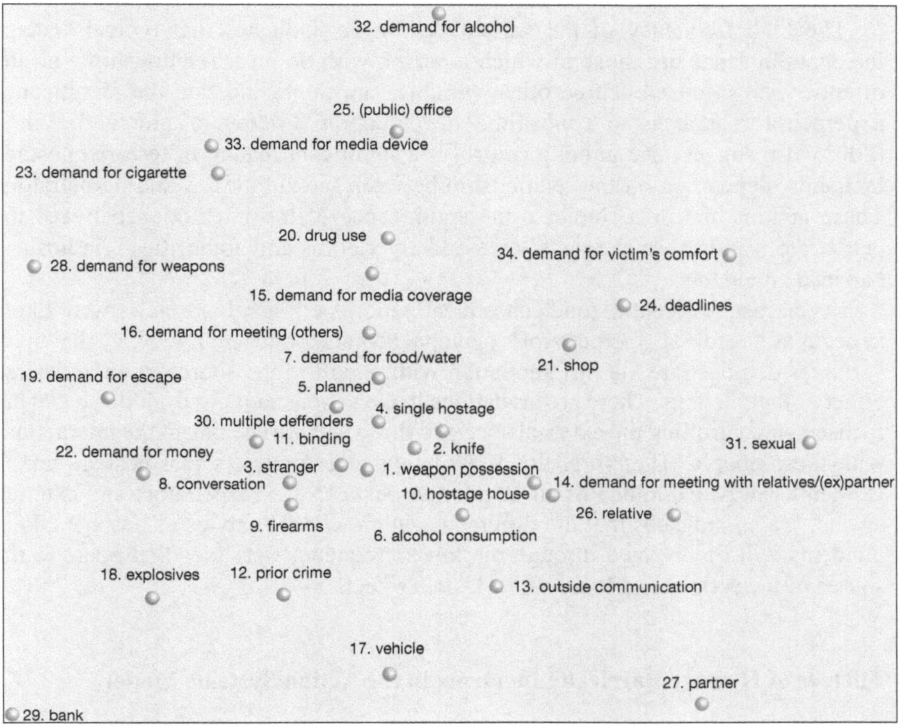


**Figure 4.1 SSA of 34 offence variables**

the frequency of its occurrence was lower (8%). It is due to the interrelationship of a variable 'multiple offenders' with every other variable.

In the configuration of Figure 4.1, a modular facet was identified as a pattern resembling a set of concentric bands. Actions at the centre are the general aspects of the sorts of crimes that are the particular focus (Canter and Alison, 2000). A number of specific hypotheses can therefore be proposed about the actions that will be found in the centre of the configuration. One is that they will provide some indication of the degree of significance of the offence to the offender. Another hypothesis is that actions typical of most criminals will appear at the centre (Canter, 2000; Canter and Youngs, 2002).

The variables that occurred in 50% or more of all incidents were:

- The offender possessed a weapon beforehand (1. weapon possession).
- The offender possessed a knife (2. knife).
- The offender held a stranger a hostage (3. stranger).
- The offender held only one hostage (4. single hostage).

The high frequency of the variable 'stranger' indicates that typical hostage incidents in Japan are those in which a person with no prior relationship with the offender is victimised. Three other variables appear to indicate the significance a perpetrator attaches to controlling the situation. Fritzon, Canter and Wilton (2001) also suggest that gaining control is a significant feature of terrorist hostage incidents, depending on the relationship between the authorities and perpetrators. These actions appear to indicate the significance of the interaction between the perpetrators and external agents – most likely victims and authorities – in hostage barricade incidents.

In contrast, less central (and consequently more peripheral) variables were likely to occur as a result of a perpetrator's personal demand or desire. It is likely that these variables demonstrate the differentiation with regard to the source and the desired effect of their actions. There are gradations in the actions ranging from those that are focused on controlling the external agents to those that are specific to the interactions with these people. Therefore, this modulating facet indicates that hostage taking incidents can be examined as an interaction between the perpetrators and external agents. It also indicates that the differences in the criminal styles of hostage taking incidents will be revealed through the lower frequency variables that relate to the source of the actions and locus of its desired effects.

## Themes of Hostage Barricade Incidents in the Action Systems Model

In the current analysis, each of the four modes of the hostage incidents proposed by the action systems framework was expected to bring together variables with similar implication into the same region of the multi-dimensional space. Figure 4.2, which depicts the same configuration as Figure 4.1, shows the result of the SSA with regional interpretation. Among the 34 variables in the current sample, two facets were recognised: (a) the sources of actions and (b) the desired target of actions.

### *Source of Actions*

The source of action is determined by whether the incidents emerge from within the individual or from an external cue from the environment. When the source of action lies within the individual, the incident is expressively triggered by his/her emotional needs. Variables such as 'drug use', 'sexual', 'alcohol consumption' or 'demand for a meeting with relatives/(ex-) partner' belong to this region and indicate the expressive nature of the offences, revealing internal psychological aspects of the perpetrators. On the other hand, when the source of actions is external, hostage taking is triggered by the external environment, such as a police siege in a bank robbery, or compliments to political issues. Variables that relate to instrumental demands, such as 'demand for media coverage' or 'demand for escape' were found to belong to this region. Variables that imply that hostage takings or other

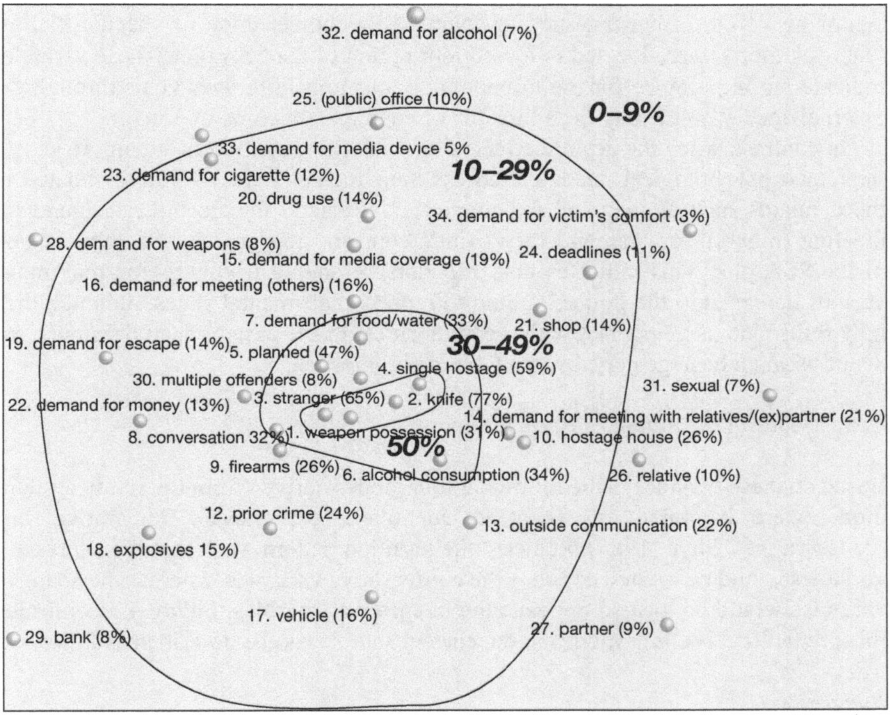


**Figure 4.2 SSA of 34 offence variables by frequency distribution**

kinds of incidents (e.g., robbery) were planned beforehand, such as 'planned' or 'weapon possession', were also plotted within this region. These variables indicate that instrumental incidents may be more sophisticated in terms of criminality as opposed to the impulsive nature of expressive incidents.

Furthermore, variables related to interactions with victims, such as 'demand for victims' comfort', 'sexual assault of victims' or prior relationships with them (i.e., 'partners' or 'relatives') appear in the right region of the SSA plot. This indicates that offenders whose actions are internally precipitated might pay more attention to the victims than those whose actions are externally triggered.

### *Target of Actions*

It is possible to differentiate between the targets of hostage taking incidents based on whether the desired effect of the act is internal or external. This is the second facet. Perpetrators who require any observable rewards seek an external effect from the authorities and/or the victims. Variables related to the physically threatening behaviour of the offenders, such as 'binding' or the selection of specific victims (e.g., 'partner'), were located in the bottom region of the SSA plot. These variables indicate the importance for the offenders of accomplishing their goals through the external agents; some may even threaten or coerce the victims by force.

In contrast, when the desired effect is internal, the perpetrators attempt to satisfy their own psychological needs or redress their mental states. Variables related to the demands such as 'demand for cigarettes', 'demand for alcohol', 'demand for meeting (others)', or 'demand for victim's comfort' appeared in the upper region of the SSA plot. This indicates that offenders belonging to this region may make various demands to the police, aiming to redress their mental states, although they may refuse intensive contact with the authorities. In the case of such offenders, the act of taking a hostage may, by itself, be of significance.

*Four Modes of the Action Systems Model*

Based on these two facets, the following four modes derived from the action systems model were identified as expected: 'adaptive', 'expressive', 'integrative' and 'conservative'. Shye (1985) predicted the partition pattern, such that the expressive variables would be located opposite the conservative variables, whereas the adaptive variables would be located opposite the integrative variables. Figure 4.3 confirmed this prediction. The four modes in the current sample can be described as follows:

*Integrative*

'Integrative' hostage situations reveal the most disturbed styles in relation to destructive and interpersonal forms of criminal activity. No substantive demands appeared in this mode, and variables such as 'drug use', 'sexual', 'demand for alcohol' or 'demand for victim's comfort' were found to belong to this region. Furthermore, variables such as '(public) office' and 'shop', which also belong to this region, indicate that the locations of integrative hostage situations are often public places.

In the current sample, it was found that in the case of the integrative mode, perpetrators with emotional or mental problems were likely to take hostages. Criminal acts in the integrative mode may include those 'which appear to be senseless in that there is no obvious way in which the perpetrator can stand to gain anything or in which the act is clearly self-destructive' (Miron and Goldstein, 1979; p. 10). In the current sample, it was found that some perpetrators in this mode did not carry any weapons to take hostages. Others were under the influence of drugs. Similar to the 'expressive' mode of hostage situations, many perpetrators made no clear demands to the police, only demanding that the negotiators should leave the scene. Such perpetrators usually refused direct communication with the authorities. In the current sample, the variable 'deadline' also appeared within this region, suggesting that the deadline set by the perpetrators was likely to be an irrational one.

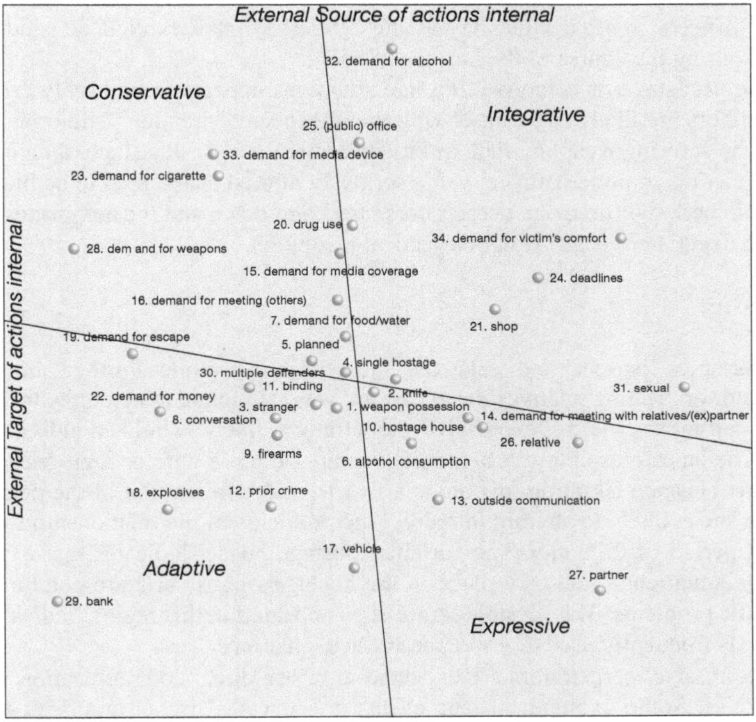


**Figure 4.3 SSA of 34 offence variables with four themes**

*Adaptive*

In 'adaptive' situations, the perpetrators react to an unprepared environment and take hostages in order to obtain tangible rewards. In the current sample, it is likely that the perpetrators held hostages as a consequence of their failure to carry out a crime successfully. The following is a typical example of such a situation: perpetrators commit a bank robbery prior to the hostage event, and these results in a siege by the police. The variable 'bank' was plotted in this region, suggesting that 'bank' is one of the common barricading settings for this style of hostage incidents. In such situations, the offenders often demand assistance to escape, such as an automobile to leave the barricade scene.

Although hostage taking is not planned in such cases, a perpetrator usually makes a clear demand to the police. In this situation, a hostage may be identified merely as a 'vehicle' and a threat towards the victim is simply a means of achieving cooperation from the police. This is similar to the 'conservative' situations described later. However, in 'adaptive' situations, the interaction between perpetrators and police officers is often intensive, as the offenders make explicit demands to the police during the course of the hostage incident.

The first stage of 'adaptive' hostage situations appears to be highly critical, as perpetrators are likely to be upset with the unexpected situation. Additionally, they might be carrying weapons such as knives or firearms. At this stage, the possibility of the victims or police officers being seriously injured is assumed to be high. After a certain period of time, the perpetrators may calm down and the authorities may be able to negotiate a successful, non-tactical resolution.

*Expressive*

The variables 'partner' and 'relatives' fall within this mode. Further, the variable 'demand for meeting relatives/ (ex-) partner' was also found to belong to this region. In the current sample, an 'expressive' perpetrator is likely to hold an individual with whom he has a close but troubled relationship – often a wife or a girlfriend – as a hostage. Hostage taking in this mode arises from the frustration of the perpetrator, and he/she is likely to attempt to redress the problems of the relationship following a long period of difficulty. The variable 'hostage house' indicates that expressive hostage situations often take place in the hostage's house and are combined with domestic problems. The variable 'knife' also appeared in this region, indicating that a knife is frequently used as a weapon in such situations.

'Expressive' perpetrators are expected to refuse direct communication with the authorities. Some of these hostage events are preceded by an argument with the victims, such as an estranged wife. In cases where (ex-) partners are victimised, perpetrators may put forward no clear demands to the police; occasionally, they do demand that the negotiators should leave the scene, especially at the first stage of the incident. In such situations, the threat is likely to be directed at the victims. An expressive hostage taking incident may include cases in which perpetrators hold the relatives of their partners as hostages, demanding a meeting with the partners.

*Conservative*

In 'conservative' situations, perpetrators tend to have objectives that are related to their own systems of beliefs and values. They may plan hostage barricade incidents in advance, anticipating the impact on the external environment. In the current sample, variables related to various demands in such situations appeared under this region. Perpetrators in conservative situations have various goals, each of which might differ from the other; however, these are often related to their own beliefs or values and their political backgrounds. In these cases, the methods of threatening victims are determined in advance. Most perpetrators have little personal interest in their victims and view them merely as means of achieving the goals.

In the case of conservative offenders, the act of taking a hostage may, by itself, be of significance. However there appears to be some variation within 'conservative' incidents, although the configuration of the SSA strongly suggests that they share common features in criminal actions and styles. Some perpetrators aim to publicise their political opinions and demand media coverage or interviews with the media in order to do so. In contrast, in other cases, emotional motives might play a role and the perpetrators may demand media coverage expecting to become the object of public attention, although they may not interact intensively with the authorities. In such instances, the perpetrators are likely to have similar characteristics with 'integrative' incidents, in which the perpetrators' main goal is to solve internal emotional difficulties.

## Classification of Hostage Barricade Incidents

The SSA is based on co-occurrence across events; therefore, if all variables had the same likelihood of co-occurrence, the plot would be random. The structured SSA plot indicates that it is far from the random; therefore assigning incidents to one of the modes would be possible. The validity of the action systems approach can be further confirmed if each incident can be classified.

One of the simplest ways to assign an incident to one of the four modes is by developing scales for hostage barricade incidents. Based on an assumption formulated from a set of actions belonging to each mode, scales could be developed for each mode by analysing the actions of that mode, because co-existing actions indicate the likelihood of an underlying pattern. One direct way of testing whether scales for the four modes can be developed or not is to calculate the Cronbach's $\alpha$ for a set of actions that were included in each mode.

Table 4.2 shows the Cronbach's $\alpha$ for each of the four modes in the current sample. The adaptive theme has the highest Cronbach's $\alpha$ ($\alpha = 0.54$), revealing that it is the most clearly represented theme in the present sample. This is followed by the conservative theme ($\alpha = 0.45$). In the case of incidents that belong to the adaptive and the conservative themes, the source of the perpetrators' actions is external to the individual; the acts of the perpetrators are likely to be instrumental, making tangible demands to the external. The higher values of Cronbach's $\alpha$ imply that a set of criminal actions in these incidents form more coherent criminal styles than those in the expressive incidents.

On the other hand, the integrative theme has the lowest Cronbach's $\alpha$. Although a set of actions within the region of the integrative theme describes a formed style of hostage incidents that reflect a perpetrator's disturbed behaviour, it is supposed that various sub-styles might exist within this mode. For instance, some perpetrators may

**Table 4.2 Cronbach's α for each of four themes**

| | Adaptive | Expressive | Integrative | Conservative |
|---|---|---|---|---|
| α VALUE | .54 | .39 | .14 | .45 |

take illegal drugs during their hostage events and make no demands, while others might be schizophrenic and may make specific demands to the police and set a deadline. Although both the types of perpetrators are expected to behave impulsively and irrationally, the actions of these two groups differ from each other.

The $\alpha$ values in Table 4.2 were not sufficiently high to develop scales for each theme ($\alpha$ = 0.14–0.54), even when the data derived from official reports, in which there is considerable scope for omission and ambiguity, is taken into account. Even taking into account that the Cronbach's $\alpha$ may underestimate the reliability of dichotomous variables, the low Cronbach's $\alpha$ suggests that a few sub-styles may exist within each of these themes.

The SSA configuration in Figure 4.3 demonstrates that each of the four themes represents a distinct style of hostage taking. This leads to the hypothesis that each theme can be identified by a certain type of perpetrator or situation, which emerges from a set of criminal actions in one region of the SSA plot. For instance, variables such as 'bank', 'weapon possession', 'prior crime', 'demand for escape' and 'demand for money' appeared in the region of the adaptive mode. The combination of these variables gives rise to a typical 'adaptive' situation in which the perpetrators hold hostages as a consequence of their failure to successfully carry out a crime. This adaptive situation can be appropriately explained in terms of the cause and the target of criminal actions within the action systems framework; the crimes are opportunistically precipitated by the perpetrator's external environment, while the perpetrators seek instrumental gain from the external agents.

The same is equally true of the integrative, expressive and conservative modes. Based on the results of the SSA, typical profiles of perpetrators representing the four themes were described as follows:

- A typical profile of an 'integrative' perpetrator is someone '*mentally ill*', i.e., someone with a psychiatric disorder or drug addiction that shows delusional thinking during the course of a hostage incident.
- A typical picture of an 'adaptive' perpetrator is a '*criminal*', who holds hostage(s) after failing at another crime, such as robbery.
- A typical picture of an 'expressive' perpetrator is a '*desperate lover*', who holds his wife, girlfriend, or family member as a hostage.
- A typical picture of a 'conservative' perpetrator is a '*planner*', who deliberately takes a hostage and makes a tangible demand to the police for the purpose of fulfilling his/her goal.

These four figures may not cover all the types of hostage barricade incidents; they are only the 'typical' sub-groups for the four themes. However, if all hostage barricade incidents can be assigned to any of the four distinct sub-groups, these sub-groups can constitute the classification of the hostage barricade incidents. Rather than developing a scale, it may be more appropriate to represent each incident by a certain type of perpetrator or situation.

Some incidents have characteristics which fall under several themes. As an example, a person suffering from a mental illness may attempt to commit robbery, and may take hostages as a result of being surrounded by the police. This case can be assigned either to 'integrative' (considering the mental illness) or 'adaptive' (considering the attempted robbery). However any case committed by the mentally ill is likely to have a stronger affinity to 'integrative' as his/her internal psychological/psychiatric process plausibly influences the whole process of hostage situations and his/her actions are expected to be 'integrative' rather than 'adaptive'. In addition, some perpetrators in the current sample planned to hold strangers as hostages to demand the police to look for their girlfriends or wives who had left them. Such cases have similar features with 'expressive' situations, in which hostage incidents were precipitated by the interpersonal troubles a perpetrator had with his wife or girlfriend. However, they can also be classified under the 'conservative' category, so long as the perpetrator plans the incident in advance. In such cases, hostages are just means to fulfil the offender's tangible goals, and there is always a clear demand to the police (e.g., to meet with the perpetrator's wife or girlfriend).

Based on examples like those just described, a procedure for classification was proposed as follows (also see Figure 4.4):

- If a hostage incident was committed by the mentally ill, it was assigned to the 'integrative' category.
- The remainder of incidents were labelled 'adaptive', when hostage incidents were unexpectedly committed by people who failed at another crime.
- The rest of incidents were labelled 'expressive', when hostages were a perpetrator's (ex-) girlfriend, spouse or family member.
- Finally, incidents were labelled 'conservative' if the incident was planned beforehand and any tangible demands were made to the police.

In the course of classification, the first priority was given to the mental status of the offender; the second to the failure at another crime; the third to the hostage's relationship to the offender; and the fourth to the existence of tangible demands and preparations for the incident.

Classification of the current sample resulted in 13 out of 116 incidents which were not assigned to any of the four modes. However, among seven of these unclassified incidents, the perpetrator had an obvious, tangible goal which motivated the hostage event. Therefore these seven incidents were classified as 'conservative'. In the other six cases that were not assigned to any mode, the perpetrators apparently had no tangible goal. These six cases were assigned to the 'integrative' category, as their behaviours were deemed to be senseless and the perpetrators did not expect to get any tangible rewards.

The flowchart in Figure 4.4 assigns each of the 116 hostage barricade incidents in the current sample to one of the four modes. This confirms the validity of the classification framework described in Figure 4.4. The most frequent category of incident was 'conservative', representing 35% (n = 41) of all incidents. This was followed by 'integrative' (31%; n = 36), 'adaptive' (22%; n = 25) and 'expressive' (12%; n = 14).

The action systems framework attempts to explain all human behaviours using two dominant modes as the sources of the incidents: (a) the sources of actions and (b) the effect or desired target of actions. The result of the SSA configuration demonstrated that the criminal actions of hostage barricade incidents can be interpreted within this action systems framework. Four modes derived from the model were found in the SSA space: 'adaptive', 'expressive', 'integrative' and 'conservative'. Furthermore, each of the incidents in the current sample was assigned to each of the four modes. The clear distinction among the four modes strengthens the validity of the action systems approach derived from the SSA analysis.

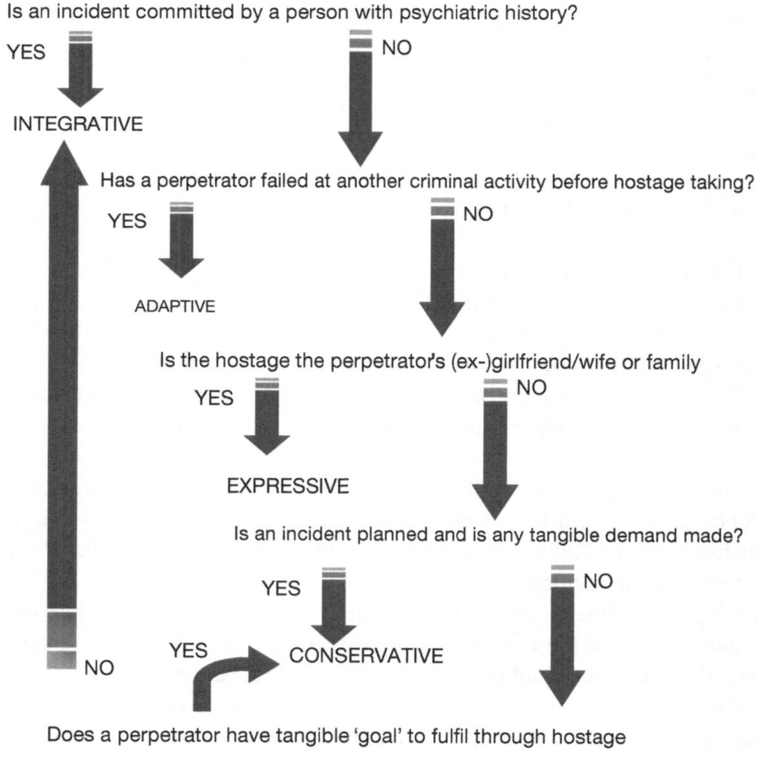


**Figure 4.4 Procedure for classifying hostage barricade incidents**

## Discussion

The current methodology of assigning each incident to any given theme may be applied to other types of incidents, such as terrorist attacks or arson, so long that the incident can be characterised by a distinct feature corresponding to each of the mutually exclusive sub-categories. For instance, in the study of arson by Canter and Fritzon (1998), each of the four modes derived from the action systems model represents a distinct offending style, such that the fire-setting by the conservative mode is revenge for a real or imagined wrong-doing, whereas the fire-setting by the expressive mode tends to be of a serial nature. This distinct differentiation among the different modes may enable to classify fire-setting incidents into one of the 'sub-categories'.

This study has a number of psychological and practical implications. However it should be noted that there are some limitations to these findings. The problem associated with police data is the potential bias arising from the requirement of the representation, where the sample needs to be representative of the general population of hostage barricade incidents that occurred in Japan in the past. The police records are usually destroyed after stipulated periods. However the records of the incidents in which hostages were seriously injured or killed are often retained in the police; therefore, surveys of serious incidents are often possible even after several years have passed. This could possibly create a bias in the characteristics of the sample in favour of more serious incidents.

Nevertheless, findings in the current research can contribute to the police investigation in many ways. In practice, police officers can develop their strategies or tactics for hostage barricade incidents, depending on each of the four modes. In addition, the model proposed here does provide a framework within which diverse perspectives as indicated in the literature can be shown to complement one another, rather than being in conflict. The identification of the four criminal modes in hostage taking behaviours has a number of implications for further study. Future research should elaborate the current model further, examining the process of how the dynamic is developed between different factors in hostage events.

## References

American Psychiatric Association (1994). *Diagnostic and Statistical Manual of Mental Disorders (4th ed.)*. Washington, DC: American Psychiatric Association.

Brun, A. (2000). School associated violent deaths. Proceedings of the sixth International Investigative Psychology Conference.

Canter, D. and Alison, L. (2000). Profiling property crimes, in *Profiling Property Crimes*, edited by D. Canter and L. Alison. Aldershot: Ashgate.

Canter, D. and Fritzon, K. (1998). Differentiating arsonists: a model of firesetting actions and characteristics. *Legal and Criminological Psychology*, 3(1), 73–96.

Canter, D. and Youngs, D. (2002). Beyond offender profiling: the need for an investigative psychology, in *Handbook of Psychology and Legal Contexts*, edited by R. Bull and D. Carson. Wiley & Sons.

Fesbach, S. (1964). The function of aggression and the regulation of aggressive drive. *Psychological Review*, 71, 257–272.

Fish, J. (2004). The neglected element of human emotion in Talcott Parsons's the structure of social action. *Journal of Classical Sociology*, 4, 115–134.

Fritzon, K. (1998). *Differentiating Arson: An Action Systems Model of Malicious Firesetting*. Dissertation submitted for PhD Investigative Psychology at the University of Liverpool.

Fritzon, K. (2000). The application of an action systems model to destructive behaviour: the example of intrafamilial homicide. Proceedings of the sixth International Investigative Psychology Conference.

Fritzon, K., Canter, D. and Wilton, Z. (2001). The application of an action system model to destructive behaviour: the examples of arson and terrorism. *Behavioural Sciences and the Law*, 19, 657–690.

Fuselier, D. (1986). A practical overview of hostage negotiations. *FBI Law Enforce Bulletin*, 56(11), 1–11.

Greenstone, J.L., Kosson, D.S. and Gacono, C.B. (2000). Psychopathy and hostage negotiations: some preliminary thoughts and findings, in *The Clinical and Forensic Assessment of Psychopathy: A Practitioner's Guide*, edited by C.B. Gacono. NJ: Lawrence Erlbaum Association Inc.

Hammer, M.R. and Rogan, R.G. (1997). Negotiation models in crisis situations: the value of a communication-based approach, in *Dynamic Processes of Crisis Negotiation: Theory, Research, and Practice*, edited by R.G. Rogan, M.R. Hammer and C.R. Van Zandt. Westport: Praeger.

Lutes, C. (2001). Al-Qaida in Action and Learning: A Systems Approach. The George Washington University. Accessed 13.6.06 <http://www.au.af.mil/au/awc/awcgate/readings/al_qaida2.htm>.

Marth, D. (2003). *Hostage Taking (Geiselnahme)*. Luchterhand. (German with English abstract).

Miron, M.S. and Goldstein, A.P. (1979). *Hostage*. New York: Pergamon Press.

Noesner, G.W. (1999). Negotiation concepts for commanders. *FBI Law Enforcement Bulletin*, 68, 6–14.

Parsons, T. (1978). *Action Theory and the Human Condition*. Detroit: The Free Press.

Salfati, G. and Canter, D.V. (1999). Differentiating stranger murders: profiling offender characteristics from behavioural styles. *Behavioural Sciences and the Law*, 17, 391–406.

Shye, S. (1985). Nonmetric multivariate models for behavioural action systems, in *Facet Theory: Approaches to Social Research*, edited by D. Canter. New York: Springer-Verlag.

Strentz, T. (1986). Negotiating with the hostage-taker exhibiting paranoid schizophrenic symptoms. *Journal of Police Science and Administration*, 14, 12–16.

Thompson, D. (2000). The decision to burgle: target selection in burglary. *Proceedings of the sixth International Investigative Psychology Conference.*
Webster, M.C. (1997). Process vs. outcome in the management of hostage/barricaded persons' incidents. *Gazette*, 59(5), 24–27.
Wilton, Z. (2000). Terrorist barricade-hostage incidents: classifying control using an action systems approach. Proceedings of the sixth International Investigative Psychology Conference.
Yokota, K., Iwami, H., Watanabe, K., Fujita, G. and Watanabe, S. (2004). High risk factors of hostage barricade incidents in a Japanese sample. *Journal of Investigative Psychology and Offender Profiling*, 1(2), 139–151.

## Appendix

*List of variables*

1. *Weapon possession* This variable refers to instance where the offender possessed a weapon before the incident.
2. *Knife* This variable refers to instance where the offender possessed a knife.
3. *Stranger* This variable refers to instance where the offender held a stranger hostage.
4. *Single hostage* This variable refers to instance where the offender held only one hostage.
5. *Planned* This variable refers to instance where the offender planned the hostage incident.
6. *Alcohol consumption* This variable refers to instance where the offender consumed alcohol prior to/during the incident.
7. *Demand for food/water* This variable refers to instance where the offender demanded food/water.
8. *Conversation between offender and hostage* This variable refers to instance where there was a conversation between the offender and hostage.
9. *Firearms* This variable refers to instance where the offender possessed firearms during the hostage incident.
10. *Hostage house* This variable refers to instance where the offender barricaded inside the hostage's house.
11. *Binding* This variable refers to instance where the offender bound a hostage.
12. *Prior crime* This variable refers to instance where the offender committed another crime prior hostage taking.
13. *Outside communication* This variable refers to instance where the offender had communication with outside citizens during the hostage incident.
14. *Demand for meeting with relatives/ (ex-) partner* This variable refers to instance where the offender demanded a meeting with relatives/ (ex-) spouse/girlfriend.
15. *Demand for media coverage* This variable refers to instance where the offender demanded media coverage.

16. *Demand for meeting (others)* This variable refers to instance where the offender demanded a meeting with a specific person, such as a mayor. It excludes demands for meeting with relatives/ (ex-) spouse-girlfriend.
17. *Vehicle* This variable refers to instance where the offender barricaded himself/ herself inside a vehicle.
18. *Explosives* This variable refers to instance where the offender possessed explosives.
19. *Demand for escape* This variable refers to instance where the offender demanded escape assistance, such as a car to escape.
20. *Drug use* This variable refers to instance where the offender consumed illegal drugs prior to/during the hostage incident.
21. *Shop* This variable refers to instance where the offender barricaded himself/ herself inside a shop.
22. *Demand for money* This variable refers to instance where the offender demanded money.
23. *Demand for cigarette* This variable refers to instance where the offender demanded cigarettes.
24. *Deadlines* This variable refers to instance where the offender set a deadline for demands.
25. *(public) office* This variable refers to instance where the offender barricaded himself/herself inside (public) office.
26. *Relative* This variable refers to instance where the offender held a relative hostage.
27. *Partner* This variable refers to instance where the offender held a (ex-) spouse-girlfriend hostage.
28. *Demand for weapons* This variable refers to instance where the offender demanded a weapon.
29. *Bank* This variable refers to instance where the offender barricaded himself/ herself inside a bank.
30. *Multiple offenders* This variable refers to instance where there were multiple offenders.
31. *Sexual* This variable refers to instance where the offender sexually violated a hostage.
32. *Demand for alcohol* This variable refers to instance where the offender demanded alcohol.
33. *Demand for media device* This variable refers to instance where the offender demanded media device, such as a television.
34. *Demand for victim's comfort* This variable refers to instance where the offender demanded items for the victim's comfort, such as blankets for victim.

Chapter 5

# Test of Canter's Sexual Behaviour Models in a Sample of Young People who had Sexually Harmed

Louise Almond

## Editor's Introduction

In this Chapter, Louise Almond develops one of the earliest theoretical frameworks in IP, the Victim Role model (Canter, 1995), developed by Professor Canter during his earliest involvement in cases. This was the idea that as part of the narratives that underpin their crimes, offenders allocated one of 3 abbreviated and sub-human roles to their victims (see Canter and Youngs, 2012 paper on Sexual and Violent Offenders' role assignments for a detailed specification of Professor Canter's original theory). It is a framework that has proved remarkably durable.

## Previous Research

In 1994, Canter utilised narrative theory in order to explore adult criminal behaviour. He suggested that through their actions a criminal tells us about how he has chosen to live his life. Canter goes on to argue that criminal activity can only be understood through in-depth analysis and understanding of an individuals' "inner-narratives". These narratives can be connected to characteristic roles and actions. It is hypothesised that in any given criminal context there will be a dominant role the criminal will take, which relates directly to a recognisable overall narrative. In particular, Canter argued that sexual assault involves interpersonal behaviour, with the variations in offending behaviour indicating differences in the roles that the victims have for their offenders. It is argued that these styles of offender-victim interactions vary from each other in terms of interpersonal distance, and they represent underlying themes of offence behaviour (Canter, Hughes and Kirby, 1998).

Canter (1994) analysed 105 cases involving rape in order to establish whether there was a coherent pattern to the behaviour displayed by perpetrators. Canter's 1994 model identified three distinct behavioural themes which related to the role the victim plays for the offender. These themes were defined as: *Victim as Object*, *Victim as Person* and *Victim as Vehicle*. The *Victim as Object* theme refers to the perpetrators lack of empathy for their victim. They do not aim to cause any great discomfort but they have no empathy for their victim's reactions. These perpetrators view their victims as objects to be exploited for their own personal gain, not only sexual but also instrumental, by using the opportunity to steal items from the victim. The victims are not expected to play any active part in the assault. The *Victim as Person* theme refers to perpetrators who view their victim as a significant individual. These perpetrators attempt to develop a pseudo-intimate relationship with the victim by treating them as a reactive individual rather than a sexual object. Therefore the victim is important in the formulation and meaning of the abuse. For some of these perpetrators the desire for social contact is the primary purpose for the assault. The third behavioural theme is that of *Victim as Vehicle*, which refers to the perpetrator viewing the victim as a representation or surrogate for some generalised other rather than being targeted as a specific person or treated as an object. These perpetrators use their victims as a vehicle for venting their anger and frustration. These incidents are characterised by verbal and physical violence and often involve humiliation and the demeaning of the victim. The abuse is therefore seen as a displacement of anger and a need for power rather than an uncontrollable desire for sexual gratification.

Canter (1994) also argued that rape is essentially a crime of violation; the victim experiences a range of violations from the highly intrusive penetrative sexual violation to personal humiliation, and physical assault. He went on to show that a pattern of frequencies exists among the behaviours that occur during sexual assaults, which correspond to this scale of violation. In general, Canter found that sexually violating behaviours were high frequency variables, and personally violating behaviours were low frequency variables with physically violating variables represented in between.

Canter's (1994) model has since been refined by Canter, Bennell, Alison and Reddy (2003). The refined model has four behavioural themes: *Hostility*, which relates to Canter's original *Victim as Vehicle* theme and *Involvement*, which relates to the *Victim as Person* theme. The *Victim as Object* theme was differentiated in this more recent model into two themes: *Control*, which refers to the perpetrator exerting power over the victim by demobilising them and *Theft*, which refers to the perpetrator using the opportunity for instrumental gain. As in Canter's (1994) model, Canter et al. (2003) showed that a pattern of frequencies exist amongst the behaviours, which corresponded to the various levels of violation (sexual, physical and personal).

Canter, Hughes and Kirby (1998) developed a multivariate model of offence behaviour in child sexual abuse; they analysed 97 cases involving a child victim. Canter, Hughes and Kirby's (1998) findings indicated that sexual offences against children could be conceptualised into three distinct behavioural themes, which are characterised by aggressive, intimate, or criminal-opportunist modes of offender-victim interaction. The *Aggressive* style of interaction involves the perpetrator perceiving the child as a focus or vehicle for their aggression. The incidents often involve threats of harm and physical aggression greater than that necessary to control the victim. The sexual activity is characterised by domination and anger and necessarily involves the degradation of the victim. This *Aggressive* theme is therefore similar to Canter's (1994) *Victim as Vehicle* theme.

A second behavioural theme found in the behaviour of paedophiles is the *Intimate* style of interaction, which involves the perpetrator perceiving the child as an alternative to an age-appropriate partner. They view their relationship with the victim as comparable with conventional sexual relationships between adults. These perpetrators use methods such as enticement, affection and the giving of gifts in order to develop a consenting sexual relationship with the child. This is often referred to as "grooming". The sexual behaviour develops over time from non-sexual physical contact into sexual touching in order to desensitise the victim. The perpetrator performing sexual acts on the victim such as oral sex and mutual masturbation characterises this sexual activity. This *Intimate* theme is therefore similar to Canter's (1994) *Victim as Person* theme.

The third theme found by Canter, Hughes and Kirby (1998) is a *Criminal/Opportunist* style of interaction, which involves the perpetrator using the victim solely as an outlet for their sexual gratification. It is not the intention of these perpetrators to hurt their victim and the force used will not exceed that necessary to control the victim. These incidents are opportunistic in nature with little emotional attachment involved, these individuals have a general disregard for the rights of others and sexual abuse is just one of the criminal activities they are involved in. These perpetrators are often intoxicated, which results in the lowering of their impulse control and enhances their perception of opportunities to offend. This *Criminal/Opportunist* theme is therefore similar to Canter's (1994) *Victim as Object* theme.

However, these studies have only investigated the behaviour of adult offenders; the question arises as to whether the behaviour of young people reveals a similar multivariate model. Descriptive studies carried on UK samples have found that there is no single behaviour displayed by the majority of young people who sexually harm (Manocha and Mezey, 1998; Richardson, Graham and Bhate, 1995). Therefore, there is no "typical" behaviour displayed by youths who sexually harm. This observed heterogeneity suggests that there may be identifiable subgroups of young people who sexually harm each with distinct behavioural characteristics. However, systematic analysis at the behavioural level is currently an underdeveloped area in the research literature of youths who sexually harm. Researchers predominately identify subgroups of youths on the basis of particular perpetrator or victim characteristics. They then investigate how these particular subgroups differ in terms of the behaviour they display, generally failing to find significant differences (Richardson, Kelly, Graham and Bhate, 2004; Worling, 2001).

## Aims of the Chapter

Canter's studies into the behaviour of perpetrators of Rape (Canter, 1994; Canter, Bennell, Alison and Reddy, 2003) and Child abuse (Canter et al., 1998) have therefore found empirical support for a composite model of sexual behaviour consisting of three modes of interaction (*Victim as Object*, *Victim as Person* and *Victim as Vehicle*) which occur at various levels of violation (*personal*, *physical* and *sexual*). This chapter aims to investigate whether the behaviour of young people who sexually harm has some comprehensible coherence, as has found to be the case in Canter's adult sexual behaviour models.

The first hypothesis proposed in this chapter is that the frequency patterns of behaviours across a set of sexual abusive incidents committed by young people will conform to a scale of violation, as is the case in adult sex offender models of behaviour. This pattern will have a common order of increasing violation with increasing frequency of behaviour. High frequency variables will relate to sexually violating behaviours, low frequency variables will relate to personally violating behaviours and physically violating behaviours will be represented in between.

The second hypothesis proposed is that the behaviour displayed by young people who sexually harm can be differentiated into three distinct themes: *Victim as Object*, *Victim as Person* and *Victim as Vehicle* which relate to the differing modes of interaction between a perpetrator and their victim, as is the case in adult sex offender models of behaviour. If these three themes are distinct, then each theme will contain a set of conceptually related behaviours that will consistently occur together.

A third hypothesis proposed in this chapter is that the behaviours an individual perpetrator exhibits will reflect one dominant theme of interaction, as the three themes represent different modes of interpersonal interaction between the perpetrator and the victim.

This chapter therefore aims to utilise Canter's sexual behavioural models as a basis to help identify the underlying structure of the behaviour of young people who sexually harm. The resulting multivariate model will help distinguish one set of assaults from another. This has possible implications for investigative process, both in the apprehension of an unknown perpetrator and in the linking of a series of offences. In addition, as each theme of behaviour reflects a different mode of interaction with the victim, it would therefore be proposed that each mode of interaction would benefit from distinctly different treatment approaches.

## Procedure

Information was obtained from two specialist agencies that work with children and young people who sexually harm: 170 cases from G-Map and 130 from the 5A project. The youths were referred to the agencies between 1988 and 2002. G-Map is an independent provider that offers a range of services for young people who sexually harm. The agency was established in 1988 and is based in Greater Manchester, however the service is accessible on a national basis. The 5A project has, since 1994, provided a systematic and consistent service for young people in Liverpool with problematic sexual behaviour. Additional funding in 1999 meant that the project could extend its services to young people throughout the Merseyside area.

The data is based on an extensive and detailed review of subject files. A data collection form was used to collect information regarding the behaviour of the perpetrator during the abusive incident. In total, 33 behavioural characteristics were coded as present or absent for each individual. Full details of these characteristics are outlined in the content dictionary (Appendix). An independent observer was used to investigate the inter reliability of the coding dictionary. Ten randomly selected files were independently coded resulting in a Cohen's Kappa value of .770, which is significant at the $p<.0001$ level, indicating acceptable inter-rater reliability.

### *Sample*

There was a total of 300 youths in the sample. All were aged 18 or under at the time of their referral to the specialist agencies. The mean age of the cohort was 14.3 (SD = 1.79) years with a range of 9–18 years. Of these youths 292 (97%) were males and 8 (3%) were females. The data consisted of behavioural information concerning the abusive incident for which the perpetrator was referred. These incidents had previously been defined as abusive by the specialist agencies from which the data were collected. If the perpetrator was referred for more than one incident then the information pertaining to the first incident was recorded. Canter, Bennell, Alison and Reddy (2003) in their study of stranger rape used this one offence per perpetrator method to ensure that the empirical structure revealed by the analysis was not biased, by weighting being given to frequent perpetrators who may be displaying a particular pattern of behaviour.

### *Statistical Analysis*

This chapter aimed to examine the behaviour displayed by young people who sexually harm by utilising multidimensional statistical procedures, which have previously been used by Canter to examine the behaviour of adult sexual offenders (Canter, 1994; Canter, Bennell, Alison and Reddy, 2003). In order to do this the data was analysed using a multi-dimensional scaling procedure known as Smallest Space Analysis (SSA) (Lingoes, 1973). SSA is based on the assumption that any underlying structure will be most readily appreciated by examining the relationship each variable has with every other variable (Canter, 1985).

In order to test the relationship, each behaviour has to every other behavioural characteristic, a measure of association is calculated that indicates the degree of co-occurrence between every behaviour and every other. In the present case Jaccard's coefficient was used as this has been found to be appropriate for this kind of data in the earlier studies cited. These measures of association between all variables are then rank ordered to enable the SSA to represent the relationships between the characteristics as effectively as possible in a low dimensionality. These rank ordered correlations are then represented as ranked distances in an abstract "space". This allows the underlying structure of the behaviour to be examined enabling any themes within the characteristics to be identified.

The visual representation is generated such that the higher the correlation between any two characteristics, the closer together the points representing them will appear on the spatial plot (Guttman, 1968). The resulting patterns of characteristics can hence be examined and thematic differentiations can be delineated. The aims of this chapter were built upon the assumption that characteristics with similar underlying themes will be more likely to co-occur than those that imply divergent themes. As mentioned earlier this regional hypothesis has previously been viewed as an appropriate way of interpreting co-occurrences of variables, and has successfully been used to interpret related areas such as paedophilia (Canter, Hughes and Kirby, 1998) and rape (Canter, Bennell, Alison and Reddy, 2003).

## SSA of Behavioural Characteristics

An SSA was carried out on 33 behaviours across the 300 cases. The three-dimensional SSA solution has a Guttman Lingoes coefficient of alienation of 0.16 indicating a good fit between the SSA plot and the original association matrix. In both figures, vectors 1 and 2 of a three-dimensional space are shown. Each point represents a behaviour displayed by the perpetrator during the abusive incident. The closer any two points are, the more likely it is that the behaviours will co-occur in comparison with other behaviours. For illustration, it is very likely that if the incident involved a co-perpetrator then there will be multiple acts of violence. In contrast, it is unlikely that if a youth physically coerces their victim that they will also use some form of inducement.

## Levels of Violation

The first hypothesis stated that the frequency patterns of behaviours across a set of sexually abusive incidents committed by young people would conform to a scale of violation. Canter et al. (2003) in their study of stranger rape argued that as an SSA plot is derived from the correlations between the behaviours and there is no inevitable link to their frequencies. Therefore any frequency structure that emerges is an empirical finding. As indicated in Figure 5.1, it is possible to draw contours on the SSA that represent a general frequency pattern. This pattern ranges from medium frequency actions in the centre of the plot to lower frequency actions that radiate out towards the edges of the plot. As found by Canter, Bennell, Alison and Reddy. (2003) the frequencies serve as a summary of actions displayed during the abusive incident, showing that those actions further out from the core are the most differentiated, giving any particular incident its specific characteristics while those at the centre are conceptually central to youths' sexually harmful behaviour.

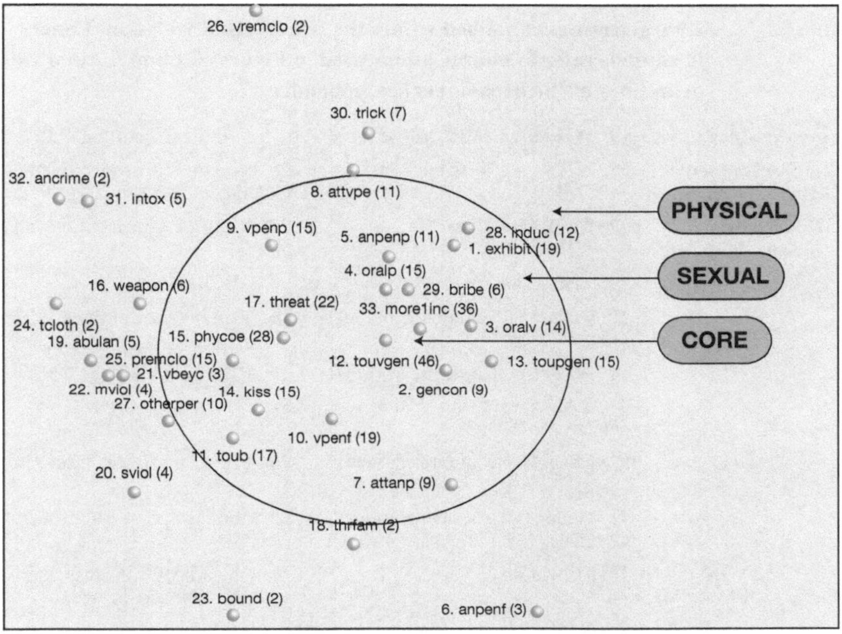


**Figure 5.1** **A three-dimensional SSA, vectors 1x2, indicating the degrees of violation in the behaviour of youths who sexually harm. Numbers indicate behavioural characteristics as listed in the Appendix. Parenthesis contain the percentage frequency of each characteristic**

An examination of the behaviours within these general frequency contours provides evidence for the facet of increasing violation. The variables "perpetrator touches victims genitals" (46%) and "more than one incident with the victim" (36%) were found to form the core region of the SSA, indicating that these two variables are the defining variables of youth sexually harmful behaviour. In addition, a medium frequency band (10–30%) could be identified that generally consists of sexually violating behaviours and a lower frequency band (<10%) could be identified that consists of physically violating behaviours (see Table 5.1).

Unlike the stranger rape research carried out by Canter, Bennell, Alison and Reddy, (2003) this model does not have a set of personally violating behaviours. The only personally violating behaviours recorded in the case files of young people who sexually harm was the behaviour "concurrently with another crime" was a low frequency behaviour as was the case in the adult model. The lack of personally violating behaviours may be a result of the fact that young people are at a different developmental, emotional and behavioural stage of their life than adults, it may also be an indication that young people are less sophisticated when compared to

**Table 5.1 Characteristics contained within the two levels of violation. Letters in capitals refer to abbreviations used in Figures 5.1 and 5.2. For full definitions of the behaviours see Appendix**

| Core variables >30% | Sexual violation 10–30% | Physical violation <10% |
|---|---|---|
| 12. TOUches Victims GENitals (46%) | 15. PHYsical COErcion (28%) | 25. Perpetrator REMoves victims CLOthes (15%) |
| 33. MORE than 1 INCident (36%) | 17. THREAT (22%) | 27. OTHER PERpetrators involved (10%) |
| | 1. EXHIBITionism (19%) | 30. TRICKery (7%) |
| | 10. Vaginal PENetration with Finger (19%) | 16. WEAPON use or threat of (6%) |
| | 11. TOUched victims Breasts (17%) | 19. ABUsive LANguage (5%) |
| | 4. ORAL contact with Victims genitals (15%) | 31. INTOXicated (5%) |
| | 9. Vaginal PENetration with Penis (15%) | 20. Single act of VIOLence (4%) |
| | 13. Victim TOUches Perpetrators GENitals (15%) | 22. Multiple acts of VIOLence (4%) |
| | 14. KISS (15%) | 21. Violence BEYond that necessary to Control the victim (3%) |
| | 3. ORAL contact with Perpetrators genitals (14%) | 6. ANal PENetration with Finger (3%) |
| | 28. INDUCement (12%) | 18. THReat to FAMily (2%) |
| | 5. ANal PENetration with Penis (11%) | 23. BOUND (2%) |
| | 8. ATTempted Vaginal Penetration (11%) | 24. Tears CLOTHes (2%) |
| | 2. GENital CONtact (9%) | 26. Victim REMOves own CLOTHes (2%) |
| | 7. ATTempted ANal Penetration (9%) | 32. concurrently with ANother CRIME (2%) |
| | 29. BRIBE (6%) | |

adult offenders. It is also possible, of course, that differences in procedure when interviewing youths about the abusive incident may have different emphasis from those carried out with adults. Therefore, the behaviours "implies knowing the victim", "forces victim to make sexual comments" and "compliments the victim" may either not be occurring or the information regarding these behaviours is not being requested during the referral process.

*Sexual Violation*

As indicated by Figure 5.1, actions that constitute sexual violation form a central region in the SSA plot. Sexually violating behaviours found in this moderate frequency band include: "vaginal penetration with penis", "attempted vaginal penetration", "anal penetration with penis", "attempted anal penetration", "exhibitionism", "victim makes oral contact with perpetrator genitals", "perpetrator oral contact with victims genitals", "victims touches perpetrator genitals", "genital contact without penetration", "vaginal penetration with finger", "touches victims breasts", "perpetrator kisses victim". The region also includes behaviours such as "inducement", "bribe", "verbal threat", "physical coercion" and "perpetrator removes victims' clothes". These variables relate to the methods of coercion the perpetrator used to ensure the victims compliance in order that the sexual behaviours are carried out successfully.

*Physical Violation*

Within the lower frequency region, these lesser frequent behaviours reflect the physical violation of the victim. The physically violating actions in the region include: "weapon", "tearing of clothes", "abusive and/or sexual language", "single act of violence", "multiple acts of violence", "violence beyond that necessary to control the victim", "threats to harm victims family", "binding of the victim", "trickery", "anal penetration with finger". This region also included variables such as "other perpetrator involved", "incident occurred in conjunction with another crime" and "perpetrator intoxicated". These behaviours may relate to why the incident occurred.

## Theme of Behaviour

The second hypothesis stated that the behaviour displayed by young people who sexually harm can be differentiated into three distinct themes: *Victim as Object*, *Victim as Person* and *Victim as Vehicle*, which relate to the differing modes of interaction between a perpetrator and their victim. Figure 5.2 illustrates how the co-occurrences of behaviours of young people who sexually harm can be partitioned into three thematically similar subgroups.

*Victim as Object Perpetrator*

As can be seen from Figure 5.2, there is a collection of behaviours in the top left of the plot that imply that the perpetrator is interacting with their Victim as an Object. These perpetrators are using their victim to satisfy their own gratifications; sexual gratification as indicated by the variable "vaginal penetration with the penis" and instrumental gratification, indicated by the variable "another crime committed at

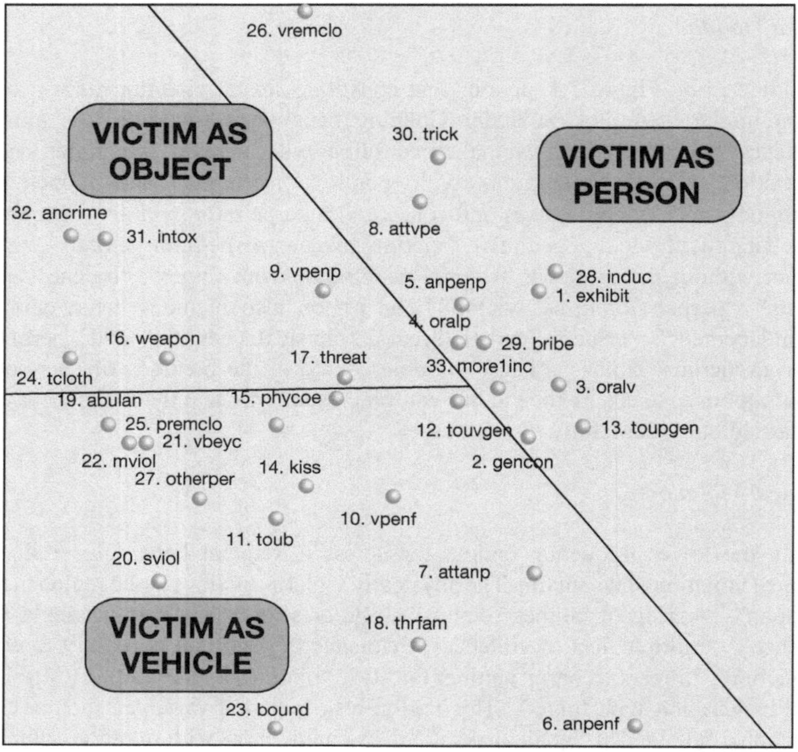


**Figure 5.2** **A three-dimensional SSA, vectors 1x2, shows themes of behaviour displayed by youths who sexually harm. Numbers indicate perpetrator characteristics as listed in Table 5.1. Parenthesis contains the percentage frequency of each characteristic**

time of the abusive incident". This accord's with Canter's (1994) Victim as Object mode of interaction. As in Canter, Hughes and Kirby's (1998) model of paedophilic behaviour (Criminal/Opportunist region) the variable "perpetrator intoxicated" is found within this region. Canter, Hughes and Kirby. (1998) argued that alcohol and/or drug use may facilitate sexual offending by lowering impulse control and enhancing the perception of opportunity. The lack of other sexual behaviours in this region indicates that the sole motivation for these perpetrators is the accomplishment of the sexual act. As is the case in Canter's (1994) model, these perpetrators control their victims through "verbal threats" and "threat and/or use of a weapon". These behaviours are used to force the victim into a non-participative role. The behaviour "tearing of victims clothes" also indicates the perpetrators attempt to exert control over his victim.

*Victim as Person Perpetrator*

Behaviours in the top right of the plot indicate that the perpetrator is interacting with the Victim as a Person. The presence of the behaviour "more than one sexually abusive incident occurred" within this region indicates (as is the case in Canter's 1994 and 2003 models of rape and in Canter, Hughes and Kirby.'s (1998) model of paedophilic behaviour (Intimate region), these perpetrators view their relationship with the victim as a conventional sexual relationship and therefore interact with them as a person. This is also implied by the reciprocal sexual behaviours contained within this region, which include; "perpetrator makes oral contact with the victims genitals", "victim makes oral contact with perpetrators genitals", "victim touches perpetrators genitals", "exhibitionism" and "victim removes own clothes". These behaviours imply that the perpetrator views their victim as a reactive individual. In the adult behaviour models, however, the variable "oral contact with perpetrators genitals" was contained within the Victim as Vehicle region indicating that adults use this behaviour in an aggressive manner whilst young people use it as a form of reciprocal contact.

These perpetrators also use psychological methods of coercion as opposed to physical methods indicated by the behaviours "inducement", "trickery" and "bribes". However, due to the fact that these incidents may occur over a period of time, as seen by the variable "more than one incident", this results in the escalation of the seriousness of the behaviours being displayed as indicated by the behaviours "genital contact without penetration", "attempted vaginal penetration with the penis" and "anal penetration with the penis". This results in the variable "anal penetration" with the penis being placed in a different region in this model than in the adult behaviour models where it indicated a Victim as Vehicle or Aggressive behaviour.

*Victim as Vehicle Perpetrator*

Behaviours in the bottom of the plot indicate that the perpetrator is interacting with the Victim as a Vehicle. These perpetrators are using their victim to vent their anger and frustration. As is the case in Canter's 1994 and 2003 models of rape and Canter et al's 1998 model of paedophilia (Aggressive region) behaviours in this region indicate the aggressive manner in which these perpetrators interact with their victim. These behaviours include "physical coercion", "single act of violence", "multiple acts of violence", "violence beyond that necessary to control the victim" (which included, in one, case attempted murder), "perpetrator removes victims clothing" and "victim is bound". These perpetrators also utilised language as a method of aggression, as indicated by the presence of "abusive and sexually explicit language" as well as "threats to harm the victims' family". These verbally aggressive behaviours were also found in the Victim as Vehicle region in the adult sexual offender models (Canter, 1994; Canter, Hughes and Kirby, 1998; Canter, Bennell, Alison and Reddy, 2003). These aggressive behaviours are used by the perpetrator to physically and mentally intimidate their victim.

The sexual behaviours in this region mainly involve penetration, "vaginal penetration with the finger", "anal penetration with the finger" and "attempted anal penetration". The behaviours "perpetrator touches victim genitals" and "touches victim breasts" were also contained within this region. These sexual behaviours are used by the perpetrators to humiliate and demean their victims. This region also contained the characteristic "more than one perpetrator involved". Amir (1971) found that gang rape was significantly associated with violence especially in its extreme forms. Interestingly the behaviour "perpetrator kisses the victim" is contained in the Victim as Vehicle region. In both Canter et al.'s (2003) model of rape and Canter et al.'s (1998) model of paedophilia it is located in the regions comparable with Victim as Person. Therefore, young people in this sample are kissing their victim as an aggressive action, (the behaviour correlates highly with other aggressive behaviours as indicated by its location in this region), and this is not comparable with the behaviour of adult sexual offenders.

Table 5.2 shows the behaviours contained within each theme and their relative frequencies. The highest frequency behaviours within each theme help define that theme. The highest frequency behaviours in the Victim as Object theme are "verbal threat" and "vaginal penetration with the penis"; in the Victim as Person theme they are "more than one incident with the victim" and "exhibitionism" and in the Victim as Vehicle theme the high frequency behaviours are "touches victims genitals" and "physical coercion".

Kuder-Richardson 20 (K-R 20) coefficients were calculated in order to provide an index of internal reliability. The K-R 20 is equivalent to the more common Cronbach's alpha coefficient but can be used with dichotomous data. Table 5.2 gives the K-R 20 coefficients for each of the three themes, these values are reasonable considering the data was not collected for research purposes. They also equate with other published models in this area which have used this coefficient such as Canter, Bennell, Alison and Kirby, (2003) and Porter and Alison, (2004). These coefficients are not sufficiently high enough to demonstrate clear evidence of a scale therefore the characteristics within each theme do not represent a scale of increasing behaviours within each theme. However, they are sufficiently high enough to indicate that the themes are meaningful and coherent (Alison and Stein, 2001).

In summary, visual examination of the SSA plot confirmed that the behaviours displayed during the abusive incident by young people that sexually harm indicate a common order of increasing violation with increasing frequency of behaviour. Frequency contours were superimposed on the plot to reflect these differences in sexual and physical violation (Figure 5.1). The behaviours can also be differentiated in terms of three themes of interaction with the victim. Behaviours that co-occur in the top left of the plot reflect a Victim as Object theme, behaviours in the top right of the plot reflect a Victim as Person theme and behaviours at the bottom of the plot reflect a Victim as Vehicle theme. A linear partition was superimposed onto the plot to reflect these distinct thematic differences (Figure 5.2).

**Table 5.2 Characteristics contained within the three themes of behaviour. Letters in capitals refer to abbreviations used in Figures 5.1 and 5.2. For full definitions of the behaviours see Appendix**

| Victim as object | Victim as person | Victim as vehicle |
|---|---|---|
| 17. THREAT (22%) | 33. MORE than 1 INCident (36%) | 12. TOUches Victims GENitals (46%) |
| 9. Vaginal PENetration with Penis (15%) | 1. EXHIBITionism (19%) | 15. PHYsical COErcion (28%) |
| 16. WEAPON use or threat of (6%) | 4. ORAL contact with Perpetrators genitals (15%) | 10. Vaginal PENetration with Finger (19%) |
| 31. INTOXicated (5%) | 13. victim TOUches Perpetartors GENitals (15%) | 11. TOUched victims Breasts (17%) |
| 24. Tears CLOTHes (2%) | 3. ORAL contact with Victims genitals (14%) | 14. KISS (15%) |
| 32. concurrently with ANother CRime (2%) | 28. INDUCement (12%) | 25. Perpetrator REMoves victims CLOthes (15%) |
| | 5. ANal PENetration with Penis (11%) | 27. OTHER PERpetrators involved (10%) |
| | 8. ATTempted Vaginal Penetration (11%) | 7. ATTempted ANal Penetration (9%) |
| | 2. GENital CONtact (9%) | 19. ABUsive LANguage (5%) |
| | 30. TRICKery (7%) | 20. Single act of VIOLence (4%) |
| | 29. BRIBE (6%) | 22. Multiple acts of VIOLence (4%) |
| | 26. Victim REMoves own CLOThes (2%) | 6. ANal PENetration with Finger (3%) |
| | | 21. Violence BEYond that necessary to Control the victim (3%) |
| | | 18. THReat to FAMily (2%) |
| | | 23. BOUND (2%) |
| K-R 20 .511 | K-R 20 .561 | K.R 20 .622 |

## Classifying Youths who Sexually Harm

The third hypothesis in this chapter proposed that the behaviours an individual perpetrator displays will reflect one dominant theme of interaction. Indeed, the utility of the thematic structure proposed above is considerably enhanced if such dominant themes are found for most perpetrators. In order to test this hypothesis as well as test whether the proposed framework serves as a useful way to classify youths who sexually harm, each of the 300 cases in the dataset were individually examined to ascertain if they could be assigned to a dominant theme of behaviour. A perpetrator may display behaviours from more than one theme, although because the themes represent psychologically distinct behaviours, it is hypothesised that the majority of behaviours a perpetrator displayed would be contained within one dominant theme. Every incident was assigned a score for each of the three themes reflecting the percentage of Victim as Object, Victim as Person and Victim as Vehicle behaviours that occurred in that incident. The criteria used for assigning an individual to a particular theme were taken from Salfati and Canter (1999) who used this method to classify stranger murders. To be assigned to a dominant theme, the percentage score for that theme has to be greater or equal to the sum of the other two themes combined. The incident could also be classified as a hybrid if the percentage score for more than one theme were similar.

Using this procedure 86% (258 of the 300) of abusive incidents perpetrated by a young person could be assigned to a dominant theme. As Figure 5.3 shows, out of the 258 (86%) incidents that could be assigned a dominant theme, 124 (41%) were classified as Victim as Person, 89 (30%) Victim as Vehicle and 45 (15%) Victim as Object perpetrators. If an individual had similar frequency scores on more than one theme they were classified as a hybrid. There were only a small number of individuals who were classified as a hybrid. There were 10 (3%) classified as Victim as Object/ Victim as Person perpetrators, 5 (2%) classified as Victim as Object/Victim as Vehicle perpetrators and 2 (1%) classified as Victim as Person/Victim as Vehicle perpetrators.

The fact that the majority of cases belong to one of the three main behavioural themes is empirical support for the hypothesis that the SSA structure represents the dominant processes underlying the sexually harmful behaviour of young people and this structure is similar to that found by Canter in his models of adult sexual behaviour (Canter, 1994; Canter, Hughes and Kirbyl, 1998; Canter, Bennell, Alison and Reddy, 2003).

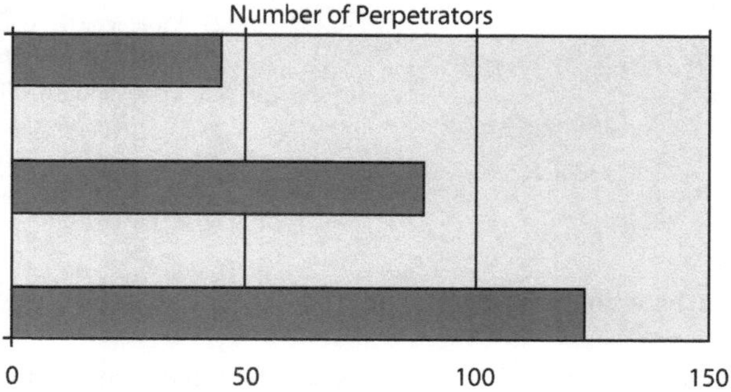


**Figure 5.3 Distribution of cases across dominant themes of behaviour**

## Chapter Summary

This Chapter has shown that Canter's sexual behaviour models are productive when examining the sexually harmful behaviour of young people. The pattern of behaviour of youths who sexually harm has been found to have a common order of increasing violation with increasing frequency and the behaviour displayed by these young people could also be conceptualised as various modes of interpersonal interaction, Victim as Object, Victim as Person and Victim as Vehicle. More studies, however, are required, utilising different sources to further strengthen the applicability of this model for young people.

The model proposed by Canter has almost entirely been replicated with an entirely different sample. Except for a very small number of behaviours, which are in different regions, the majority comply with Canter's models of sexual behaviour. The main difference in this model and Canter's models was the lack of a personal violation region. This is either a reflection of the data collection procedure, in that these behaviours are just not recorded in the case files of young people or it could indicate that young people are less sophisticated than adults in their sexually offending behaviour. There were two variables in this model which were positioned in the Victim as Person region whilst in the adult models they were found in the Victim as Vehicle regions, "anal penetration with penis" and "oral contact with perpetrators genitals" this is probably due to the high number of male victims found in this sample (31%) and due to many of these incidents occurring over a period of time resulting in escalation to serious penetrative behaviours. There was one behaviour which was located in the Victim as Vehicle region whilst in the models it was found in the Victim as Person region, "perpetrator kisses the victim" therefore unlike adults this behaviour when displayed by young people correlated highly with aggressive and violent behaviours.

The fact that the majority of cases involving young people, 86%, could be assigned to one dominant theme of behaviour is empirical support for the hypothesis that this multivariate model represents the underlying structure of the behaviour displayed by young people during the sexually abusive incident. This multivariate model therefore allows one set of assaults to be distinguished from another.

To further test the validity of these three themes the typical characteristics of people within the sample who have committed the different types of sexual abuse needs to be examined, in order to test the hypothesis that individuals who sexually harm in a particular theme of behaviour will also differ in their characteristics, as found to be the case in other crimes such as arson (Canter and Fritzon, 1998) and Homicide (Salfati and Canter, 1999).

The emergence of a multivariate model of behaviour in youths who sexually harm has number of important implications. The current model will aid practitioners who work with these young people as it will allow the majority of individuals to be classified as one of three themes of behaviour as opposed to the current method of classifying all youths who sexually harm as one group. Effective classification schemes can help criminal justice agents in their decision making, improve service delivery and make more effective use of the limited resources made available to specialist agencies.

This model could also potentially enable the identification of young people who are at a high risk of recidivism, by examining the re-offending rates of the different themes. Using this model it may also be possible to identify whether the risk is of further sexual, violent or non-sexual offending. For example young people who interact with their Victim as a Vehicle may be more likely to commit further violent offences due to the high levels of aggression shown during the abusive incident. Whilst youths who interact with their Victim as an Object may be more likely to commit further sexual offences as their sole motivation was the accomplishment of the sexual act.

There also exists considerable potential for the development of treatment programmes for these young people that are responsive to the variations that exists between individuals based on differences in their dominant behavioural theme. For example, youths who recognise the human, personal qualities in their victims require a different sort of treatment from that of youths who treat their victims as inanimate objects.

## Acknowledgments

The author would like to thank all the staff at G-MAP and the 5A project for all their assistance and for allowing them access to their files.

## References

Alison, L. and Stein, K. (2001). Vicious circles: accounts of stranger sexual assault reflect abusive variants of conventional interaction. *The Journal of Forensic Psychiatry*, 12, 515–538.

Amir, M. (1971). *Patterns in Forcible Rape*. Chicago: University of Chicago Press.

Beckett, R. (1999). Evaluation of adolescent sexual abusers, in *Children and Young People Who Sexually Abuse Others*, edited by M. Erooga and H. Masson. *Challenges and Responses*. London: Routledge.

Canter, D., Bennell, C., Alison, L. and Reddy, S. (2003). Differentiating sex offences: a behaviourally based thematic classification of stranger rapes. *Behavioural Sciences and the Law*, 21, 157–174.

Canter, D., Hughes, D. and Kirby, S. (1998). Paedophilia: pathology, criminality, or both? The development of a multivariate model of offence behaviour in child sexual abuse. *The Journal of Forensic Psychiatry*, 9, 532–555.

Canter, D. and Fritzon, K. (1998). Differentiating arsonists: a model of firesetting actions and characteristics. *Legal and Criminological Psychology*, 3, 73–96.

Canter, D. (1994). *Criminal Shadows*. London: Harper Collins Publishers.

Canter, D. (1985). *Facet Theory Approaches to Social Research*. New York: Springer Verlag.

Guttman, L. (1968). A general nonmetric technique for finding the smallest co-ordinate space for a configuration of points. *Psychometrika*, 33, 469–506.

Lingoes, J. (1973). *The Guttman Lingoes Nonmetric Program Series*. Ann Arbor, MI: Mathesis.

Manocha, K. and Mezey, G. (1998). British adolescents who sexually abuse: a descriptive study. *The Journal of Forensic Psychiatry*, 9, 588–608.
Porter, L. and Alison, L. (2004). Behavioural coherence in violent group activity: an interpersonal model of sexually violent gang behaviour. *Aggressive Behaviour*, 30, 449–468.
Richardson, G., Kelly, T., Graham, F. and Bhate, S. (2004). A personality-based taxonomy of sexually abusive adolescents derived from the Millon Adolescent Clinical Inventory (MACI). *British Journal of Clinical Psychology*, 43, 285–298.
Richardson, G., Graham, F. Bhate, S. and Kelly, T. (1995). A British sample of sexually abusive adolescents; abuser and abuse characteristics. *Criminal Behaviour and Mental Health*, 5, 187–209.
Salfati, G. and Canter, D. (1999). Differentiating stranger murders: profiling offender characteristics from behavioural styles. *Behavioural Sciences and the Law*, 17, 391–406.
Worling, J. (2001). Personality-based typology of adolescent male sexual offenders: Differences in recidivism rates, victim-selection characteristics and personal victimization histories. *Sexual Abuse: A Journal of Research and Treatment*, 13, 149–166.

## Appendix

*Content Dictionary*

| Behaviour | Short name | Definition |
|---|---|---|
| 1. Exhibitionism | Exhibit | The perpetrator shows their genitals to the victim |
| 2. Genital contact without penetration | Gencon | The perpetrator simulates having intercourse without penetrating the victim |
| 3. Perpetrator makes oral contact with victim's genitals | Oralv | The perpetrator makes contact with the victims genitals using his/her mouth |
| 4. Victim makes oral contact with perpetrator's genitals | Oralp | The victim makes contact with the perpetrators genitals using his/her mouth |
| 5. Anal penetration with penis | Anpenp | The perpetrator penetrates the victims anus with his penis |
| 6. Anal penetration with finger | Anpenf | The perpetrator penetrates the victims anus with his/her finger |
| 7. Attempted anal penetration | Attanp | The perpetrator attempts to penetrate the victims anus with penis |
| 8. Attempted vaginal penetration | Attvp | The perpetrator attempts to penetrate the victims vagina with penis |
| 9. Vaginal penetration with penis | Vpenp | The perpetrator penetrates the victims vagina with his penis |
| 10. Vaginal penetration with finger | Vpenf | The perpetrator penetrates the victims vagina with his/her finger |

| Behaviour | Short name | Definition |
|---|---|---|
| 11. Touches victims breasts | Toub | The perpetrator touches the victims breasts |
| 12. Perpetrator touches the victims genitals | Touvgen | The perpetrator touches the victim genitals |
| 13. Victim touches perpetrators genitals | Toupgen | The victim touches the perpetrators genitals |
| 14. Perpetrator kisses the victim | Kiss | The perpetrator kisses the victim |
| 15. Physical coercion | Phycoe | The perpetrator uses physical force during the incident (e.g. hitting, slapping, restraining) |
| 16. Threat/use of weapon | Weapon | The perpetrator threatens and/or uses a weapon in order to control the victim |
| 17. Verbal threat | Threat | The perpetrator verbally threatens the victim |
| 18. Threat to victims family | Thrfam | The perpetrator threatens to harm victims family |
| 19. Perpetrator uses abusive or sexually explicit language | Abulan | The perpetrator uses abusive and/or sexually explicit language during the incident |
| 20. Single act of violence | Sviol | The perpetrator carries out a single act of violence against the victim (e.g. single slap) |
| 21. Violence used beyond the level necessary to control the victim | Vbeyc | Violence is used beyond the level necessary to control the victim. i.e. for gratuitous purposes |
| 22. Perpetrator carries out multiple acts of violence against victim during one incident | Mviol | The perpetrator carries out multiple acts of violence against the victim (e.g. multiple punches) |
| 23. Victim is bound | Bound | The victim is bound at any time during the incident with any material (not including restraint by perpetrators hands) |
| 24. Tears clothing | Tcloth | The perpetrator damages the victims clothing by removing them in a violent manner |
| 25. Perpetrator removes victims clothing | Premclot | The perpetrator forcefully removes the victims clothing |
| 26. Victim removes own clothing | Vremclot | The victim removes their own clothing |
| 27. Another perpetrator involved | Otherper | Another perpetrator/s were involved in the incident |
| 28. Inducement | Induc | The perpetrator uses some form of inducement to coerce the victim |
| 29. Perpetrator bribes the victim | Bribe | The perpetrator buys the victims gifts or gives them money |
| 30. Trickery | Trick | The perpetrator tricks the victim by playing "games". |
| 31. Perpetrator intoxicated at time of the offence | Intox | The perpetrator was intoxicated with alcohol/and or drugs when the incident occurred |
| 32. Sexual assault occurred in conjunction with another crime | Ancrime | The incident occurred in conjunction with another crime (e.g. burglary) |
| 33. More than one incident with the same victim | more1inc | The perpetrator was involved in more than one sexually abusive incident with the same victim |

# Chapter 6
# Emotions as Explanation of Crime

Maria Ioannou

## Editor's Introduction

The next Chapter focuses on one of the central tenets of David Canter's approach to crime; that we need to understand the meaning and significance of the action for the offender, in the offender's own terms and as it sits within the offender's broader purview. In short, we need to understand the experience of the crime. Typically, in encouraging Maria Ioannou and other supervisees to pursue this line, Professor Canter had pinpointed an area where understanding was lacking, perhaps because it is such a challenge to study. He found a way. The 'crime experience' paradigm that we are currently pursuing looks at cognitive and interpersonal identity, as well as the emotional, components of the roles offenders see themselves playing. This work is causing much interest not only as an approach to exploring differentiation in offending style, but also to exploring the much neglected question of the immediate instigators, the direct activators of criminal action (Canter and Youngs, 2012a; Ward, 2011; Youngs and Canter, 2011, 2012).

## Background to the Research

Humans have always formulated theories to explain the occurrence of criminal activity and to understand the criminal. These theories have been drawn from several scientific disciplines with the major contributions coming from sociology, psychology, psychiatry, criminology, anthropology, biology. Although there is an abundance of literature associated with the aetiology of crime and criminals and a number of researchers and theorists looked into the situational dynamics of crime, a neglected area of research within criminality has been that of the actual experience of the offence for the offender (Canter and Ioannou, 2004). The actual experience of offending such as feelings has received little attention and the internal dynamics of the offending itself have not been systematically studied. It is actually remarkable how little attention has been paid in criminological theory to emotions experienced while offenders commit their crimes.

Most existing social science explanations of crime emphasise societal context, antecedent events or personality characteristics of offenders. All processes that are external to the choices and decisions the offender makes as an active agent. By contrast both the legal processing of offenders and rehabilitation efforts focus on the purposes of the offender and his/her intentions, on the conscious intent and agency of the individual in committing the criminal act rather than causes external to the individual (Canter, 2008; Canter and Ioannou, 2004). There is, however, very little understanding of what the emotional experience of crime is and how it varies from crime to crime or person to person. This experience is what encourages the offender to carry out the crime, providing the phenomenological, internal, reasons for the crime and the emotional benefits that help to sustain the criminal activity. A better understanding of these influences will assist the modelling of the processes through which the external causes are internalised by criminals. The emotions associated with crimes can be seen as central to this process whereby context and personal characteristics are translated into actions.

Katz (1988) in his work *Seductions of Crime* took up the challenge of discussing the sensual aspects of deviant experience. His central thesis is that criminal behaviour cannot possibly be understood or explained without grasping how it is experienced or what it means to the actor. Empirical research has to focus on the foreground, the immediate, sensual aspects of crime, rather than the background. Background factors such as age, gender and material conditions of the offence don't get at the essential experiential facts of crime. He reports that too often, we impose our own interpretations on what the criminal is doing without bothering to find out what he or she feels. These sensual dynamics are the deciding factors in whether or not a crime is committed.

Studies into the emotional aspects of crime may also help in understanding the qualities of experience that distinguish different forms of criminality. An explanation for murder cannot possibly address burglary; motivations for shoplifting rarely impel someone to rape. Each crime has its own distinctive appeals. On the basis of narrative descriptions from university students, and some field research, Katz (1988) proposes that there are a variety of emotional states that entice the offender to offend. Such seductions range across a variety of crimes including murder, theft and robbery. In violent crime, e.g., he identifies feelings such as humiliation, righteousness, arrogance, ridicule, cynicism, defilement and vengeance that, in effect, give the offender the feeling that s/he had a moral right to attack; what Katz calls 'righteous slaughter'. The perpetrator of the violent offence believes that it is he or she who has been wronged and, in gaining revenge, is defending moral equality. In murder, e.g., it would be the experience of anger that would compel the murderer to commit the crime. One feature of the typical homicide is its character as a self-righteous act undertaken within the form of defending communal values. For property crimes, Katz sees the dominant emotion of a 'sneaky thrill'. Offenders feel propelled into action seduced by objects, people and most compellingly by the act of crime itself. The excitement provided by some devious property crime is undeniably seductive. With sneaky thrill property crimes such as shoplifting a conventional object becomes fascinating seductively drawing the would-be shoplifter to it.

**Previous Research on Emotions and Criminality**

To the author's knowledge before the recent work from Canter and colleagues (Canter and Ioannou, 2004; Youngs and Canter, 2012) there hasn't been any systematic study of the actual emotional experience of crime experienced by individuals whilst they are committing a crime and how this experience may induce or sustain criminal activity. Although there exists a vast body of research for the emotions and feelings that are experienced by a 'normal' population, research into the emotions that criminals experience while committing their crimes has been scarce. With the exception of Katz (1988) in his book on the *Seductions of Crime*, who is only offering hypotheses, based mainly on reports and narrative descriptions by university students, and not any systematic research or solutions, there are very few studies of what the offender feels when in the process of committing a crime. The emotion of anger is widely evoked in studies of violence, but in an unsystematic way. Unacknowledged grief has been posited to be a cause of violence, but only on theoretical and clinical grounds (Mitscherlisch and Mitscherlisch, 1975). Of all the emotions that might be involved in the genesis of crime and violence, shame has got the most attention (Luckenbill, 1977; Scheff and Retzinger, 1991; Sherman, 1993; Hagan and McCarthy, 1997).

Even though there have been few recent studies of the emotions experienced by criminals the emotional significance for perpetrators of their criminal actions have long been recognised. In her study of Victorian theft, Albelson (1989) notes that several early 20th century writers promoted the idea that shoplifters, particularly women, were seduced into theft. As early as 1901 the French psychologist Dubuisson explained why some women shoplift:

> Temptation is so strong, surging desire so powerful, so impervious, so irresistible that the act (shoplifting) is accomplished before reason has time to plead its cause … for the moment pleasure is everything (quoted in Albelson, 1989, p. 46).

Matza (1964) discussing delinquency suggested that sensual dynamics might be the motivating force behind an individual offending. In 1961, Bordua recognised theorists' failure to acknowledge that enjoyment was a factor in the undertaking of many offences. McCarthy (1995) has shown that most young thieves do not steal to get essentials like food, but luxuries, drugs, ostentatious clothing and other items that reflects fashion rather than necessity. An Australian Study by Indermaur (1996) looked at offender's perspectives on violent property crime in which they examined offenders self-reported thoughts and feelings before, during and after the use of violence. He found that offenders felt a range of emotions. Tension, fear, excitement, anger, frustration were some of the feelings they reported. Fleming (1999), when he looked at young car thieves in British Columbia, found that most youthful auto theft was carried out for recreational purposes, as opposed to stealing for profit. Excitement and thrills were the motives behind most of the thefts he analysed.

Feeney (1999) reported that in robbers the decision to commit such a crime was often not simply to obtain money; fewer than 60% said that money was the primary motivation to commit a crime. On the contrary, any of the criminals indicated that they committed the crime to achieve a particular emotional state. Wright et al. (1999) also found evidence that the decisions made by offenders during crimes are influenced by emotions. Åkerström (1993) proposed that many criminals see their lives as more exciting and adventurous than those of non-criminals; 72% of the offenders said that non-criminals lead a boring life. Adler (1993) considered the careers of drug dealers and found that emotions played an important part in the description of their experiences. She noted themes of glamour and excitement in the lives of many drug dealers and that thrill seeking characterised their lifestyles.

## Canter and Ioannou Research

Canter and Ioannou (2004) used existing models of emotions that illustrate how emotions are experienced by 'normal' non-criminal populations in order to provide hypothesis that can be applied to the criminal population. This hypothesis is based on the premise that criminality reflects the full range of human activities and experiences. The focus on emotions is part of a general approach to understanding criminal activity, which sees it as an extreme form of non-criminal behaviour. Therefore the general approach to studying day-to-day emotions that has an established history in psychology is worth testing in the criminal context. In many other psychological areas there are validated models of emotions and rich theories that are productively drawn on to explicate human agency. One approach in particular appears fruitful for considering criminals' emotional experiences: the Circumplex of Emotions (Russell, 1997), which provides a starting point for characterising the emotions experienced by criminals.

One important aspect of the structure of the circumplex rarely noted is that it implies a degree of variation in intensity from the centre outwards. In studies of emotion the neutrality at the centre of the space is mentioned, but the implication that as the variable gets further from the centre so it is more intense has often not been considered. In the context of criminal actions this consideration is important because it is possible that whilst criminality runs the full gamut of emotions it may be hypothesised that they would be more extreme in intensity, that intensity being what encourages the criminal to take action. More information on the Circumplex of Emotions (Russell, 1997) is provided in Figure 6.1.

Many researchers do agree that most feelings can be categorised as one of two hedonic values, either pleasant or unpleasant. Several major lines of research on affective structure indicate the presence of two major bipolar dimensions. These include analyses of facial and vocal emotional expressions (e.g. Albelson and Sermat, 1962; Schlosberg, 1954), and judged similarities among mood words (Russell, 1979). In these studies Pleasantness–Unpleasantness (terms such as happy, enthusiastic and content, versus afraid, sad) and Degree of Arousal or Activation (excited, tense versus relaxed) have regularly emerged as the two major dimensions of mood (Watson and Tellegen, 1985). These dimensions adequately describe human affective (emotional) responses to all types of stimuli. These dimensions are defined as bipolar such that pleasure is a continuum ranging from extreme pain or unhappiness at one end to extreme happiness or ecstasy at the other end. Arousal ranges from sleep through intermediate states of drowsiness and then alertness to frenzied excitement at the opposite extreme. Pleasure–displeasure distinguishes positive affective states from negative ones. Arousal–nonarousal is defined in terms of a combination of mental alertness and physical activity.

Research is discovering, increasingly frequently, that the structure of the categories of emotions can be schematically represented as a circumplex (Schlosberg, 1941; Plutchik, 1962; Russell, 1980; Fisher, Heise, Borhnstedt and Lucke, 1985; Watson and Tellegen, 1985; Feldman, 1995; Feldman Barrett and Russell, 1998; Remington, Fabrigar and Vissar, 2000). Russell (1979, 1997) has developed this framework further by hypothesising a circular order of emotions, or 'circumplex' that incorporates these two bipolar axes, whilst recognising that emotional states merge into one another, a proposal that has been supported in a number of studies (Fisher, Heise, Borhnstedt and Lucke, 1985; Plutchik, 1962; Russell, 1979; Schlosberg, 1954; Watson and Tellegen, 1985). In these studies Pleasantness-Unpleasantness (terms such as happy, enthusiastic, content vs. afraid, sad) and Degree of Arousal or Activation (excited, tense vs. relaxed) have considerably emerged as the two major dimensions of mood (Watson and Tellegen, 1985).

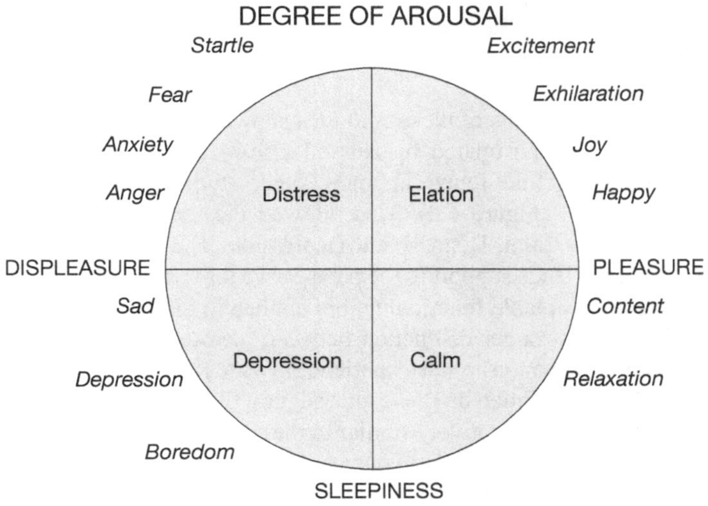


**Figure 6.1 Russell's (1997) circumplex of emotions**

Figure 6.1 is a schematic representation of a circumplex that illustrates how emotions, feelings, moods and related states fall in a continuous order around the perimeter of a two-dimensional space. The centre of the space establishes a neutral point or adaptation level. This circular model is one example of a general class of models for aspects of human experience and personal attributes first proposed by Guttman (1954) as the basis of his Facet Theory (Canter, 1984). Such circular models have now been demonstrated for a wide range of interpersonal behaviours, both normal and pathological, intelligence, social interactions, vocational interests, facial expressions, social acuity or empathy and aspects of personality, as well as criminal behaviour (e.g. Canter and Heritage, 1989). They are all characterised by the relationship amongst the variables having a circular order in the sense that it is without beginning or end, similar variables being closer to one another on the circle. Variables that are semantic or behavioural opposites are located directly across the circle (i.e., through the origin) and variables that are unrelated or orthogonal are separated by angles of 90 degrees. The model gives rise to the identification of four quadrants that capture four broad classes of mood; distress, elation, calmness, and depression. In summary, the circumplex model of emotions has been among the most widely studied representations of affect and an extremely valuable paradigm for understanding personality, psychopathology and interpersonal relations over the past 30 years (Plutchik, 2000).

Canter and Ioannou (2004) interviewed 83 incarcerated offenders who indicated, on a forced choice questionnaire, the emotions they had experienced whilst committing a specific crime they remembered well. The questionnaire consisted of emotions statements, representing emotions selected to cover the full gamut of Russell's (1997) circumplex and was developed from pilot research (Oldale, 1997; Cross, 1998; Murray, 1998; Ioannou, 2001) that had shown that emotions made sense to criminals as possible descriptions of their feelings during a crime they could clearly remember.

Smallest Space Analysis of these emotions showed they reflected the circumplex structure of emotions postulated by Russell (1997) for non-criminal experiences supporting the distinction found in many other studies with dominant axes of pleasure and arousal (Figure 6.2). This allowed the identification of four modes of emotion: Elation, Calm, Distress and Depression. The existence of these within criminal experience lends support to the perspective that criminal reactions are but an aspect of normal acceptable functioning, but applied to different contexts. However, emotions showed a stronger distinction between pleasure and displeasure than for the normal range of non-criminal experiences, with Russell's 'arousal' dimension being less clearly differentiated. The results suggest that the emotional element of the criminal experience is qualitatively similar to the emotional experience of the normal population but they differ quantitatively, as the emotions that were experienced by criminals, while they were committing their crimes, were found to be more intense and extreme. From the graphic representation of the data, Canter and Ioannou (2004) showed that the most distinct and significant emotions of the crimes are on the extreme sides of the axis, thus proving the idea of having a pleasant or unpleasant association with a committed crime. In summary the findings showed that crimes have dominant emotions, elation, calm, distress, depression, but these are extremely distinct and experienced much stronger in criminals. It is also interesting to note that some of the emotions introduced as of particular relevance to criminal experiences find their place within this division. Emotions such as being out of control or annoyed are clearly negative, whereas calm and excited are positive. Russell's dominant axis is therefore clearly relevant to the experience of crimes. Criminals are indicating that their experiences are either pleasurable or not with little in the way of gradations between these extremes. The full circular structure of emotions is therefore not recovered in this context but what might be regarded as a version that reflects more extreme differences.

Further analysis showed that different subsets of crimes were more like to be associated with different emotions. It was found that the different types of crimes could be differentiated on the basis of whether they were perceived to be a positive or negative experience for the offender. Offenders that committed property offences, drug offences and fraud all regarded their experience to be positive or pleasant while offenders who committed robbery, violence, sexual offences and murder regarded their experience to be negative or unpleasant with fraud strongly at one end of the scale and murder at the other. The almost neutral experience of drug offences, which

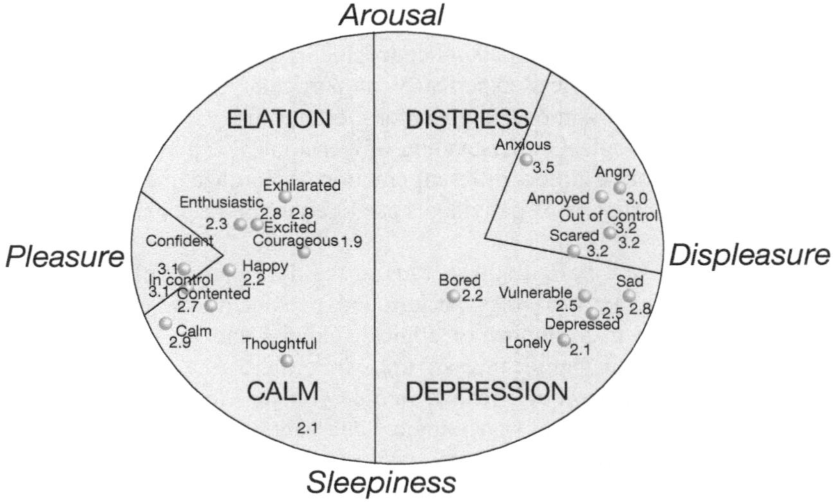


**Figure 6.2 Two-dimensional Smallest Space Analysis (SSA) of emotions with regional interpretation and mean values indicated (the regions of extreme values are indicated). Coefficient of alienation = 0.15598**

*Source*: Canter and Ioannou (2004).

are not clearly property or person oriented is also interesting in this regard, raising the possibility that the emotional tone of a crime is a product of the nature of the transaction with others. In broad terms, property crimes were found to be more pleasurable than crimes against the person indicating that the more interpersonal the crime, the more negative or unpleasant the emotional experience.

A number of papers derived mainly from my PhD thesis but also from other studies which are under preparation not only on the emotional experience of offending but also into the relationship between the roles that offenders act out while they commit their crimes and the associated emotions (previous research by Canter, Kaouri and Ioannou (2003) and Ioannou (in prep.), Youngs and Canter (2011, 2012) have found that the narrative roles acted out by criminals were derived from narratives dominant in our culture and could be categorised into four distinct themes that supported a circular order of criminal roles identifying four themes: *Adventurer*, *Professional*, *Revenger* and *Victim*), on how different classes of crime, mainly burglary, robbery, rape, murder, relate to different emotions and roles, on the association of different backgrounds, styles of interpersonal interaction (personality) and criminal histories with different roles and related emotions.

## The Importance of the Study of Emotions

The study of the criminal emotional experience represents an important development in the understanding of crime and therefore generates a number of significant implications for our general conceptualisation of crime as they advance an understanding of offenders' experiences, in particular, and of crime in general, by moving away from traditional explanations. Intellectually, the study of emotions enhances the psychological understanding of a criminals' experience while he/she is committing a crime and how different emotions encourage and sustain criminal activity but also what sorts of individuals are likely to be responsible for different types of crimes.

Practically, the study of emotions leads to the development of valid scales of emotions which together with roles, background, personality and criminal histories can then be utilised in a number of clinical, judicial and investigative settings. Beyond the theoretical significance of this work there is a practical relevance particularly to the treatment of offenders and programmes to reduce offending. For although the dominant form of psychological intervention with offenders, cognitive behavioural therapy (CBT), goes some way to addressing the offender's agency through the exploration of the understanding the offender has of his/her crimes and their consequences, many commentators recognise that the emphasis on cognitive processes in CBT undervalues the emotional significance of crimes to offenders. By linking CBT approaches of the offender's understanding to their personal emotions and their links with their narratives a variety of other forms of intervention is possible. The therapist can uncover the offenders' emotions and recognise their significance for the individuals. Conceiving of offenders' emotions and narrative roles while he is committing his crimes provides the therapist with an understanding of his perception of reality/crime. It indicates which emotions, feelings, actions and roles are likely to feature prominently in the person's conceptualisation of what happened. Crime represents just one of a range of reactions or tools in acting out a role or experiencing an emotion and this has to be addressed during treatment or intervention programmes. Suggestions for tailoring treatments to individual cases can be developed. As therapy is aimed at modifying behaviour, knowledge of the emotional experience, is a powerful tool in enhancing the effectiveness of treatment. Therapy can help a criminal invest energy and care into new and more promising aspects or domains.

A model of criminal experience has also implications for the ways in which the courts understand crime, with consequent influence on sentencing decisions. This association of feelings and narrative roles with crimes can broaden the legal perspective by providing a richer understanding of the notion of 'intention' so crucial to jurisprudence. In addition, it has a number of implications for police investigations. It aids law enforcement agencies to better understand the actions of those they seek to detect, capture and control. They provide police officers with an alternative framework for thinking about crime, which has direct implications for the handling of cases and management of offenders in different ways. Offender's accounts of corresponding emotions and narrative roles, which can be applied to experience themes, may be mapped onto offence, offender characteristics and actions during a crime. This would result in a more elaborate picture aiding 'offender profiling' techniques.

It offers the foundations for a bridge between the concern with agency that is central to the legal process and the concern with cause that is at the heart of social science studies of crime. Furthermore, it applies models that are used in other areas of psychology to the investigation of crime demonstrating the usefulness of existing models or theories applied on 'normal' population to try to explain criminality. The explanation of criminal activity in terms of the emotions set out within theories of 'normal' non-criminal behaviour is of great importance. Particularly interesting is the way in which it is possible to tie emotions felt by a 'normal' population to the emotions that offenders experience while they are committing their crimes.

## The Future of the Research on the Emotional Experience of Offending

Such research should continue into the future. The studies by Canter and Ioannou (2004), Canter, Kaouri and Ioannou (2003), Ioannou (in prep.), Youngs and Canter (2011, 2012) can only be regarded as a first step towards understanding the role that the Criminal Narrative Experience plays in the development and continuation of offending. These studies have highlighted a number of issues important to the understanding of the criminal experience in particular and of crime in general and the offenders responsible for it. However, these results have also highlighted areas that still need to be investigated in order to gain a fuller understanding of the different emotions and roles that lead to crime. An important priority, as Ioannou's study shows, is the development of a model that takes into account both the roles and the emotions as the roles provide the psychological framework for making sense of the emotions as well as connecting with the broader life narratives that underlie the person's actions. It is also important to establish to what extent offenders experience different or the same emotions and act out different or the same roles when they commit the same and/or different type of crime. Especially interesting would be to see the differences or similarities in emotions and roles of an offender who committed an offence against property and an offence against a person. Further studies employing larger data sets with other populations, e.g. female, young offenders etc. would add to the findings of current research findings.

Canter (1994) proposed that narrative theory, can interpret the stories criminal activities reveal. 'Inner narratives' of offenders are shaped by their past, their experienced present and they are then reflected in their future offending, revealing the psychological basis for sequences of criminal activities over time. Emotions and narrative roles have much to offer in the comprehension and analysis of criminal behaviour. An understanding of why individuals commit crimes requires an analysis of these internal stories. 'We need to learn to identify the distinguishing features of these evil narratives in order to recognise the men who write them' (Canter, 1994).

## References

Adler, P.A. (1999). Dealing careers, in *In Their Own Words: Criminals on Crime* (2nd ed., pp. 186–197), edited by P. Cromwell. Los Angeles: Roxbury Publishing Company.

Åkerström, M. (1999). Looking at the squares: comparisons with the square Johns, in *In Their Own Words: Criminals on Crime* (2nd ed., pp. 23–31), edited by P. Cromwell. Los Angeles: Roxbury Publishing Company.

Albelson, E.S. (1989). *When Ladies Go A-thieving: Middle Class Shoplifters in the Victorian Department Store*. New York: Oxford University Press.

Albelson, R.P. and Sermat, V. (1962). Multidimensional scaling of facial expressions. *Journal of Experimental Psychology*, 63, 546–554.

Bordua, D.J. (1961). Delinquent subcultures: sociological interpretations of gang delinquency. *The Annals of the American Academy of Political Science*, 338, 119–136.

Canter, D. (1984). (ed.) *Facet Theory: Approaches to Social Research*. New York: Springer – Verlag.

Canter, D.V. (1994). *Criminal Shadows*. London: Harper Collins.

Canter, D.V. and Heritage, R. (1989). A multivariate model of sexual offence behaviour: developments in offender profiling. *Journal of Forensic Psychiatry*, 1, 185–212.

Canter, D. and Ioannou, M. (2004). Criminals' emotional experiences during crimes. *International Journal of Forensic Psychology*, 1, 71–81.

Canter, D., Kaouri, C. and Ioannou, M. (2003). The facet structure of criminal narratives, in *Facet Theory: Towards Cumulative Social Science* (pp. 27–38), edited by L. Shlomit and D. Elizur. Ljubljana, Slovenia: University of Ljubljana.

Canter, D. and Youngs, D. (2012). Narratives of Criminal Action and Forensic Psychology. *Legal and Criminological Psychology*, 00, 1–17.

Cross, C. (1998). *The Experience of Crime: Associated Roles and Emotions*. Unpublished BSc thesis. University of Liverpool, UK.

Feeney, F. (1999). Robbers as decision makers, in *Their Own Words: Criminals on Crime* (2nd ed., pp. 119–129), edited by P. Cromwell. Los Angeles: Roxbury Publishing Company.

Feldman, L.A. (1995). Variations in the circumplex structure of emotion. *Personality and Social Psychology Bulletin*, 21, 806–817.

Feldman Barrett, L. and Russell, J.A. (1998). Independence and bipolarity in the structure of affect. *Journal of Personality and Social Psychology*, 74, 967–984.

Fisher, G.A., Heise, D.R., Bohrnstedt, G.W. and Lucke, J.F. (1985). Evidence for extending the circumplex model of personality trait language to self-reported moods. *Journal of Personality and Social Psychology*, 49, 233–242.

Fleming, Z. (1999). The thrill of it all: youthful offenders and auto theft, in *In Their Own Words: Criminals on Crime* (2nd ed.) edited by P. Cromwell. Los Angeles: Roxbury Publishing Company.

Guttman, L. (1954). A new approach to factor analysis: the radex, in *Mathematical Thinking in the Social Sciences*, edited by Lazarsfield. New York: Free Press.

Hagan, J. and McCarthy, B. (1997). *Mean Streets: Youth Crime and Homelessness*. New York: Cambridge University Press.

Intermaur, D. (1996). Offenders' perspectives on property crime, in *In Their Own Words: Criminals on Crime* (1st ed.), edited by P. Cromwell. Los Angeles: Roxbury Publishing Company.

Ioannou, M. (2001). *The Experience of Crime: Emotions and Roles Experienced while Committing an Offence*. Unpublished MSc thesis. Liverpool: The University of Liverpool.

Ioannou, M. (2006). *Hero or villain? Criminals' Experience of Crime*. Unpublished Doctoral thesis. Liverpool: The University of Liverpool.

Katz, J. (1988). *Seductions of Crime: Moral and Sensual Attractions in Doing Evil*. USA: Basic Books.

Luckenbill, D.F. (1977). Criminal homicide as a situated transaction. *Social Problems*, 25, 176–86.

Matza, D. (1964). *Delinquency and Drift*. New York: John Wiley & Sons.

McAdams, D.P. (1988). *Power, Intimacy and the Life Story*. New York: The Guildford Press.

McCarthy, B. (1995). Not just 'for the thrill of it': an instrumentalistic elaboration of Katz's explanation of sneaky thrill property crimes. *Criminology*, 33, 519–538.

Mitscherlisch, A. and Mitscherlisch, M. (1975). *The Inability to Mourn*. New York: Grove.

Murray, K. (1998). *An Investigation into the Experience of Crime: A Multidimensional Scalogram Analysis of the Emotions and Roles Experienced while Committing an Offence*. Unpublished BSc thesis. University of Liverpool, UK.

Oldale, K. (1997). *The Experience of Crime*. Unpublished BSc thesis. University of Liverpool, UK.

Plutchik, R. (1962). *The Emotions: Fact, Theories and a New Model*. New York, USA: Random House.

Plutchik, R. (2000). *Emotions in the Practice of Psychotherapy: Implications of Affect Theories*. Washington, DC: American Psychological Association.

Remington, N.A., Fabrigar, L.R. and Visser, P.S. (2000). Reexamining the circumplex model of affect. *Journal of Personality and Social Psychology*, 79, 286–300.

Russell, J.A. (1979). Affective space is bipolar. *Journal of Personality and Social Psychology*, 37, 345–356.

Russell, J.A. (1980). A circumplex model of affect. *Journal of Personality and Social Psychology*, 39, 1161–1178.

Russell, J.A. (1991). In defence of a prototype approach to emotion concepts. *Journal of Personality and Social Psychology*, 60, 37–47.

Russell, J.A. (1997). How shall an emotion be called? in *Circumplex Models of Personality and Emotions* (pp. 205–220), edited by R. Plutchik and H.R. Conte. Washington, DC: American Psychological Association.

Scheff, T.J. and Retzinger, S. (1991). *Emotions and Violence*. Lexington, MA: Lexington Books.

Schlosberg, H. (1941). A scale for the judgment of facial expressions. *Journal of Experimental Psychology*, 29, 497–510.

Schlosberg, H. (1954). Three dimensions of emotion. *Psychological Review*, 61, 81–88.

Sherman, L. (1993). Defiance, deterrence and irrelevance: a theory of criminal sanction. *Journal of Research in Crime and Delinquency*, 30, 445–473.

Watson, D. and Tellegen, A. (1985). Toward a consensual structure of mood. *Psychological Bulletin*, 98, 219–235.

Ward, T. (2011). Commentry – Narrative identity and forensic psychology: a commentary on Youngs and Canter. *Legal and Criminologcal Psychology*, 1–12.

Youngs, D. and Canter, D. (2011). Narrative roles in criminal action: an integrative framework for differentiating offenders. *Legal and Criminological Psychology*, 16(2), 99–119.

Youngs, D. and Canter, D. (2012). Offenders' crime narratives as revealed by the Narrative Roles Questionnaire (NRQ). *International Journal of Offender Therapy and Comparative Criminology*, 1–23.

Wright, R.T., Decker, S.H., Redfern, A.K. and Smith, D.L. (1999). A snowball's chance in hell: doing fieldwork with active residential burglars, in *In Their Own Words: Criminals on Crime* (2nd ed., pp. 1–7), edited by P.Cromwell. Los Angeles: Roxbury Publishing Company.

# SECTION 2
# On David Canter's IP Methodologies

# Chapter 7

# Introducing a Common Range Index of Inter-variable Similarity for the Analysis of Radex Structures

*Sean Hammond*

When asked to produce a chapter for David Canter's Feschrift, I had to think long and hard about what part of his eclectic and wide ranging contribution to psychology I would focus on. In the end, I chose to concentrate on his forensic work and in particular, his pioneering role in developing replicable structures of offending behaviour through application of multidimensional scaling. In this chapter I attempt to address the Achilles heel of such work, the choice of an appropriate index of object association that minimises artefact distortion in the coordinate space. In doing so I have developed a new coefficient of dichotomous association that, I argue, utilises the best features of the Jaccard index as well as minimising distortion due to skew in the data. This makes the coefficient particularly useful when exploring the radex structure of behavioural or symptom data. I name the coefficient the Jaccard–Canter Index (JC), and I hope David approves.

The purpose of this chapter is to introduce a new index of inter-variable similarity for use in the dichotomous case. The index was developed specifically with multidimensional scaling in mind and, in particular, the exploration of radix structures. In doing so, it summarises a strand of my own work that has been bubbling along since it was inspired by David Canter in the 1980's shortly after I had joined the Department of Psychology at the University of Surrey (Hammond and Leinert, 1992; Hammond, 1993; Hammond and Leinert, 1995). The specific catalyst for this work was a discussion on the most appropriate means of evaluating similarity between the dichotomous variables in David's newly established database on sexual assaults prior to performing Smallest Space Analyses. We concluded that the Jaccard Coefficient was a particularly useful index for this purpose for reasons that I will explain later in this chapter.

This discussion prompted an abiding interest in the problem of identifying analytic methods that fit the data in question, rather than bludgeoning sensitive data with analyses whose primary reason for use is their easy accessibility in canned computer programs. The problem of identifying the appropriate similarity coefficient is particularly pertinent in this regard. Firstly, because the similarity matrix is the starting point for most techniques used for exploring underlying structure and if we get this matrix wrong, our subsequent analysis is compromised and, second because the use of the Pearsonian correlation is ubiquitous in such analyses while, at the same time, being often inappropriate.

In the first part of this chapter we will briefly describe the issue of exploring underlying structure and demonstrate that the choice of inter-variable association coefficient is critical in this enterprise. We will then discuss the Jaccard Coefficient in some detail highlighting its advantages and limitations. In the third part we will introduce a new coefficient based upon the principles of Jaccard's original coefficient that we will name the Jaccard–Canter (or JC) Index. Finally, we will explore the use of this index on a dataset drawn from the BADMAN database of sexual assaults.

Psychologists historically have tended to explore multivariate structure in terms of underlying latent traits and, following Spearman's (1904) work, this has generally involved the use of factor analysis. Barring a number of technical caveats (Guttman, 1955; Steiger and Schonemann, 1978; Hammond, 1986, 1987), factor analysis is a very useful technique for evaluating the existence of putative latent traits. Such traits should explain the relationships between the given variables. The relationships in question are defined by product moment correlations or inter-variable covariances (the former simply being a standardised form of the latter). A factor analysis begins by generating a correlation matrix between the relevant variables and then identifies a factor matrix of weights or loadings linking each variable to one or more underlying latent traits. The relationship between the original correlation matrix and the resulting factor matrix is expressed in the factor analysis model as.

$$\Sigma = \Lambda'\Lambda + \Psi$$

Where

$\Sigma$ = the original correlation or covariance matrix
$\Lambda$ = the resulting factor loading matrix
$\Psi$ = a diagonal matrix of error terms

Thus the resulting structure may be used to reproduce the original correlations. Although factor analysis in itself is a useful and powerful technique for exploring underlying structure it is very often misused and misapplied. Like all data analytic strategies it has strict limitations but these are so often ignored that a great many published factor analytic studies are of limited value.

One problem with factor analysis is that the researcher must buy in to the notion that the underlying structure they are exploring is defined by bipolar traits. This is familiar territory for psychometricians whose focus is largely upon latent trait modelling in one form or another. However, many published factor analyses are more concerned with simply clustering groups of variables into superordinate sets, for which a more defensible strategy would be some form of cluster analysis. However, not all psychological structures are conceived in bipolar traits or discrete clusters. Birtchnell, (2002) for example has proposed an interpersonal relating octagon that implies a polar structure while Guttman (1957, 1992) has demonstrated that a polar-modular, or radex, structure explains the relationship between ability tests. While it is possible to extrapolate these structures to some extent by using some form of factor analysis, it is generally a complex and indirect task.

A second and more fundamental problem confronting researchers using factor analysis is its reliance on the Pearsonian product moment correlation coefficient, and this coefficient has limitations itself (Gourlay, 1951; Carroll, 1961). Firstly, it assumes a linear relationship between the two variables considered and it also assumes bivariate normality in the variable distributions. It is surely not disputable that most psychological data does not support these assumptions (Micceri, 1989). We usually get around this uncomfortable fact by arguing that there is a degree of robustness in the correlation coefficient and we can tolerate some deviation from the assumptions. However, this is unfortunately not the case (Dunlap, Burke and Greer, 1995).

Deviations from normality will truncate the range of the correlation and, in the multivariate case, the fact that one correlation has a differing range from another in the same correlation matrix means that they are not directly comparable, so exacerbating the initial insult to the method. In fact, this state of affairs is not incompatible with correlation theory because the correlation coefficient is actually an index of prediction and this is indeed adversely effected by skew. Nevertheless, where the focus is upon underlying structure, the relationships between variables are assumed to be of common range so this limitation is incompatible with such analyses.

In addition, much data in psychology is recorded in ordinal (rating scales) or categorical (present vs absent) form. The correlation coefficient is not designed for such cases although Pearsonian estimates known as polychorics and tetrachorics have been designed for each one respectively. However, these coefficients make further assumptions about the underlying distribution of the scale implied by the categories and so move us further from our original data. Simpler solutions have been suggested, but these only apply to some forms of factor analysis (Vegelius, 1978; Zegers, and Ten Berge, 1986; Hammond and Leinert, 1992).

A radical change from the factor analytic perspective came in the form of multidimensional scaling (MDS). The point of an MDS analysis is to represent the relationships between variables in n-dimensional spatial coordinates. These coordinates describe a configuration X of points within Cartesian space where each point represents a variable (Borg and Groenen, 1997). The Euclidean distance between these points can be readily derived by:

$$d_{ij} = \sqrt{\sum_{k=1}^{m} \left(x_{ik} - x_{jk}\right)^2}$$

$$i=1,2\ldots.n;\ j=1,2\ldots.n$$

Where

n = the number of variables
m = the number of dimensions

MDS analyses are carried out such that the distances derived from a low dimensional space are maximally congruent with the original relationships between the variables. The data are fitted to the smallest meaningful space bearing in mind that a perfect fit will usually require a dimensionality of one less than the number of input variables. Nevertheless, a less than perfect fit can generally provide meaningful patterns in a much reduced dimensionality that provide insights or confirm expectations.

The relationship of d to the original data, δ, is defined by a function that varies depending upon the kind of MDS model one wishes to use.

$$\delta_{ij} = f\left(d_{ij}\right)$$

$$d_{ij} = \alpha + bd_{ij}$$

One of the simplest functions is the linear, or interval one in which:

Where $\delta_{ij}$ is the empirical distance between variables i and j derived from the raw data and $d_{ij}$ are the derived inter-point distances in Cartesian space. However, reliance on the linear relationship between δ and d seems unnecessarily restrictive in light of the work of Shephard (1964), Kruskall (1964) and Guttman (1968) who laid the foundations of a non-metric approach. Here the relationship between δ and d is simply construed as an ordinal or monotonic one.

If $s_{ij} > s_{kl}$ then $d_{ij} < d_{kl}$

OR

If $\delta_{ij} < \delta_{kl}$ then $d_{ij} < d_{kl}$

Where:

$s_{ij}$ = similarity measure between object i and j

$d_{ij}$ = distance measure between object i and j

$d_{ij}$ = derived distance between object i and j in n-dimensional space

Thus, for the general non metric MDS model it is sufficient to be able to reproduce the order of the original input matrix from the spatial coordinates.

The main point to be made here is that MDS liberates the researcher whose focus of interest is the underlying structure of his or her data in two important ways. First, the researcher is no longer constrained to consider underlying structure in terms of latent traits and second the relationships between his or her variables need not be constrained by the theoretical straightjacket of the product moment correlation. Of course, what this liberation does is to provide a new challenge because now the researcher must make an appropriate choice of the coefficient of association that best fits the data in question and the question he or she is trying to answer. For the remainder of this chapter we will concentrate upon the challenge of analysing dichotomous data representing the present or absence of a particular feature.

Where a variable is measured in one of two categories (i.e. Yes–No, True–False, Present–Absent, Male–Female) it is known as dichotomous. Typically, one category is ascribed the code of 0 while the other is given the code of 1 and it should not matter which category gets which numerical code. In fact there are two forms of dichotomous data that may have implications for the kinds of coefficients of association one might apply.

The first form relates to dichotomised data in which two categories have been imposed upon a continuum. For example, a researcher may have a set of test scores and s/he decides to code the scores as 'above the mean' and 'below the mean'. This is not a generally advisable thing to do as an obvious drawback is the loss of information. However, it is often done and it results in dichotomised data that may be appropriate for tetrachoric correlations where a normally distributed underlying continuum for the variables is assumed (Muthen and Hofacker, 1988).

The second form is the true dichotomy where the categories describe the true character of the variable. Thus, being dead or alive is a true dichotomy as is being pregnant or not pregnant. A common form of true dichotomy in psychological data is the variable recording presence or absence of some feature; in fact this defines a true dichotomy (i.e. presence or absence of life, presence or absence of a Y chromosome, presence or absence of an embryo).

The point of this distinction between dichotomised and true dichotomies is that it is hard to justify assuming an underlying continuum for a true dichotomy. This point was made by Yule (1912) in promoting his own strategy for measuring association and was countered by Pearson and Heron (1913) who launched their rejoinder with the statement:

> we believe that, if Mr Yule's views are accepted, irreparable damage will be done to the growth of modern statistical theory (Pearson and Heron, 1913, p. 159).

It is up to the reader to decide whether a statistical theory that depends upon the notion of every woman lying on a continuum between not at all pregnant, through slightly pregnant, to very pregnant is appropriate for real-world analysis.

Whatever your views on that point, and of course there are a larger number of niceties in the argument than I have time to relate here, the relationship between two dichotomous variables can be represented in a 2x2 contingency table, sometimes called a four-point table. In Table 7.1, an example of such a table is presented that represents the relationship between two variables X and Y. In this table ***a*** represents the number of cases in which X and Y are present, ***b*** represents the number of cases in which X is absent but Y is present, ***c*** represents the number of cases in which X is present but Y is absent and ***d*** represents the number of cases where both X and Y are absent.

**Table 7.1 A fourfold contingency table between two dichotomous variables X and Y**

| | | X Present | X Absent | |
|---|---|---|---|---|
| Y | Present | a | b | a + b |
| Y | Absent | c | d | c + d |
| | | a + c | b + d | N |

The reader should be able to see that a very simple way of determining the strength of a relationship between the two variables is to simply take the sum of cells where there is agreement (***a*** + ***d***) and divide this value by the total number of entries in the table (***a***+***b***+***c***+***d***). Thus, the proportion of observations where the two variables are in agreement can be used as a simple similarity index (Sokal and Sneath, 1966). However, there are situations where the joint absence of a feature (***d***) cannot be meaningfully applied to real data. An example of this is where coexistence is the primary focus of our similarity judgement. Thus, if we were looking to explore the coexistence of certain symptoms, the fact that two symptoms (say headache and in-growing toenail) do not co-occur does not imply a relationship between them. This can only be gauged if they consistently occur together. The same logic operates in the forensic area where we may be looking at coexistence of certain crime features in order to identify syndromal behaviour or linkage. This leads us to consider the Jaccard Coefficient.

## The Jaccard Coefficient

Given that there are only four values defining the relationship (a, b, c and d) it is astonishing how many ways in which the relationship between two dichotomous variables may be measured (Sokal and Sneath, 1963; Holley and Guilford, 1964;

Cheetham and Hazel, 1969; Lienert, 1972; Janovitz, 1980; Jackson Somers and Harvey, 1989). Hubalek (1982) identified 43 coefficients but this is not an exhaustive list. The simple probability of two features being present, conditional on at least one of them being present, was first proposed by the botanist Paul Jaccard (1902) as a Genus to Species ratio for exploring botanic diversity. The formula is extremely simple:

$$J = \frac{a}{a+b+c}$$

Here it is readily apparent that Jaccard has done away with ***d*** altogether so the coefficient is not spuriously inflated by lack of coexistence. A number of researchers have remarked upon the usefulness of J. Goodall (1973) who, for example, states that its sampling bias is very small while Hubalek (1982), after a rigorous evaluation of 43 coefficients, recommended Jaccard among five others for practical use. Jansen and Vegelius (1982) judged 20 coefficients according to six practical criteria and judged that J was one of three coefficients to meet all six.

One interesting feature of J is that, for any dichotomous dataset, the mean inter-item J will equal the mean inter-case J. In formal terms:

$$\frac{\sum_{i=1}^{N-1}\sum_{j=i+1}^{N} J_{ij}}{N(N-1)\times 0.5} = \frac{\sum_{x=1}^{m-1}\sum_{y=x+1}^{m} J_{xy}}{m(m-1)\times 0.5}$$

This is clearly seen because for any number of coefficients the sum of the numerators divided by the sum of the denominators will always equal the sum of the coefficients. This property makes J particularly useful when examining shared representations within groups of individuals (Hammond, 1993).

## The Distribution of J

One possible drawback for the Jaccard Coefficient is that it does not yield mean values near the mid-point of its range (i.e. 0.50) (Archer and Maples, 1987). Indeed, it can be demonstrated that the expected value under randomisation for the Jaccard Coefficient is:

$$\bar{J} = \frac{1}{\hat{a}\left(\hat{a}+\hat{b}+\hat{c}\right)}$$

Where $\hat{a}$, $\hat{b}$ and $\hat{c}$ signify population estimates of proportion (Janson and Vegelius, 1981). This is generally closer to zero than 0.5 and has led some to argue that it is a major caveat in the use of the coefficient (Pierce, 1989). However, since the Jaccard Coefficient is a measure of co-incidence it would appear to be eminently sensible that the 'null' or random result should be to produce a mean around zero.

When n is large the coefficient is normally distributed about this mean with a standard error defined as:

$$SE = \sqrt{\hat{a}(\hat{b}+\hat{c})\left(\frac{1}{\left(\hat{a}+\hat{b}+\hat{c}\right)^3}\right)\left(\frac{1}{n}\right)}$$

Thus, should the researcher wish to examine the coefficient inferentially the following formula might be applied:

$$z = \left(\hat{a}\cdot\hat{a}\left(\hat{a}+\hat{b}+\hat{c}\right)-\hat{a}-\hat{b}-\hat{c}\right)\cdot\sqrt{\hat{a}+\hat{b}+\hat{c}}\cdot\frac{\sqrt{n}}{\left(\hat{a}\left(\hat{a}+\hat{b}+\hat{c}\right)\cdot\sqrt{\hat{a}\left(\hat{b}+\hat{c}\right)}\right)}$$

Where z is distributed normally with a mean of zero and variance of unity and describes deviation from $\overline{J}$. Confidence intervals can be obtained by the standard convention of taking: $J \pm z_{\alpha/2}\cdot SE$. Other strategies for estimating the significance of J can be found in Baroni-Urbani (1980) and Real and Vargas (1996).

## The Effect of Marginal Distributions

Despite its very useful heuristic and statistical properties, however, the Jaccard Coefficient comes with caveats. The most important of these, for the researcher interested in MDS, is that the range of the coefficient is dependent upon the distribution of the variables in question. This point was made very early on in a slightly different way and led to a spirited debate between Jaccard (1922) and Palmgren (1921, 1925) on the utility of the coefficient in species distribution studies (See Järvinen (1982) for an account of this debate). From the perspective of a research psychologist, the problem arises when the two variables being correlated have dissimilar prevalence rates.

It can be shown that the maximum size of the Jaccard Coefficient is the ratio of the smaller prevalence to the larger one. Thus, if two variables X and Y have prevalence rates of 0.50 and 0.70 respectively the maximum J between these two variables will be 0.71. As the two prevalence rates diverge so the maximum Jaccard index falls. The maximum Jaccard Coefficient given the prevalence of X and Y (a+c and a+b respectively) can be estimated as:

$$Max\ J = \frac{Mn}{Mx}$$

Where:

Mx = Max (a+b, a+c)
Mn = Min (a+b, a+c)

As we have seen, this problem is not unique to the Jaccard Coefficient. Most measures of association are in some way effected by the distributions of the variables. Thus, the commonly used Phi coefficient (the Pearson Correlation for dichotomies) is known to manifest a truncated range when the distributions of the variables deviate from a 50:50 split.

As mentioned previously, the problem of truncated range becomes particularly challenging when multivariate analyses of structure are undertaken. This is because the starting point for such analyses is matrices of inter-variable associations. If all of the association coefficients were equally truncated there would be no problem as the coefficients in the matrix would have a common range. However, in the real-world this is not likely to be the case.

In Table 7.2 the maximum J coefficient is shown for five variables with different prevalence rates. Thus, it may be possible for a relationship between A and E to reach 0.43 (a perfect association) but a coefficient of 0.44 between D and E although larger actually reflects a lesser association.

**Table 7.2 Matrix of maximum J coefficients for various variable prevalences**

| | A | B | C | D | E |
|---|---|---|---|---|---|
| Prevalence | 0.30 | 0.40 | 0.50 | 0.60 | 0.70 |
| A | 1.00 | | | | |
| B | 0.75 | 1.00 | | | |
| C | 0.60 | 0.80 | 1.00 | | |
| D | 0.50 | 0.67 | 0.83 | 1.00 | |
| E | 0.43 | 0.57 | 0.71 | 0.85 | 1.00 |

It should be emphasised that in MDS analyses the effect of restricted range need not be a problem because the researcher may be interested in observing the effect of distribution or prevalence rate on the structure. Since extreme prevalence rates truncate the association coefficients, such variables tend to be moved to the outer regions of the MDS plot. This is because their relationship with the other variables will tend to be smaller due to the distributional artefact of the association coefficient being used. Thus, researchers examining modular or radex structures should be aware of this potential artefact. We will present an example of such an analysis later in this chapter.

## Adjustment for Common Range

A number of solutions have been suggested to adjust for common range and most have related to the Pearsonian phi coefficient because the problematic effect of truncation has a severely distorting effect on factor analytic outcomes. These solutions include point-symmetry or axial-symmetry adjustment of the fourfold tables, (Hammond and Leinert, 1996; Leinert, von Eye and Rovine, 1987; Wall and Leinert, 1976) and range adjustment by division by maxima (the so-called phi/phimax) proposed, among others, by (Loevinger, 1947) and used heavily in non-parametric item response theory applications (Mokken, 1971).

In the case of the Jaccard Coefficient, symmetry adjustment of the four-point table is made difficult by the fact that the two marginals that involve joint absence (d) are unspecified. However, it is clear from Table 7.2 that maximum J provides a symmetric and well-ordered simplex structure and this is reflected in the surface plot of the maximum J as a function of the prevalence rates of two variables, presented in Figure 7.1. It's smooth and predictable form suggests that it may be a relatively simple task to adjust the coefficient to have a common range across all prevalence combinations by using a division by maximum strategy. Thus, we propose a new index that, in deference to the catalyst for this work, we label the Jaccard–Canter Index:

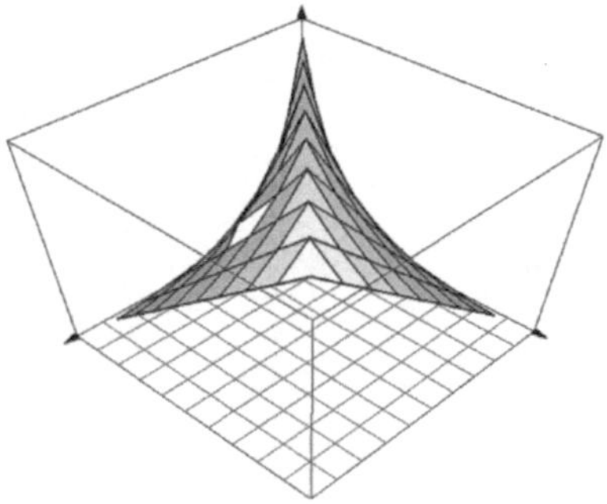

**Figure 7.1 Surface plot of maximum J as a function of $p_x$ and $p_y$**

$$JC = \frac{J}{Max\ J}$$

Which may be written in a more complete form as:

$$JC = \frac{\left(\dfrac{a}{a+b+c}\right)}{\left(\dfrac{Mn}{Mx}\right)}$$

Or, more simply as:

$$JC = \left(\frac{a}{Mn(a+b+c)}\right)Mx$$

If a distance rather than a similarity index is required, it is a simple matter to generate a distance coefficient that ranges between zero and one and is perfectly monotonic with JC by using the following formula:

$$JC_D = \frac{(MaxJ - J)}{Max\ J}$$

An Example

**Table 7.3 Example data to demonstrate the calculations for the JC index**

| | | X<br>Present | | Absent | |
|---|---|---|---|---|---|
| Y | Present | 72 | 26 | 98 | |
| | Absent | 66 | | 136 | 202 |
| | | 138 | | 162 | 300 |

Let us assume that we have obtained the data summarised in Table 7.3. We can see that variable Y is rather skewed with a prevalence of 32.67%, while X is more evenly distributed with a prevalence of 46.00%. These are not wildly skewed data but they are fairly typical of the kinds of distributions that occur in psychological data. If we use the standard Jaccard formula we arrive at the following:

$$J = \frac{72}{72+26+66} = \frac{72}{164} = 0.44$$

However, as we have seen the variables do not have equivalent prevalence, thus this Jaccard Coefficient is not bound between 0 and 1 and the maximum coefficient available for this data can be estimated as follows:

$$a+b=98=Mn;\ a+c=138=Mx$$

$$JMax = \frac{98}{138} = 0.71$$

This means that given the prevalence rates of these two variables a perfect association can only reach 0.71. Given the fact that the prevalence rates for these two variables is not highly skewed, the reader should be able to see the potential problem with real data where greater skew is very common. In order to rescale the coefficient to range between 0 and 1, we utilise formula 3 as follows and obtain the Jaccard–Canter Index.

$$JC = \left(\frac{72}{98\times(72+26+66)}\right)\times 134 = \frac{0.44}{0.71} = 0.62$$

Not only is this coefficient larger than the raw Jaccard Coefficient, it is also directly comparable to all other JC indices because they are all measured on a common range between 0 and 1. The raw Jaccard Coefficients on the other hand each have a unique range depending upon the prevalence of the variable pairs that they represent.

## A Practical Application of the JC Index

In order to demonstrate the effect of using the JC index we will carry out an analysis on sexual assault data collected as part of the BADMAN database. This dataset was initiated by David Canter and Rupert Heritage and formed the basis of their seminal paper on the use of MDS for the typology of sexual assault behaviours (Canter and Heritage, 1990). Since that time, until his retirement from the Surrey Police Behaviour Science Section, Rupert Heritage and his colleagues continued collecting cases and adding them to the database. The analysis I will report here is based upon 716 cases.

Twenty nine variables were used for the analysis and these are presented in Table 7.4. The sexual behaviour variables used in the original Canter and Heritage paper were excluded because they do not manifest much discriminating power (Heritage, *Personal Communication*).

**Table 7.4 Sexual assault variables and their prevalence rates (%)**

| Variable | % | Variable | % |
|---|---|---|---|
| 1. A disguise was worn | 17 | 15. Reveals something personal tovictim | 31 |
| 2. A weapon was seen | 37 | 16. Is verbally violent | 9 |
| 3. Threat of an unseen weapon | 12 | 17. Demands something | 20 |
| 4. Extends contact withafter assault | 25 | 18. A blitz attack | 6 |
| 5. Steals something personal to victim | 6 | 19. Blndfolds the victim | 18 |
| 6. Steals something of monetary value | 21 | 20. Binds the victim | 15 |
| 7. Steals something easily identifiable | 6 | 21. Gags the victim | 11 |
| 8. Demonstrates forensic awareness | 25 | 22. A single act of violence | 31 |
| 9. Uses a con approach | 35 | 23. Multiple acts of violence | 15 |
| 10. Is inquisitive about victim | 25 | 24. Was deterred by victim | 28 |
| 11. Compliments the victim | 16 | 25. Removed victim's clothing | 92 |
| 12. Reassures the victim | 24 | 26. Removed own clothing | 20 |
| 13. Is verbally demeaning | 13 | 27. Tears victim's clothing | 17 |
| 14. Apologizes to the victim | 11 | 28. Physically demeaning | 4 |
| | | 29. Kisses the victim | 38 |

A 29×29 matrix of Jaccard Coefficients was generated using all 716 cases and a smallest space analysis was carried out. The result is summarised in Figure 7.2. The resulting distances in 2D space map onto the original Jaccard indices reasonably well although there is a degree of misfit as revealed by the stress indices. Nevertheless, the interpretability of the structure is good and replicates the Canter–Heritage model very closely. A polar structure emerges in which the three regions are readily defined as, Criminal, Aggression and Intimacy.

However, a radex structure can be superimposed upon the substantive polar one when we take the prevalence of each behaviour into account. It is possible to create three modular structures in which the outer region contains variables with prevalences of less that 10%, and the inner region contains variables with prevalence rates over 25%. The region in between contains variables with a 10 to 25% prevalence. Thus, the modular structure observed in this solution owes much to the prevalence rates of the variables. The researcher interpreting this solution should beware of trying to place a substantive interpretation on the putative radex unless the prevalence rates are part of that interpretation.

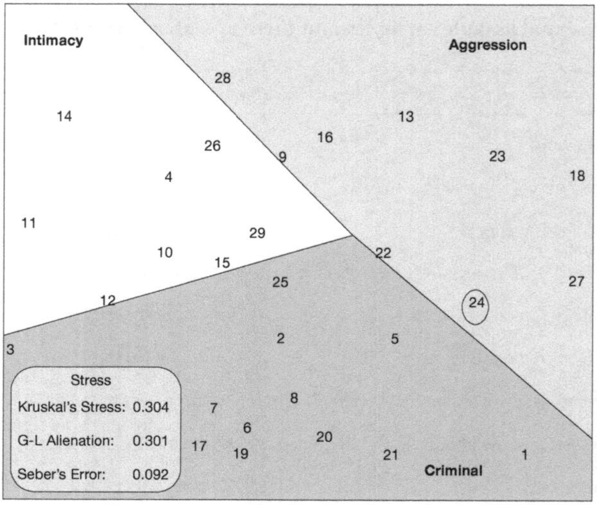


**Figure 7.2** **SSA solution for sexual assault features based upon Jaccard–Canter indices**

When the same data are analysed using the JC index of similarity rather than the simple Jaccard Coefficient, the solution summarised in Figure 7.3 is found. The first thing to notice is that the stress indices are higher than for the simple Jaccard solution, although the polar regions are still readily interpretable. Note also that variable 24 (deterred by the victim) now falls within an anomalous region.

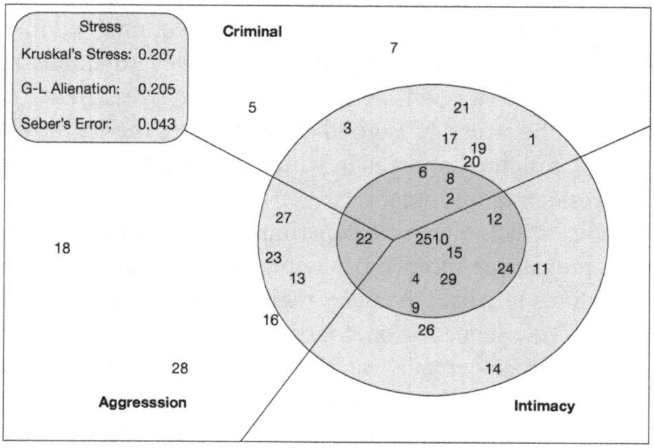


**Figure 7.3** **Solution for sexual assault features based upon Jaccard coefficients**

This solution may, at first sight, be slightly less satisfying than that produced by the simple Jaccard Coefficient. It should be clearly stated that this is not a necessary result of using the JC index since the removal of prevalence bias may reduce stress levels in some data. The researcher has now to ask the question as to whether the removal of prevalence bias in this case necessitates a higher dimensional solution and presumably a better fit. Unfortunately, it is beyond our remit to pursue this further with the present data at the present time. However, comparing the performance of JC with other coefficients of similarity is relevant to our thesis and this is the topic of the last section in this chapter

## The Jaccard–Canter Index in Relation to Other Coefficients

As mentioned previously, the fact that the MDS user is not constrained to use a product moment correlation provides great freedom, but also a number of challenges because it is now necessary for the researcher to select and justify the coefficient of similarity or distance that best fits their own data. The list of possible coefficients is enormous and here we briefly discuss only seven indices that have been widely used for dichotomous data.

Simpson (1943) identified two very simple measures of coexistence:

$$\left(\frac{a}{a+c}\right),\left(\frac{a}{a+b}\right)$$

These formulae may be simply defined as the proportion of times that one variable is endorsed in the presence of another. These formulae are not symmetric, however, so they do not constitute useful indices for a typical MDS analyses. Nevertheless, a number of coefficients utilise Simpson's formulae in producing indices that are symmetric and do not consider joint absence as a function of similarity.

1. Kulczinczi's (1927) Coefficient is the mean of Simpson's two formulae. It ranges between 0 and 1 and has been used largely in taxonometric analyses in the natural sciences.

$$Kulc = \frac{\left(\left(\frac{a}{a+c}\right)+\left(\frac{a}{a+b}\right)\right)}{2}$$

2. The Ochiai (1957) Coefficient is similar to Kulczinczi's index but it uses the geometric mean of Simpson's two formulae rather than the arithmetic mean. This provides a stronger measure in terms of its Euclidean metric, and has the interesting geometric property of being the cosine between two variables represented as radiating vectors (Imbrie and Purdy, 1962). It ranges between 0 and 1.

$$Ochai = \frac{a}{\sqrt{(a+b)(a+c)}}$$

3. Dice (1945) proposed another coefficient that does not consider joint absence and this turns out to be the harmonic mean of Simpson's formulae. It shares the nice metric properties of the Ochai Coefficient and ranges between 0 and 1. The formula for the Dice coefficient reveals its similarity to the Jaccard measure for, while the latter is simpler, Dice gives joint presence a double weight thereby emphasising similarity.

$$Dice = \frac{2 \cdot a}{2 \cdot (a+b+c)}$$

5. The Pearson Correlation Coefficient has been briefly discussed previously. In the dichotomous case it is known as the φ (phi) coefficient. It is the most widely used measure of inter-variable association. It ranges between −1 and +1 and has a number of very attractive statistical properties. However, these come at the cost of some pretty demanding assumptions not least that the variables have approximately 50/50 distributions.

$$\varphi = \frac{ad - bc}{\sqrt{(a+b)(a+c)(b+d)(c+d)}}$$

Yule's Q (Yule, 1900) is based upon the cross-product ratio:

$$\frac{ad}{bc}$$

And it is a symmetric coefficient ranging between −1 and +1. In fact, it is a special case of Guttman's μ (mu), a measure of simple montonicity between two variables and in its ordinal case it is often known as the Goodman–Kruskal γ (gamma) coefficient. Q gives equal weight to joint absence (d) as joint presence (a). It is ill-conditioned if b or c equal zero, taking a value of +1 in this case and −1 if a or d equal zero. This problem has been addressed by Leinert and Sporer (1982) who simply advocate adding 1 to each cell in the four-point table. Q has advantages over φ because it is not as sensitive to marginal skew so it is not truncated by low prevalence rates.

$$Q = \frac{ad - bc}{ad + bc}$$

The Baroni-Urbani-Buser Coefficient (Baroni-Urbani and Buser, 1976) was developed to address some of the weaknesses of φ and Q. This coefficient ranges between 0 and 1 and has good inferential statistical properties. It uses joint absence but it is worth noting that if d is zero it reduces to the Jaccard Coefficient.

$$BUB = \frac{\sqrt{ad} + a}{\sqrt{ad} + a + b + c}$$

Loevinger's (1947) H Coefficient is sometimes known as 'phi over phimax'. It represents an attempt to equalize the range of φ coefficients by dividing the raw φ by its maximum possible value given the observed marginal distributions. This maximum is calculated using:

$$\varphi \max = \sqrt{\frac{\max p * (1 - \min p)}{\min p * (1 - \max p)}}$$

Where max p is the proportion present for the most prevalent variable and min p is the proportion present for the least prevalent variable. The H coefficient is then calculated by dividing φ by fmax. In this way φ is rescaled to range between −1 and +1 irrespective of the distribution of the variables in question.

In order to see where the JC index fits in relation to these other coefficients of similarity the BADMAN data was utilised. A 29×29 matrix of coefficients was generated for each coefficient including raw Jaccard and the JC index. This resulted in nine similarity matrices. The lower triangular part of each matrix, excluding the diagonal, was taken and turned into a column vector of order (29*(29-1))/2 or 406. This resulted in a rectangular data matrix of nine columns each representing a coefficient and 406 rows each representing an association between two variables. The columns of this data matrix were correlated using Guttman's μ, a measure of ordinal relationship. The resulting matrix is presented in Table 7.5. A smallest space analysis was then carried out on this matrix and the resulting solution is sumarised in Figure 7.3.

The solution reveals a very good fit in 2D space and there is a clear diagonal axial partition between those coefficients in which joint-absence is considered, above the diagonal, and those where it is zero-weighted or excluded, below. There is also a clear order along this diagonal where the degree of marginal sensitivity is represented. The H coefficient and the JC coefficient occupy the low sensitivity region while the raw Jaccard, Dice and Baroni-Urbani-Buser coefficients occupy the high sensitivity region. The solution found here corresponds entirely with expectation and demonstrates that the new JC index is doing exactly what is expected of it in terms of removing prevalence bias.

**Table 7.5 Measures of monotonicity (μ) between nine coefficients of similarity**

| | 1 | 2 | 3 | 4 | 5 | 6 | 7 | 8 | 9 |
|---|---|---|---|---|---|---|---|---|---|
| 1 JACCARD | 1.000 | | | | | | | | |
| 2 JC | 0.779 | 1.000 | | | | | | | |
| 3 KULC | 0.958 | 0.984 | 1.000 | | | | | | |
| 4 OCHIAI | 0.997 | 0.919 | 0.992 | 1.000 | | | | | |
| 5 DICE | 0.999 | 0.773 | 0.955 | 0.997 | 1.000 | | | | |
| 6 Q | 0.839 | 0.745 | 0.841 | 0.855 | 0.833 | 1.000 | | | |
| 7 PHI | 0.902 | 0.664 | 0.846 | 0.891 | 0.896 | 0.994 | 1.000 | | |
| 8 BUB | 0.908 | 0.067 | 0.566 | 0.803 | 0.904 | 0.872 | 0.956 | 1.000 | |
| 9 H | 0.804 | 0.782 | 0.840 | 0.839 | 0.795 | 0.992 | 0.967 | 0.693 | 1.000 |

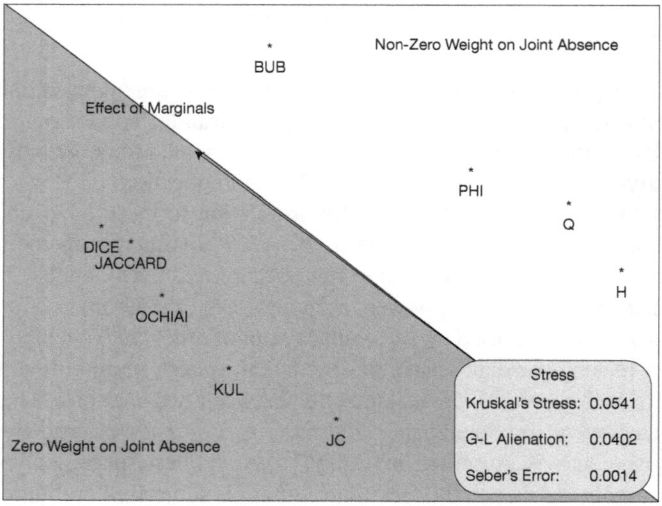


**Figure 7.4 Smallest space analysis performed on the relationships between nine similarity coefficients**

## Conclusion

A new index of similarity for dichotomous data has been introduced and has been named for the person who inspired its development. It is recommended for use in situations where joint absence of features is not considered relevant to the appraisal of inter-variable similarity and where there is a need to remove prevalence rate bias or marginal distortion from the measure. It has been demonstrated that it does indeed remove prevalence bias and that it falls into place alongside other measures of similarity as expected.

However, a final caveat should be raised. This is not a general purpose coefficient for 'doing MDS'. It should be clearly understood that no coefficient serves that purpose. The researcher needs to be selective and careful in choosing the coefficient s/he uses in order to ascertain that the analytic tool suits the data. To do otherwise results in the risk that MDS research will fall into the same sub-optimality trap that much factor analysis is prey to.

## References

Archer, A.W. and Maples, C.G. (1987). Analysis of binary similarity coefficients: effects of sample sizes upon distributions. *PALAIOS*, 2, 609–617.

Baroni-Urbani, C. (1980). A statistical table for the degree of coexistence between two species. *Oecologia*, 44, 287–289.

Baroni-Urbani, C. and Buser, M.W. (1976). Similarity of binary data. *Systematic Zoology*, 25, 251–259.

Birtchnell, J. (2002). Psychotherapy and the interpersonal octagon. *Psychology and Psychotherapy*, 75, 349–363.

Borg, I. and Groenen, P. (1997). *Modern Multidimensional Scaling*. Springer: New York.

Canter, D. and Heritage, R. (1990). A multivariate model of sexual offence behaviour: developments in 'offender profiling'. *Journal of Forensic Psychiatry*, 1, 185–212.

Carroll, J.B. (1961). The nature of data, or how to choose a correlation coefficient. *Psychometrika*, 26, 347–372.

Cheetham, A.H. and Hazel, J.E. (1969). Binary (presence-absence) similarity coefficients. *Journal of Paleontology*, 43, 1130–1136.

Dice, L.R. (1945). Measures of the amount of ecologic association between species. *Ecology*, 26, 297–302.

Dunlap, W.P., Burke, M.J. and Greer, T. (1995). The effect of skew on the magnitude of product-moment correlations. *Journal of General Psychology*, 122, 365–378.

Goodall, D.W. (1967). The distribution of the matching coefficient. *Biometrics*, 41, 647–656.

Gourlay, N. (1951). Difficulty factors arising from the use of tetrachoric correlations in factor Analysis. *British Journal of Statistical Psychology*, 4, 65–73.

Guttman, L. (1955). The determinacy of factor score matrices with implications for five other basic problems of common factor theory. *British Journal of Statistical Psychology*, 8, 65–81.

Guttman, L. (1957). Empirical verification of the radex structure of mental abilities and personality traits. *Educational and Psychological Measurement*, 17, 391–407.

Guttman, L. (1968). A general nonmetric technique for finding the smallest coordinate space for a configuration of points. *Psychometrika*, 33, 469–506.

Guttman, L. (1992). The irrelevance of factor analysis for the study of group differences. *Multivariate Behavioral Research*, 27, 175–204.

Hammond, S.M. (1986). Some pitfalls in the use of factor scores: the case of the KAI. *Personality and Individual Differences*, vol. 6, 401–407.

Hammond, S.M. (1987). DETFAC: a program for assessing factor indeterminacy. *Behaviour Research Methods, and Instruments and Computers*, vol. 19, 485–486.

Hammond, S.M. (1993). The descriptive analyses of shared representations, in G.M. Breakwell and D.V. Canter (eds), *Empirical Approaches to Social Representations*. Oxford University Press: Oxford.

Hammond, S.M. and Lienert, G.A. (1992). Point symmetry adjustment of phi coefficients in the factor analysis of psychometric test items. *Personality and Individual Differences*, 13, 211–219.

Hammond, S.M. and Lienert, G.A. (1995). Modified phi correlation coefficients for the multivariate analysis of ordinally scaled variables. *Educational and Psychological Measurement*, 55, 225–236.

Holley, J.W. and Guilford, J.P. (1964). A note on the G index of agreement. *Educational and Psychological Measurement*, 24, 749–753.

Hubálek, Z. (1982). Similarity based on binary (presence-absence) data: an evaluation. *Biological Review*, 57, 669–689.

Imbrie, J. and Purdy, E.G. (1962). Classification of modern Bahamian carbonate sediments. American Association of Petroleum Geologists, 1, 253–272.

Jaccard, P. (1908). Nouvelle researches sur la distribution floraie. *Bulletin de la Société Vaudoise des Sciences Naturelles*, 44, 223–270.

Jaccard, P. (1922). La chorologie selective et sa signification pour la sociologie vegetale. *Mémoires de la Société Vaudoise des Sciences Naturelles*, 2, 81–107.

Jackson, D.A., Somers, K.M. and Harvey, H. (1989). Similarity coefficient: measures of co-occurrence and association or simply measures of occurrence? *The American Naturalist*, 133, 436–453.

Janowitz, M.F. (1980). Similarity measures on binary data. *Systematic Zoology*, 29, 342–359.

Janson, S. and Vegelius, J. (1981). Measures of Ecological Association. *Oecologia*, 49, 371–376.

Järvinen, O. (1982). Species-to-genus ratios in biogeography: a historical note. *Journal of Biogeography*, 9, 363–370.

Kruskal, J.B. (1964). Nonmetric multidimensional scaling. A numerical method. *Psychometrika*, 29, 1–27.

Kulczyński, S. (1927). Die Pflanzenassoziationen der Pienmen. *Bulletin Internationalde lAcadémie Polonaisedes Sciences et des letters, Classe des Sciences mathématiques et naturelles*, 37, 242–272.

Lienert, G.A. (1972). Note on tests concerning the G index of agreement. *Educational and Psychological Measurement*, 32, 281–288.

Lienert, G.A. and Sporer, S.L. (1982). Interkorrelationen seltner Symptome mittels Nullfeldkorrigierter Yule-Koeffizienten. *Psychologische Beitrage*, 24, 411–418.

Lienert, G.A., von Eye, A. and Rovine, M.J. (1986). Factor analysis: difficulty adjustments of item intercorrelations using symmetry transformations. *EDV in Medizin und Biologie*, 18, 118–124.

Loevinger, J. (1947). A systematic approach to the construction and evaluation of tests of ability. *Psychological Monographs*, 61, 1–49.

Micceri, T. (1989). The unicorn, the normal curve and other improbable creatures. *Psychological Bulletin*, 105, 156–166.

Mokken, R.J. (1971). *A Theory and Procedure of Scale Analysis: With Applications in Political Research*. Walter de Gruyter: Mouton.

Muthén, B. and Hofacker, C. (1988). Testing the assumptions underlying tetrachoric correlations. *Psychometrika*, 48, 563–577.

Ochiai, A. (1957). Zoogeographical studies on the Soleoid fishes found in Japan and its neighbouring regions II. *Bulletin of the Japanese Society of Science and Fisheries*, 22, 526–530.

Palmgren, A. (1921). Die entfernung als pflanzengeographischer faktor. *Acta Societatis Pro Fauna et Flora Fennica*, 49, 1–113.

Palmgren, A. (1925). Die artenzahl als pflanzengeographischer character sowie der zufall und die sekulare landhebung als pflanzengeographischer entwurfbasiert auf materialaus dem alandischen sarenarchipel. *Acta Botanica Fennica*, 1, 1–143.

Pearson, L. and Heron, D. (1913). On theories of association. *Biometrika*, 9, 159–315.

Pierce, H.G. (1989). Monte Carlo simulation of selected binomial similarity coefficients(I): effect of number of variables. *Palaios*, 4, 101–103.

Real, R. and Vargas, J.M. (1996). The probabilistic basis of Jaccard's index of similarity. *Systematic Biology*, 45(3), 380–385.

Shepard, R.N. (1964). Attention and the metric structure of the stimulus space. *Journal of Mathematical Psychology*, 1, 54–87.

Simpson, G.G. (1943). Mammals and the nature of continents. *American Journal of Science*, 241, 1–31.

Sokal, R.R. and Sneath, P.H. (1963). *Principals of Numerical Taxonomy*. W.H. Freeman & Co.: San Fransisco.

Spearman, C.E. (1904). 'General intelligence' objectively determined and measured. *American Journal of Psychology*, 5, 201–293.

Steiger, J.H. and Schonemann, P.H. (1978). A history of factor indeterminacy, in S. Shye (ed.), *Theory Construction and Data Analysis in the Behaioural Sciences*. Jossey-Bass: San Francisco.

Vegelius, J. (1978). On the utility of the E-correlation coefficient concept in psychological research. *Educational and Psychological Measurement*, 28, 605–611.

Wall, K.D. and Lienert, G.A. (1976). A test for point symmetry in J-dimensional contingency cubes. *Biometrical Journal*, 18, 259–264.

Yule, G.U. (1900). On the association of attributes in statistics. *Philosophical Transcriptions of the Royal Society*, 194, 257–319.

Yule, G.U. (1912). On the methods of measuring association between two attributes. *Journal of the Royal Statistical Society*, 75, 579–652.

Zegers, F.E. and Ten Berge, J.M.F. (1986). Correlation coefficients for more than one scale type: an alternative to the Janson and Vegelius approach. *Psychometrika*, 46, 549–557.

# Chapter 8
# Homicide Crime Scene Analysis: An Investigative Psychology Approach

C. Gabrielle Salfati

## Editor's Introduction

In this chapter, Gabrielle Salfati, one of the original IP team, describes some of the basic premises behind one of the approaches within David Canter's general methodological paradigm (see Chapter 1). She outlines one IP approach to investigative inferences, that is the relating of offence actions to offender characteristics. This question of what used to be called 'offender profiling' as Gabrielle explores, is an issue on which David Canter is particularly adamant; there is no special 'profiling' process (see Canter 2011; also Section 4, this volume). His focus then rather than on evaluating and assessing a mythical process, has been on developing the theoretical and empirical models that relate the action and characteristic domains, in much the same way that particular relationships are established in many less glamorous areas of science (Canter, 1993, 1995; Canter and Youngs, 2009).

This chapter traces the developments of the empirical analysis of homicide using the main approaches from Investigative Psychology, from early studies focusing on developing classification systems differentiating between different types of crime scenes, to studies linking these distinct crime scene types to distinct offender characteristics. A specific focus will be taken to how Investigative Psychology has informed these studies in terms of its methodological framework. The focus will be to show how the Investigative Psychology approach to focusing on behaviours as the first stages of analysis has enabled first steps towards establishing a solid empirical foundation. The chapter will then move on to discuss how this early work has provided the foundations for recent empirical work on linking homicide crime scenes within cases of serial homicide. The chapter will conclude by outlining where the work on profiling homicide is going in the future.

## Introduction

The 1970s–1990s saw the field of profiling develop and, with its increased popularity, reach a point where, by virtue of its increased use, the method came under close scrutiny by scholars. Specifically, there was an increasing demand for demonstrating its validity in terms of how well it does what it claims to do, i.e. identify differences in types of crime scenes and identify the most likely offender responsible for the crime. It was with this need in mind that the field of Investigative Psychology was developed by David Canter in the late 1980s who, as part of this discipline, began looking at how psychology may help understand the various inference processes used in offender profiling. Determining what evidence can be used from the crime scene and exactly how it links to the offender's personality characteristics became the main steps to establish, using both psychological theory and empirical study.

The recognition of inherent perceptual bias, combined with a lack of empirical support of subjective profiles based on case evidence, have been the main causes for questioning the accuracy of profiling as an applied psychological tool in police investigations. In the first study done on the validity of profiling, Pinizzotto and Finkel (1990) concluded that much of the psychological profiling used in criminal investigations, though based on years of investigative experience, had been more a matter of guesswork and the use of anecdotal information that is vulnerable to errors and misinterpretation. Numerous other studies since have reiterated this issue (see review in Salfati, 2012)

When we additionally look at the psychological literature on how people make decisions, we find that people are apt to believe they are unbiased in the way they analyse evidence regardless of how subjectively they perceive the world. When people are faced with a complicated judgement or decision, they tend to rely on general 'rules of thumb', based on their experiences in similar situations, which can oversimplify a complicated situation and lead to the wrong answers (for a review, see Plous, 1993). Skewed, and biased, opinions on the characteristics of offenders, based on case evidence, can thus be seen to be a key issue to deal with when looking at how valid profiles have been.

Alison, Smith, Eastman, and Rainbow (2003), in an early study looking at the content of profiles, and working within the Investigative Psychology framework, examined the validity and reliability of 21 investigative profiles which sought to construct identifiable characteristics of suspects based on behavioural indices at the crime scene. They showed that of nearly 4,000 claims of the characteristics of the offender made in the 21 profiles, as much as 80% of the information provided was not supported by evidence. There was also a great lack of substantiation to the claims that were made. In short, it did not appear that the offender profiles were very valid or reliable in providing well-substantiated and accountable support, ultimately to be used to help investigations to narrow down the suspect pool of the most likely offender responsible for the crime. Alison et al. concluded by emphasising the importance of backing up any claims as to the characteristics of the offender, and how important it is that these are based on empirically validated research regarding the link between the actions of an offender at the crime scene, and their corresponding characteristics.

It is the premise of Investigative Psychology that in order to provide valid profiles, it is important to provide profiles which include conclusions about the characteristics of the offender based on their behaviour at the crime scene. This in turn needs to be backed by relevant, valid, and reliable research showing this connection in the empirical literature. With the introduction of the field of Investigative Psychology, research was started with the aim of establishing a scientific basis for profiling by thoroughly analysing criminal behaviour and the offenders responsible for engaging in such activities. More specifically, studies endeavoured to distinguish between different types of criminals and the way they commit their crimes. The idea was that this greater understanding of criminal behaviour as it applies to the crime scene could then be used to substantiate and back-up the conclusions made in offender profiles, regarding the link between the crime scene and the possible offender responsible.

This chapter will go on to specifically deal with the part of this work that has been done on profiling the crime scene actions and characteristics of homicide offenders.

## Profiling Homicide Offenders

Owing to the seriousness of the charges, homicide offenders are more likely to be referred for psychiatric examination and treatment than are most other offenders, and so it is not surprising that a number of the earlier taxonomies and typologies that were offered often reflected psychiatric and psychoanalytical frames of reference (Bartol, 1995). Similarly, because the individuals studied in these samples are undergoing assessment with the aim of plea-bargaining within the court-system, motive became another organising principle upon which offenders were classified.

Until recently, our understanding of homicide and the homicide offender was therefore based on these psychiatric classifications of pathological conditions leading to the offence. However, little coherence or agreement was present in this literature (see Bartol, 1995 for an overview). These classifications are often based on internal psychological processes which in addition to being subjective, contain motivational components often not observable at the crime scene, and so can only vaguely purport to aid the police in their investigations of homicide through providing ways of narrowing down the type of offender responsible for the crime. There has thus been a real need to develop models that are not only valid, but which are also based on more useful units of analysis, such as observable actions at the crime scene, in order to be more helpful to police investigations.

### *The FBI Approach to Profiling*

The earliest study in the field which laid the groundwork for focussing on behaviours at the crime scene, and which aimed to link differences in an offender's crime scene patterns with difference in their background characteristics, came from the Federal Bureau of Investigation (FBI) in the US in the 1980s (for a review, see Ressler, Burgess, and Douglas, 1988).

Early work by the FBI on profiling homicide focused on interviewing offenders in order to access the information of what happened at the crime scene, and combined this with an analysis of the evidence left by the offenders at the crime scenes themselves. This led to a model which, based on differences in the individual components, identified two different types of sexual homicide crime scenes, notably Organised and Disorganised. This was the first study that aimed to look at identifying patterns and subtypes in the actual offender's murder crime scene behaviour. Their work highlighted the idea of looking at subtypes, and then linking these to identifying differences between the characteristics of the offenders themselves, based on which subtype of crime scene they had left behind. They went on to suggest that offenders exhibiting a particular behavioural theme at the crime scene (Organised or Disorganised) are also likely to exhibit the same theme in their background. In other words, an Organised crime scene will indicate a greater possibility that the offender will have what they identified as Organised characteristics, and the same with the Disorganised type.

This original work in the field of profiling very much lay the foundations for future work by alerting us to the fact that crime scenes are rich sources of information for analysing the psychology of homicide. However, this work, which the authors themselves stated that 'at present there have been no systematic efforts to validate these profile-derived classifications' (Ressler, Douglas, Burgess, and Burgess, 1992, p. 22), i.e. stressing that their work was very much in the pilot stage and had not been tested, was still later picked up and used in profiling practice by both the FBI themselves, as well as other people. As the model grew in popularity and started being integrated in much other work (see Meloy, 2000 for an overview), other authors started highlighting the necessity to actually test the validity or the model in delineating differences between offenders.

## Identifying Methodological Issues based on Examination of the Early Work on Profiling Homicide

### *The FBI Work on Profiling Homicide*

Upon examination, several difficulties with this early work in profiling have been pointed out by later literature. Of particular note in terms of its empirical foundations, is the fact that the Organised/Disorganised classification system does not take into account the inherent ability of the frequencies of each individual behaviour to discriminate between individuals. As Canter, Alison, Alison and Wentink (2004) show in their study which aimed to evaluate the FBI classification study, many of the behaviours which were originally used to differentiate between the two types, were ones which were found to be common to most offenders. However, any behaviour which occurs in the majority of all cases is unlikely to aid differentiating between offenders, as high frequency behaviours denote behaviours which are *common* to most offenders, and as such define what is common to the group as a *whole*. Furthermore many of the variables which were used to discriminate between the Organised and the Disorganised typology were ones which came from the offender's own testimony, and were variables which often included a motivational aspect (i.e. an internal aspect of the offender's thinking and intent), which is not only difficult to measure at the crime scene, but involves a great deal of subjective interpretation which at the stage of developing an empirical model could bring in biases that would render the model invalid and unreliable. Some of the behavioural aspects of the models also included behaviours which although important in understanding the finer points of the pattern of offending (see Ressler, Burgess, and Douglas, 1988) were of the kind that were more difficult to observe, or at least obtain information about unless asking the offender about what had happened. These elements included behaviours such as 'controlled behaviour' and 'minimal conversation'.

What the FBI's work did importantly draw attention to however, was the very real possibility of using crime scene behaviours as a unit for analysis in the classification of homicide. They stressed the hypothesis that behaviours left at the crime scene, which are the result of certain actions of the offender, can be used to interpret the specific sub-style the offender engaged in, and in this way, identify the most likely type of offender associated with this style, which they highlighted could provide a first step to prioritising the most likely type of suspect the investigation needs to focus on at the primary stage of the investigation.

This early work was significant and provided the key directions for later studies in Investigative Psychology, by showing that behaviours lent themselves well to empirical analysis. Today, psychological researchers within the field of Investigative Psychology using an empirical approach to profiling are therefore less likely to rely on interviewing during the *initial* stages of research, and focus less on motivational aspects of the offence. Although interviews may be used later to add depth of understanding, Investigative Psychology approaches specifically focus on identifying variables that are useful to investigators in terms of being objective to allow for reliable measurement, and observable at the crime scene.

During the initial stage of any research using these objective measures provides a more valid basis upon which to make assertions. The offender's internal motivations or mental reasonings, which are often the focus of interviews, although interesting and useful in psychological treatment, are less reliable in understanding the differences between types of offences in terms of how the offender acted at the crime scene. What is needed is the physical measure of internal motivations. If we can ascertain how certain motivations are physically exhibited at crime scenes, we will ultimately, further down the road, be able to much more accurately account for why the offender committed the crime.

### *Other Models of Profiling Homicide*

There are a number of other early models in the early profiling literature that are often referred to and which aim to use crime scene indicators to identify subtypes of homicides. Few of them however have been validated either by the authors themselves, or by others. The only other one, apart from the FBI model, which has since been evaluated to date, is the one by Holmes and Holmes (1988), which was evaluated by Canter and Wentink (2004). The issues brought up during Canter and Wentink's critique backs up many of the conclusions provided by Canter et al. (2004) when they evaluated the FBI model, and again highlights key methodological issues regarding the necessary steps we need to take in attempting to produce empirically valid models on homicide, ultimately to be used for profiling.

In their attempt to evaluate the Holmes and Holmes (1988) typology of serial homicide through replicating it, they make the important note that the nature of the measures, or the behaviours themselves, are highly important. In addition to issues to do with selecting variables that are more objective, and that are not common to most offenders, they further discussed the issues of the definition of the variables themselves. Without clear guidelines of what each measure is, interpretation of even the more objective crime scene evidence introduces an element of interpretation and thus possible subjectivity.

This issue of defining the specific measures used as crime scene behavioural indicators specifically becomes important when we aim to test, or replicate, previously established models, or even create new models. For this reason, we have needed to focus much of the current work in homicide on creating reliable measures that we can use for research.

## The Methodology of Data Collection in Homicide Research

Currently, there are many approaches to collect data, and there are a number of available databases that researchers have available to them which each have their own variables. However, the common issue with most of these is the inclusion only of a certain number of variables, mostly demographic ones, and a lack of more detailed information. There is also a scarcity of variables that include pertinent details useful for profiling and crime scene classification, notably the actions of the offender at the time of the crime, the nature of the victims, and the characteristics of the offender. Most systems also include different subsets of variables, and include or exclude types of homicide cases, thereby also reducing any possibilities for comparisons of data from different systems. In addition, many of the current data collection tools do not have clear definitions of what constitutes each of the items or variables contained within the tool. Indeed, as stated before, this has been found to be a common problem in much of the research (e.g. Canter, Alison, Alison, and Wentink, 2004; Canter and Wentink, 2004).

The initial problems identified by these studies have been the theoretical, and consequently, methodological frameworks the original studies on profiling have used. Notably, as previously shown, most of these studies rely on motivational or internal cognitive and psychological features of the offenders as some of the key components of their classification systems. Although pertinent to the area of psychology, the obvious problem with this in relation to research pertaining to crime scene investigation, is that these motivational components are not only difficult to assess, but are also difficult to measure in an objective and reliable way.

There exist a number of large police databases which have aimed to collect information for operational use, and which include hundreds of variables pertaining to the crime scene, but evaluation studies have shown that these have suffered from many of the same methodological issues (see Salfati, 2012 for a review).

Because of these problems, we created a coding framework in the early years with the aim of creating an objective measurement tool to record the actions as they occur at the crime scene. This early work was based on an initial set of variables highlighted by Holden (1993), a police investigator with additional Investigative Psychology training who identified a subset of useful behaviours for an investigation. The expanded dictionary of behaviours (Salfati, 1998, 2000) created has been found useful to construct behavioural models of crime scene behaviours (Salfati and Canter, 1999; Salfati, 2000; Salfati, 2003) and the tool has been used by a number of different researchers in an attempt to replicate these earlier studies (e.g. Santilla, Elfgren, and Hakkanen, 2001; Salfati and Dupont, 2006; Salfati and Haratsis, 2001; Salfati and Park, 2008), and over the next 20 years been developed into a thoroughly reliability tested data collection tool for collecting data relevant to studies on profiling, the *Homicide Profiling Index Revised (HPI-R)* (for details see Salfati, 2012).

### *The Homicide Profiling Index Revised (HPI-R)*

Since this early work on classification systems (Salfati, 1994, 1998, 2000; Salfati and Canter, 1999), the work has moved forwards to deal with focusing on the more detailed components of the crime to gain a deeper understanding of the actions of the offender at the crime scene, as well as a clearer understanding of the measurement issues themselves. For this purpose, a number of new measures have been identified and all of these have been extensively defined to increase the definitions of each variable for ease of use in data collection, and to make the process of data collection from crime files a more reliable process. These developments have led to the creation of the *HPI-R*, which includes a detailed number of behavioural indicators of crime scene actions, as well as detailed demographics of both the victim and the offender. Since its beginning, the *HPI-R* has undergone several generations of testing for both validity and reliability, and a thorough training protocol for the use of the *HPI-R* has been developed to increase reliability measures (Salfati, 2012).

## The Psychological Theory behind the Work on Homicide

Having established a reliable data collection process which deals with many of the original concerns in the literature, it is important to next go back to look at the more theoretical issues relating to analysis of homicide in relation to profiling. Specifically, this includes understanding the psychological differences between different types of homicides in terms of how the offender acted during the crime scene. This has been referred to as understanding the very important first step in profiling, notably *Individual Differentiation* (Canter, 2000). Secondly, issues relating to how we may understand the psychological link between how an offender acts at the crime scene, and the type of person they are, and ultimately how each *different* subtype of crime scene actions relate to *different* types of offenders, what Canter (2000) refers to as the *Actions-to-Characteristics (Canonical) equation*, what is often referred to as the $A \rightarrow C$ equation.

### *Individual Differentiation*

David Canter, in his original book *Criminal Shadows* (1994) which outlines the basic psychological principles of Investigative Psychology that we can use towards profiling, as well as in his later papers (e.g. Canter, 2000), states that the most important goal of behavioural profiling is to devise a method for determining this individual differentiation, or comparing individuals in terms of conceptual categories.

In behavioural profiling, that means differentiating among behavioural styles at the crime scene, and then matching these behavioural subtypes to various offender lifestyle and criminal background patterns. The idea behind this is that offenders engage in a number of different ways of acting at the crime scene. These subtypes generally include subgroups of behaviours with the same underlying psychological theme or meaning to the offender. In the first paper ever published in the field of Investigative Psychology, Canter and Heritage (1990) analyzed 66 stranger rapes committed by 27 offenders in order to establish whether the behaviours as they occurred at crime scenes had any coherent patterns of co-occurrences to them. Their results indicated several thematic subtypes of offending styles. One example of different types were offenders who may have been interested in forming a pseudo-intimate relationship with the victim, who engaged in a different subset of behaviours at the crime scene such as kissing or complimenting the victim, versus offenders whose aim was to control the victim, who engaged in behaviours such as binding and gagging.

### *Analysis of Consistency and Linking Serial Homicide*

The impact of theme based models become particularly important in the understanding and linking of serial crime. In order to link a series of crimes to one-another, and then subsequently connect them to the characteristics of the offender, we need to demonstrate that offenders act in a similar way across their crime series. Imagine a situation in which a number of rapes have been committed, and have been linked to one offender because in each case, the offender used the single identifying behaviour of gagging his victim. Similarly another series have been identified by the offender binding the victim. By using a single behaviour like this a series has been identified.

However, it has also excluded us from linking these two series to each other, and so to the same offender. Canter and Heritage (1990) in their work show that there is a subgroup of offenders whose primary psychological theme is one of Control, and these offenders will engage in a certain subset of behaviours that physically demonstrate this psychological theme.

To clarify how this process works, I often use the example of a plumber and his toolbox, where the toolbox is made up of tools specifically made for plumbing. However the plumber won't know which exact tool he needs until he gets to the job. Once at the house where the job needs to be done, he will use the most appropriate one to get the job done. Using Canter and Heritage's (1990) work, we can then understand how an offender might use gagging if the victim is screaming, and binding if the victim is trying to escape – both behaviours which illustrate the offender trying to control the victim so that he can get his job done of raping the victim. If we recognise the underlying psychological meaning behind gagging and binding, we get a different perspective. While the physical behaviour is different, the psychological meaning behind the behaviour remains the same – Control. In the same vein, we may compare the plumber to the electrician. The electrician also has his own toolbox, but his toolbox is filled with a different set of tools from the plumber, each of which has its own purpose, but all relating to electrical work, rather than plumbing. Put another way, we may say that the offender possesses a variety of offending behaviours with the same function, but which are used for a different psychological reason. As such, relying on psychological themes allows for establishing context-victim connections which are typically ignored in offender-focused approaches when analysing behaviour. In this way we use our understanding of the interpersonal interaction between the offender and victim in a way that is more reliable, and allow for the measurement of this whilst keeping the focus on the offender.

## Homicide as an Interpersonal Transaction

As a first step in identifying the pertinent psychological issues that may help us understand homicide, the literature points us in the direction of understanding the interpersonal dimension that leads to homicide. Interpersonal normally refers to a two-way interaction, but in the case of homicide we don't have reliable information available as to this interaction, and so we must aim to understand it through looking only at the actions of the offender, without inferring what may or may not have influenced them. What we can establish, however, is that merely knowing the relationship between the offender and victim, that the homicide will show discernible and different patterns.

Homicide has been shown to often grow out of a transaction between individuals and that it is the nature of the relationship between the offender and the victim that can tell us something about the type of homicide we are dealing with. It is thus the hypothesis that more may be understood about the nature of homicide, its varieties and causes, by considering how the relationships between the participants may differ (Salfati, 1998;

Salfati, 2000; Salfati, 2003). Early psychiatric classifications have not dealt with this in detail, however early theories on aggression and differences in behavioural patterns in aggressive behaviours have discussed this in detail. Understanding this literature can take us a long way in establishing a baseline for us to take into account when analysing homicide. Specially, theories focussing on Instrumental and Expressive subtypes of aggression (Fesbach, 1964; Block, Devitt, Donoghue, Dames, and Block, 2000) and theories focussing on the issues of Impulsivity and Control (see Berkowitz, 1993) have dealt with the interpersonal issues in aggression. These broad theories were therefore chosen in the early stages to help interpret and understand differences between subgroups of actions of homicide and characteristics of homicide offenders (Salfati, 1998; Salfati, 2000; Salfati, 2003; Salfati and Canter, 1999).

Using these theories, Salfati and Canter (1999), and Salfati (2000) proposed that different forms of interpersonal transactions, and thus variations in murders, will be reflected in the murder crime scene itself, through the victim the offender chooses and the behaviours they do onto the victim. Given that the basic hypothesis in Investigative Psychology is that there will be some consistency between the way an offender acts and their past, behaviours as they are left at a homicide crime scene can then be analysed to help us understand both the action of homicide and the type of person responsible. The starting point in identifying such information was thus to look at what these behaviours consisted of, how they could be differentiated in terms of subtypes, or themes, of behaviour, and how each of these themes then differed in terms of what type of offender would be responsible for engaging in them.

Using these principles of consistency, the early work on homicide aimed to understand how different homicide offenders act differently towards their victims at the crime scene.

*The Expressive–Instrumental Model of Homicide*

The literature on aggression has consistently suggested that most violent episodes can be traced to well-learned, systematic strategies of violence that some people have found effective in dealing with conflict, interpersonal relationships (e.g. Toch, 1969; Huessman and Eron, 1989). Fesbach (1964) proposed a classification between different types of crimes such as person crimes and property crimes, each respectively being distinguished by Expressive and Instrumental types of aggression. Hostile (Expressive) and Instrumental aggression, are distinguished by their goals or the rewards they offer the perpetrator. The Expressive type of aggression occurs in response to anger-inducing conditions such as insults, physical attack or personal failures. The goal is to make the victim (the person) suffer. Most homicides, rapes, and other violent crimes he suggests are directed at harming the victim and are precipitated by hostile aggression and anger. The Instrumental type of aggression comes through the desire for objects or the status possessed by another person, such as jewelry, money or territory. Here the offender tries to obtain the desired object regardless of the cost. Usually there is no intent to harm anyone, although if someone interferes with the thief's objective, he may feel forced to harm that person or risk losing the desired goal.

The literature aiming to use this theoretical base to help distinguish between different types of aggressive episodes have, however, raised the issue of how these different aggressive strategies can be understood within violent interactions such as homicide, (e.g. Block, Devitt, Donahue, Danes, and Block, 2001; Salfati, 2000) and how these different types can consequently be linked to the different types of offenders associated with each type (e.g. Salfati, 2000).

Much of this work has aimed to go back to grassroots in order to more clearly define the concepts of Expressive and Instrumental aggression as it pertains to actual behaviour during homicides. Block et al. (2001), following up on their early work on understanding differences in Expressive and Instrumental homicide, highlight a number of issues regarding the Expressive–Instrumental dichotomy that are important to take into account when using it as the basis for any research. Notably they put forward that it is important to fully define what these types mean theoretically, and second it is important to be able to use this differentiation to very specifically be able to distinguish between cases. In particular, they highlight again how important it is to move away from indicators that are motivational only, which are difficult to measure, towards more objective measures such as actual behavioural actions. Their research also points to the fact that the Expressive–Instrumental divide is not as clear as previously thought. Both types not only occur in homicide in general, but also in very congruent subgroups such as intimate partner homicides. This highlights the very real problem of doing research in this area, as it is both theoretically and behaviourally complex.

Building on some of this original work in homicide classification, Salfati and Canter (1999) provided the original pilot work to a later long series of studies developing this area of research. They proposed that different forms of interpersonal transactions, and thus variations in murders, will be reflected in the murder crime scene itself, through the victim the offender chooses and the behaviours they do onto the victim. Given the assumption that there is a consistency between the way offenders act and their past, manifestations of behaviour which are left at a homicide crime scene can then be analysed to help us understand both different styles of homicide and the kind of person responsible for each one of these styles.

The different meanings aggressive actions have to the offender in a violent assault they suggested can be distilled from the general literature on aggression talking about expressive and instrumental aggression (Fesbach, 1964; Toch, 1969; Zillman, 1979; Megargee, 1966) into the idea of a victim being either a person onto whom the aggression is impulsively and expressively vented, or being a target secondary to the offender's instrumental motivations of ulterior criminal actions. They argued that this differentiation would be indicated through investigating particular subsets of actions that could be identified at the crime scene. Furthermore, they proposed that the processes which give rise to these differences would also be evident in the characteristics of the offender (Canter, 1994; Salfati and Canter, 1999).

This study of 82 British single-offender single-victim solved homicides found that the Expressive–Instrumental dichotomy could successfully be used in order to classify cases to specific behavioural themes. In addition, their behavioural model allowed 65% of the cases to be assigned to one of the dominant styles and a further 36% to be assigned to appropriate hybrids.

Salfati 2000 followed this initial study up with a larger sample of 247 British single offender-single victim solved homicide cases, showing similar results. This study showed that with expressive homicides, there was often an extreme physical attack. Moreover, these behaviours, when looked at together are suggestive of actions centred on the needing to separate themselves from the victim, and the place of crime, as these elements might have aided the identification of the killer. All of these behaviours were suggested to show a prior relationship between the two parties, or at least suggest that the offender knew the victim to some extent. Actions in the instrumental theme on the other hand centred on behaviours that were not singularly directed at the victim as a person. Rather, the actions were part of a larger theme of the offender using the victim to further attain an ulterior aim such as sex or money. When taken together, these actions suggested a behavioural theme where the offender regarded the victim not as a person with whom they were personally interacting, but as an object ultimately to be used for personal gain.

Through the analysis of the co-occurrences of the actual behaviours used by offenders at homicide crime scenes, these first studies in the area of Investigative Psychology brings attention to the actual behavioural components that make up different themes of homicide such as Expressive and Instrumental crime scenes. These behavioural components suggest that there are certain behaviours, which taken singularly, and out of context of the other behaviours could be interpreted much differently. However, by interpreting the actual meaning of these behaviours in relation to other behaviours with which they coincide, the thematic meaning of not only the behaviour, but also each of the two subgroups (Expressive and Instrumental), procures a more subtle definition than hitherto suggested. The behavioural components of Expressive and Instrumental homicides can thus be understood through a more subtle analysis and interpretation than hitherto put forward (Salfati, 2000). Consequently, 'expressiveness' and 'instrumentality' are reinterpreted to be not only more behaviourally subtle but also more thematically specific.

Using the same classification criteria as Salfati and Canter (1999), Salfati (2000) reported that 62% of the cases could be seen to exhibit a dominant behavioural style, and a further 30% being assigned as hybrids of the two proposed styles. Considering the stringent classification criteria used (where an offender had to exhibit at least twice the percent in the dominant theme, as compared to the percent in the other theme), these results are notable and show that not only are behaviours a useful unit of analysis, but that the Expressive–Instrumental dichotomy is a useful theoretical basis upon which to make these distinctions.

*Reliability of the Expressive–Instrumental Dichotomy across Samples*

Flewelling and Williams (1999) state that common classification systems across studies will greatly enhance our ability to interpret findings from multiple studies and thereby advance our knowledge regarding the causes and correlates of homicide.

As stated previously, one of the problems that the literature on classification of homicide has met with is the fact that studies have used different databases which each have different subgroups of variables, and which each use a different focus, notably demographics or motivations, neither of which helps in understanding differences in homicide crime scene action for the use for profiling. The work in Investigative Psychology on homicide has established a framework which overcomes some of these limitations by not only establishing a model outlining subtypes of behaviourally based crime scene actions, but also providing a data collection framework that meets with stringent reliability standards.

A number of studies have since been done, using the same methodological and theoretical framework, aiming to replicate the original Salfati and Canter (1999) and Salfati (2000) with different datasets of homicide in different countries. These studies include Greece (Salfati and Haratsis, 2001), Finland (Santilla, Canter, Elfgren, and Hakkanen, 2001), Canada (Salfati and Dupont, 2006), Korea (Salfati and Park, 2008), and the US (Salfati and Bateman, 2005). These replication studies are continuing, and all these have helped to test the Expressive–Instrumental classification system, by allowing to factor out possible national differences and by so doing, testing the robustness of the classification in terms of what each theme consists of in terms of individual behaviours, and whether these subgroups of behaviours can be understood using the same classification scheme across nations. In particular, these studies have continued to test the idea that it is the offender's actions against the victim that defines the differences between Expressive and Instrumental homicides, and these studies have shown that homicide in different countries retain the Expressive–Instrumental structure, but show intra-theme differences which differ by the country. This growing body of replication studies continues to build on the validity and reliability of this model, and the methodological approaches taken.

Of note however, is that these studies, following the lead of Salfati and Canter (1999) and Salfati (2000), provide very clear data on how accurate the model is in classifying crime scenes. Across the board, the studies show that only about 62–68% (Salfati, 2000; Salfati and Canter, 1999; Salfati and Haratsis, 2001; Santtila, Canter, Elfgren, and Hakkanen, 2001) can be seen to show a dominant theme. Most of these studies use stringent criteria to establish this figure, and considering this criteria, this is a high percent this early on in the field. However, what it also very clearly shown, is that there is an element of non-consistency which needs to be evaluated and studied further, so that we may start focusing on how to improve our models to further develop models on homicide crime scene profiling. Other studies have also highlighted that as part of this process we also need evaluate the best methodological approaches to classification and allocation to a theme, as this process in itself has key implications to the results obtained (see Trojan and Salfati, 2009).

### Linking the Crime Scene to Offender Characteristics

The main psychological premise behind profiling is that there will be consistency between the way offenders act at the crime scene and who they are. This is based on the broader findings from longitudinal studies and cross-situational consistency in general as well as from findings on the development of criminal behaviour. By understanding consistencies in offenders' development and change over time, the suggestion is that we can link the way they behave at the crime scene with how they have previously behaved in different contexts, what Canter (2000) calls the A→C equation. Providing this link, provides the backing that Alison et al. (2003) highlighted when they outlined the necessary structure of empirical backing that needs to go into any claims regarding the characteristics of the offender based on the crime scene evidence at hand. This in turn can then ultimately be used as a primary tool for the police to narrow their suspect pool down to statistically the most likely type of offender.

In terms of our primary focus in empirically based profiling, we are not focusing on the internal attributes of what an offender is thinking about or their psychological processes, but rather what the police can use in a very objective and practical way to narrow down the suspect pool. We are thus looking at characteristics like gender, possible age or age range, whether they had a criminal record and if so what type, and importantly with respect to searching for the suspect, the distance they may have travelled from home or the location of their home with respect to the crime scene. We may also want to include in this list a number of other factors such as mental illness or drug abuse as these may influence the offender's behavior to the extent that they may not adhere to clear patterns normally associated with specific crime scene themes due to influencing factors on their cognition (Salfati, 2012).

In the first study on homicide profiling done from an investigative psychology perspective, Salfati and Canter (1999) found that the Expressive–Instrumental dichotomy could successfully be used in order to classify offenders in relation to their Expressive and Instrumental crime scene actions. This study also provided the first study aiming to empirically link these crime scene behavioural types with the most likely background characteristics of offenders responsible for each type, and by so doing, testing the A→C profiling equation, and showing that there were distinct co-occurrences between specific subgroups of background characteristics with each crime scene theme. The results from this empirical study of actions and characteristics of homicide offenders helped set an empirical agenda to establish a classification system of homicide crime scenes and its related offenders that go beyond the individual experience any one 'profiler', and by so doing, Salfati and Canter (1999) helped take the first steps towards demystifying the hitherto shrouded process which has been called offender profiling.

The A→C link was also shown in Salfati (2000), even when the methodology to examine this was changed (see Trojan and Salfati, 2009 for a review). However as both of the studies showed this A→C link as part of a general analysis of associations, in this subsequent study, further analysis was also done to look at how many offenders actually displayed the same dominant theme at the crime scene as they displayed in their background characteristics.

The analysis of the link between an offender's crime scene style and their background characteristics further showed that when we attempted to look at consistency in theme between how an offender acted at the crime scene and their background characteristics, that only 55% of cases could be classified as exhibiting the same dominant style (Salfati, 2000). Further analysis highlighted that there was a substantial mix between crime scene themes and themes of background characteristics.

Having established that although 55% of cases could be classified as exhibiting the same dominant them at the scene as in their backgrounds, this was still lower than when cases are classified purely on crime scene actions or purely on offender characteristics. The same issues are thus present in the examination in the A→C link as there is in classification itself, both pertaining to both methodological issues as well as theoretical issues.

These two factors remain the two key issues that are at the centre of offender profiling or crime scene analysis work within Investigative Psychology (for more details on this, see Block, 1977; Berkowitz, 1993; and Cornell, Warren, Hawk, Stafford, Oram, and Pine, 1996; Salfati, 2012).

Figures from these two first baseline studies outlined here show that we are only capturing a portion of offenders in terms of identifying their patterns. We must now establish whether this is due to the fact that the models need to be further refined, or whether it is due to the fact that offenders are simply not consistent. One of the issues we need to further investigate is whether the behaviours which we use to define each theme need to be refined. In particular we need to understand whether individual behaviours which make up each theme accurately identifies those variables which are the strongest in identifying the offender, or whether they are variables that depend more on situational and changing factors at the crime scene. Replication studies have helped us in the first step in identifying these problem variables and further studies are in progress to refine the model in light of this.

### *How 'Profilable' is a Homicide Using Classification Models?*

In line with some of the issues that were originally brought up in critiquing early studies on profiling homicide (Canter, Alison, Alison, and Wentink, 2004; Canter and Wentink, 2004), we have conducted studies looking into the influence of the frequency of variables on building reliable models of homicide for use in profiling. Studies such as Salfati (2003) have provided important findings in terms of the parameters in terms of what we can profile and what we cannot.

Salfati (2003), using the same data and model used in the 2000 paper, identified four behaviours that were of high frequency, i.e. that occurred in over 50% of the sample, and as such defined what was common to the sample, and what could not be used to differentiate between crime scenes. These four high frequency behaviours were indicative of impulsive with no great degree of planning and seeming with the main purpose of killing the victim. They all represent behaviours suggestive of a more frenzied and emotional attack than an organised and intentionally planned attack. This is consistent with the idea in the literature in general that homicide is for the most part, an act of impulsive aggression, most probably spurred on by an argument of some description. The study further showed that almost 69% of the sample had three or four of the high frequency variables present. As such, this further validates the idea that these high-frequency behaviours should not be used to attempt to differentiate between cases. The study thus further highlights how important it is to identify the commonalities in the sample before attempting to identify the variables most effective in differentiating between subtypes of homicide.

Of more crucial importance to the issue of how useful such models are for profiling, further analysis showed that 57% of the sample had a higher percent of variables present in this high frequency band, than for the rest of the 32 variables in the analysis. This suggests that in this particular sample, almost 60% showed a pattern that is common to most homicides. Essentially what this shows is that 60% of the sample would not lend itself to being profiled as we cannot identify a specific subgroup of offenders associated with these cases, rather they exemplify the most common type of homicide, and do not provide any further details (in terms of other behaviours) that can be used to help identify a subtype of crime scene. This is still the only study to date in the literature that highlights this very simple, yet very important issue, by providing data to back up what types of homicide can more easily be profiled, versus others.

Salfati (2003) shows that what is common to homicides is the level of impulsivity, and the type and level of wounding, which all makes sense when we consider the type of crime we are looking at, notably homicide. What the study also shows however, is what Canter, Alison, Alison and Wentink (2004) also highlight, namely that it is the more rare subgroup of behaviours that may prove more useful in differentiating between types of crime scenes. In this particular study, these less common behaviours all centre on activities that are not necessary to kill the victim (i.e. commit the homicide), but rather illustrate the activities the offender engages in that deal with their possible ulterior agenda, which includes different ways of how they interact with the victim, how they use the victim, control them, sexually abuse them, steal from them, and dispose of the victim's body after the crime.

Looking at the nature of these variables, we can start to understand them in line with other theories in the literature which have attempted to understand what the most productive subgroups of behaviours are in terms of identifying an offender's unique behavioural pattern at the crime scene. Some of this work centres on the idea of Signature.

*Signatures*

Bateman and Salfati (2007) talk about the work of Douglas and Munn (1992) who define signature as the 'calling card' left by the offender that is unique to the offender's pattern of behaviours throughout their offences. For example, this signature may be related to the ritualistic acts committed by an offender perhaps to fulfil a specific fantasy. The authors explain that the signature aspect of the violent offence is a constant behaviour performed by an offender during their offences but that it may evolve and become more developed throughout the series of offences. They provide the example of the degree of post-mortem mutilation and indicate that the behaviours of post-mortem mutilation will be pervasive throughout the series of homicides by the same offender but that the degree of mutilation may increase as the series continues. Unfortunately, Bateman and Salfati (2007) state that researchers do not explain in detail how they arrived at these conclusions so the validity of their statements is left un-tested. Indeed, much of the literature on signatures they state, is not backed up by empirical studies, but instead, is a collection of theoretical and practice-led papers that propose these patterns, and although this wealth of experience provides a great basis for understanding behaviour, a detailed examination and definition of what a signature consists of needs to be developed based on this work, as well as an empirical testing of their inherent ability to account for consistency across an offender's series.

However, although the literature has talked about the idea of signatures, there have been no solid empirical studies until recently that have aimed to test this theoretical concept. Keppel and Walter (1999) went some way towards explaining signatures, and put forward a model on sexual homicide discussing how signatures may be seen to fall into four subtypes of offending, but as highlighted in Salfati (2012) this model like many early ones, remain theoretical and do not hold up to methodological and empirical testing. So for the purposes of further developing our understanding of the usefulness of signatures, we need to go back to establishing baselines, and actually look at how often these signatures occur, and additionally examine how these may be displayed consistently across time such as in cases of serial homicide, where the understanding until recently has been that offenders remain consistent in psychological theme or signatures as they move through their series.

## Linking Serial Homicide

Salfati and Bateman (2005) and Bateman and Salfati (2007), both working within the Investigative psychology framework, are the first two empirically based studies published on the issues of behavioural linking of serial homicide.

Bateman and Salfati (2007) provides the first empirical study looking at testing the concept of signatures, by looking at how it can be used to link cases of serial homicide, thus testing the psychological idea of consistency *across time*, i.e. first of all testing if offenders 1) *do* display what has been defined as signature behaviours, and if so, what these consist of, and 2) whether they display them *consistently* across their series, and as such, provides a justification for using these behaviours to link individual crimes.

The results from Bateman and Salfati (2007) shows that there are inherent difficulties in using individual behaviours to identify consistency patterns across a series, and consequently link cases. The results from the study further indicated that serial homicide offenders do not seem to show consistency in their use of the same crime scene behaviours throughout their series of homicides, nor does this consistency increase when behaviours are looked at as general groups, i.e. the offenders showing the use of *any* kind of sexual behaviour, *any* kind of body disposal behaviour etc., i.e. offenders do not even adhere to general behavioural patterns that we can identify. This study thus provides the first wave of empirical testing which questions current theories in the literature on serial homicide which has suggested that signatures or specific key behaviours are not only obvious, but key in understanding the consistency in an offender's behaviour across their crimes. It also highlights the importance in identifying which of these key behaviours are more indicative of the offender and their psychology, rather than behaviours which change depending on the situation, such as the environment, the interaction with the victim, and through learning and maturation that occurs throughout an offender's series.

As the initial work which focused on individual behaviour may be more problematic in terms of identifying consistency, Salfati and Bateman (2005) did another study where, using the principles of Investigative Psychology, they focused more on how consistency may be identified through the use of psychological themes. They based their work on the original work on *single* homicides (e.g. Salfati and Canter, 1999; Salfati, 2000), and tested whether the Expressive/Instrumental typology was valuable in distinguishing between different subtypes of *serial* homicides. Having found that the Expressive–Instrumental typology holds in serial homicide (for a more thorough discussion of this, see Salfati and Bateman, 2005) they went on to test the consistency with which offenders offended according to the same theme across their series, the idea being that by focusing on themes, we can factor out more of the situational factors that looking at individual behaviours cannot do. Results from this study showed that although this general homicide classification was more productive in analysing consistency than single behaviours, consistency levels were still not high. One of the issues the study highlighted was the same as that highlighted in the literature on Expressive–Instrumental single homicides, notably that the individual behaviours which make up each theme still needs to be refined to factor out behaviours that are more dependent on the situation than on the offender's psychology. The study therefore highlighted that it is important to further investigate the nature of individual behaviours themselves so that the understanding of the consistency and stability of these can be fed back into a more thematic model, which in the current literature has been shown to be more effective and reliable at classifying crime scenes. The subsequent studies in Investigative Psychology have focussed on these issues specifically in the study of serial homicide (see Sorochinski and Salfati, 2012; Salfati, 2012).

## The Future of Investigative Psychology and the Analysis of Homicide

This chapter has given a brief overview on how work on homicide in the area of Investigative Psychology has developed since its beginning, and how it has attempted to establish a more reliable and solid methodological framework identifying more reliable behavioural indicators at the crime scene, as well as a building a more valid theoretical framework that has been tested across many different groups of homicide. This work has provided a way to establish a baseline of good research practice in the area of homicide crime scene analysis. Although we are still at this time at the stage of establishing what we know about offenders who commit homicide, having taken an approach of closely scrutinising and monitoring the key methodological steps in the advancement of this research, it has enabled us to identify what the key theoretical and methodological questions are in terms of taking this research forwards.

In a way we have now come full circle. Having identified key methodological issues with work that originally used motivational indicators to form models of homicide, we have now developed methodologies which aim to address this by providing a framework for doing the same work from a more empirically objective standpoint. However, for the work to progress, we now need to go back to looking at the explanations given by the offenders themselves so that we may test out these behavioural models to see if the individual differentiations we have established based on purely behavioural measures, can now be combined with what Canter (1994) already in his early work on Investigative Psychology talked about, notably the narrative explanations that offenders give of their own actions. Once we have done this, we can then move on to test some of the questions we have highlighted in the course of this work, notably the issues of cross-situational consistency and the influence of external factors on the behaviours by the offender.

By now having a more methodologically sound baseline and framework, it will allow a more formal structure against which to test early ideas in the field relating to offender motivations, theoretical models looking at offender narratives and ultimately, we can bring together the best of all approaches to date towards analysing homicide under one all-encompassing approach, which will provide a more in-depth and refined model of how and why different types of offenders act differently during the crime.

## References

Alison, L., Smith, M.D., Eastman, O., and Rainbow, L. (2003). Toulmin's philosophy of argument and its relevance to offender profiling. *Psychology, Crime & Law*, 9, 173–183.

Bartol, C.R. (1995). *Criminal Behavior: A Psychosocial Approach (4th ed.)*. New Jersey: Prentice Hall.

Bateman, A.L. and Salfati, C.G. (2007). An examination of behavioral consistency using individual behaviors or groups of behaviors in serial homicide. *Behavioral Sciences and the Law*, 25, 527–544.

Berkowitz, L. (1993). *Aggression: Its Causes, Consequences and Control.* Philadelphia: Temple University Press.

Block, C.R., Devitt, C.O., Donoghue, E.R., Dames, R.J., and Block, R.L. (2000). 92–11, in *Diversity of Homicide: Proceedings of the 2000 Homicide Research Working Group*, edited by P.H. Blackman, V.C. Leggett, and J.P. Jarvis. Washington, DC: Federal Bureau of Investigation.

Canter, D.V. (2000). Offender profiling and criminal differentiation. *Legal and Criminological Psychology*, 5, 23–46.

Canter, D. (1994). *Criminal Shadows*. London: Harper Collins.

Canter, D.V., Alison, L.J., Alison, E., and Wentink, N. (2004). The organized/disorganized typology of serial murder: myth or model? *Psychology, Public Policy, & Law*, 10, 293–320.

Canter, D. and Heritage, R. (1990). A multivaraite model of sexual offence behavior: developments in 'offender profiling'. *Journal of Forensic Psychiatry*, I, 2, 185–212.

Canter, D.V. and Wentink, N. (2004). An empirical test of Holmes and Holmes's serial murder typology. *Criminal Justice & Behavior*, 31, 489–515.

Cornell, D.G., Warren, J., Hawk, G., Stafford, E., Oram, G., and Pine, D. (1996). Psychopathy in instrumental and reactive violent offenders. *Journal of Consulting and Clinical Psychology*, 64, 783–790.

Douglas, J.E. and Munn, C. (1992). Violent crime scene analysis: modus operandi, signature, and staging. *FBI Law Enforcement Bulletin*, 61, 2.

Fesbach, S. (1964). The function of aggression and the regulation of aggressive drive. *Psychological Review*, 71, 257–272.

Flewelling, R.L. and Williams, K.R. (1999). Categorizing homicides: the use of disaggregated data in homicide research, in *Homicide: A Sourcebook of Social Research* (pp. 96–106), edited by M.D. Smith and M.A. Zahn. Thousand Oaks: Sage.

Holden, R. (1993). *Facet Theory Approach to Homicide Crime Scene Analysis*. Unpublished M.Phil. thesis. University of Surrey, UK.

Holmes, R.M. and Holmes, S.T. (1998). *Serial Murder* (2nd ed.). California: Sage Publications.

Huesmann, L.R. and Eron, L.D. (1989). Individual differences and the trait of aggression. *European Journal of Personality*, 3, 95–106.

Keppel, R.D. and Walter, R. (1999). Profiling killers: a revised classification model for understanding sexual murder. *International Journal of Offender Therapy and Comparative Criminology*, 43, 417–437.

Megargee, E.I. (1966). Undercontrolled and overcontrolled personality types in extreme antisocial aggression. *Psychological Monographs*, 80, 611.

Meloy, J.R. (2000). The nature and dynamics of sexual homicide: an integrative review. *Aggression and Violent Behavior*, 5, 1–22.

Pinizotto, A.J. and Finkel, N.J. (1990). Criminal personality profiling: an outcome and process study. *Law and Human Behavior*, 14, 215–234.

Plous, S. (1993). *The Psychology of Judgment and Decision Making*. New York: Mcgraw-Hill.

Ressler, R.K., Douglas, J.E., Burgess, A.W., and Burgess, A.G. (1992). *Crime Classification Manual*. London: Simon and Schuster Ltd.

Ressler, R.K., Burgess, A.W., and Douglas, J.E. (1988). *Sexual Homicide: Patterns and Motives*. Massachusetts: Lexington Books.

Salfati, C.G. (2012, in press). *Profiling Homicide: A Sourcebook for Students and Researchers*. Offender Profiling Series. Aldershot: Ashgate.

Salfati, C.G. (2003). Offender interaction with victims in homicide: a multidimensional analysis of frequencies in crime scene behaviors. *Journal of Interpersonal Violence*, 18, 490–512.

Salfati, C.G. (2000). Profiling homicide: a multidimensional approach. *Homicide Studies*, 4, 265–293.

Salfati, C.G. (1998). *A Behavioural Analysis of Homicide Crime Scene Actions and Associated Offender Characteristics*. Unpublished Ph.D. thesis. University of Liverpool, UK.

Salfati, C.G. (1994). *Homicide: A Typology of Crime Scene Behaviours and Offender Characteristics*. Unpublished Masters dissertation. University of Surrey, UK.

Salfati, C.G. and Bateman, A. (2005). Serial homicide: an investigation of behavioral consistency. *Journal of Investigative Psychology and Offender Profiling*, 2, 121–144.

Salfati, C.G. and Canter, D.V. (1999). Differentiating stranger murders: profiling offender characteristics from behavioral styles. *Behavioral Sciences and the Law*, 17, 391–406.

Salfati, C.G. and Dupont, F. (2006). Canada homicide: an investigation of crime scene actions. *Homicide studies*, 10, 118–139.

Salfati, C.G. and Haratsis, H. (2001). A behavioral analysis of Greek homicide. *Homicide Studies*, 5, 335–362.

Salfati, C.G. and Park, J. (2008). Korean homicide crime scene analysis. *Journal of Interpersonal Violence*, 23.

Santilla, P., Canter, D., Elfgren, T., and Hakkanen, H. (2001). The structure of crime-scene actions in Finnish homicides. *Homicide Studies*, 5, 363–387.

Toch, H. (1969). *Violent Men: An Inquiry into the Psychology of Violence*. Chicago: Aldine.

Trojan, C. and Salfati, C.G. (2009). Methodological considerations of determining dominance in multi-dimensional analyses of crime scene behaviors and offender characteristics. Special issue: debates and critiques within investigative psychology (D.V. Canter, ed.). *Journal of Investigative Psychology and Offender Profiling*, 5, 3, pp. 125–146.

Zillman, D. (1979). *Hostility and Aggression*. Hillsdale, NJ: Erlbaum.

# Chapter 9

# Investigative Psychology and Suicide: The Facet Structure of Investigative Material

Susan Giles

## Editor's Introduction

As outlined in Chapter 1, for David Canter research is fundamentally about solving problems. To really do this, he argues researchers need to integrate their studies directly with the issues and the material as these present themselves in the real world. Susan Giles' chapter provides an interesting example of working with the naturally-occurring material central to many important IP studies (see Canter and Alison, 2003). She describes a study that drew directly upon coroner's reports then used the methodological process David Canter innovated to make conceptually and statistically sophisticated empirical research with this sort of material possible. Susan shows how this process allowed the development of a sophisticated, multidimensional model of suicide precursors that nonetheless had the potential to feed directly into decision making. In so doing, Susan illustrates the potential that the Canter IP methodology opens up in broader domains. This certainly has always been David Canter's position – that IP is not simply investigative because it pertains to criminal (or civil) investigations. IP is also investigative in the sense of being about problem-solving.

## Investigating Suicide and Sudden Death

Operating in discreet geographical districts throughout England and Wales, Coroners are legally or medically qualified judicial officers of the Crown whose functions include enquiring into cases of accidental, sudden and unexplained or suspicious death, including all incidences of suspected suicide or self-harm. A formal process of investigation may often be required and where necessary an inquest held. In 1999 inquests were held in 12% of all cases reported to a Coroner (Dorries, 1999).

### *Initial Information Gathering and Assessing Environmental Cues*

Although operational procedures may vary from force to force, police officers invariably act on behalf of the Coroner in attending sudden deaths, making an initial assessment based on environmental cues at the scene and information from witnesses, then conducting further investigations as appropriate in the apparent circumstances of each particular case. For example, protocols and procedures involved in the launch of a murder inquiry are much more extensive and complex than those required when death is thought to have occurred from natural causes such as old age. As a form of homicide, all cases of suspected suicide are subject to formal investigation and detailed reports, usually under the supervision of a Detective Inspector and in liaison with a Coroner's Officer, resulting in a substantial corpus of investigative material.

Initial information gathering in cases of suspected suicide is focused on discounting the possibility of criminal involvement by other people. This is particularly important where the scene of death is ambiguous. For example, there may be signs of violence or disturbance, more than one victim or the deceased may be female. Providing these concerns are met, and then the focus will shift to establishing, so far as is evidentially possible, whether or not the individual actually intended to take their own life. Here the mode of death, presence or absence of a suicide note and its content, direct evidence from witnesses and information about previous expressed suicidal attempts or intent may all be important factors.

*Investigative Material Available in the Inquest File*

These comprehensive files contain a variety of different kinds of material. For example, descriptions of the scene will usually be supplemented by a photographic record and scenes of crime or forensic reports. A pathologist will provide a written record of their post-mortem examination with a considered judgement about the cause of death, and there may be associated toxicology reports where relevant. Suicide is often a secretive affair and so investigating officers may interview relevant persons including witnesses at the scene, family members, colleagues, neighbours and friends. Each will often have their own points of view about the deceased, giving rise to different opinions about the likelihood of suicide and their written statements may complement direct factual accounts from, e.g. police officers or rescue and recovery personnel. Finally, those involved in the health of the individual, psychiatrists and general practitioners, may provide their own record of contact and considered professional opinion about the probability of self-harm.

*The Inquest Procedure and Decision Making*

A Coroners' inquest, sometimes held with a jury, is a formal public enquiry into the medical cause and circumstances of a death. Inquests must be held into all violent or unnatural deaths and those where the cause of death still remains uncertain after a post-mortem examination. Although not always necessary, witnesses may be called to give sworn evidence and be asked questions about their testimony. This will usually include relatives, the pathologist and police officers. However, the purpose of the inquest is not to apportion blame or guilt but to come to a decision or verdict about how an individual died: the *mode* of death.

Five possible verdicts are available in cases of suspected self-harm. Of these '*killed him or herself*' carries the highest burden of proof beyond reasonable doubt that death occurred as a result of a deliberate act by the deceased performed with an intention to cause their own death (Dorries, 1999). Where a reasonable doubt does exist then, *open*, *misadventure*, *accidental* or *narrative* verdicts may be recorded as appropriate on the balance of probabilities in each particular case. *Misadventure* verdicts require an awareness of risk, as in the case of a habitual drug user who died by overdose, e.g. whereas *accidental death* might be recorded where an individual was unaware of the likely consequences of their actions. If a Coroner is only satisfied on the balance of probabilities that a suicide has occurred then an *open* verdict must be recorded (Matthews and Foreman, 1993). Where contentious issues surround a case, e.g. alleged failures in a hospital's or prison's duty of care, a short storied or *narrative* verdict is increasingly being seen as appropriate.

Even from this brief description, it can be seen that the Coroners task is to make a judgement about whether a person had deliberately acted with the *intention* to take their own lives, whilst recording verdicts within a tightly drawn decision set. Coroners' legal verdicts are therefore unreliable indicators of actual suicide epidemiology, and in order to make the most appropriate inferences possible from the available evidence it would be helpful for scholars and practitioners to be able to uncover and reconstruct as accurately as is possible the motivations and intentions of the individual in question.

### *Death is Often Equivocal*

Reconstructing an individual's thoughts and actions is a difficult task for police officers and psychologists alike. Rarely are deaths and suicide straightforward, and there may be equivocal elements to nearly all such deaths. For example, family members may not have known the extent of an individual's distress and so may be adamant that their loved one would not have taken their own lives. There are many puzzles to cases of fatal self-harm, exactly because it is a series of actions that often has no witnesses. Equally, there are inherent problems of 'knowing' when one comes to reconstruct the actions of someone who is no longer able to provide detailed accounts themselves (Canter, 1999; Leenaars, 2002), leading Canter (1999) to draw parallels between reconstructions of this type and the task of a literary biographer or historian. Frustratingly, not everyone leaves clear clues behind. For example, living within invisible networks (Canter and Youngs, 2002), consciously and unconsciously managing ourselves and the relationships we share with others there may be gaps of days or weeks when an individual had not been seen, or if they had been, they appeared normal to those around them. According to Maris (1981) 'one of the major problems in understanding self-destructive behaviours is that the data base for such potential explanations is conspicuously absent'. Researchers, police officers and Coroners have to be particularly opportunistic and take advantage of any available intelligence (Alison, Snook and Stein, 2001;

Canter and Alison, 2003; Leenaars, 2002). In coming to a decision about whether an individual had intended to take their own lives, inferences must be made on the basis of this available information.

### *A Hierarchy of Evidence*

Often, a hierarchy of evidence exists in which forensic material is the most objective indicator. This may consist of physical material available at the scene, such as drug paraphernalia or a suicide note. Further forensic information may become available at post-mortem. For example, toxicology reports can indicate the amount of drugs an individual had consumed, or whether particular quantities of drugs or alcohol may have affected an individual's ability to form a rational judgement. Indeed in some cases, e.g. a concealed paracetamol overdose, forensic evidence may be the only indicator of suicide. However, questions of intent cannot be addressed by these means and in other cases forensic evidence may be completely absent even though intent to self-harm has been expressed. Clearly then, any advice that can be given to improve psychological inferences would complement and in some cases stand in place of the more objective inferences that can be made from the physical evidence that is available.

## Potential for an Investigative Psychology

There is huge variation amongst individuals known to have taken their own lives. For some, the prospect of suicide may have been a long term and frequently communicated plan. For others, despair might have been kept secret from those around them, or they might have acted fatally on an impulse. In the words of Kay Redfield Jamison, an academic who has written widely on the subject, and who battles herself with manic depression 'each way to suicide is its own: intensely private, unknowable, and terrible. Suicide will have seemed to its perpetrator the last and best of bad possibilities, and any attempt by the living to chart this final terrain of a life can be only a sketch, maddeningly incomplete' (Jamison, 2001, p. 1). However, through research the ways we have for understanding the psychological underpinnings of suicide do provide us with grounds for a beginning. For example, retrospective analysis of those who have died by suicide and those whom survive a suicide attempt has identified many of the correlates of suicide behaviour (c.f. Hawton and van Heeringen, 2000). And there is more work that can be done in examining how suicide is investigated by considering how material is collected, how lives are reconstructed and how appropriate inferences and decisions are made in relation to cases of self-harm.

### *Quality of Investigative Material in Inquest Files*

Canter and Alison (2003) discuss at length the strengths and weaknesses of the various kinds of unobtrusive archival material that is increasingly being opened up for study by applied psychologists. This material is unobtrusive in the sense that they are records that are pre-existing and do not involve the direct elicitation of information from research subjects (Lee, 2000; Webb et al., 1966). They are also non-reactive in that the researcher was not there when the information was generated, thus removing possibility for direct influence by the researcher (Lee, 2000; Webb et al., 1966). Indeed, Webb et al. (1966) advocate the use of unobtrusive and non-reactive measurements generally to supplement traditional controlled research methods. However, sources of this kind have not always been held in such high regard by academics and researchers. For example, Allport expressed reservations about the use of personal documents in the social sciences, despite acknowledging their importance in fulfilling psychology's commitment to increase 'man's understanding of man' (Allport, 1942). Leenaars (2002), a leading figure in suicide research, sees the idiographic approach to suicide, including the study of qualitative documents as being a necessary strand of parallel study in an event that is multifarious and complex.

However, there is no doubt there are many weaknesses to the material held in inquest files. Perhaps the defining and most frustrating of these from a research point of view is the lack of consistency from case to case, making comparisons difficult. This may arise from differences between investigating officers, but it may also relate to other biases. For example, as is the case with many elderly individuals, there may not be anyone available to provide a detailed history of the individual. In other cases, people may not have presented themselves to health professionals leading to a paucity of information in relation to their mental or physical wellbeing. Issues of this kind raise questions about the validity of documentary case comparisons and make it even more vital that the material is scrutinised within a scientific remit so that the comparative quality of the material can be improved.

However, there are also undoubted benefits to working directly with the kinds of material that are collected by the police. In addition to increased face validity noted by Alison, Snook and Stein (2001) and Canter and Alison (2003) the study of police statements reveals the way in which crimes are investigated and evidence collected, in effect opening up the investigative process. This makes the findings of any study fundamentally more relevant and applicable. In addition to what inquest files can tell us about suicide we can ask what they tell us about how suicide is investigated and conceived. This can be fed back into the investigative process and highlight areas where training is needed for more effective reconstructions of individuals.

A final note should be made about the many strengths of this material. Research using inquest files has the benefit of being conducted on written material that is the result of a long and considered investigation, including interviews with many witnesses and the considered judgements of professionals. Taken together they can sometimes amount to more than just pen portraits of an individual but can provide a holistic profile taken from many different perspectives. Triangulation and corroboration is possible to ensure that the bias inherent in any one source of information does not necessarily distort the whole picture (Canter, 1999). Indeed, the fact that useful research findings are making their way into the literature despite these weaknesses is testimony to the potential of this material (e.g. Canter, Giles and Nicol, 2004; Gregory, 1999). Substantial variation, however, does still exist. The challenge to researchers then is be aware of the various potential biases and to use research designs and analyses that can reveal useful underlying themes in behaviour despite weaknesses in material (Alison, Snook and Stein, 2001; Allport, 1942; Canter and Alison, 2003). I shall now turn to a worked example that indicates one way in which this can be achieved.

## Canter, Giles and Nicol (2004): Suicide without Explicit Precursors

In this paper we wanted to contribute to evidence that suicide can occur without overt, explicit precursors, amongst individuals who constitute a low suicide risk (Robins et al., 1959; Robins, 1981). We wanted to consider whether 'anything was possible' or whether there were limits to the processes by which people can bring themselves to suicide. This would be particularly important in investigating cases where the cause of death is equivocal. It could also aid in the rare number of murder trials where the suicide of an individual forms part of the defence (e.g. Regina v Gilfoyle; Canter, 2005) since jurors may have misplaced assumptions about precursors and expressions of intent. In the Coroners court too, relatives may raise questions about suicide intent in individuals that had kept their despair secret. Our aim was to establish clear indications of the possible pathways to suicide and how they might be present without being overt or explicit.

### *Suicide is a Multi-dimensional Malaise*

A large number of precursors to suicide are identified in the epidemiological research literature which have identified categories of risk such as psychiatric illness (e.g. Guze and Robins, 1970; Hawton, 1992; Henrikkson et al., 1993), medical illness (e.g. Hendin, 1999; Stenager and Stenager, 2000), stressful life events (e.g. Heikkinen et al., 1994; Rich et al., 1991), marital status (e.g. Cantor and Slater, 1995) and gender (e.g. Cantor, 2000). However, these risk factors are not alone explanatory. Although they are often at the forefront of the mind of those who attempt suicide they are only part of the complexity. Suicide is a multi-dimensional malaise (Shneidman, 1985; Leenaars, 1996). Many events may co-occur creating a route to suicide or be co-morbid with psychiatric disorders. There has been little research to date which examines the multi-faceted nature of suicide risk factors in concert. How might risk factors co-occur to create suicide pathways? Developing a framework for understanding any distinct routes or specific sub-sets of indicators that may be present across cases of suicide would be of value for examining emerging cases of equivocal death where the precise pathway to suicide may not be strongly apparent. In the investigative domain we are limited by the kinds of information that is routinely collected by the police. Given the weaknesses in this material methods of analysis that place too many constraints on the data may lead to important trends and patterns being overlooked.

## Canter's Approach to Uncovering the Patterns of Human Action

In the past few decades Professor Canter has been advocating and developing methods of analysis that reveal important trends in human action, whilst imposing minimal constraints on material that is inconsistently and unreliably recorded. After years of research he advocates Facet Theory as the most satisfying way of maintaining scientific rigour when working with multivariate complex real world data, without falling into the trap of scientific rhetoric (Canter, 2000b).

### *The Value of the Correlational Method in Applied Research*

Facet theory is a metatheory for research design and analysis (Canter, 1983) that allows researchers to consider the relational structure of multivariate data. Research methodologies make fundamental assumptions about the nature of human beings (Canter, 1983; Canter, 2000b) and statistics designed to test differences in average responses of subgroups to a limited range of variables, such as T-tests and analysis of variance, can lead to restricted models of human behaviour that have little practical applicability for practitioners working with real world problems. Facet theory is concerned with the overall pattern of relationship between variables (Canter, 1983). It relies on the study of internal correlations which can 'reveal the co-variance within individuals summarised as general trends across individuals' (Canter, 2000b, p. 202). According to Canter (2000b) 'it is the patterns of co-occurrence that reveal the underlying meanings of what people say and what people do'. Further, the 'real answers to pressing problems may be best answered by an indication of the mixture and variety of experiences that relate to the problems to be solved' (Canter, 1993, p. 34). As such, the relational design has long been advocated as being of more direct utility in the study of applied problems and qualitative concerns (Benjafield, 2002; Canter, 1993; Cronbach, 1957, 1978).

### *Benefits of the Facet Approach for Archival Qualitative Material*

Facet theory procedures are non-metric. This means that they can be applied to the categorical concerns of practitioners, making for more applicable results. They work with the ranked associations between variables which are unaffected by mathematical transformations, therefore they can also tolerate more weaknesses in the data and can greatly facilitate the interpretation of what is often less than clear data (Canter, 2000a) For researchers this means that they can take account more of the context within which data is collected and 'draw upon that context in a clear sighted way rather than planning research in relation to pure and abstract notions of elegant design' (Canter, 1993, p. 28). Imposing a minimum set of assumptions on data means that the facet approach is more 'honest in representing the underlying material' (Canter, 2000b, p. 203).

Multidimensional scaling procedures provide visual spatial representations of qualitative data at a glance (Guttman, 1944; Lingoes, 1968) which 'offers ways of summarising research material that allows decision makers to conceptualise the results in a form that is salient to them while still staying close to the original empirical results' (Canter, 1993, p. 30). These are also without reference to any arbitrary dimension or cluster as in factor analysis (Shye, 1998) so that the patterns of co-occurrence can be examined directly (Canter, 1983). These visual spatial summaries therefore serve some mnemonic advantage (Guttman, 1944). In analysing the relationship between variables facet theory reveals the structural similarity between variables that commonly co-occur, i.e. that share the same facet element (Guttman's principle of contiguity). There is a formal language for defining what you expect those relationships to be, but equally facet theory can be used in a more exploratory way to reveal underlying patterns of relationships and elucidate problems being studied.

### *The Structure of Human Action*

Facet theory and its attendant multidimensional scaling procedures allow for models of human action derived from an examination of variable intercorrelation, (2002). MDS combined with facet interpretation gives the researcher a visual representation which allows an interpretation of the dominant themes that can be used to classify behaviour. Examining behaviour at this thematic level has advantages since it is more tolerant of variables being missing because they had been unreliably recorded (Canter and Youngs, 2002).

This structural radex model has been found in a variety of studies of criminal behaviour (Bennell et al., 2001; Canter and Heritage, 1990; Canter, 2000), which rather than offering evidence for criminal 'types' help to develop an understanding about how differentiation between criminals needs to have foundations in understanding the processes that give rise to co-occurring patterns of criminal activity (Canter, 2000a; Canter and Youngs, 2002). Similarly, in Canter, Giles and Nicol (2004) we wanted to explore any underlying structure to suicide risk factors that might reveal the dominant themes that differentiate pathways to suicide. This would provide a model of suicide that might further understanding about action in cases where despair had been kept secret.

## The Structure of Suicide Pathways

After searching the literature on suicide, and bearing in mind the kinds of information police routinely collect we identified in Canter, Giles and Nicol (2004) 14 overt precursors to suicide (Suicide Precursor Scale) and noted the presence or absence of these precursors from case files of 128 cases returned with a suicide verdict. These precursors were:

- Male gender
- Marital status of divorced, separated or widowed

- Unemployed/retired
- History of depression
- History of substance abuse
- Schizophrenia
- Other psychiatric disorder
- Physical illness
- Bereavement
- Stressful Life Event (not including bereavement)
- Previous suicide attempt
- Previous communication of suicidal intent (>1 week prior to death)
- Communication of suicidal intent in the week preceding death
- Note found at scene of death.

*Establishing Suicide without Explicit Precursors*

Individuals scored between 2 and 10 on the SPS scale, with a mean score of 6. Seven individuals achieved a score equal to or less than three, indicating that the absence of many precipitating factors did not preclude a verdict of suicide. In the sample, 107 individuals were suffering from one or more psychiatric disorder at the time of death with depression being the most common disorder occurring in 96 individuals. This leaves 17% of the sample who had not presented to mental health services and who were 'psychiatrically undiagnosed'. Further, only 28 individuals communicated their intent via statements to family or friends in the week prior to their death. Fifty four had made some form of threat in the months before their death. Suicide intent was communicated, at some point preceding death by only half of the sample, indicating that suicide can happen with little warning. However, by considering the intercorrelation of these variables in concert we were able to establish evidence for distinct routes to suicide that could further understanding about suicide risk.

*Modes of Expressiveness of Suicide Behaviour*

Although these precursors are common correlates of suicide they do vary in how closely or directly they connect to the suicide event. A note found at the scene, and a previous communication of intent is more indicative or expressive of suicide than is gender, depression or employment status. But there is increased risk for suicide amongst individuals belonging to these more distal categories. This suggests there might be a behavioural hierarchy of suicide pathways in the same way that has been postulated for individuals who commit crimes (Canter, 2000a; Canter and Youngs, 2002). Some indicators would be expected to be fairly common across all suicides, being conceptually central to the process of suicide. A further hypothesis is that the distinctions in pathways would be a product of the lower frequency and perhaps more expressive indicators. The consequent hypothesis is that there would be discrimination between different sub-sets of precursors and that it would not be expected that all precursors would provide distinct routes to suicide. These questions about the overall structure of suicidal indicators were addressed using smallest space analysis (SSA-I) (Lingoes, 1973), a multidimensional scaling technique that shows the relationship every variable has with every other variable (Borg and Shye, 1995).

Plotting the frequency of occurrence of each of the variables onto the SSA-I projection above it can be seen that there are variables that occur in more than 45% of cases, in 30% to 45% of cases, and in less than 30% of cases. At the core of this structure are those variables that capture the typical context of suicide; being male, unemployed, depressed and having suffered a recent stressful life event. Moving out from this are those indicators that reflect increasing 'expression' of suicide. The variables lying at the periphery of the plot portray suicide precursors that are more directly related to expressions of actions related to suicidal potential, such as communicating immediate suicidal intentions (PresComm), getting involved with alcohol or drugs (SubAbuse), and being diagnosed as suffering from schizophrenia (Schizo). The variations in the frequencies of the variables give rise to a modulating facet constituting forms of active expression of behaviours fostering suicide.

This serves to clarify the distinctions in the pathways to suicide as being aspects of the way in which the ideation relating to suicide is expressed. It is the variations in these modes of expression that make up the dominant themes of suicide. They have been indicated on the SSA-I plot through three conceptually distinct regions

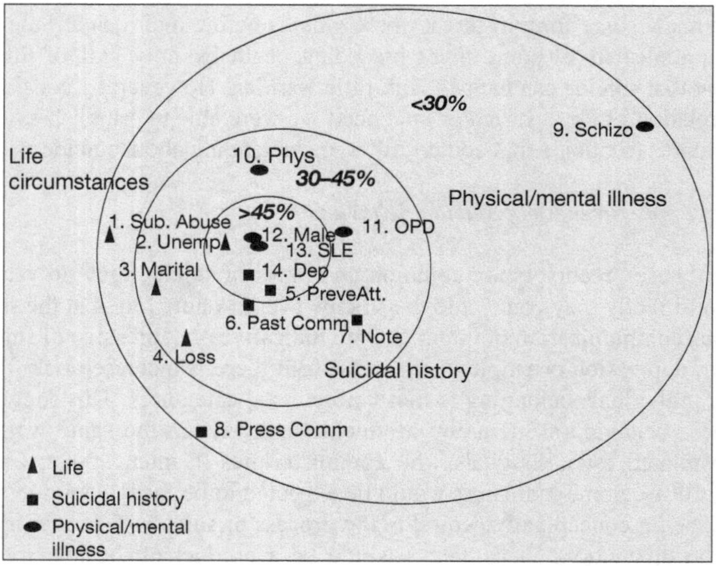


**Figure 9.1 SSA-I of suicide precursor**

representing modes of expression: 'Life Circumstances', 'Physical/Mental Health', and 'Suicidal History'. For a more thorough discussion of each region, consult with the original paper. Each region contains variables that share a common theme, showing that there are different 'routes' into suicidal behaviour. This model indicates that there are distinct behavioural routes along which those who are prone to suicide may travel. Although for some people many of the observable precursors indicated here might be present, the structure revealed in the SSA-I and the frequency distribution of variables shows that most suicides have a limited number of observable precursors. It therefore follows that for each of these pathways there will be individuals with a limited number of that sub-set of precursors.

In equivocal cases some attempt to identify these limited sub-sets of indicators may be of value in recognising cases for which the major expression of despair is kept secret. The overt characteristics of suicidal precursors may be very limited indeed. Although not offered as distinct 'types', the framework proposed here may act as one further basis for evaluating the psychological issues being considered. Coroners may use frameworks such as these to consider how a pathway to suicide might be apparent without being overt or explicit. It is important therefore that the constituents of a potential pathway, the risk factors an individual had experienced are recorded as accurately as possible.

## Replication

Canter, Giles and Nicol (2004) looked only at cases where a suicide verdict had been returned. However, it may be that other cases receive an alternative verdict precisely as a result of the absence of overt precursors. In a second study, using the same methodology we looked at 101 cases of suicide, open verdicts and accidental/misadventure deaths (Canter, Giles and Collins, in prep).

In this study we again tried to connect with the kinds of information that is available to the police but expanded the range of variables to include other suicide correlates. In their consultation for research in suicidology, Leenaars et al. (1997) argue for more work on interpersonal features of suicide. We were able to get a measure of those individuals who were no longer in contact with their children or whose children had been placed into care. As well as those individuals who came from a broken home or who had lost contact with their family. It may further be possible that suicide verdicts relate to the context of an individual's attempt and that certain contextual features are indicative of higher suicide intent, e.g. expectations for rescuability (e.g. Beck et al., 1979) therefore we included two variables 'deliberate or immediate method' and 'died alone and at a time or place where there were not expecting to be interrupted'. The importance of these variables has long been known to suicide researchers. And although they may be features that are taken into account when practitioners make decisions about a death, their precise significance in suicide investigations may not be consistently realised.

As in Canter, Giles and Nicol (2004) at the core of this structure were depression, unemployment, and a single life style. We again found evidence of a radex structure for suicide precursors that could be seen to be partitionable into regional facets similar to the findings from Canter et al. (2004). These were labelled 'life circumstances', 'psychiatric illness', and 'co-contributory risk factors'. In both studies substance abuse, a single lifestyle, and unemployment form part of the 'life circumstances region'. The region 'suicidal history' from Canter et al. (2004) is incorporated into the 'psychiatric illness' region of Canter, Giles and Collins (in prep) which may reflect the increase in previous attempts and prior communication that occurs more in the lives of those with enduring mental illness. There are therefore similarities in the structures of each SSA-I plot which points towards the reliability of there being distinct pathways to suicide that can be seen across individuals, irrespective of verdict. It is probable that the overt precursors to suicide are even more lacking here than in Canter et al. (2004) who only used suicide verdicts, making the replications in structure even more interesting.

## Discussion

### *Investigative Psychology and Suicide*

Both of the studies cited are based on reasonably objective characteristics of the person and his/her death derived from official records. The studies show that people do take their own lives in the absence of many overt precursors but that there are limits to the processes by which people can bring themselves to this desperate act. The clear results do illustrate how these sources of information can be fruitful bases for quantitative and qualitative analysis despite their many weaknesses (Canter and Alison, 2003). However, increased care needs to be taken in substantiating the exact absence or presence of these precursors and there are many ways in which the retrieval, evaluation and utilisation of investigative material may be improved.

There may also be more subtle precursors that come from knowledge of the considerable literature on suicide that it may be possible for police officers and coroners to consider. The pathways to suicide, identified here in cases with few precursors, and receiving a variety of verdicts suggest that there are super-ordinate categories that together show distinct routes to suicide that it may also be fruitful to consider when precursors are not overt or explicit. There may also be precursors to suicide that are more expressive although the subtlety of their significance may not be appreciated in any one individual case. Continued work looking at the co-occurrence of risk factors in concert would be clearly beneficial.

### *A Scientific Approach to Gathering Information*

There are weaknesses in all sources of information or data that practitioners work with, be it statistics, case analyses or detailed interviews. There are problems of inference and access to data that are common across disciplines and which researchers are well aware. What sets apart researchers from practitioners is their training in a scientific method which encourages them to set out a systematic process for asking questions, and finding evidence that both supports and refutes these questions. According to Canter and Youngs (2002) 'It is the simple task of enhancing the quality of the material officers must work with that is perhaps the most important contribution psychologists can make to police activities' (p. 8). Suicide enquiries are unlike other areas of interest for investigative psychologists because they are focussed upon a known individual whose inner mental life is central to their intention to act against themselves. This is a complex area of investigation where a clearer and more scientific standard of reconstruction could be provided by incorporating findings from suicide research and principles from 'psychological autopsy'.

### *The Use of Psychological Autopsy in Investigations*

Psychological autopsy, a procedure that has been developed over the last forty years (Canter, 1999), aims at revealing the state of mind of a deceased person through detailed and structured document analysis, and interviews with relatives, friends and health professionals. Shneidman and Farberow (1961) describe psychological autopsy as 'A retrospective reconstruction of an individual's life that focuses on lethality, that is, those features of his life that illuminate his intentions in relation to his own death, clues as to the type of death it was, the degree (if any) of his participation in his own death, and why the death occurred at that time' (p. 351). Canter (1999) calls for increased systematisation in the area, citing as support the wide and varied ways in which researchers and investigators have approached the task. In the United Kingdom, Professors Appleby and Hawton have gone further in publishing a detailed 'How to' guide informed by the many obstacles researchers have faced in attempting reconstructions (Hawton et al., 1998). According to Selkin (1994) the promise of the procedure is that it 'provides the opportunity to cloak an investigation concerned with the soft data of attitudes and feelings in the mantle of exactitude conveyed by medical and physical science'.

Typically conducted by psychologists and psychiatrists it aims to consider a broader range of information than is normally collected during police interviews, such as the individuals typical actions, reactions to stress, interpersonal relationships, thought processes, exposure to suicide, and experiences surrounding the death (e.g. Shneidman, 1976; Brent, 1989). It uses information from those close to the deceased as intelligence about the historical and recent developments and behaviours of the individual and combines this with study of any available archival data. In addition to the wider range of more detailed information it is designed to elicit it provides suggestions for overcoming the problems of bias which are especially important in investigating equivocal death, e.g. corroborating with as wide a range and variety of sources of information and prudent choice of informants.

According to Canter (1999) the contribution of psychological autopsy to equivocal death investigations may best be regarded as the development of an organised framework for indicating the issues to be considered when forming a view about the deceased. A psychologist or behavioural scientist may also draw on sources that are not normally considered by legal professionals, police officers, or physicians. There is value in bringing in an expert witness for some equivocal deaths since researchers and psychologists can draw on what is known of people and processes similar to that demonstrated in the case, taking the individual being considered as an illustration of people and processes that are known to have carried out similar actions (Canter, 1999). They may also provide more systematic detail and clearer evidence for conclusions reached.

However it may be productive and reasonable to consider appropriate training of police officers and coroners in the use of psychological autopsy. Neither are trained clinicians; however it is likely that further training in the correlates of suicide behaviour (developed and informed by research) would make investigative information more thorough and ultimately more comparable. The investigation of suicide is a challenging area of police work requiring a great deal of personal resources in meeting and dealing with the needs of relatives. There may be many factors, including the relationship that officers can develop with relatives that may impact on the quality of the investigative material collected. Therefore having a standardised list of areas of interest, as could be offered from psychological autopsy would be of real benefit. At present, police officers have no training or conceptual system for considering suicide (Canter, 1999) and yet 'there is indeed much that a layman can do in forming a view about a dead person that will parallel the opinion of a professional psychologist' (p. 143). In the first instance, increased training in the clues to and correlates of suicide would be the first step forward. It would also have benefits for coroners by adding to more objective processes for systematic decision making which others could also be trained to use. Jobes et al., (1986) e.g. showed that 95 medical examiners who received reports containing only physical and circumstantial evidence about a fatality, gave distinctly different judgements compared with 100 who had the same reports augmented with psychological opinion. Increased knowledge about the processes involved in suicide would complement and enrich decisions that are typically based upon physical, contextual and contemporary information. It is also possible then, that the inductive reasoning afforded by a more grounded knowledge about suicide could serve to improve the deductive reasoning that a Coroner must invariably apply to each individual case.

### *Science Should not Offer More than it Can Deliver*

Canter (1999) discusses the possibilities for psychological contribution to investigation of equivocal death, arguing that it is essential that science does not offer more than it can deliver. He goes on to say that it is clear that psychologists have much to offer to reduce the bias and improve clarity of judgements. But there is more work and thought needed here before the technique is translated for use by investigating practitioners. For example, there is no well-developed conceptual or theoretical basis for deriving conclusions from the various sources of information (Canter, 1999). The studies considered here suggest that it may be prudent to consider the co-occurrence of proximal and distal suicide risk factors, rather than each risk factor in isolation. Further research and guidance would be useful here. There is also little research that examines the reliability or validity of psychological autopsies. At present it would be wise to take on the recommendations it carries for a more scientific approach, i.e. the effective collection and corroboration of information. Inferences are no better than the information and informants on which they are based (Canter, 1999) and there is much work that can be done in improving the information that is collected. There are other lessons that can be borrowed from psychological autopsy and a scientific approach, such as the importance of reducing bias, by clearly recording sources, the potential validity of these sources and the extent to which they corroborate with each other. Informally, these requirements may be met by individual officers, however, formal adherence to more scientific strategies and evaluations of the evidence would be useful additions to police training. One interesting feasibility study in this area would be to compare inquest files and decisions made in cases where coroners and police officers are trained in the principles of psychological autopsy, compared with naturalistic cases where they are not. A variant of this may be a longitudinal design where the inquest files and decisions of officers and coroners are compared before and after training.

There are other aspects of suicide cases where a systematic approach or notional checklist born from research could be of real benefit to practitioners. For example, the legal system is based upon the notion of intention and its relationship to the purpose that the individual had in mind when carrying out an action. According to Canter (2000b) motivations and intentions are difficult areas for psychologists, since what follows an action is not unequivocally the cause of it. Further work here in the mental representations of intent (e.g. Fairburn, 1995; McAuliffe, 2002) is one area for further consideration and research but it may be that the increased systematisation that is offered by suicide intent scales, such as that of Beck et al. (1979) may be a useful addition to the investigative process.

There would also be implications for those involved in suicide prevention research. Through a more detailed consideration of those aspects of suicide that are relevant to establishing intent where few precursors exist, and in making the investigation of cases more consistent and comparable by adopting a more scientific approach it may also be feasible to align the investigation of self-harm with the requirements of suicide research that would serve huge benefits for those engaged in the suicide prevention strategy.

## Conclusions

Reconstructing the lives of an individual to establish whether they had acted with the intention of taking their own lives is a difficult task for investigators and psychologists. And yet there is much that research psychologists can offer investigators in making their material more consistent and comparable, and their decisions more systematic. In spite of the weaknesses of the material that police officers work with they can be used to examine pathways to suicide, irrespective of verdict or where clear indications of suicide might not be overt or explicit. Continued collaboration between researchers and practitioners could help to elucidate the pathways to this multi-dimensional malaise and develop the conceptual system for suicide that legal practitioners operate under.

## References


Alison, L.J., Snook, B., and Stein, K.L. (2001). Unobtrusive measurement: using police information for forensic research. *Qualitative Research*, 1, 241–255.

Allport, G. (1942). *The Use of Personal Documents in Psychological Science*. New York: Social Science Research Council.

Beck, A.T., Kovacs, M., and Weissman, A. (1979). Assessment of suicidal intention: the scale for suicidal ideation. *Journal of Consulting and Clinical Psychology*, 47, 343–352.

Benjafield, J.G. (2002). Research methods: a history of some important strands. *Archives of Suicide Research*, 6, 5–14.

Bennell, C., Alison, L.J., Stein, K.L., Alison, E.K., and Canter, D.V. (2001). Sexual offenses against children as the abusive exploitation of conventional adult child relationships. *Journal of Social and Personal Relationships*, 18, 155–171.

Borg, I. and Shye, S. (1995). *Facet Theory; Form and Content*. London: Sage.

Brent, D.A. (1989). The Psychological autopsy: methodological considerations for the study of adolescent suicide. *Suicide and Life Threatening Behaviour*, 19, 43–57.

Canter, D.V. (1983). The potential of facet theory for applied social psychology. *Quality and Quantity*, 17, 35–67.

Canter, D.V. (1993). The wholistic organic researcher: central issues in clinical research methodology, in *The Wholistic Organic Researcher: Central Issues in Clinical Research Methodology*, edited by G. Powell, R. Young, and S. Frosh. Curriculum in clinical psychology, Leicester: BPS, pp. 40–56.

Canter, D.V. (1995). Psychology of offender profiling, in *Handbook of Psychology in Legal Contests*, edited by R. Bull and D. Carson. Chichester: Wiley, Chapter 4.5, pp. 343–335.

Canter, D.V. (1999). Equivocal death, in *Profiling in Policy and Practice*, edited by D. Canter and L. Alison. Aldershot: Ashgate, 123–156.

Canter, D.V. (2000a). Offender profiling and psychological differentiation. *Journal of Criminal and Legal Psychology*, 5, 23–46.

Canter, D.V. (2000b). Seven assumptions for an investigative environmental psychology, in *Theoretical Perspectives in Environmental Behaviour Research: Underlying Assumptions, Research Problems and Methodologies*, edited by S. Wapner, J. Dmick, T. Yamamoto, and H. Minami. New York: Plenum, pp. 191–206.

Canter, D.V. (2005). Suicide or murder? Implicit narratives in the Eddie Gilfoyle case, in *The Forensic Psychologist's Casebook*, edited by L.J. Alison. Willan publishing, pp. 315–333.

Canter, D.V. and Alison, L.J. (2003). Converting evidence into data: the use of law enforcement archives as unobtrusive measurement. *The Qualitative Report*, 8, June.

Canter, D.V., Giles, S.P., and Nicol, C. (2004). Suicide without explicit precursors: a state of secret despair? *Journal of Investigative Psychology and Offender Profiling*, 1, 227–48.

Canter, D.V., Giles, S.P., and Collins, S. (in prep). The ambiguous verdict: the influence of suicide risk factors on the coroners verdict of suicide. International Research Centre for Investigative Psychology, University of Huddersfield.

Canter, D.V. and Heritage, R. (1990). A multivariate model of sexual offence behaviour: developments in 'offender profiling'. *Journal of Forensic Psychiatry*, 1, 185–212.

Canter, D.V. and Youngs, D.E. (2003). Beyond 'offender profiling'. The need for an investigative psychology, in *Handbook of Psychology in Legal Contexts*, edited by D. Carson and R. Bull. Chichester: John Wiley and Sons, pp. 171–208.

Cantor, C.H. (2000). Suicide in the western world, in *The International Handbook of Suicide and Attempted Suicide*, edited by K. Hawton and K. van Heeringen. John Wiley & Sons Inc.

Cantor, C.H. and Slater, P.J. (1995). Marital breakdown, parenthood and suicide. *Journal of Family Studies*, 1, pp. 91–102.

Cohen, A. (2003). The identification of underlying dimensionality in social sciences: differences between factor analysis and smallest space analysis, in *Facet Theory: Towards Cumulative Social Science*, edited by S. Levy and D. Elizur. Ljubljana: Faculty of Arts, Center for Educational Development.

Cronbach, L.J. (1978). The two disciplines of scientific psychology, in *American Psychology in Historical Perspective*, edited by E.R. Hilgard. Washington, DC: American Psychological Association (Original work published 1957), (285–308).

Dorries, C. (1999). *Coroner's Courts: A Guide to Law and Practice*. Chichester: John Wiley & Sons.

Gregory, A. (1999). The decision to die: the psychology of the suicide note, in *Interviewing and Deception. Offender Profiling Series*. Vol I, edited by D.V. Canter and L.J. Alison. Aldershot: Ashgate.

Guttman, L. (1944). A basis for scaling qualitative data. *American Sociological Review*, 9, 139–150.

Guze, S.S. and Robins, E. (1970). Suicide and primary affective disorders. *British Journal of Psychiatry*, 117, 437–438.

Hawton, K. (1992). Suicide and attempted suicide, in *Handbook of Affective Disorders: 2nd Edition*, edited by E.S. Paykel. London: Churchill Livingstone.

Hawton, K., Appleby, L., Platt, S., Foster, T., Cooper, J., Malmberg, A., and Simkin, S. (1998). The psychological autopsy approach to studying suicide: a review of methodological issues. *Journal of Affective Disorders*, 50, 269–276.

Hawton, K. and van Heeringen, K. (2000). *The International Handbook of Suicide and Attempted Suicide*. Chicester: John Wiley & Sons.

Heikkinen, M.A. and Lönnqvist, J. (1994). Recent life events, social support and suicide. *Acta Psychiatrica Scandinivicia*, Supplement, 377, 65–72.

Hendin, H. (1999). Suicide, assisted suicide and medical illness. *Journal of Clinical Psychiatry*, 60, 26–50.

Henriksson, M.M., Aro, H.M., Marttunen, M.J., Heikkinen, M.E., Isometsä, E.T., Kuoppasalmi, K.I., and Lönnqvist, J.K. (1993). Mental disorders and comorbidity in suicide. *American Journal of Psychiatry*, 150, 935–940.

Jobes, D.A., Berman, A.L., and Wright, D.G. (1991). Empirical criteria for the determination of suicide manner of death. *Journal of Forensic Sciences*, 36, 1, 244–256.

Lee, R.M. (2000). *Unobtrusive Methods in Social Research*. Buckingham: Open University Press.

Leenaars, A.A. (1996). A multidimensional malaise. *Suicide and Life-threatening Behaviour*, 26, 221–235.

Leenaars, A.A. (2002). In defense of the idiographic approach: studies of suicide notes and personal documents. *Archives of Suicide Research*, 6, 19–30.

Leenaars, A.A., De Leo, D., Diekstra, R.F., Goldney, R.D., Kelleher, M.J., Lester, D., and Nordstrom, P. (1997). Consultations for research in suicidology. *Archives of Suicide Research*, 3, 139–151.

Lingoes, J.C. (1968). The multivariate analysis of qualitative data. *Multivariate Behaviour Research*, 3, 61–94.

Lingoes, J. (1973). *The Guttman-Lingoes Non-metric Program Series*. MA Thesis, University of Michigan.

Maris, R.W. (1981). *Pathways to Suicide: A Survey of Self-destructive Behaviours*. Baltimore, MD: The John Hopkins University Press.

Matthews, P. and Foreman, J. (1993). *Jervis on the Office and Duties of Coroners*. 11th Edition. London: Sweet & Maxwell.

Redfield, J.K. (2001). *Night Falls Fast: Understanding Suicide*. Picador.

Rich, C.L., Warsradt, G.M., Nemiroff, R.A., Fowler, R.C., and Yound, D. (1991). Suicide, stressors and the life cycle. *American Journal of Psychiatry*, 148, 524–527.

Robins, E. (1981). *The Final Months. A Study of the Lives of 134 Persons Who Committed Suicide*. New York: Oxford University Press.

Robins, E., Gassner, S., Kayes, J., Wilkinson, R., and Murphy, G. (1959). The communication of suicidal intent: a study of 134 consecutive cases of successful (completed) suicide. *American Journal of Psychiatry*, 115, 724–733.

Selkin, J. (1994). Psychological autopsy: scientific psychohistory or clinical intuition. *American Psychologist*, 49, 64–75.

Shye, S. (1998). Modern facet theory: content design and measurement in behavioural research. *European Journal of Psychological Assessment*, 14, 160–171.

Stenager, E.N. and Stenager, E. (2000). Physical illness and suicidal behavior, in *The International Handbook of Suicide and Attempted Suicide*, edited by K. Hawton and K. van Heeringen. John Wiley and Sons Inc.

Shneidman, E.S. (1976). *Suicidology: Contemporary Developments*. New York: Grune and Stratton.

Shneidman, E.S. (1985). *Definitions of Suicide*. New York: Wiley.

Shneidman, E.S. and Farberow, N.L. (1961). Sample psychological autopsies, in *The Psychology of Suicide*, edited by E.S. Shneidman, N.L. Farberow, and R.E. Litman. New York: Science House.

Webb, E.J., Campbell, D.T., Schwartz, R.D., and Sechrest, L. (1966). *Unobtrusive Measures: Non-reactive Research in the Social Sciences*. Chicago: Rand McNally and Company.

# Chapter 10
# Questions and Answers about the Faceted Analysis of Criminal Actions

Jamie Lee

## Editor's Introduction

Although many IP studies do not use the facet approach, using the approach has facilitated developments in understanding that might not have come so readily otherwise (see Canter, 1983, 1985). The particular IP use of the approach to work with challenging, non-research generated (and often qualitative) data (see Canter and Youngs, 2009) has allowed insights and answers to debates that more traditional approaches have not, in particular facilitating the modelling of human behaviour as systemic structures and producing conceptual frameworks that can tolerate unreliable data. The integrated facet modelling approach, first proposed by Professor Canter in the early 1990s, to map multivariate domains, such as offence actions to offender characteristics, remains the most conceptually sophisticated approach to establishing these inferential relationships (see Canter and Youngs, 2009; Youngs, 2008). The use of MSA in the linking or 'comparative case analysis' task, is a further illustration of the potential of this innovative use of the facet approach in the investigative domain.

## Introduction

Investigative Psychology (IP) has been highly successful in applying sound psychological principles to police investigations and many other forensic contexts (e.g, Canter, 2004a; for a review see Canter, 2004b; Canter and Fritzon, 1998; Canter and Heritage, 1990; Canter, Hughes and Kirby, 1998). Critical to this success is IP's use of Facet Theory (FT), an approach to systematic research in psychology and the social sciences (e.g. Canter, 1985; Donald, 1995; Shye and Elizur, 1994), along with the use of non-metric Multidimensional Scaling (MDS) computational statistical procedures (e.g. Kruskal, 1964; Lingoes, 1968; Lingoes, 1973). This marriage of IP and FT is somewhat unusual given their respective family histories. FT began in attitude measurement and intelligence testing, where data is typically gathered through structured quantitative questionnaires with participants found specifically for this purpose. Participants in these contexts are usually motivated to take part, are open and honest with their responses and have no reason to conceal their intentions. It's quite the opposite for the typical IP context of criminal actions.

I believe that a hangover from the wedding is that forensic audiences of IP research can be unfamiliar or uncertain about FT, its vocabulary and its practices. A possible consequence is becoming stuck on issues of methodology rather than working through the insights. Therefore in this chapter, I address some key methodological issues in the faceted analysis of criminal actions by asking and then answering questions I have often heard from different audiences.

## What is the Facet Theory of Investigative Psychology?

Many opening questions broadly ask what FT is and why it is being used to study criminal actions. The first point of the answer is to clarify that FT is a theory about the process of doing research, not a theory of the content of research. So when IP studies draw similar conclusions or find similar patterns of behaviour then this is a *consequence* of FT but is not actually FT itself. Therefore a rephrase of the question is; 'What is done when using FT in IP?' which is answered by exploring the usual steps taken by the FT researcher.

## The Steps of Facet Theory in Investigative Psychology

Though other authors have explored FT in much greater detail (e.g. Shye and Elizur, 1994; Borg and Shye, 1995; Donald, 1995), research using FT in IP usually have the following common steps:

### *Step 1: Review Accumulated Knowledge*

After developing the idea for research, the researcher identifies and critiques previous literature and studies to see how previously accumulated knowledge can give clues to possible structures or patterns of behaviour. This review of the 'domain' is essential in FT and is also a feature of other research processes.

### *Step 2: Propose Structural Hypotheses*

In FT these thoughts on structure are formalised explicitly into *structural hypotheses* by proposing Facets and then ideally constructing Mapping Sentences as a framework for the hypotheses. The researcher here begins to hypothesise what the structures may be within the Facets. For example, a Facet of 'Aggressiveness' may be hypothesised with a quantitative structure increasing from verbal abuse to threats of violence to physical violence. Alternatively, a broad Facet of 'Mode' may have qualitative structure in bipolar opposites of 'Instrumentality' versus 'Expressiveness'.

*Step 3: Create Faceted Design*

To turn the structural hypotheses into concrete variables that can be used to explore the domain, the researcher ideally will create a *faceted design* by combining different Facets to create an optimal template for variables. For example, combining the Facets in Step two of 'Aggressiveness' and 'Mode' would create six templates for variables. If participants or case studies can be used specifically for the purpose of the research with structured formats, then all the combinations can usually be covered. However, if using pre-existing and unstructured data sources such as witness statements or crime scene photographs then this may not be possible so the researcher may need to be careful to ensure Facets are fully explored.

*Step 4: Consult Sources and Critically Assess Data*

When *consulting real world sources* to gather data, the source is not a passive subject or static record. Many potential biases and distortions in the domain of criminal actions create noisiness in the data. For example, a witness or victim of crime might (understandably) forget or not notice certain details of a highly traumatic event; an investigating officer might be sure to record certain details deemed useful at the time but not even ask about others; and a suspect or convicted prisoner might mislead or conceal some behaviours during an interview. Therefore the researcher at this step is transparent about assumptions made about sources and possible interactions with the source, giving a *critical assessment* of the resulting data. This assessment is especially important where existing data are used for secondary purposes.

*Step 5: Analyse Data and Create Data Representation*

When *analysing the data* and preparing it for interpretation, the researcher uses the previous critical assessment to make decisions about how best to find meaning. For example, should whole cases be compared qualitatively or can the data be analysed meaningfully for similarity with coefficients and with which coefficient? Then consideration switches to how to *create a data representation* that is adequate to show any structure in the data. Typically representations are created with Non-Metric Multidimensional Scaling (MDS) procedures using programs like HUDAP which has the MDS procedures of SSA-I (Lingoes, 1973) and MSA1 (Lingoes, 1968).

*Step 6: Interpret Regions to Evaluate Structural Hypotheses*

Finally, the interpretation of the representation must show if the structural hypotheses from step 2 can find and demonstrate the structure in the domain given the data collected on the real world source. In FT this usually means a *regional interpretation* to detect meaning in the plot (e.g. Shye and Elizur, 1994).

But why follow these steps – what is the benefit? This requires a quick review of why FT was developed.

*Guttman and the Transparency of Facet Theory*

Canter suggests that FT was originally designed by Louis Guttman as a reaction specifically against inadequate methodologies such as factor analysis and more generally with 'the lack of clarity of existing approaches to the definition of research problems' (Canter, 1983, p. 37). Guttman abhorred the use of item analysis to create internally reliable but completely artificial scales by simply deleting meddlesome items that didn't fit, as if they were 'throwing away evidence that the world is round' (Guttman, 1977, p. 100). Guttman was also scathing about the 'arbitrariness' of fixed cut-off points that could scupper meaningful research like setting $p = 0.05$ for significance testing or ignoring item-factor loadings below $\pm 0.3$ in factor analysis. Concerned by a casual regard for the interplay between theory and methodology, Guttman tried deliberately to make the role of methodology transparent in building theory stating that 'one must conceptualise – in substantive terms – what is being studied before one proceeds to design tests, gather data, and go through elaborate statistical analyses' (Guttman, 1967, p. 438).

The consequence of this transparency – and I believe the benefit too – is that the researcher feels empowered to make decisions about the research him/herself, rather than rely on permissions from test values and statistics. This confidence can only come from being fully immersed in the whole research process. I believe the openness to challenge and possibility for reinterpretation paradoxically makes FT research stronger because any weaknesses become more apparent and can be built upon with further research. This transparency of the research process and the relentless emphasis on theory building rather than statistical manipulation makes the use of FT powerful in studying criminal actions.

## Is that Plot Significant?

Probably the most familiar statistical technique in psychology is hypothesis testing using a $p$ value to indicate the risk of rejecting the null hypothesis and accepting the alternative hypothesis when in fact the null hypothesis is true. More commonly – but misleadingly – researchers use the $p$ value as the 'significance of the result'. Therefore when a faceted analysis uses a plot which has no $p$ value, people often ask 'Is that plot significant?' which is primarily a challenge to step 5 of the research process above. It is a challenge to data analysis and the representation as an MDS plot, perhaps asking if the result can be taken seriously and searching for a comparison to a test statistic and cut-off value.

*The p Value and Alienation/Stress*

Probably the most similar feature of an MDS plot to a *p* value is *alienation* (Guttman, 1968; Lingoes, 1973) or its close relative, *stress* (e.g. Kruskal, 1964). Alienation and stress are badness of fit measures from 1 to 0 where 1 means 'completely error ridden' and 0 means 'perfect'. Kruskal (1964) has given influential cut-offs that show if the result in the plot is acceptable for different stress values, such as a plot with stress 0.05 being 'good' but 0.20 being 'poor'. But unfortunately these simple guidelines ignore the diversity of research situations and the same alienation or stress value for a plot could be terrible if it contained 15 input variables but excellent for 40 input variables (Shye and Elizur, 1994). This is analogous with doing correlation analyses under different conditions and getting the same Pearson's *r* value but have different *p* values due to different degrees of freedom.

'Monte Carlo' studies attempt to overcome the problem by determining the badness of fit for sets of random data on parameters such as the number of variables and dimensions (e.g. Klahr, 1969; Spence, 1972; Stenson and Knoll, 1969; Wagenaar and Padmos, 1971), enabling comparison of fit with substantives sets of data from real world sources. A favourable comparison means the researcher can reject the 'nullest hypothesis' (Cliff, 1973) that the data are sampled from an utterly random universe of observations and to conclude that the real world source is worthwhile investigating.

However, it requires a leap of faith to use the comparison alone to then conclude that the representation has legitimacy and can be interpreted and that the research is substantive and rich in meaning. The same alienation can be found in two analyses with vastly different parameters and input data but the research can still be meaningful in both situations. For example, Canter, Bennell, Alison and Reddy (2003) found alienation of 0.24 with their two dimensional SSA1 of 27 male-to-female stranger rape behaviours but Canter, Alison, Alison and Wentink (2004) found a similar alienation of 0.25 with their two-dimensional SSA1 of 39 male-to-female stranger serial murder variables in the 'Missen Corpus' data set. In both cases the research was profoundly meaningful, with Canter *et al.* (2003) using their SSA-I to support their hypotheses of structure while Canter *et al.* (2004) have used their SSA-I to refute the FBI research hypothesis that there are 'organised' and 'disorganised' types of murderers (e.g. Ressler, Burgess, Hartman, Douglas and McCormack, 1986). In other words, trying to answer the question of a 'plot's significance' by using alienation misses firstly the point of alienation as a dynamic function and secondly the importance of the researcher's judgement of substantive significance over statistical significance which was central to Guttman's development of FT.

*The Role of Alienation and Substantive Significance*

Alienation/stress is a dynamic measure at the heart of MDS programs, not a one-off statistic produced at the end of an analysis like a *p* value. Its role is to enable programs to evaluate how well each piece of input data (e.g. associations between two variables coding witness statements) has been represented in the output plot (e.g. the distance between the two variables in a plot) and to indicate where errors have been made. Based on this information, iterative MDS programs can then begin improving things in the next iteration until no more improvements to be made. It's as if alienation is the altimeter for the program as it blindly clambers up a foggy mountain so it can raise the flag when it thinks it's at the top and give the final alienation value.

Based on this, Borg and Lingoes (1987) suggest a different and more useful way to think of alienation. For them, alienation acts as a measure of how much variation is unexplained so far, with high alienation suggesting large amounts of the unexplained variation (it is similar to variance explaining functions in other iterative computational procedures like factor analysis or principal components analysis). This 'variance explaining' links to the calculation of alientation from $\mu$, Guttman's coefficient of monotonicity which measures how closely two sets of numbers are ordered together. (Under certain circumstances Guttman's $\mu$ is identical to Pearson's $r$.) SSA-I is designed to use alienation to improve the relationship between input and output, given the parameters and data set by the researcher. Therefore there is a straightforward but somewhat flippant answer to the question about the 'significance of a plot': the plot is as *statistically* significant as the program could make it given the input data and the decisions made by the researcher. But whether the plot is *substantively* significant is a decision that must be made by the researcher.

There are times when the pursuit of substantive significance means deliberately choosing solutions that are higher in alienation and strictly speaking greater in error overall. For example, using local monotonicity in MDS means that points that are close together are prioritised by the program to be placed more accurately; in other words, error is pushed out to variables that are distant from each other. Doing this may minimise error locally with close variables but increases error overall and drives up the alienation. For example Lee (1998) shows that increasing the weighting of local monotonicity in FSSA (Shye, 1991) with a substantive data set systematically increases alienation as shown in Figure 10.1.

| Weighting for Local Monotonicity | –5 | –4 | –3 | –2 | –1 | 0 | +1 | +2 | +3 | +4 | +5 |
|---|---|---|---|---|---|---|---|---|---|---|---|
| Coefficient of Alienation | 185 | 199 | 215 | 229 | 244 | 260 | 276 | 291 | 305 | 303 | 309 |

**Figure 10.1 Alienation values for different local monotonicity weightings in FSSA with substantive data values for alienation are without decimal points**

If the objective is minimising alienation then the decision is to choose the −5 weighting. Yet local monotonicity is very useful where the lines of regional interpretation may appear to 'bisect' close variables. Thus the exact positioning of close variables is important since it can determine their region within a facet and potentially change conclusions about structural hypotheses. Therefore if the objective is to maximise substantive significance decision then the decision is to choose positive local weighting even up to +5.

In summary, Guttman (1978) suggests the blind pursuit of significance values (what he called 'star-worshipping') – and by implication the blind pursuit of minimising error – is counter-productive when it means ignoring the potential value of research. This substantive value comes from considering how carefully the domain was conceptualised and put into a structured design; the reliability of the consultation of the real world source; the suitability of the data analysis and the data representation; and the power of the interpretation to detect meaning. These aspects determine the significance of a plot in FT.

## Aren't those Lines Subjective?

An MDS plot does not interpret itself (though FSSA from Shye (1991) may assist under the strict guidance of the researcher). Therefore researchers themselves usually interpret an MDS plot to make sense of it and to show others what they believe is happening. In the case of FT the plot is divided or 'partitioned' into different regions, each of which has a distinct meaning to create a 'regional interpretation'.

At face value, regional interpretation appears to involve drawing lines on the plot and attaching labels around them. This can seem somehow unscientific and not objective, especially given the dominant 'methodological monist' notion that the social sciences and psychology should share similar empiricist ideals to the natural sciences. Therefore it's not surprising when regional interpretation becomes contentious and people ask 'Aren't those lines subjective?' It's almost as if the faceted researcher is just not playing by the rules. Specifically, I understand the question to be: 'Is it legitimate for you to interpret the plot in that particular way?'

### *The 'Compelling Reason' for Regional Interpretation*

The first point is that FT researchers do not look at an MDS plot and read it like tea leaves at the bottom of a cup – making sense out of nothing. Though researchers can interpret plot in other ways such as dimensional interpretation or clustering (Coxon, 1982), faceted research lends itself easily to regional interpretation. The choice of regional interpretation flows naturally from the formalised links between theory, structure and representation in FT and is for a specific reason. As Lingoes put it, 'Each partitioning of the space imposed by the investigator implies a particular classification of subsets of points … In constructing these partitions it is crucial that there be some compelling reason for doing so'. (Lingoes, 1977, p. 115, emphasis in original). The compelling reason for regional interpretation is Contiguity.

Foa (1958) suggests Contiguity is the property of different objects having aspects in common and therefore being conceptually similar but still distinct. In Canter *et al.* (2003), e.g. gagging, binding and blindfolding are crime scene behaviours that seem contiguous together during male-to-female stranger rape. Contiguity becomes useful for MDS because it 'suggests the following hypothesis: 'The larger the number of contiguous facets between two variables, the higher their intercorrelations' (Foa, 1958, p. 233, emphasis in original). This is useful because variables which have high intercorrelations are placed close together by programs like SSA-I. If the variables were created in a faceted design and used to explore a real world source, then the variables would assemble themselves in regions in the plot according to the faceted definitions, assuming the structural hypotheses were accurate in the first place (but also see the answer to question five).

This idea, the 'Contiguity Principle' (Foa, 1965), is 'an absolutely critical assumption' of Facet Theory (Brown, 1985, p. 20) and it is expanded and updated in Borg and Shye (1995). Nevertheless, in its original sense, it remains simple but powerful: a faceted researcher first hypothesises some structure and designs a study based on that hypothesis; the original structure will be found with regional interpretation in a suitable representations of data provided that Contiguity holds true in the research. The 'subjectivity' of performing regional interpretation is merely the researcher using the plot to assess the original structural hypotheses, just as the non-faceted researcher uses a test statistic or working with confidence values to assess the null or experimental hypotheses.

But what actually happens during the detection of meaning in MDS plots with regional interpretation and how does this make for a legitimate conclusion for the original hypotheses of structure?

### *The Mechanics of Regional Interpretation*

By partitioning a plot into regions and performing regional interpretation, the researcher is asserting that variables within a region are more conceptually similar together than they are to variables in other regions. However, the researcher performing regional interpretation is not saying that variables in different regions have zero conceptual similarity and are unrelated or even are inversely related. A quick check on the association matrix shows that variables that are close but partitioned into different regions are often related (although when coefficients have a minimum value of 0 then the researcher has decided that information about negative relations between variables is irrelevant). What is being stated is that the variation within variables in a region is more important conceptually than the variation between variables in other regions.

When a research domain can be understood in more than one way – meaning there is more than one facet proposed to describe the structure – then FT is flexible enough to allow the researcher to look for variation between and within the same pair of variables to make decisions on multiple conclusions. The structural hypotheses derived from accumulated knowledge, perhaps from previous literature, are fundamental in making decisions about what's in and what's not in a region and if a facet can be supported.

To take an example, Canter and Ioannou (2004) propose that the circumplex of emotions of Russell (1997) can be extended to how people feel when committing crimes. The hypothesised circumplex facet of 'Emotion' had themes of Elation, Distress, Calm and Depression with 20 variables to cover the space, including variables of Exhilaration, Anxious, Thoughtful and Depressed for the four themes respectively. Canter and Ioannou analysed information given to them by a sample of convicted offenders on how they felt during a particularly significant criminal act; this supported their structural hypotheses of a circumplex with the four variables named above in four distinct regions.

In another example, Canter *et al.* (2003) build on previous research to propose that male-to-female stranger rape is an act of violation with the crimes varying in both level and type of violation. A facet of 'Level of Violation' is hypothesised to have Personal, Physical and Sexual levels and another facet is hypothesised of 'Variation of violation' with themes of Hostility, Control, Theft and Involvement. A faceted design based on these two facets means that 'acts of physical violence towards the victim' is proposed to be a 'Physical Hostility', 'forced anal penetration of the victim' is a 'Sexual Hostility' and 'forcing the victim to make a sexual comment' is a 'Personal Hostility'. While these three behaviours have distinctions between them, namely the Level of Violation, they also have something in common, namely the Type of Violation to the victim of Hostility. In other words, these three variables are proposed to have both high between variation and low within variation respectively. Canter *et al.* find however that though these variables do not partition perfectly, there is still enough evidence from the configuration of other variables to support their structural hypotheses of two facet.

Some themes and dimensions are often proposed and found across different areas of IP, such as 'Instrumental vs Expressive' or 'Object vs Person'. But as shown when examining the steps of doing FT, this replication is not an automatic consequence of using FT. Instead it is more suggestive that there are a few repeating patterns for how people cumulative knowledge contrasts with other techniques, as shown in Guttman's critique in question 1. (Consider 'perform' crime and that different crimes are not unique and disconnected from the social context which creates criminals.

Therefore regional interpretation is the mechanism for testing the contiguity between structural hypothesis and representation. The regional interpretation is as 'scientific' and 'objective' as the researcher him/herself wants to be – assuming these are prized attributes – when doing the literature review and faceted design. This transparency about the decision to select variables as 'in' or 'out' of a region on the basis of conceptual similarity and practices such as item analysis within scales to cull items that push Cronbach's α below some arbitrary cut-off or delegating the selection of variables to a computational statistical function for 'within variance minimising/

between variance maximising'.) And if people query 'Why doesn't the line stretch over there?' or 'Could it loop back around here?' then these alternative interpretation should be accepted or at least tested, provided of course the questioners can find greater and overwhelming conceptual support for their interpretation. And though the questioners may not realise it, they have discovered Guttman's intentions in building a cumulative approach to knowledge through transparency in methodology and empowering the researcher to make decisions.

## How Does this Analysis Account for Error?

Error and unreliability are inevitable when the complex actions of human beings are boiled down into fewer – but more convenient – generalities using various analysis techniques. While 'accidental' error is a feature of many domains, deliberate confusions are a particular feature of real world sources of information on criminal actions, such as when crime scenes are staged in some way. As Canter and Alison (2003) note, IP researchers face numerous challenges when using police files to derive information that is 'unobtrusive' and 'non-reactive' (Lee, 2000). Importantly, though, IP research doesn't use explicit statistical functions to identify and extract either random or measurement error in such information sources. Consequently the researcher is often invited to explain how these issues of error were addressed. I believe the answer begins with a substantive examination of how decisions in the research process before the creation of data and interpretation.

### *Inclusion and Exclusion in Creating Data*

Ackroyd and Hughes (1992) state that 'data are always the result of a selection from what can possibly be said about some phenomenon' (p. 5). Decisions about what to select for inclusion happen throughout the research process, with each decision resulting in only a subset of possibilities being captured. Building on Coombs (1964), the subsets created by the selections in a typical research interview are:

> Decisions about potential sources – how are real world sources identified by the researcher as being 'worthy of research'?
>
> Decisions about potential questions – how is the real world source consulted by the researcher deciding 'what it a good question'?
>
> Decisions about potential answers – what does the real world source reveal about himself/herself by deciding 'what shall I say in reply'?
>
> Decisions about recorded answers – what does the researcher decide counts as a 'noteworthy reply'?

Decisions about data – how does the researcher turn information into data and analyse it?

Decisions about interpretation – which meaning does the researcher detect from the analysis and on what basis?

These decisions stack on top of each other like a pyramid, with lower levels carrying the tremendous weight of decisions made much further up. In a classic FT study of attitudes, the layers of this pyramid are usually well constructed: a structured questionnaire used with a random sample from a well-characterised population which in turn gives robust data and clear interpretations of structure. While some IP research has much in common with classic FT studies (e.g. Canter and Ioannou, 2004; Youngs, 2006), most IP research has these decisions frequently made by external people and not the researcher, making the analysis in a sense from secondary data sources. As Canter and Alison (2003) have shown, this brings numerous challenges with it. In particular, the decisions made are not always transparent, especially what was excluded and why. For example, what did the scenes of crime officer not photograph? Why are witness statements gathered from one heavily urbanised constabulary and one large rural constabulary? What state of mind was the convicted prisoner during the interview based on unknown events in the previous week? It's as if the pyramids of IP research frequently have their foundations buried in the sand, with some higher levels weathered and shaped by unknown influences.

Canter and Alison (2004) describe ways IP researchers can get around these influences and minimise the effects of external decisions. In particular, IP research has used Jaccard's association coefficient to account for what was excluded from research (e.g. Canter and Heritage, 1990; Canter, Hughes and Kirby, 1998; Canter, Alison, Alison and Wentink, 2004). Jaccard's creates associations between variables coded dichotomously with a weighting on what was recorded as present in the research and less weighting on absence and is calculated as $J=a/(a+b+c)$ if presence and absence in two dichotomous variables is shown in Figure 10.2.

In other words, information where there is absence for both variables (cell d) is excluded. (Other association coefficients could be used to emphasise the importance of *a* even further, such as the double weighting of *a* in Dice's measure or even ignoring absence altogether in cells *b* and *c*.) This is useful because in IP if something was

| | | Variable 2 | |
|---|---|---|---|
| | | Yes/present | No/absent |
| | Yes/present | A | b |
| Variable 1 | No/absent | c | d |

**Figure 10.2 Framework for pairs of dichotomous variables**

recorded as happening then it usually happened. However if it wasn't recorded as happening then this may be either because it didn't happen, or it did happen and it wasn't recorded. This may occur, e.g. in coding witness statements, where the absence of a specific piece of information may mean the question wasn't asked by the interviewer or it was misunderstood by the witness, or the witness chose not to answer the question. Therefore it is critical to think about how data are created from real world sources – such as choice of association coefficient – in order to design research that detects meaning.

Lee and Canter (2004) examine the impact of different parameters such as choice of association coefficient using the Kirby data set (see Canter, Hughes and Kirby, 1998). In this analysis, the choice of association coefficient is equally or even more important than the dimensionality of the solution within a coefficient. Specifically, the role of the *d* cell in calculating similarity is critical, with multiplicative roles (in Pearson's phi and Yule's Q) strongly distinguished against the additive role (in Russell and Rao) or absence (in Jaccard's). Therefore there are key decisions to be made by the researcher other than just the dimensionality of the solution.

To recap, IP research can account for error by careful consideration of how data are created (Canter and Alison, 2004). Though IP researchers could still potentially use techniques such as factor analysis with FT, there are further beneficial characteristics of MDS program suites such as LiFA to help recover structure. These additional advantages include 'gap analysis' of plots, gentleness in data handling and plot smoothing through regional interpretation.

*Finding Gaps, Being Gentle and Smoothing the Bumps*

In MDS plots there are 'gaps' in the space where there are no variables. Under the Continuity Principle of Borg and Shye (1995), the variables show where questions were asked and the 'gaps' are not actually empty but places where questions were *not* asked. For example, if there are large gaps in the 'Intimacy' region of the plot then maybe the researcher or information gatherer did not ask many questions about how (pseudo) Intimacy was expressed during the offence. Or maybe it was expressed but wasn't recorded or conceptualised, such as a burglar who spends extra time in the bedroom or looking at family photos in residential break-ins. The Continuity Principle is useful because it allows the researcher to identify where the interpretation may be inaccurate due to fewer 'known' reference points (e.g. variables on the plot). It is also useful in pursuit of cumulative knowledge since subsequent research can create designs that will create variables that may fit the gaps. This is harder with techniques such as factor analysis which relentlessly boils the meat off the bones of data but without indicating what seasonings might need to be added before serving.

For example, Canter *et al.* (2003) use data on serial murder from the 'Missen Corpus' to challenge successfully the FBI notion that there is a distinct 'Organised/Disorganised' typology of murderers (e.g. Ressler *et al.*, 1986). Though cautious about then using the SSA-I plot to go snooping for structure *post hoc*, they suggest tentatively that a better conceptualisation instead is a circumplex facet of 'Offender-

Victim Interaction'. Interestingly, the plot is dense with data points in the 'Mutilation' and 'Sexual Control' regions of the tentative circumplex. By contrast, 'Plunder' and 'Execution' are relatively sparsely populated – there are large gaps. This begs the question of what types of information are missing in this particular sampling of the Missen Corpus. Based on the tentative circumplex, what variables could be proposed in a fully faceted design to test the tentative circumplex by 'filling the gaps' and making the findings more robust – perhaps finding structure in a second modulating facet. In this way, producing MDS plots is not the end of the story but potentially the opening of a new chapter towards cumulative knowledge.

Another beneficial feature of such MDS programs as HUDAP is that they can be quite 'gentle' in the way they deal with data and transform them into plots – much more so than factor analysis. For example, the transformation from input associations into output plot uses the ranked order of input values rather than the absolute values (hence '*non-metric* MDS') and some transformations allow the untying of any tied values in the input. The benefits are that systematic error and outliers in the data are less influential and the gentle transformations make the plot lower in dimensionality. This in turn means low (e.g. two- or three-) dimensional representations allow structure to be detected more easily than higher dimensional representations. But as Coombs (1964, p. 5) observes, 'we buy information with assumptions'. Potentially then information is lost by avoiding assumptions like 'input data are meaningfully measured as interval' and 'tied input values are identical therefore must remain tied'.

It turns out that these assumptions are actually unnecessary and would buy little information despite the considerable cost. Young (1970) shows it is easily possible in *non-metric* MDS to 'back translate' from representation into the original input data with little loss of the original information. In other words, the assumption that the input data have systematically spaced intervals in them is unnecessary. Considering the noisy information sources often found in IP, this seems also a highly reasonable step towards a good representation. Furthermore, the association coefficients often used with these noisy information sources do not have the same precision and assumptions that would benefit from preserving ties in input data. Stricter (i.e. less 'gentle') transformations would only be appropriate for more controlled situations such as with sensory evaluation data of similarity judgements between colours, or survey data from taken representative samples correlated with Pearson's $r$.

But perhaps the most important point way that MDS accounts for error is the way the plot is interpreted. Regional interpretation in MDS plots (explored in question three) further reduces the impact of error. This is because variables positioned in the 'wrong place' in the plot – maybe they should be 'up a bit' or 'over to the left' – are still usually found in the same region, assuming Contiguity holds in the research. This power of regional interpretation to smooth out the bumps in the plot also holds when error in variable positioning is introduced by the program itself, such as by local minima where the program gets stuck in a computational rut while trying to represent the data.

Lee and Canter (1999) explore how three different substantive IP data sets in SSA1 produced plots with varying alienation values and output plots depending on different starting dimensionalities in the program. (The use of substantive data and the starting dimensionality are missing from Monte Carlo studies.) For example, Lee and Canter found that when creating a two dimensional representation of the Kirby data set (see Canter, Hughes and Kirby, 1998), if SSA1 was instructed to start at one dimension then finish at two, the alienation in two dimensions was 0.275; but if SSA-I started *and finished* in two dimensions then the alienation in two dimensions was 0.223. Lee and Canter termed this phenomenon termed 'dimensional slurring'. But despite these changes in alienation and changes in how the plot actually looked due to dimensional slurring, the regional interpretation of the different plots was still the same. Therefore regional interpretation could cope with dimensional slurring in SSA-I and shows how FT in IP can account for error.

## How Can you be Sure this Research is Valid and not an Artefact?

Probability values with statistical tests are intended to guide the researcher draw valid conclusions, though objections have been raised objected on the grounds of their questionable role in the scientific process (e.g. Guttman, 1977; Schmidt, 1996). Furthermore there is frequent misunderstanding – even in some introductory psychology texts – on the exact meaning of the probability value for the null hypothesis (Dracup, 1995). To be specific there is an ongoing myth that the probability value is the 'chance that the effect happened at random', which Booth (1994) forcefully stated was highly misleading. Nevertheless the two approaches of hypothesis deduction by statistical significance and structural hypothesis by faceted research have important other similarities. I believe exploring these similarities can show the validity of faceted research by building on how they showing validity in statistical significance testing when used appropriately.

### *Connecting Statistical Significance and Faceted Research*

According to Fisher's original ideas, 'statistical significance' actually meant one of two things: that the sample taken from the population was extremely rare or that the theory of random distributions did not hold for this sample. What it did *not* mean was the independent variable 'caused' the change in the dependent variable; however, if all other external influences were controlled such as respondent fatigue then the researcher would be justified in concluding there was an experimental effect (Macdonald, 1997). Macdonald states: 'All statistical tests do is to provide a researcher with an answer to the skeptical challenge that some particular effect could have resulted from sampling variation'. (Macdonald, 1997, p. 334). This is also an important challenge in faceted research.

I believe the most important similarity between statistical significance testing and faceted research however is the conditional nature of the test. The acceptance or rejection of the null hypothesis using probability depends entirely upon the true state of the data, as theorised by Neyman and Pearson as an alternative to the null hypothesis (Macdonald, 1997). In other words, it is the probability that the test statistic will lead to the rejection of the null hypothesis when in fact the null hypothesis is true – the Type I Error or False Positive. At the same time, the risk of false negative when the null hypothesis actually is false but the sample leads the researcher to accept the null hypothesis – the Type II Error or False Negative. Figure 10.3 summarises the interplay between the reality of the population and the conclusion drawn from the sample in statistical hypothesis testing.

By analogy with faceted research, what is under investigation is the structural hypothesis about the population of some domain. The decision in faceted research is whether or not it is possible to conduct a regional interpretation. For example, Youngs (2006) proposes that young offenders are motivated by three different incentives while committing criminal actions. Youngs decides that regional interpretation in the plot is possible and therefore concludes the structural hypothesis is true based on these data. Therefore the analogous table for faceted research is in Figure 10.4.

| | | Population | |
|---|---|---|---|
| | | **Null Hypothesis False** | **Null Hypothesis True** |
| **Decision based on test statistic** | **Reject Null Hypothesis** | True Positive (Power) | False Positive (Type I Error) |
| | **Accept Null Hypothesis** | False Negative (Type II Error) | True Negative |

**Figure 10.3 Interplay between population and decision based on test statistic from sample in statistical hypothesis testing**

| | | Domain | |
|---|---|---|---|
| | | **Structural Hypothesis True** | **Structural Hypothesis False** |
| **Decision based on representation** | **Regional interpretation possible** | Contiguous Positive (Power) | False Positive (Type I Error) |
| | **Regional interpretation not possible** | False Negative (Type II Error) | Contiguous Negative |

**Figure 10.4 Interplay between domain and decision that regional interpretation is possible based on sample in faceted research**

This figure also shows a more formal link between structure and representation, introduced previously: Contiguity. Evaluating the link can answer the question about the validity of the research.

*Linking Structure and Representation*

Contiguity suggests that if variables are taken from the same facet then they will be statistically related (Foa, 1958), indicating a logical flow from conceptual closeness to statistical closeness. This means such that variables which are conceptually close and taken from the same facet will be statistically related (i.e. being from the same facet is sufficient for being statistically related) under Contiguity. By way of counter-example, Canter *et al.* (2004) propose that if the FBI typology of 'Organised' and 'Disorganised' criminal was conceptually meaningful then sets of variables representing 'Organised' and 'Disorganised' murderers should be highly statistically related. Canter *et al.* find a *lack* of statistical relation among such variables and on this basis conclude that the typology is not useful.

In a perfect MDS data representation with a reliable real world source and sound methodology and statistics, such conclusions would be immediately obvious to the researcher that the original structural hypotheses were accurate because the decision would be 'regional interpretation is possible'. But as previously shown in answer to question four, there are many influences making IP research much more complicated than this and the representations are far from perfect. (Consider the effects of coefficient, dimensionality, data noise, computational error, etc.) Therefore there are extra conditions to be considered before a Contiguous Positive can be concluded.

Additionally, it is fallacious to invent facets *post hoc* for sets of variables in a regional interpretation even if they are statistically related and close in a representation (in practical terms, this would like look coding data into variables and then analysing the variables in MDS *without* a thorough review of cumulative knowledge in the literature and some clear structural hypotheses in a faceted design). Statistical closeness is necessary but not sufficient for conceptual closeness. The logical flow is the other way around: begin first with structural hypotheses based on theory and then go to faceted design and then to regional interpretation in a representation. This is a key condition towards sufficiency in faceted research with primary *ad hoc* data: the researcher must have a clear faceted design specified in advance of the data analysis to ensure conceptual closeness comes from statistical closeness.

This minimises the risk of Type I Error where the researcher does not create meaningful structural hypotheses or inadequately conceptualises the domain but still declares meaning in the plot by making a regional interpretations. This means that even greater caution is required when working with secondary data, where decisions about conceptual inclusion and exclusion have not been made by the researcher. Although secondary data sources are extremely useful, transparency is clearly required to keep the integrity of the research by indicating where decisions where taken by others that may influence the current research.

To minimise the chance of Type II Error – where the researcher fails to recover the underlying structure – the representation must be adequate to show the true structure. For example a structural hypothesis of a (three-dimensional) cylindrex requires three dimensions in the representation (e.g. Porter and Alison, 2004). But this principle introduces the dilemma that usually the variance retained in a plot can be increased, and the chance of finding structure assuming Contiguity exists, by increasing the number of dimensions. So attempts to minimise Type II Error by tactics such as using dimensionality greater than necessary could suggest there is structure that the researcher has missed. By the principle of parsimony the least number of dimensions should be used, as should the least number of restrictive assumptions. If the representation is 'over-specified' in any way for the structure recovered then it begs the question: could there be something missing in the regional interpretation? Without data snooping and risking Type I Error, is there meaning in another projection or in a rotation of the MDS plot that could be followed up or built upon by another researcher?

Bringing this all together, finding a Contiguous Positive is as much about eliminating the chance of decisional errors and critically assessing how data are created as it is about a thorough literature review and a sound faceted design. For these reasons – which must be candidly presented with the transparency that FT can allow – the conclusion of a Contiguous Positive is essentially a statement that the research cannot be artefactual and that the results are valid.

## Conclusion

I believe Guttman's critique of the way theory and methodology are usually separated out is still relevant today. Perhaps is it even more relevant given the invitations to 'fire and forget' in statistics packages that remove explicit researcher decision making, such as by offering default options and make it easy to repeat analyses until the right result appears – 'gerrymandering the data' as Loevinger put it (cited by Coombs, 1964). Researcher decisions are more open to challenge when using Guttman's solution to the problem, namely using FT. Consequently the marriage of FT and IP – initiated by Professor Canter and now enthusiastically taken up by others – means that researchers find they too are frequently challenged on methodology by those both new and familiar with FT. I have tried to explore from my perspective some of those most frequent questions. I don't believe the integrity of IP using FT has so far been undermined by such questions. So my final thought is that if even these answers do not satisfy questioners then I suggest to them: why not just try FT and answer the questions for themselves!

**References**


Ackroyd, S. and Hughes, J. (1992). *Data Collection in Context* (2nd edition). London: Longman.

Booth, D. (1994). 'Tricky stats' no. 2. *The Psychologist*, 7, 533.

Borg, I. and Lingoes, J.C. (1987). *Multidimensional Similarity Structure Analysis*. New York: Springer-Verlag.

Borg, I. and Shye, S. (1995). *Facet Theory: Form and Content*. Newbury Park, CA: Sage.

Brown, J. (1985). An introduction to the use of facet theory, in *Facet Theory: Approaches to Social Research*, edited by D.V. Canter. New York: Springer-Verlag.

Canter, D.V. (1983). The potential of facet theory for applied social psychology. *Quality and Quantity*, 17, 35–67.

Canter, D.V. (1994). *Criminal Shadows*. London: Harper Collins.

Canter, D.V. (2004a). A partial order scalogram analysis of criminal network structures. *Behaviormetrika*, 31, 1–21.

Canter, D.V. (2004b). Offender profiling and investigative psychology. *Journal of Investigative Psychology and Offender Profiling*, 1, 1–15. Retrieved 15th January 2006 from <http://www3.interscience.wiley.com/cgi-bin/fulltext/106599596/PDFSTART>.

Canter, D. and Alison, L.J. (2003). Converting evidence into data: the use of law enforcement archives as unobtrusive measurement. *The Qualitative Report*, 8, 151–176. Retrieved 15th January 2006 from <http://www.nova.edu/ssss/QR/QR8-2/canter.pdf>.

Canter, D.V. and Ioannou, M. (2004). Criminals' emotional experiences during crimes. *International Journal of Forensic Psychology*, 1, 71–81.

Canter, D.V. and Fritzon, K. (1998). Differentiating arsonists: a model of firesetting actions and characteristics. *Legal and Criminological Psychology*, 3, 73–96.

Canter, D.V. and Heritage, R. (1990). A multivariate model of sexual offences behaviour: developments in 'offender profiling'. *Journal of Forensic Psychiatry*, 1, 185–212.

Canter, D.V., Hughes, D.T. and Kirby, S. (1998). Paedophilia: criminality, pathology or both? *Journal of Forensic Psychiatry*, 9, 532–555.

Canter, D.V, Alison, L.J., Alison, E. and Wentink, N. (2004). The organized/disorganized typology of serial murder: myth or model? *Psychology, Public Policy, and Law*, 10, 293–320.

Cliff, N. (1973). Scaling. *Annual Review of Psychology*, 24, 473–506.

Coombs, C.H. (1964). *A Theory of Data*. New York: Wiley.

Coxon, A.P.M. (1982). *The User's Guide to Multidimensional Scaling*. London: Heinemann.

Donald, I. (1995). Facet theory: designing research domains, in *Research Methods in Psychology*, edited by G.M. Breakwell, S. Hammond and C. Fife-Schaw. London: Sage.

Dracup, C. (1995). Hypothesis testing – what it really is. *The Psychologist*, 8, 359–362.

Foa, U. (1958). The contiguity principle in the structure of interpersonal relations. *Human Relations*, 11, 229–238.

Foa, U. (1965). New developments in facet design and analysis. *Psychological Review*, 72, 262–274.

Guttman, L. (1967). The development of nonmetric space analysis: a letter to Professor John Ross. *Multivariate Behavioral Research*, 2, 71–82.

Guttman, L. (1968). A general nonmetric technique for finding the smallest coordinate space for a configuration of points. *Psychometrika*, 33, 469–506.

Guttman, L. (1977). What is not what in statistics. *The Statistician*, 26, 81–107.

Guttman, L. (1978), Cyril Burt and the Careless Star Worshippers. Reprinted in Levy, S. (1994). *Louis Guttman on Theory and Methodology*. Aldershot: Ashgate.

Klahr, D. (1969). A Monte Carlo investigation of the statistical significance of Kruskal's nonmetric scaling procedure. *Psychometrika*, 34, 319–330.

Kruskal, J.B. (1964). Multidimensional scaling by optimizing goodness of fit to a nonmetric hypothesis. *Psychometrika*, 29, 1–27.

Last, S.K. and Fritzon, K. (2005). Investigating the nature of expressiveness in stranger, acquaintance and intrafamilial homicides. *Journal of Investigative Psychology and Offender Profiling*, 2, 179–193.

Lee, J. (1998). *Structure and Representation of Criminal Actions*. University of Liverpool: Unpublished PhD Thesis.

Lee, J. and Canter, D. (2004). The impact of starting dimensionality on alienation in SSA1 with substantive data. Internal report; IRCIP.

Lee, J. and Canter, D. (1999). The impact of association coefficient, dimensionality and monotonicity on SSA1 with substantive data. Internal report; IRCIP.

Lee, R.M. (2000). *Unobtrusive Methods in Social Research*. Buckingham: Open University Press.

Lingoes, J.C. (1968a). The multivariate analysis of qualitative data. *Multivariate Behavioral Research*, 3, 61–94.

Lingoes, J.C. (1973). *The Guttman-Lingoes Nonmetric Program Series*. Ann Arbor, MI: Mathesis.

Lingoes, J.C. (1977b). Identifying regions in the space for interpretation, in *Geometric Representations of Relational Data: Readings in Multidimensional Scaling*, edited by J.C. Lingoes. Ann Arbor, MI: Mathesis.

Macdonald, R.R. (1997). On statistical testing in psychology. *British Journal of Psychology*, 88, 333–347.

Porter, L.E. and Alison, L.J. (2004). Behavioural coherence in violent group activity: an interpersonal model of sexually violent gang behaviour. *Aggressive Behavior*, 30, 449–468.

Ressler, R.K., Burgess, A.W., Hartman, C.R., Douglas, J.E. and McCormack, A. (1986). Murderers who rape and mutilate. *Journal of Interpersonal Violence*, 1, 273–287.

Russell, J.A. (1997). How shall an emotion be called? in *Circumplex Models of Personality and Emotions*, edited by R. Plutchik and H.R. Conte. Washington, DC: American Psychological Association.

Schmidt, F. (1996). Statistical significance testing and cumulative knowledge in psychology: implications for the training of researchers. *Psychological Methods*, 1(2).

Shye, S. (1991). *Faceted Smallest Space Analysis (FSSA) version 3.01*. Jerusalem: Israel Institute of Applied Social Research.

Shye, S. and Elizur, D. (1994). *An introduction to Facet Theory*. Newbury Park, CA: Sage.

Spence, I. (1972). A Monte Carlo evaluation of three nonmetric multidimensional scaling algorithms. *Psychometrika*, 37, 461–486.

Stenson, H.H. and Knoll, R.L. (1969). Goodness of fit for random rankings in Kruskal's nonmetric scaling procedure. *Psychological Bulletin*, 71, 122–126.

Wagenaar, W.A. and Padmos, P. (1971). Quantitative interpretations of stress in Kruskal's multidimensional scaling technique. *British Journal of Mathematical and Statistical Psychology*, 24, 101–110.

Young, F.W. (1970). Nonmetric multidimensional scaling: recovery of metric information. *Psychometrika*, 35, 455–473.

Youngs, D.E. (2006). How does crime pay? The differentiation of criminal specialisms by fundamental incentive. *Journal of Investigative Psychology and Offender Profiling*, 3, 1–19. Retrieved 15th January 2006 from <http://www3.interscience.wiley.com/cgi-bin/fulltext/112278387/PDFSTART>.

# SECTION 3
# IP: A Problem-solving Discipline

# Chapter 11
# Offenders' Spatial Behaviour and Geographical Offender Profiling

Laura Hammond and Donna Youngs

## Editor's Introduction

In this chapter, Laura Hammond and I provide an overview based on a couple of books David Canter and I put together, of what has become a highly active area of Investigative Psychology: Geographical Offender Profiling (see Canter and Youngs, 2008a, 2008b). It is an area of IP that has particular applied potential, leading to the development of software systems to support the decisions of investigators and law enforcement analysts about where to search for a perpetrator (see Canter's commentary on the debate about the utility of such systems in Section 4).

David Canter's approach to understanding offender spatial behaviour has always been psychological, including a particular emphasis on the environmental psychological. This has distinguished him from many in the area who have privileged a geometric perspective on offence location patterns or general criminological frameworks such as routine activities or rational choice 'theories' that describe some of the relevant issues but do not explain offenders' specific or particular spatial choices. It is an emphasis that has been tremendously fruitful. It is giving rise to current work from Canter's team on the individual variations in offender spatial behaviour and the processes that may underpin these (Canter and Youngs, 2009; Canter et al., 2012).

## Historical Roots of Research into the Spatial Patterning of Crime

The foundations of procedures for making inferences as to the possible areas in which police should search for an offender based on the locations of their crimes come from studies of criminal spatial behaviour that can be traced back over a century and a half. Early criminological works, such as those of Guerry (1833) and Quetelet (1942), explored the geographical distributions of crimes and criminals at an aggregate level. They demonstrated that offenders tended to live in distinct areas of a city and did not travel very far to commit their crimes. The most graphic early description of this process was in the writings of Mayhew (1861) in which he described the areas in which there was a high concentration of criminals as 'Rookeries'. These criminal areas were located close to places that offered attractive opportunities for crime. For example, the St Giles rookery was situated between the City of London boundary and Oxford Street, which was then, as now, one of the major shopping streets in the capital. From the Rookery, less than half a mile away, thieves could commit crimes in Oxford Street and never be too far from the sanctuary of home (Canter and Youngs, 2008a).

In the early part of the 20th century sociologists expanded the study of the spatial distribution of crime, showing that crimes, and criminals, will be more prevalent in some areas of a city than others. For example, White (1932) found that the frequencies of offender residences and crime locations were higher in some parts of the city of Indianapolis than others. Further, he illustrated that criminals typically travelled less than two miles to commit their offences, although some variations across offence categories were noted. Shaw and McKay (1942), part of the 'Chicago School' of researchers, also examined crime rates across various parts of the city, proposing that the organisational geometry of cities generates spatial patterns in criminal behaviour.

In the 60s and 70s studies emerged that explored directly how people imagined and interacted with their surroundings, examining the ways in which individuals understood the geography of their cities. One of the most important works in this area was that of Lynch (1960), who demonstrated extensively that a person's experience of a city relates to how they perceive and remember it. Building upon Lynch's findings, researchers went on to examine in more depth the mental representations that individuals have of their environs. These 'schemata', it was proposed, were governed by knowledge of an area or region, and would therefore be unique to each individual, generated by their own personal experiences, with these internal representations determining where that person did what. This more in-depth understanding of the ways in which people make sense of, and relate to, their surroundings led to the development of the concept of 'Mental Maps' (Canter, 1977); the internal conceptualisations that people have of the world around them.

Following his contribution to the police investigation of a series of rapes and murders in the 1980s, in which he predicted the home location of the perpetrator on the basis of the geographical locations of the offences, Professor Canter began to examine the spatial behaviour of the individual offender. This earliest geographical offender profiling work (Canter and Larkin, 1993; Canter and Gregory, 1994) drew on basic psychological processes including earlier ideas from environmental psychology. While earlier research had explored aggregate patterns in the geographical distribution of crime, these studies began to map out the spatial behaviour and decisions of the individual offender to explore the offender's selection of offence locations.

## The Origins of Geographical Offender Profiling

In the mid-1980s scientists assisting police investigations (Canter, 1994; Canter, 2004; Kind, 1999; Rossmo, 1995) realised that they could estimate where an offender was likely to be based from an analysis of the geographical locations of that individual's crimes (Canter and Youngs, 2008a).

Kind (1987) was probably the first person to recognise the investigative potential of geographical analysis of crime locations. In 1980 he produced a report on the locations of the crimes attributed to 'The Yorkshire Ripper' who, over a five year period starting in July 1975, in the North of England, had murdered 13 women. As an ex-RAF navigator (Kind, 1999) saw the task of locating the offender as a navigational task, likening the offence locations to fuel depots, with the challenge of discovering the optimal location of an aircraft's base by calculating the 'centre of gravity' of the crime locations. This proved reasonably accurate in determining where the convicted offender, Sutcliffe, was eventually found to live. Sutcliffe was arrested before the report could be acted upon, so Kind's discovery lay dormant until Canter rediscovered it independently five years later (Canter, 2004; reported in Canter and Youngs, 2008a).

In the late 1980s, Canter (2004) was asked to provide advice to the police investigation into the crimes of the 'Railway Rapist', John Duffy. A series of violent sexual assaults had occurred throughout the west of London, all committed close to railway lines (hence the moniker), which had eventually culminated in three murders. Using his knowledge of environmental psychology and the ways in which people interact with the environment around them, and drawing on the ideas presented by those such as Kind (1987), Canter made recommendations as to the ways in which the police might focus their resources and where they may wish to concentrate their investigative efforts. The value of his ideas in solving the case, and their accuracy when related to the individual who was convicted of committing these crimes, laid the foundations for the development of the discipline that Canter later named 'Investigative Psychology'. One of the core strands of this approach is the spatial analysis and geographical offender profiling of serial crime.

## An Emerging Sub-discipline within Investigative Psychology

The early work of those such as Kind (1987), Canter (1995) and Canter and Larkin (1993) served to show that police data could be used to test systematic hypotheses, even on something as fundamental as where a crime has occurred (Canter, 2004). A body of research began to emerge which explored directly statistical regularities in offenders' travel patterns and the distributions of their offences. Empirical findings on consistencies in spatial aspects of criminal activity, such as the distances between home and offence locations and characteristic ranges of offending, led to the recognition that, under some circumstances, using relatively simple geometrical calculations a criminal's base could be inferred from their crime sites with a useful degree of accuracy (Canter and Youngs, 2008a).

This process of indicating the possible area in which police should search for an offender eventually became known as 'Geographical Profiling' (Canter, 2004), or in North America – 'Geographic Profiling' (Rossmo, 1995). Geographical profiling is, in essence, concerned with the operational utility of spatial measures of crime. It involves making inferences as to aspects of the offender, usually where they are likely to reside and in which location(s) they are most likely to operate, on the basis of the spatial distribution of crime series.

Whilst published accounts of such predictions date back to the 1970s and 1980s and the work of those such as Kind (1987), Newton and Swoope (1987), Newton and Newton (1989), and Canter (as discussed in Canter, 1995), the early 1990s marked the emergence of the field of geographical profiling as we now know it, with the advent of computerised geographical profiling systems (cf. Canter and Gregory, 1994) allowing such predictions to become more systematic and sophisticated (Bennell and Corey, 2007).

A variety of geographical profiling systems are becoming increasingly commonplace within the investigative domain. They are based upon published accounts and models of criminal spatial behaviour, and apply geometric functions derived from such findings to crime scene locations in order to prioritise the locations at which an offender may have a base (Canter and Hammond, 2007).

The works of Canter et al. (2012), Canter, Coffey, Huntley and Missen (2000), Canter and Hammond (2006) and Canter and Youngs (2008c) provide detailed descriptions of geographical profiling systems and the fundamental characteristics of their operation, and Paulsen (2006; 2007) compares the main systems that are currently available.

Since the early 1990s a growing body of research into the geography of crime and geographical profiling has explored where offenders live, where they carry out their crimes, and the relationships between these locations. Some of these studies have helped in the identification of principles that are being drawn on for more and more police investigations worldwide (Canter and Youngs, 2008a).

In their discussion of the development of progression of geographical offender profiling Canter and Youngs (2008a; 2008b) discuss how early works, such as those detailed above, have generated what is now a recognisable, scientific field; this discipline – the study of criminal spatial behaviour and geographical offender profiling – they propose consists of three central components:

Studies of criminal spatial behaviour – basic research
Development of decision support tools that incorporate research findings
Explorations of how such tools may help police investigations

Each of these is considered in more detail over the course of this chapter.

## Key Components of Field of Geographical Offender Profiling

### *A. Studies of Criminal Spatial Behaviour*

Most crime has a distinct geographical location, as well as a number of behavioural and related psychological characteristics. Therefore, as Canter and Youngs (2008a) observe; the process of studying the interplay of offence actions and locations is an interesting route into understanding the psychology of crime. Canter (2004) suggests that the secret of geographical profiling, the essence of the approach that makes it stand apart from other statistical procedures, is to consider beyond the dots on the map, just the locations of the crimes in space, and to understand how and why they relate to the perceptual and psychological processes of the offender.

There are two distinct qualities of criminal spatial behaviour that make the inference of an offender's home location possible from examination of where the crimes are committed. One is the common finding that the assumed journey from a base to a crime location, rather than being a lengthy one to an alternative city or locality, is often very short. This was well illustrated in a detailed study of young criminals in Philadelphia, drawn from a 10% sample of police records for 1960 by Turner (1969). The results of this study demonstrated that offenders often do not travel far to commit their crimes. He reports that three quarters of offences took place within one mile of the juvenile's place of residence. Although Turner does not seem to be aware of the practical implications of his results, his study is the starting point for a more systematic and scientific contribution to criminal investigations. Such findings are the first step towards combining informal experience and academic scholarship into investigative support tools (Canter and Youngs, 2008a).

If we consider burglary, we can see a consistency in the average distance travelled from home to crime across many different places and time periods (as discussed in detail by Canter and Youngs, 2008b). Mean distances reported in the literature vary from, for example; 0.89 kilometres on the small island of Barbados to 3.87 kilometres in a small town in Southern England, with many other studies from different places give mean distances that tend to fall within the same range. For other types of crime there are different ranges of distances, but as Gabor and Gottheil (1984) report for Ottawa, quite different crimes such as sex offences, robbery or even auto theft are often carried out within the same overall range of distances that are found for burglary. The only crimes that typically appear to be carried out at much longer distances from home are serial murders and serial stranger rapes. Canter et al. (2000) report a mean of 46 kilometres for US serial killers, for example. Similarly, Warren et al. (1998) give a mean of 23 kilometres for US serial rapists.

The discovery and rediscovery over the years, that many offenders often do not travel far to commit their crimes can form the basis of a decision support tool for investigators, because, if for example, 75% of offenders are found to travel less than 2 kilometres to commit their crimes, then it must be the case that 3 out of 4 actual offenders will travel less than 2 kilometres. This is not a perfect prediction but it gives an investigator some framework within which to evaluate possible suspects. It suggests, for example, that all else being equal suspects who live less than 2 kilometres from the crime scene should be given higher priority in the follow up investigation (Canter and Youngs, 2008a).

Beyond average home-crime distances, researchers have explored the distributions of the frequency of different offenders' distances travelled to offend. This distribution typically follows a curve in which the rate of change in frequencies is not constant. As Turner (1969), describing the frequency of crimes against distance from home, puts it; 'the proportion wanes with distance'. Such a shape to the distribution of journeys to crime has been repeatedly found in many subsequent studies (e.g. Canter et al., 2000; Rhodes and Conly, 1981; Van Koppen and Jansen, 1998). The further away a crime is from home, the greater the distance has to be for a similar reduction in frequency. This rapid drop-off in frequencies is usually referred to as a 'decay' in the frequencies, and the shape of any mathematical formula that describes this curve is known as a decay function.

'Distance decay' is a universal pattern, observed in varied non-criminal spatial behaviour, whether shopping trips, recreational journeys as well as offenders seeking out potential crime locations. The locations for all these tend to be disproportionally close to home [Le Comber et al., 2006]. An aggregate concept, distance decay essentially captures the tendency for people to take trips most frequently to places nearby and less and less frequently as distance from the origin of the trip increases (Golledge, 1987]) There is an inverse relationship between distance travelled to an activity and frequency of participation in that activity (Jackle, Brunn and Roseman, 1976), and this generates what Canter and Youngs (2008a) have termed the 'propinquity' of offenders' spatial activity.

As Rengert, Piquero and Jones (1999) observe, the relations between interaction, activity and distance are some of the most fundamental relationships in human geography. The decay in activity or event occurrence in relation to distance has been examined in relation to many different spatial and behavioural phenomena, including areas a far-ranging as; shopping trips (Gärling and Gärling, 1988; Hansen and Solgaard, 2006); international travel flows (McKercher and Lew, 2003); political voting (Gimpel, Karnes, Mctague and Pearson-Merkowitz, 2007); similarity in ecological communities (Soininen, McDonald and Hillbrand, 2007) and even dental health care (Bradley, Kirby and Taylor, 1978).

Research exploring the home to crime distances of offenders has unsurprisingly supported the notion of distance decay in criminal journeys (Santilla et al., 2008), showing that aggregate distributions of these distances can by characterised by a 'distance decay function' (Turner, 1969). Essentially, as the distance from an offender's home or base increases, the likelihood and frequency of their offending decreases (Canter et al., 2000; Phillips, 1980; Rhodes and Conly, 1991; Rengert et al., 1999). Whilst some variation in the degree of distance decay exhibited by different offending sub-sets has been shown (Van Koppen and De Keijser, 1997), the distance decay function does fit all crime types, with very few exceptions (Phillips, 1980). Evidence for this pattern has been found over a variety of cultures and situations (Capone and Nichols, 1976; Phillips, 1980; Rhodes and Conley, 1991; Turner, 1968; Van Koppen and De Keijser, 1997).

The significance of the decay function for geographical profiling is that it implies that a simple averaging of the distances between offences, i.e. calculating their 'centre of gravity', or in other words the location that is the average minimum distance from all of the crime locations, will give too much emphasis to those offences committed at longer distances. The decay function leads to the hypothesis that the locations nearer a crime should be given more weight than those further away (Canter and

Youngs, 2008b). Some researchers have consequently begun to explore exactly what mathematical function may best characterise the decay in frequencies of distances from home to crimes (e.g., Canter et al., 2000; Canter and Hammond, 2006).

A second important aspect of criminal spatial behaviour that has notable implications for geographical profiling strategies is the possibility that offenders will often have a base within the area circumscribed by their crimes (Canter and Larkin, 1993). This has been shown to be quite a distinct from the shortness of the distance between home and crime (Canter et al, 2000). Indeed, the finding that criminals tend to operate over a particular size of area, having a particular 'criminal range' (Canter and Gregory, 1994) helped to broaden the whole perspective beyond just those offenders who travel small distances. This, as Canter and Youngs (2008b) observe, opened the way to considering the patterns of offending in relation to the home rather than simply focusing on offenders whose base is close to the crime.

Research studies have established that for many offenders the home is located within the area of their criminal activity (e.g. Canter and Larkin, 1993; Canter and Gregory, 1994), with, in some instances, a criminal's offences literally surrounding their residence (Bennell and Corey, 2007). As Canter and Gregory (1994) discuss, this provides a starting point for utilising the crime sites in an offence series to make predictions about where the home of the perpetrator of those offences may be located.

These spatial patterns of offending, notably the significance of the home and the characteristic range of offending, led to the recognition that under some circumstances the offender›s base could be inferred with a useful degree of accuracy from relatively simple geometrical calculations (Canter, 2008). This encouraged the development of software systems that allowed precise predictions to be made, and tested, applying various geometrical models to the distributions of crimes (Canter, 2004).

One suggestion is that offenders spatial behaviour is influenced by general mental schemata (Bartlett, 1930) of how offenders conceptualise their environment. These internal representations, as observed previously, are often referred to as 'mental maps' (cf. Canter, 1977), and have been explored extensively by environmental psychologists such as Ladd (1970) using the device of getting people to draw a sketch map of an area. As Down and Stea (1977) and many others have shown, building on the seminal work by Lynch (1960), these mental representations do differ from person to person, relating closely to their actual experience of particular environments.

According to Canter (1977), however, this is only one aspect of how people come to understand and make sense of places. He emphasised that there are two interacting psychological processes that contribute to a person's internal model of his/her surroundings. One is the process of encoding the information. This leads to various forms of distortion in the mental image. The second is how people make use of their surroundings.

The mental image or 'map', in Canter's opinion, is derived from the interaction between the active storing of information and the passive availability of environmental cues. The mental image that is formed influences what a person thinks is possible and where that possibility lies. This is a developing, cyclical process. The direct interaction with the surroundings in turn shapes the person's conceptualisations. Where a person does various things is consequently partly a product of what that person knows to be possible and where. Their experience shapes what they know to be possible. This will be a dynamic process that takes the offender beyond their 'routine activities' as they get to explore the possibilities for crime. It is out of these dynamic processes that the offender selects opportunities for crime (Canter and Youngs, 2008a).

The direct exploration of offenders' 'Mental Maps' (Canter and Hodge, 2000) as a way of predicting and understanding the spatial distribution of their activities has become a distinct research focus (see Canter and Youngs, 2009). Canter and Shalev (2000) and Canter and Hodge (2000) explored the mental representations people have of their surroundings, following up key studies conducted with non-criminal populations (Canter, 1977; Downs and Stea, 1977). They studied the strategies offenders use for choosing crime locations by asking them to draw 'mental maps' of their offence areas. Their findings, they proposed, were illustrative of the mixture of locational decision processes on which offenders draw, ranging from impulsive, opportunistic strategies to those that are carefully planned.

Canter's (1977) model, with its greater emphasis on the person's internal representations, gives more weight to where the people live, as this is likely to be at the core of their cognitive representation of the places they know and are familiar with. Some support for this stress on 'domocentricity' can be derived from the finding, discussed previously, that in many cases the offender's home or base is within the geographical distribution of his offences (Canter and Youngs, 2008b).

Canter and Gregory (1994) proposed that the simplest way to define the area circumscribed by the crimes was to identify the two crimes furthest from each other and use the line joining them as the diameter of a circle. They then hypothesised that the offender's home would be within the circle so defined. They never implied that the circle was necessarily the most precise geometry for describing an offender's domain, just that it was the simplest and most direct way of indicating the area covering offenders' 'mental maps' of criminal opportunities.

This 'Circle Hypothesis' (Canter and Larkin, 1993; Canter and Gregory, 1994) enables offenders to be classified into one of two categories, based on the spatial relations between their home and crime locations; those offenders whose homes fall within their criminal range and are bounded by their offences are known as 'Marauders', as they maraud out from their base to the places where they commit their crimes. Offenders whose homes are not contained within the area defined by their crime sites are known as 'Commuters', as they commute outwards from their home region, travelling into a separate area to commit their offences (Canter and Larkin, 1993).

Various studies have supported the existence of these dichotomous offending styles, with the proportions of each varying for different criminal subsets. The reasons for such variations have not been explored, but as more studies emerge a clearer picture will become possible. However, even at lower proportions there are still enough offenders with bases within the areas of their crimes for this finding to provide a systematic basis for prioritising offenders, or the places to look for them. This assumption of 'domocentricity' helps to demarcate the areas to be searched in order to find an offender. As a consequence, the general principle of crimes being centred on the home of the offender has been at the heart of geographical profiling systems. Thus most of geographical decision support systems work on the assumption that the offender is operating within the area of his/her crimes.

*B. Decision Support Tools*

The findings that have emerged from various studies have been drawn upon to develop decision support systems, as discussed in Canter et al. (2000). These can be distinguished from 'expert' systems because they do not aim to give the investigator a direct answer of where to find the offender. Rather, their objective is to systematise the information available to the police in a way that facilitates detectives' understanding of the crimes and the patterns within them (Canter and Youngs, 2008b). This support can then be drawn upon and combined with the investigators' specialist and local knowledge to reach a decision about how to proceed.

Stages in the development of a decision support system. Canter and Youngs (2008b) outline the stages in the development of a decision support system (for a more detailed discussion see also; Canter et al., 2000; Canter and Larkin, 1994):

1. The first is the indication that an offender is likely to live within an area related to any given crime (Figure 11.1).

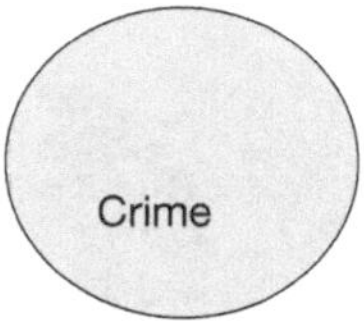


**Figure 11.1 An area around a crime indicating where the offender might live**

2. If there is more than one crime then it is possible to combine the areas around the crimes and give more weight to those areas that overlap (Figure 11.2).

**Figure 11.2 Two crimes with overlapping areas**

3. Adding further crimes can increase the detail in the distribution of probabilities of where the home/base may be. This pattern of probabilities can be developed further by adjusting for the distance from the crime, taking account of the frequent finding that there are likely to be fewer crimes further from the offender's home. This adjustment can take the form of a decay function so that the probabilities decrease more rapidly as the distances get further away.

   The third stage in the process is therefore to assume that the offender's home is within the area circumscribed by the crimes linked to him (Figure 11.3).

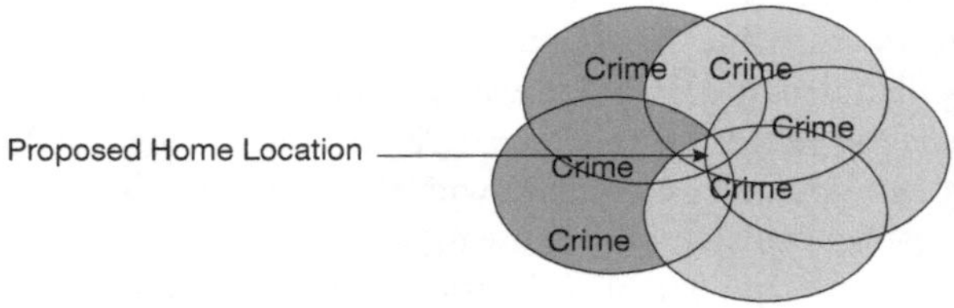


**Figure 11.3 An offender's home lying within the area circumscribed by his crimes**

4. The actual shape of the probability surface is then modified by the actual decay functions incorporated into the software (Figure 11.4)

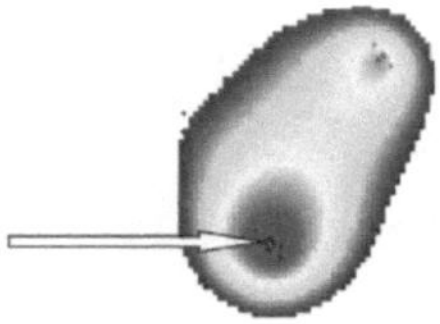

**Figure 11. 4 Probability surface, modified by decay function (area of highest probability is indicated by the arrow)**

*C. The Use of Geographical Offender Profiling Within the Investigative Context*

As Canter and Youngs (2008b) note in assessing the use and value of geographical profiling within the investigative domain, it is useful to consider the actions that law enforcement agencies can take as a result of geographical profiling analysis. The fictional idea that the computer gives a name and address so that all the police have to do is knock on a door, is of course very misleading, although there have been cases that get close to that, as discussed by Canter (2005). It is also important to emphasise that geographical profiling systems offer a probability surface, i.e. they indicate an area with different degrees of probability that the offender has some association with that area, not just a point with distances from it.

The probability of different locations being of significance provides a set of priorities that can be acted on in a number of different ways. The particular action will depend on the nature of the crimes and the circumstances under which they occur. Canter and Youngs (2008b) identify five main tactics that investigators may employ on the basis of a 'geographical profile':

> Surveillance – the high priority areas can become the focus of attention for overt or covert police observation, watching for offenders going to or returning from a crime.
>
> Arrest and Questioning – if there is clear evidence of who is likely to be involved, derived from geographical and other analyses, then suspects can be arrested and interviewed.
>
> TICs – geographical profiling principles can be used to identify other offences (that are 'Taken into Consideration' known as TICs) potentially committed by the same offender for consideration. These may be unsolved crimes identified on the basis of their relationship to the offender's home or linked by their proximity to the initial offence under investigation.
>
> Covert Development – the area of focus can be used as a basis for seeking out further information, for example, from local informants or house to house enquiries.
>
> Prevention or Disruption – geographical profiling can also serve to highlight those areas most at risk and possibly the sorts of criminals they are at risk from. This can therefore be drawn on for crime reduction and other forms of disruption of criminal activity.

Finally, an analysis that shows the geographical distribution of crimes and links that to the base of a known offender can strengthen the case presented in court. It is possible even that this information could be used by the defence if the defendant can demonstrate a lack of association or access to that area. But to date it has not been possible to identify any actual cases in which this strategy has been used.

## References


Bartlett, F. (1932). *Remembering: A Study in Experimental Social Psychology*. London: Cambridge University Press.

Bennell, C. and Corey, S. (2007). Geographic profiling of terrorist attacks, in *Criminal profiling: International Theory, Research and Practice*, edited by R.N. Kocsis. Tolowa, NJ: Humana Press.

Bradley, J.E., Kirby, A.M. and Taylor, P. (1978). Distance decay and dental decay: a study of dental health among primary school children in Newcastle upon Tyne. *Regional Studies*, 12, 529–540.

Canter, D. (1977). *The Psychology of Place*. London: The Architectural Press.

Canter, D. (1995). *Criminal Shadows*. London: HarperCollins.

Canter, D. (2004). *Mapping Murder*. London: Virgin Books.

Canter, D. (2008). Geographical profiling of criminals, in *Principles of Geographical Offender Profiling*, edited by D. Canter and D. Youngs. Aldershot: Ashgate.

Canter, D., Coffey, T., Huntley, M. and Missen, C. (2000). Predicting serial killers' home base using a decision support system. *Journal of Quantitative Criminology*, 16, 457–478.

Canter, D. and Gregory, A. (1994). Identifying the residential location of serial rapists. *Journal of the Forensic Science Society*, 34, 164–175.

Canter, D. and Hammond, L. (2006). A comparison of the efficacy of different decay functions in geographical profiling for a sample of U.S. serial killers. *Journal of Investigative Psychology and Offender Profiling*, 3, 91–103.

Canter, D. and Hammond, L. (2007). Prioritising burglars: comparing the effectiveness of geographical profiling methods. *Police, Practice and Research*, 8, 371–384.

Canter, D. and Hodge, S. (2000). Criminal's mental maps, in *Atlas of Crime*, edited by L.S. Turnball, E. Hallisey-Hendrix and B.D. Dent. Oryx Press; 187–191.

Canter, D. and Larkin, P. (1993). The environmental range of serial rapists, in *Criminal Detection and the Psychology of Crime*, edited by D. Canter and L. Alison. Aldershot: Dartmouth Ashgate.

Canter, D. and Shalev, K. (2008). Putting crime in its place: psychological process in crime site location, in *Principles of Geographical Offender Profiling*, edited by D. Canter and D. Youngs. Aldershot: Ashgate.

Canter, D. and Youngs, D. (eds) (2008a). *Principles of Geographical Offender Profiling*. Aldershot: Ashgate.

Canter, D. and Youngs, D. (eds) (2008b). *Applications of Geographical Offender Profiling*. Aldershot: Ashgate.

Canter, D. and Youngs, D. (2008c). iOPS: an interactive offender profiling system, in *Crime Mapping Case Studies*, edited by S. Chainey and I. Thompson. Wiley: Chichester.

Capone, D.L. and Nichols, W.W. (1976). An analysis of offender behaviour. *Proceedings of the American Geographer*, 7, 45–49.

Downs, R.M. and Stea, D. (1973). Cognitive maps and spatial behaviour: process and products, in *Image and Environment* (pp. 8–26), edited by R. Downs and D. Stea. Chicago: Aldine.

Gabor, T. and Gottheil, E. (1984). Offender characteristics and spatial mobility: an empirical study and some policy implications. *Criminology*, 26, 267–281.

Gärling, T. and Gärling, E. (1988). Distance minimisation in downtown pedestrian shopping. *Environment and Planning*, 20, 547–554.

Gimpel, J.G., Karnes, K.A., Mctague, J.M. and Pearson-Merkowitz, S. (2007). *Distance Decay in the Political Geography of Friends and Neighbors Voting*. Paper presented at the annual meeting of the Midwest Political Science Association; Chicago, Illinois (http://www.allacademic.com/meta/p199439_index.html).

Golledge, R.G. (1987). *Analytical Behavioural Geography*. London: Croom Helm.

Guerry, A.M. (1833). *Essai sur la Statistique Morale de la France*. Paris: Crochard.

Hansen, T. and Solgaard, H.S. (2006). Measuring the effect of distance on consumer patronage behaviour: a structural equation model and empirical results, in *New Perspectives on Retailing and Store Patronage Behavior: A Study of the Interface Between Retailers and Consumers*, edited by T. Hansen and H.S. Solgaard. International Studies in Entrepreneurship Discussion Paper Series, 4, 67–82.

Jackle, J.A., Brunn, S. and Roseman, C.C. (1976). *Human Spatial Behaviour: A Social Geography*. Prospect Heights, Il: Waveland Press.

Kind, S.S. (1987). Navigational ideas and the Yorkshire ripper Investigation. *Journal of Navigation*, 40, 385–393.

Kind, S. (1999). *The Sceptical Witness: Concerning the Scientific Investigation of a Crime Against a Human Background*. Harrogate: The Forensic Science.

Ladd, F.C. (1970). Black youths view their environment: neighbourhood maps. *Environment and Behaviour*, 2, 74–99.

Le Comber, S.C., Nicholls, B., Rossmo, D.K. and Racey, P.A. (2006). Geographic profiling and animal foraging. *Journal of Theoretical Biology*, 240, 233–240.

Lynch, K. (1960). *The Image of the City*. Cambridge, Mass: MIT Press.

Mayhew, H. (1861). *London Labour and the London Poor: A Cyclopaedia of the Condition and Earnings of Those That Will Work, Those That Cannot Work and Those That Will Not Work*. London: Griffin Bohn.

McKercher, B. and Lew, A.A. (2003). Distance decay and the impact of effective tourism exclusion zones on international travel flows. *Journal of Travel Research*, 42, 159–165.

Newton, M.B. and Newton, D.C. (1989). Geoforensic identification of localised serial crime: unsolved female homicides, Fort Worth, Texas, 1993–85, in *Principles of Geographical Offender Profiling*, edited by D. Canter and D. Youngs. Aldershot: Ashgate.

Newton, M.B. and Swoope, E.A. (1987). Geoforensic analysis of localized serial murder: the hillside stranglers located (unpublished manuscript), in D. Canter and D. Youngs (eds) *Principles of Geographical Offender Profiling*. Aldershot: Ashgate.

Paulsen, D. (2006). Human vs. machine: a comparison of the accuracy of geographic profiling methods. *Journal of Investigative Psychology and Offender Profiling*, 3, 77–89.

Paulsen, D. (2007). Improving geographic profiling through commuter/marauder distinction. *Police Practice and Research*, 8, 347–357.

Phillips, P.D. (1980). Characteristics and typology of the journey to crime, in *Crime: A Spatial Perspective*, edited by D.E. Georges-Abeyie and K.D. Harries. New York: Columbia University Press.

Rengert, G., Piquero, A.R. and Jones, P.R. (1999). Distance decay re-examined. *Criminology*, 37, 427–445.

Rhodes, W.M. and Conly, C. (1981). Crime and mobility: an empirical study, in *Environmental Criminology*, edited by P.J. Brantingham and P. Brantingham. Prospect Heights, IL: Waveland Press Inc.

Rossmo, K.D. (1995). Place, space and police investigations: hunting serial violent criminals, in *Crime and Place*, edited by J.E. Eck and D. Weisburd. New York: Criminal Justice Press.

Santilla, P., Laukkanen, M., Zapala, A. and Bosco, D. (2008). Distances travelled and offender characteristics in homicide, rape and robbery against business. *Legal and Criminological Psychology*, 13, 345–356.

Shaw, C.R. and McKay, H.D. (1942). *Juvenile delinquency and urban areas*. Chicago: University of Chicago Press.

Soininen, J., McDonald, R. and Hillebrand, H. (2007). The distance decay of similarity in ecological communities. *Ecography*, 30, 3–12.

Turner, S. (1969). Delinquency and distance, in *Delinquency: Selected Studies*, edited by T. Sellen and M.E. Wolfgang. New York: Colombia University Press.

Van Koppen, P.J. and De Keiser, J.W. (1997). Desisting distance decay: on the aggregation of individual crime trips. *Criminology*, 35, 505–513.

Van Koppen, P.J. and Jansen, R.W. (1998). The road to robbery: travel patterns in commercial robberies. *British Journal of Criminology*, 38, 230–246.

Warren, J., Reboussin, R., Hazelwood, R.R., Cummings, A., Gibbs, N. and Trumbetta, S. (1998). Crime scene and distance correlates of serial rape. *Journal of Quantitative Criminology*, 14, 35–59.

White, C.R. (1932). The relation of felonies to environmental factors in Indianapolis. *Social Forces*, 10, 498–509.

# Chapter 12
# Linking Crimes in Criminal Investigations

Craig Bennell

## Editor's Introduction

The possibility of linking those crimes committed by a common offender, along with Geographical Offender Profiling, is one of the most immediately revolutionary operational advances Investigative Psychology offers to criminal investigations. But it is also one of the most theoretically and conceptually challenging areas of the discipline, drawing as it does on core psychological issues of behavioural consistency and development. In this Chapter, Craig describes the background to the important paper outlining the highly innovative use of ROC analysis in crime linking, that he and David Canter published in 2002 (Bennell and Canter, 2002) and some of his work since. As Craig outlines, a crime linking function is an important component of the police decision support systems Professor Canter and his team have pioneered (see, e.g., Canter and Youngs' 2008 description of the original interactive Offender Profiling System -iOPS).

## Start with the Basics

To me, getting back to basics often means prioritizing research projects so that issues are dealt with in a logically ordered fashion. For example, success in criminal profiling will depend largely on our ability to link serial crimes. Therefore, it makes little sense to conduct extensive research on the topic of profiling without first examining whether it is in fact possible to link crimes. Having said this, recent reviews of the field clearly indicate that this is not happening. Over the last 30 years, there have been at least 130 published articles on criminal profiling (Dowden, Bennell, and Bloomfield, 2007). In the same time period, there are only a handful of published articles that relate directly to linking issues and it has only been in the last 10 years that any serious effort has been put into conducting empirical research on this topic. One of the first empirical tests of linkage analysis was conducted by David Canter and myself (Bennell and Canter, 2002), and the ideas put forward in that paper will form the basis of much of this chapter.

### Be Critical of Existing Research

Many people currently believe that serial offenders will modify their MO over the course of their crimes due to a range of situational and learning factors (e.g., Douglas and Munn, 1992). As a result, the use of MO analysis as a tool to link serial crimes is presently applied sparingly and with extreme caution. But, is this caution warranted given what we currently know about MO? Have researchers really examined the concept of MO to such a degree that it is possible to determine the extent to which it can be used to link serial crimes? I believe we need to be critical of what people say about MO until empirical research is available to support their conclusions. In fact, the research that my students and I have been conducting, some of which is reviewed below, indicates that the MO concept may have been dismissed prematurely. In large part, this is because people have been searching for signs of behavioural stability and distinctiveness (prerequisites for linking most would argue) in the wrong place.

### Apply What We Know from Other Fields

Part of the reason why people are sceptical about MO is that they are unaware of pertinent research from other fields of psychology. Contrary to popular view, this research suggests that it might be possible to use certain aspects of an offender's MO for linking purposes. For example, over the past 50 years or so, personality psychologists have demonstrated that people do exhibit individual differences in behaviour in a relatively stable fashion across similar situations (e.g., Epstein, 1979, 1980). Indeed, under certain conditions, the level of behavioural stability exhibited by individuals can be quite respectable (Funder and Colvin, 1990). This body of research suggests that criminals may also exhibit stability in their offending behaviour over time – we must simply identify the conditions where this is true. I have argued that an analytical technique, which is suitable for identifying these conditions, is readily available and frequently used in other fields (Bennell, 2002, 2005; Bennell and Canter, 2002; Bennell and Jones, 2005). For the remainder of this chapter, I would like to describe this technique.

### The Basic Approach to Behaviour Linkage Analysis

In my opinion, David Canter was one of the first to formally articulate the basic requirements for successfully linking serial crimes. These requirements have been dealt with most clearly in his paper *The Psychology of Offender Profiling* (1995). The first prerequisite is behavioural stability: that the way an offender commits a crime on one occasion will have some characteristic similarities to the way he or she commits crimes on other occasions. The second prerequisite is behavioural distinctiveness: that the behaviours exhibited by an offender across his crime series will be relatively distinct from those of other offenders committing similar types of crimes. In this paper, David Canter reviewed a series of early studies that tested these hypotheses. However, one study in particular has always stood out to me as providing a very straightforward illustration of the basic linking problem. In fact, it was this study that initially got me interested in the problem when I was an MSc student working with David Canter, and it was the method used in this study that formed the basis of the linking approach I proposed in my PhD.

The study I am referring to was summarized in an early report on offender profiling produced by David Canter and his colleagues in the Offender Profiling Research Unit, which at the time was housed at the University of Surrey (Canter, Heritage, and Wilson, 1991). In that report, David Canter produced a table, which for me made the basic linking process clear (see Table 12.1 later). In this table, David Canter presented Jaccard coefficients (Jaccard, 1908), which were calculated across crimes that were either committed by the same offender or different offenders. Jaccard's coefficient can range from 0 to 1 with a 1 indicating a high degree of behavioural stability across the crimes being compared. The data in this table allows for a simple, yet direct test of the two hypotheses that are central to the linking problem. Behavioural stability is reflected by large coefficients being associated with linked crimes and behavioural distinctiveness is reflected by small coefficients being associated with unlinked crimes. The degree to which it is possible to distinguish between crimes committed by different offenders can be examined by selecting a specific threshold to decide when a crime pair should be considered linked (e.g., using the adopted threshold, how many correct and incorrect linking decisions are made?).

From the data in Table 12.1, it seems reasonable to conclude that stability and distinctiveness exist to a degree within this data set. It was also possible to accurately link most of the crimes. Specifically, when Canter et al. (1991) arbitrarily selected a threshold of .30 to determine which crime pairs were linked, they correctly classified 7 out of the 12 (58.3%) linked crime pairs and 49 out of the 54 (90.7%) unlinked crime pairs. I recall being quite excited about these results when I first read this report. To me, the study indicated that there was an empirical basis for linking serial crimes. However, the data in this table, and the approach that was used to link the crimes, resulted in more questions for me than answers.

For example, it seemed to me that there was nothing in Canter, Heritage and Wilson's (1991) approach to suggest that the .30 threshold they selected was the most appropriate threshold. Why .30, and not .20 or .40? In addition, it was not clear from the study how one would go about selecting such a threshold in an *a priori* fashion, as would have to be done by the police in a criminal investigation? Related to these problems, I was unsure how the various types of linking decisions illustrated in Table 12.1 (e.g., correctly or incorrectly classifying linked versus unlinked crimes) would vary as a function of the threshold adopted. The approach also did not seem to provide an easy way of testing various moderators of linking accuracy. For instance, it was not immediately obvious to me how one could use Canter, Heritage

**Table 12.1 Jaccard coefficients for 12 sexual assaults according to 74 aspects of behaviour. Letters (A, B, C and D) refer to different offenders. Numbers (1, 2 and 3) refer to different crimes. Bolded values indicate those coefficients that exceed .30. Adapted from Canter, Heritage and Wilson (1991)**

| | Same offender | | Other offenders | | | | | | | | |
|---|---|---|---|---|---|---|---|---|---|---|---|
| | 2 | 3 | B1 | B2 | B3 | C1 | C2 | C3 | D1 | D2 | D3 |
| A1 | .11 | **.42** | .27 | **.32** | .27 | .15 | .17 | .06 | **.43** | .17 | .26 |
| A2 | | .14 | .29 | .29 | .11 | .15 | .07 | .12 | .29 | .26 | .18 |
| A3 | | | .27 | .27 | .23 | .09 | .11 | .05 | .27 | .14 | **.33** |
| B1 | **.45** | .26 | | | | .06 | .08 | .05 | .21 | .08 | .18 |
| B2 | | **.41** | | | | .07 | .07 | .02 | .27 | .07 | .16 |
| B3 | | | | | | .27 | .31 | .27 | .12 | .14 | .06 |
| C1 | **.38** | **.48** | | | | | | | .22 | **.33** | .16 |
| C2 | | **.36** | | | | | | | .10 | .11 | .02 |
| C3 | | | | | | | | | .07 | .20 | .11 |
| D1 | .21 | **.46** | | | | | | | | | |
| D2 | | .17 | | | | | | | | | |
| D3 | | | | | | | | | | | |

and Wilson (1991) approach to determine in an efficient way if certain behaviours are more suitable for linking purposes than others are. Finally, it seemed risky to place too much faith in an analysis based on just 12 offences.

## A New Approach to Behaviour Linkage Analysis

My PhD dissertation, which was supervised by David Canter, was essentially an attempt to resolve these problems and come up with a linking strategy that provided answers to each of the above questions. In my opinion, I was largely successful in doing that and the approach is now being adopted by others conducting linking research (e.g., Woodhams and Toye, 2007). The approach is also being applied to new areas of research in my own lab (e.g., Jones and Bennell, 2007). The approach I proposed was not a new approach at all, though it had never been applied to the linking problem, and rarely had it been applied to problems in the investigative area (see Swets, 1988; Whittaker, Brickley, and Evans, 1998 for exceptions). The idea to adopt this approach was sparked both by David Canter's encouragement to draw on others areas of psychology to directly address problems in investigative psychology and, in a related way, to my reading of the inaugural issue of *Psychological Science in the Public Interest*, which presented a comprehensive review of how psychological science can be used to make more accurate diagnostic decisions (Swets, Dawes, and Monahan, 2000).

Conceptually, the approach I adopted was to treat the linking problem as a diagnostic decision making task, similar to the task faced by a radiologist when diagnosing a tumour, a meteorologist when predicting a weather event, or a graduate school administrator who has to decide whether an applicant is likely to be successful (Bennell, 2002). As David Canter and I stated in our original paper on the topic in *Science and Justice*, "this analogy can be drawn because, fundamentally, the problem for the diagnostician in all of these tasks is identical: He or she must accurately and effectively identify and apply relevant diagnostic information in order to render the best possible decision" (Bennell and Canter, 2002, p. 2). Furthermore, the decisions in each of these tasks are also basically equivalent if we make predictions about whether a pair of crimes is linked – there are only two predictions that can be made (i.e., cancerous/not cancerous, tornado/no tornado, potential/no potential, linked/not linked) and two possible realties (e.g., cancerous/not cancerous, tornado/no tornado, potential/no potential, linked/not linked).

In the linking context, when the possible predictions and realities are combined, four possible decision outcomes emerge, two that are correct and two that are incorrect. Such is the case for any two-alternative, yes–no type diagnostic task (Swets, 1988). These four decision outcomes are generically referred to as hits, correct rejections, false alarms, and misses and each is evident when Canter et al. (1991) applied their threshold to the data in Table 12.1. Specifically, a hit occurs when the prediction that two crimes are linked is correct. A correct rejection occurs when unlinked crimes are accurately identified. A false alarm refers to the prediction that two crimes are linked when they are not. Finally, a miss denotes the prediction that two crimes are unlinked but they are not.

The goal for the diagnostician is to seek ways to increase the probability of rendering a correct decision and/or to decrease the probability of making an incorrect decision. Most often this is done by identifying sources of evidence that allow one to discriminate between the diagnostic alternatives to the highest degree. For example, one could imagine how calculating similarity coefficients from moderate frequency behaviours would allow one to discriminate between linked and unlinked crimes to a greater degree than calculating similarity coefficients from extremely high frequency behaviours, which every offender in the data set exhibits.

The probabilities of the various decision outcomes can be easily calculated using the frequencies of each type of outcome. Specifically, the probability of making a hit, $p$H, is equal to the frequency of hits divided by the frequency of hits and misses. The probability of making a false alarm, $p$FA, is equal to the frequency of false alarms divided by the frequency of false alarms and correct rejections. The probabilities of making misses, *p*M, and correction rejections, *p*CR, are simply the complements of *p*H and *p*FA, respectively (e.g., *p*M = 1-*p*H). However, while it is possible to calculate these probabilities from Table 12.1, the values will be specific to the threshold adopted when making linking decisions. For example, using the .30 threshold adopted by Canter et al. (1991), *p*H = .58 and *p*FA = .09. However, for a threshold of .20, *p*H = .67 and *p*FA = .41 and for a threshold of .40, *p*H = .42 and *p*FA = .02. Thus, values of *p*H and *p*FA vary across thresholds, even when basing decisions on the same evidence. This leads to a problem when we want to establish a valid measure of accuracy for the general linking approach adopted by Canter et al. (1991). In fact, the probabilities of the possible decision outcomes in the linking task will vary in a systematic and predictable fashion as the threshold is varied from strict to lenient – as the threshold becomes more lenient, *p*H will increase, but so too will *p*FA.

So how does one solve this problem? How does one compute an accuracy measure that is not threshold specific? The answer to this question is found in existing diagnostic decision making research. In that area of research, receiver operating characteristic (ROC) analysis is routinely used to solve the problem (Swets, 1996). This analytical technique was originally developed for the radar field to examine the effectiveness of radar technicians in distinguishing meaningful blips on their radar screens (i.e., signals) from background noise (Swets, 1988). Since that time, the technique has been applied to a range of fields where people have to distinguish between other sorts of "signals" (a cancerous tumour, a tornado, a high potential student, a linked crime pair) and background noise (non-cancerous tumours), no tornadoes, low potential students, unlinked crime pairs) (Swets et al., 2000).

In the current context, ROC analysis illustrates how the probability of making certain types of linking decisions is subject to change for a particular linking feature, or set of features, as thresholds are varied from lenient to strict. Essentially, once the values of *p*H and *p*FA have been calculated across a range of thresholds, the coordinates are plotted on a graph (because *p*M and *p*CR are the complements of *p*H and *p*FA, respectively, these values are rarely shown on the graph, but they reside on the axes opposite *p*H and *p*FA). As illustrated in Figure 12.1, when the points are connected, the result is typically a concave downward curve, known as a ROC curve. This curve starts at the lower left corner of the graph (where the thresholds are strict) and ends in the upper right corner (where the thresholds are lenient) (Swets, 1988). The *area under* the ROC *curve*, referred to as the AUC, can act as a measure of discrimination accuracy for the particular linking feature(s) that gave rise to that curve – the higher the curve in the graph, the greater the discrimination accuracy. AUCs can range from 1.00 (perfect discrimination between linked and unlinked crime pairs) to 0.50 (chance discrimination between linked and unlinked crime pairs). An AUC of 1.00 represents a ROC curve that follows the left and upper axes of the graph, whereas an AUC of 0.50 corresponds to a ROC curve that follows the positive diagonal on the graph, going from the bottom left corner to the upper right corner.

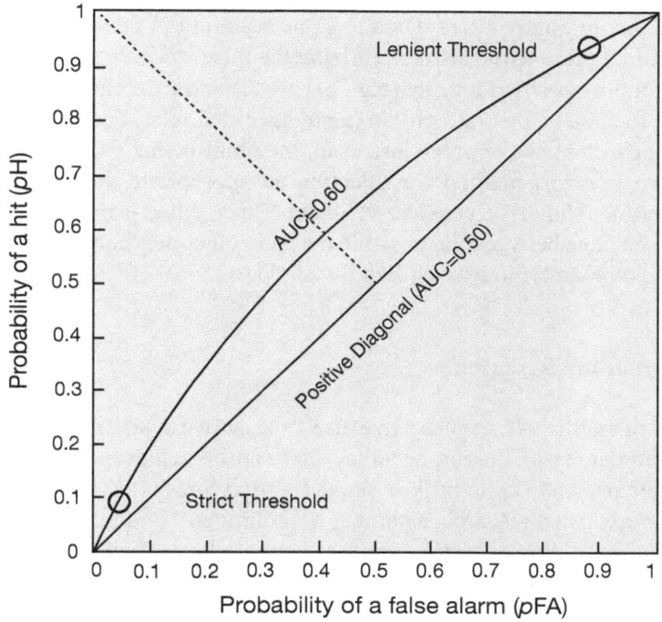


**Figure 12.1 A hypothetical ROC curve with an AUC of .60**

There are several advantages associated with the use of a ROC-derived measure of linking accuracy. One advantage is the fact that the AUC is a measure of accuracy that is independent of the particular threshold adopted. This occurs because the AUC represents the position of the entire ROC curve in its graph rather than any single point along it (Swets, 1988). Thus, the ROC curve that could be constructed from Table 12.1 would provide an accuracy score that is not specific to a threshold of .30, but rather to the general linking approach adopted by Canter et al. (1991). This curve could then be directly compared to another curve, which was constructed using a different strategy. To be sure, alternative measures of linking accuracy (e.g., percentage correct) are available, but each is biased by threshold placement. When employing such biased techniques, it is impossible to determine whether one's performance on the linking task when using a particular linking strategy is due to the inherent discriminatory power of that strategy or to the threshold adopted.

Another advantage of using ROC analysis for linking purposes is that the hit and false alarm rate (as well as the miss and correct rejection rate) occurring at each and every possible threshold along the ROC curve is preserved in the analysis and this provides a method for calculating optimal decision thresholds (Swets, 1992). One of the most common methods for selecting an optimal threshold is to identify the point along a ROC curve where the curve intersects the negative diagonal (i.e., the dashed line in Figure 12.1). The threshold resulting in this ROC point produces the maximum hit rate while also minimizing the false alarm rate. Another procedure is to select a pre-specified hit rate (e.g., pH = .80) and then choose a threshold that allows one to achieve this rate of hits (a pre-specified false alarm rate could also be chosen). Regardless of the procedure used, the point is that ROC analysis provides an objective, *a priori* method for selecting an appropriate threshold for deciding when two crimes should be considered linked. This method is more likely to result in the desired balance between the possible decision outcomes compared to what could be achieved with an arbitrarily chosen threshold.

## Findings from the Research

A number of published articles have used the above analytical approach to: (1) establish the degree of linking accuracy that can be achieved when using various linking strategies and (2) identify optimal decision thresholds for use in the linking context. Based on that research, a number of preliminary findings can be highlighted.

First, the spatial behaviour of offenders seems to be particularly useful for linking purposes. Specifically, the distance between offences appears to be an accurate indicator of whether two crimes have been committed by the same offender in that the shorter the inter-crime distance, the more likely the crimes are linked. This is found to be the case when, instead of relying on across-crime similarity coefficients, inter-crime distances are analyzed. In two of my previous studies, the AUCs found when inter-crime distances were used to discriminate between linked and unlinked burglary pairs were around .90, which is extremely high (Bennell and Canter, 2002; Bennell and Jones, 2005). Similar findings have recently been reported by others (e.g., Woodhams and Toye, 2007). This finding is important. From a theoretical perspective it suggests that offenders choose relatively distinct geographic areas (i.e., offending territories) in which to commit their crimes. This is an interesting idea that has yet to be thoroughly investigated, though I believe it is consistent with journey-to-crime research (e.g., Rossmo, 2000). Practically speaking, it appears that inter-crime distances could be used for linking purposes in an investigative context. For example, as suggested by Bennell and Canter (2002), inter-crime distances may prove to be effective as an initial filter in the linking task as a means of reducing the number of potential links that originally require consideration.

Second, behaviours that appear to be more under the control of the offender are exhibited in a more stable fashion across crimes and are thus more likely to be useful for linking purposes. For example, in my previous studies on burglary, inter-crime distances are found to be the most accurate discriminators, generally followed by similarity coefficients derived from target characteristics, entry behaviours, and property stolen, respectively (Bennell and Canter, 2002; Bennell and Jones, 2005). The explanation for this finding has been most clearly stated by Bennell and Jones (2005): "of all the various decisions made by a serial burglar during the commission of his crimes, his choice of burglary locations is possibly the most crucial, being the one decision over which the burglar has considerable control … it reasonably follows that this aspect of burglary behaviour will be the most consistently exhibited while the other, more context-dependent behaviours will be less consistent … e.g., the items an offender steals from a given property is very situation-specific, and therefore less stable, depending as it does on item availability at the particular crime scene" (p. 38). This idea originated from previous personality research where operant behaviours (i.e., behaviours that are expressed spontaneously) are found to be exhibited in a more stable fashion than respondent behaviours (i.e., behaviours that are expressed in reaction to environmental stimuli) (Funder and Colvin, 1990; Mclelland, 1984). Practically, such a finding might mean that relying on traditional MO indicators to link crimes, such as entry method and property stolen, would lead to sub-optimal linking results.

Third, and finally, all previous studies that have used the ROC approach clearly indicate that the issue of where to place the decision threshold when linking crimes is of the utmost importance, despite the fact that the issue is rarely mentioned in this context. Indeed, selecting an appropriate threshold is at least as important as identifying the features of criminal behaviour that allow serial crimes to be accurately linked. Take the finding that inter-crime distances appear to be a very effective linking feature. As Bennell and Jones (2005) have argued, "it is futile to recognize the general utility of inter-crime distances in linking a pair of burglaries in ignorance of the proximity that must be met before two crimes should be considered linked" (p. 39). Very small changes to the decision threshold can actually have a significant impact on linking results. In the study of serial burglary by Bennell and Canter (2002), e.g., adjusting the decision threshold for inter-crime distances by about 2.0 km resulted in approximately 10% less linked crime pairs and approximately 30% less unlinked crime pairs being correctly classified (per 100 crime pairs). Such results clearly indicate the need for police forces to consider the issue of threshold setting when developing linking procedures.

## Where to from Here?

Linking research is still in its infancy. Linking research using the ROC approach outlined here is even newer. Thus, there are many more studies that can be conducted to move this work forward. Rather than providing a list of all the standard future research directions I will focus instead on three lines of inquiry, each of which is linked to Professor Canter's recent research.

The first line of research that I think will be productive is to examine how the radex model of criminal behaviour described by Canter (2000) might inform the linking process. The radex model could provide a framework for testing the discriminatory power of potential linking features (and the ROC approach certainly provides the analytical tool). At least two aspects of the model warrant attention.

One relates to establishing the linking capabilities of crime scene actions comprising different behavioural themes (e.g., control, aggression, theft, and intimacy in rape; Canter, Bennell, Alison, and Reddy, 2003). This is an issue that my lab has begun to explore with respect to serial rape and homicide and it appears that behaviours from certain themes (e.g., control) are more discriminatory than behaviours from other themes (e.g., aggression) (e.g., Cao and Bennell, 2005; Taylor, Bennell, and Corey, 2006). Consistent with our serial burglary research, we have proposed that this is due to the operant nature of control-type behaviours. The second aspect of the radex model that deserves attention in the linking context relates to how the frequency of behavioural occurrence impacts the discriminatory power of crime scene actions. Canter et al. (2003), along with numerous others (e.g., Salfati and Bateman, 2005), have hypothesized that lower frequency behaviours will be the most effective for linking purposes. However, this hypothesis has yet to be adequately tested.

The second line of future research, which is more applied in nature, relates to an examination of how the ROC approach could best be implemented and evaluated as a decision aid in operational settings. The small amount of research that has examined how people perform on the linking task indicates that it is indeed a demanding task. For example, Canter et al. (1991) found that, even in a relatively simple linking exercise involving 12 crimes committed by four offenders, police officers typically performed poorly. Similar results have been reported by Santtila, Korpela, and Hakkanen (2004) and by me (e.g., Bennell, Bloomfield, Snook, Taylor, and Barnes, 2010). In each of these studies, it was also shown that actuarial decision aids could be used to improve linking accuracy, which is consistent with a large body of research demonstrating the value of using such tools (e.g., Dawes, Faust, and Meehl, 1989). Such research should continue into the future.

However, research has also demonstrated a clear reluctance on the part of front-line workers to rely on actuarial tools when making decisions, despite the increases in decision making accuracy that might be achieved through their use (e.g., Swets et al., 2000). Thus, it will be important, as a third line of research, to examine alternative ways of implementing linking tools and to evaluate these tools. One potentially useful way of implementing such tools is to incorporate them into broader, more helpful investigative management systems, developed from the ground up through researcher-practitioner collaborations. These collaborations are important because end-user involvement in system development has been found to increase end-user reliance on the system (e.g., Kaplan, Reneau, and Whitecotton, 2001). I believe that one of Professor Canter's latest achievements, an interactive offender profiling system (iOPS), which is being developed with the assistance of the London Metropolitan Police Service, might just be such a system (Canter, 2005; Canter and Youngs, 2008c). In fact, a linking component, which could potentially be improved by current and future research of the sort discussed in this chapter, is currently built into that system. In the future it will be important to carefully evaluate this aspect of iOPS.

*Postscript*

When I reflect on my own research I appear to have internalized three of Professor Canter's "take home messages":

> When conducting research, start with the basics. Putting the cart before the horse rarely advances knowledge and more often than not leads the research to draw erroneous conclusions.
>
> Be critical of existing research and do not accept at face value what other researchers say until you are sure that what they have said is correct and generalizes to the problem at hand. This is obviously true of all fields but perhaps even truer in the field of investigative psychology.
>
> Apply what is known from other fields of psychology to problems presented within our field. The problems that investigative psychologists tackle are not that different from problems examined in more traditional areas of psychology and potential answers to problems in our field often exist within these other fields.

## References

Bennell, C. (2002). *Behavioural Consistency and Discrimination in Serial Burglary*. Unpublished doctoral dissertation, University of Liverpool, Liverpool, UK.

Bennell, C. (2005). Improving police decision-making: general principles and practical applications of receiver operating characteristic analysis. *Applied Cognitive Psychology*, 19, 1157–1175.

Bennell, C., Bloomfield, S., Snook, B., Taylor, P.J., and Barnes, C. (2010). Linkage analysis in cases of serial burglary: comparing the performance of university students, forensic professionals, and a logistic regression model. *Psychology, Crime, and Law*, 16, 507–524.

Bennell, C. and Canter, D.V. (2002). Linking commercial burglaries by modus operandi: tests using regression and ROC analysis. *Science and Justice*, 42, 153–164.

Bennell, C. and Jones, N.J. (2005). Between a ROC and a hard place: a method for linking serial burglaries using an offender's modus operandi. *Journal of Investigative Psychology and Offender Profiling*, 2, 23–41.

Canter, D.V. (1995). Psychology of offender profiling, in *Handbook of Psychology in Legal Contexts*, edited by R. Bull and D. Carson. Chichester: Wiley (pp. 343–355).

Canter, D.V. (2000). Offender profiling and criminal differentiation. *Legal and Criminological Psychology*, 5, 23–46.

Canter, D.V. (2005). *Combining MO Visualization and Spatial Mapping*. Paper presented at the 8th International Investigative Psychology Conference, London, UK.

Canter, D.V., Bennell, C., Alison, L.J., and Reddy, S. (2003). Differentiating sex offences: a behaviourally based thematic classification of stranger rapes. *Behavioral Sciences and the Law*, 21, 157–174.

Canter, D.V., Heritage, R., and Wilson, M. (1991). *A Facet Approach to Offender Profiling*. London: Home Office.

Canter, D. and Youngs, D. (2008c). iOPS: An interactive offender profiling system, in *Crime Mapping Case Studies*, edited by S. Chainey and I. Thompson. Wiley: Chichester.

Cao, T. and Bennell, C. (June 2005). *The Development and Validation of a Statistical Prediction Rule for the Purpose of Linking Serial Rapes in Canada*. Poster presented at the annual meeting of the Canadian Psychological Association, Montreal, Quebec, Canada.

Dawes, R., Faust, D., and Meehl, P.E. (1989). Clinical versus actuarial judgment. *Science*, 243, 1668–1674.

Douglas, J.E. and Munn, C. (1992). Violent crime scene analysis: modus operandi, signature, and staging. *FBI Law Enforcement Bulletin*, 6, 1–10.

Dowden, C., Bennell, C., and Bloomfield, S. (2007). Advances in offender profiling: a systematic review of the profiling literature published over the past three decades. *Journal of Police and Criminal Psychology*, 22, 44–56.

Epstein, S. (1979). The stability of behavior: I. On predicting most of the people much of the time. *Journal of Personality and Social Psychology*, 37, 1097–1126.

Epstein, S. (1980). The stability of behavior: II. Implications for psychological research. *American Psychologist*, 35, 790–806.

Funder, D.C. and Colvin, C.R. (1991). Explorations of behavioural consistency: properties of persons, situations, and behaviours. *Journal of Personality and Social Psychology*, 60, 773–794.

Jaccard, P. (1908). Nouvelle recherches sur la distribution florale. *Bull. Soc. Vaud. Sci. Nat.* (*Bulletin de la Societe Vaudoise Sciénces Naturelles*), 44, 223–270.

Jones, N.J. and Bennell, C. (2007). The development and validation of statistical prediction rules for discriminating between genuine and simulated suicide notes. *Archives of Suicide Research*, 11, 1–15.

Kaplan, S.E., Reneau, J.H., and Whitecotton, S. (2001). The effects of predictive ability information, locus of control, and decision maker involvement on decision aid reliance. *Journal of Behavioral Decision Making*, 14, 35–50.

McClelland, D. (1984). Is personality consistent? in *Motives, Personality, and Society*, edited by D. McClelland. New York, NY: Praeger (pp. 185–211).

Rossmo, D.K. (2000). *Geographic Profiling*. Boca Raton, FL: CRC Press.

Salfati, C.G. and Bateman, A.L. (2005). Serial homicide: an investigation of behavioural consistency. *Journal of Investigative Psychology and Offender Profiling*, 2, 121–144.

Santtila, P., Korpela, S., and Hakkanen, H. (2004). Expertise and decision-making in the linking of car crime series. *Psychology, Crime & Law*, 10, 97–112.

Swets, J.A. (1988). Measuring the accuracy of diagnostic systems. *Science*, 240, 1285–1293.

Swets, J.A. (1992). The science of choosing the right decision threshold in high-stake diagnostics. *American Psychologist*, 47, 522–532.

Swets, J.A. (1996). *Signal Detection Theory and ROC Analysis in Psychology and Diagnostics*. Mahwah, NJ: Lawrence Erlbaum Associates.

Swets, J.A., Dawes, R.M., and Monahan, J. (2000). Psychological science can improve diagnostic decisions. *Psychological Science in the Public Interest*, 1, 1–26.

Taylor, A., Bennell, C., and Corey, S. (June 2006). The temporal consistency of crime scene behaviours in serial sexual homicide. Poster presented at the annual meeting of the Canadian Psychological Association, Calgary, Alberta, Canada.

Woodhams, J. and Toye, K. (2007). An empirical test of the assumptions of case linkage and offender profiling with serial commercial robberies. *Psychology, Public Policy, and Law*, 13, 59–85.

Whittaker, D.K., Brickley, M.R., and Evans, L. (1998). A comparison of the ability of experts and non-experts to differentiate between adult and child human bite marks using receiver operating characteristic (ROC) analysis. *Forensic Science International*, 92, 11–20.

Chapter 13

# Contemporary Challenges in Investigative Psychology: Revisiting the Canter Offender Profiling Equations

Donna Youngs and Elizabeth Spruin

## Editor's Introduction

The following is an updated version of a chapter first published by me (Youngs, 2008) in Psychology and Law: Bridging the Gap (Canter and Zikauskienne, 2008). It specifies some of the conceptual challenges that arise in developing investigative inferences: a) Criminal Pertinence, b) Contingency Destabilisation, c) Criminal Salience, d) Integrative Modelling, e) Inferential Fluency, and f) the Canonical Form of the A-C relationship. This analysis builds on David Canter's early modelling of the 'profiling' problem as the establishment of the Actions- Characteristics equations (Canter, 1993). I'm grateful to Liz Spruin for all her help in updating the references from my original chapter for this volume.

## Introduction

A quarter of a century ago the FBI drew attention to what investigators have long known: Deductions about the likely perpetrator can be drawn from a consideration, in detail, of the crime itself (Douglas, Ressler, Burgess and Hartman, 1986). Although thrown into high relief much earlier in the writings of Arthur Conan Doyle, the FBI drew particular attention to this process and gave it the label 'Offender Profiling'. Coming from a scientifically grounded psychological perspective, David Canter saw that the process being alluded to was a rather more profound one and as a first step in unpacking this, tried to specify the central question that was being implied by the profiling process. This led him to the assertion that the relationship between actions and characteristics was one that, in mathematical terms, should be represented as a canonical form (Canter, 1993).

In doing this, two things quickly became clear. The first was that if the relationships between the offending and the offender could be mapped out mathematically, these 'Profiling Equations' (Canter, 1989; Canter, 1993) could be used to systematically inform many of the tasks that comprise the whole police investigation and judicial process beyond the simple painting of suspect profiles. Moreover, the substantive remit would extend far beyond the serial murder and serial sex offences assumed to delimit offender profiling, potentially to all types and forms of criminality. The second thing that became clear in specifying the potential relationships between the offending and the offender in these formal terms was that there were many reasons why 'offender profiling' just wasn't going to be possible (see Canter and Youngs, 2009).

However, the empirical literature now boasts a growing number of studies that show that these links between offending style and offender characteristics do exist and can be established (for example, Canter and Fritzon, 1998; Lobato, 2004; Santilla, Junkkila and Sandnabba, 2005; Youngs, 2004; Zaitsu, 2010). For example, Salfati (2000) advocated that spontaneous, expressive homicides are linked to offenders most likely involved in a prior relationship with the victim. Similarly, Santtila, Hakkanen, Canter, and Elfgren (2003) linked the typical homicidal offender to a man who killed a person he knew, in familiar surroundings, furthermore, he was also more likely to be socio-economically deprived. Canter, Bennell, Alison and Reddy, (2003) established that rapes mirror either overtly aggressive offence style, control, theft or an attempt for some involvement with the victim. Alison and Stein (2003) replicated these findings with two independent samples. Clearly such findings must point to the general feasibility of the inferential process, but rather than seeing them as simple proof of profiling, we need to recognise that they have emerged despite the complexities inherent in the process.

## Criminal Pertinence

Establishing solutions to these equations requires, in the first instance, an understanding of how offenders differ in their criminal styles. But there is a range of conceptual challenges in the modelling of criminal variation that we need to find a way through if we are to pull out any differences as fully as we might. The first of these is the issue of Criminal Pertinence. This is the question of what, in the general case, should be looked at in considering a crime. The following pattern of criminal action might comprise a burglary offence:

> One Monday afternoon in November, a suburban house in Manchester is burgled. The offender disabled the alarm, then entered by smashing a downstairs window. He stole cash and jewellery without making any mess but leaving fingerprints. The larger electronic goods in the house were not stolen. Just as he was about to leave the offender encountered the occupant and reacted violently punching her in the face several times before running off (Crime Description A).

The issue of criminal pertinence is about establishing which of these component parts is relevant, indicating anything about the offenders' criminal style, and which we should ignore. The behaviours that comprise the above burglary will not all be equally revealing of the individual who carried out this offence. But deciding which are relevant is not straightforward. Does the damage done to property by the offender tell us something about him or her but not the way in which the offence was initiated or what time of day it happened? Is the offender's readiness to be violent a key consideration for Investigative Psychologists but his choice of a flat rather than a house unimportant? In part then Criminal Pertinence will relate to the nature of the behaviours.

But determining the pertinence of the behaviours also requires an overall understanding of the incident within which the individual behaviours occurred. Some behaviours may only occur in direct response to situational stimuli so that what they tell us about the offender may be limited. So, for example, is the entry method important or was this method adopted just because the window was open? Are apparently incongruous behaviours, which run contrary to the general script, particularly significant? For instance, should the fact that an offender who was experienced enough to disable an alarm in advance then also, incongruously, left fingerprints be regarded as crucial or incidental? Should we focus just on the behaviours that did happen or are there things that the offender didn't do that are relevant? For example, is it significant that the offender didn't carry any tools with him? Identifying appropriately those behaviours that have Criminal Pertinence must be an essential first step in the inference activity.

In establishing the criminally pertinent offending actions, theory is crucial because the question is not simply one of which behaviours are indicative but one of which behaviours indicate something about criminals that we actually want to know. Different behaviours are going to be indicative of different aspects of the individual. So, for example, Canter and Heritage (1990) reported that offenders with hostile and aggressive crime scene actions are more likely to have a violent crime history. While offenders with more instrumental crime scene actions (involving theft, etcetera) are more likely have a crime history of property offences. Davies, Wittebrod, and Jackson (1997) found that crime scene actions were linked to the offender's previous convictions. Most recently, Häkkänen and Pitkäniemi (2003) showed in a series of homicides that crime scene actions were associated with the offender's post-offence psychiatric diagnosis. Therefore, some crime scenes may indicate certain characteristics of offender, while failing to reveal other characteristics. For instance, while Safati (2000) suggested that spontaneous and expressive homicides are more likely to involve a prior relationship between the individuals, this involvement in a prior relationship fails to indicate the offender's interpersonal style, which may, rather, be revealed in the level of aggression displayed. The criminally pertinent subset of behaviours that investigative psychologists need to be considering should be constantly growing, expanding and being refined in response to developments in the identification of individual differences that are investigation relevant and legal process relevant. This will be a process that truly captures the investigatory rather than applied approach to science (c.f. Canter, 2005).

## Contingency Destabilisation

A second conceptual complexity in the profiling process can be most readily understood through consideration of an example:

> At 2a.m. one Saturday morning, a suburban house in Manchester is burgled. The offender disabled the alarm, then entered by smashing a downstairs window. He stole cash and jewellery without making any mess but leaving fingerprints. The larger electronic goods in the house were not stolen. Just as he was about to leave the offender encountered the occupant and reacted violently punching her in the face several times before running off (Crime Description B).

This offence differs from the previous one (A) on a single action- when the offender chose to carry out the offence. Yet this change in one behavioural detail in an entire event casts a whole new light on many of the other components of the offence. For example, the smashing of the window is rather different in the middle of the night than in the middle of the day. Similarly, the offender's violent reaction to encountering the occupant is less readily construed as a panic based reaction given that he must have expected someone to be in at that time. So, single modifications can change our view on which of the components of the offence are pertinent to the establishment of criminal style, as well as on what they actually mean.

This effect of Contingency Destabilisation is something that investigative psychologists, are highly vulnerable to because we work with real world data that are what Canter has referred to as 'patchy' (that is, incomplete but unreliably so). Yet clearly it needs to be considered in our assessments of criminal style.

## Criminal Salience

Related to the issue of Criminal Pertinence is the issue of Criminal Salience. Criminal Salience is not simply about what indicates criminal style in the general case but what allows you to define criminal style in a way that distinguishes it from other criminal styles. One complexity in establishing salience is that some of the behaviours any individual carries out will be common to all or many other offenders and so will not allow us to differentiate. Others will be carried out by a fairly large proportion of offenders. Others will be relatively rare. What is required therefore is a way of modelling differences in criminal style that can take into account these variations in the prevalence as opposed to rareness of the behaviours.

One conceptual template, which a number of investigative psychology researchers are starting to draw on that allows this and so draws attention to the salient aspects of criminal action that define distinct styles is the radex (Canter, 2000). Canter advances a conceptual model of criminal differentiation within which the variations in offenders' styles are the product of differences in two aspects of criminal behaviour.

The first, described by the 'thematic facet' are differences in qualitative aspects of the behaviour. The second, described by the 'specificity facet', are qualitative differences in the specificity as opposed to generality of the behaviours within the given area of criminal activity. Canter argues that these two processes interact such that the qualitative variations in style emerge in relation to the more 'specific' behaviours, while the more 'general' behaviours remain undifferentiated, forming a subset of behaviours that tend to be common to all offences.

The radex has facilitated tremendous progress in modelling criminal variation. Radex structures have been revealed in, for example, studies of behavioural variation in crimes ranging from homicide (Santtilla, Canter, Elfgren, and Hakkanen, 2001), rape (Canter, Bennell, Alison, and Reddy, 2003; Canter and Heritage, 1990) and paedophilia (Canter, Hughes, and Kirby, 1998) to burglary (Merry and Harsent, 2000). More specifically, Canter and Heritage (1990) were the first to demonstrate the existence of the radial structure for crime. Their study explored the actions that occurred in rapes and developed a multivariate model of rape. Specifically, the study found a co-occurrence of behaviours within 66 rapes perpetrated by 27 offenders which they analysed. Their results lead to the conclusion that there are five discernible elements of sexual offence behaviour (1) sexuality, (2) violence and aggression, (3) impersonal sexual gratification, (4) criminality, and (5) interpersonal intimacy. In general, those behaviours which were considered associated fell within the same thematic groups. For example, behaviours related to complimenting the victim or apologising to the victim were found in the same region of the radex, specifically, these variables were linked to the pseudo-intimacy theme. In contrast, behaviours such as, tearing the victim's clothes or the use of impersonal language were linked to the victim as object theme of the radex.

More recently, Canter et al. (2003) carried out a study which illustrated the power of the radex model in helping to indicate the salient aspects of crime. Their study behaviourally classified stranger rapists through victim statements and found four modes of offender–victim interaction; hostility, control, theft, and involvement, which was originally proposed by Canter and Heritage (1990). As well as proposing the likely qualitative differences of violation within stranger rape victims, there are also differences in levels (or degrees) of violation in rape. Accordingly, using the radex model, Canter et al. proposed a scale of violence ranging from personal violation, which covered the inner concentric ring, through to physical violation, and at the most extreme level, sexual violation, which covered the outer ring. These offences were differentiated in terms of one of the four themes (for example, hostile, controlling, stealing, or involving). As such, their schematic diagram indicated a model of rape consisting of the modular facet of violation (personal, physical, and sexual) and the four modes of interaction (hostility, control, theft, and involvement).

Along the same lines, recent work on differentiation at the level of the type of offence, has shown a radex structure of criminal differentiation within which variations in the salience of the behaviours relate to the particularity of the target (Youngs and Canter, 2012b). The model of criminal differentiation revealed in this work suggests that offenders show specialised styles in relation to targets that are significant or selected but not targets that are unknown or non-particular. Where the targets are significant or selected, distinct styles emerge that may be conceptualised in terms of the means through which the abuse of the other is perpetrated. Three means were identified: Stealing, Physical Assault and Damage.

This model informs the long-standing criminological debate on criminal specialisation or versatility (for example, Farrington, Snyder, and Finnegan, 1988) by showing that criminality is not either a generalised phenomenon underpinned by a single factor, or a number of distinct, specialised propensities, but both. So what the radex draws attention to is not just the idea that some offenders will be more specialised than others in the range of criminal activities that they get involved in, but more independently of this, the behaviours themselves will tend to vary in terms of how common or rare they are. By developing theoretical definitions of the specificity facet in the context of different forms of criminality and types of crime we move towards a richer understanding of criminal salience (Youngs and Canter, 2012a).

## Integrative Modelling and Inferential Fluency

The next stage in the development of investigative psychology is to relate all of these distinctions to an overall, formal psychological theory for general behavioural differentiation. This means seeking to understand different criminal styles of action, not simply in terms of ideas specific to that type of activity but rather in terms of more generic frameworks such as the Narrative framework (Youngs and Canter, 2011, 2012), Bandura's fundamental human incentives (Bandura, 1986), interpersonal behavioural style models such as Schutz's FIRO (Schutz, 1992), Shye's Action Systems (Shye, 1985) or the integrated Narrative Action Systems (Canter and Youngs, 2009). This overall approach is at the heart of addressing the other conceptual challenges of Integrative Modelling and Inferential Fluency.

General frameworks would allow us to understand crime style differences in terms that are related to recognised formal psychological process facilitating the Inferential Fluency between the ideas we use to distinguish styles and the theories we then rely on to move from those styles to infer the characteristics of the offender in the profiling process.

Drawing upon general frameworks will also allow us to understand crime style differences in terms that facilitate the direct comparability of models of criminal variation from across different cultural contexts and within different crime types. This translation of the stylistic differences within different crime types and from different cultures into a common psychological language is the challenge at the heart of Integrative Modelling.

## The Canonical Form of the Offending Actions–Offender Characteristics Relationship

The general feasibility of modelling criminal variation that all the work so far points to, does of course open up the possibility of establishing solutions to the A-C equations. Indeed, there is now quite a weight of studies showing some differential patterns of correspondence between particular styles of offending and particular sets of characteristics (for example, Canter and Fritzon, 1998; Hakkanen, Puolakka, and Santtila, 2004; Lobato, 2004; Salfati and Canter, 1999; Santilla, Junkkila, and Sandnabba, 2005; Youngs, 2004; Zaitsu, 2010). More specifically, Salfati and Canter (1999) carried out a study to test the literature on offender profiling which suggested that different styles of homicide will reflect differences in the background characteristics of the offender. The researchers examined the actions and characteristics derived from 82 stranger homicides. Their analyses revealed consistencies in the themes across actions and characteristics, it was therefore suggested that there were the existence of three distinct themes of actions: Impulsive – representing expressive aggression and an emotional attack. Offender characteristics associated with this theme included qualities such as previous impulsive offences. Opportunistic – representing instrumental aggression, where the offender's main goal may pertain to sexual gratification or material need. Offenders within this type of homicide had previously committed crimes against properties. Cognitive – representing instrumental aggression and an increase in forensic awareness. Characteristics related to this theme included the offender serving as a professional in the army and prior prison sentence. In a similar context, Davies, Wittebrod and Jackson (1997) also showed the power of the consistencies across actions and characteristics in their analysis of 210 rapes. Their results found that if an offender took measures not to leave fingerprints, stole from their victim, forced entry in the victim's home and had imbibed alcohol, there was a very high probability (over 90%), that the offender had prior convictions for burglary.

One of the most thoroughly developed empirical examinations of the links between offending style and offender characteristics, was Canter and Fritzon's (1998) study of arsonists. These researchers proposed that there will be behavioural consistencies in the actions of arsonists when committing a crime that characterise them. The themes underlying these observable differences can subsequently be utilised to help in the understanding of the offence. Drawing on Shye's (1985) Action Systems model of behaviour, the researchers proposed four styles of arson; Expressive Person, Expressive Object, Instrumental Person and Instrumental Object. These themes on the actions of arson resulted from the differences in the source of the objectives for the action (Expressive or Instrumental) combined with the differences in the direction of the effect of the action (Person or Object). To test these predictions in the differentiations of arsonists, the researchers analysed 175 solved arson cases from police forces across the UK, yielding 42 offence variables. The results from these analyses support the proposed framework which indicated four themes to arson. The researchers developed scales to measure these four themes in the actions of arsonists and developed a further four scales to measure the same themes in the background characteristics of the arsonists. Accordingly, Canter and Fritzon related the measures of the action and background scales, which indicated that the more significant relationships between the actions and characteristics were presented within the similar themes. Subsequently, Santtila and colleagues (Santtila, Hakkanen, Alison, and Whyte, 2003) found similar structural themes for crime scene actions within juvenile firesetters (aged 6–17).

This is all tremendously encouraging, indicating that offender action to offender characteristics inferences is possible. The substantive findings also start to point us towards the types of psychological and social processes that underpin the relationships between these two domains. As an exploratory phase in the defining of a discipline, it has been incredibly fruitful. But do these get us nearer to the point where we can look at any given crime and make inferences about the likely perpetrator on the basis of the style of offending exhibited? There are a number of issues about the way in which offending actions relate to offender characteristics that mean that we need to be cautious in assuming these results can be used, whether by investigators or researchers, in this way.

The central challenge relates to the canonical nature of the relationship. Particular actions do not map on to particular characteristics in any simple or direct way. The same action can, on a consistent basis, indicate more than one characteristic, and equally, the same characteristic can be inferred from different actions. So for example, extreme violence may be threatened in a robbery carried out by an inexperienced or a highly experienced offender and conversely, both rapists and robbers will tend to have criminal histories that include burglary convictions. Davies et al. (1997) looked at rape reports and found that if an offender steals from their victim or employs forced entry at the crime scene, there is a higher probability that they had previous convictions for theft and burglary. Safati and Canter (1999) found similar results in instrumental (opportunistic) homicides. Those offenders who broke into their victims home and stole from them, were also more likely to have previous convictions for theft and burglary.

The actions characteristics relationship is further complex in that the same action can indicate different characteristics in different contexts or at different points in an offender's criminal progression. So, for example, the carrying of a gun by a lone offender may indicate a rather different individual than of the carrying of a group as part of a group of an offending event. Equally, the use of an accelerant may indicate an above average intellect in a young arsonist but less so in one that was more experienced (Canter, 1993; Youngs, 2004).

What this means is that the A-C mapping does not take the form of multiple one to one relationships that accumulate to provide the description of an offender. Rather the mapping between the two domains takes the form of a given combination of interacting action variables that map on to a given combination of interacting characteristic variables. Technically this type of relationship can only be fully represented as a canonical correlation (Canter, 1993).

$$F_1A_1 + . + F_nA_n = F_1C_1 + . + F_mC_m$$

Canter's Profiling Equations

On one side of this equation are variables derived from information about the offence that would be available to investigators. On the other side, are the characteristics of the offender that are most useful in facilitating the police enquiry. So, if $A_{n...1}$ represents n actions of the offender (including, for example, time, place and victim selection) and $C_{1...m}$ represents m characteristics of the offender, then the empirical question is to establish the values of weightings ($F_{1...n}$ and $F_{1...m}$) in an equation of the above form. Solving canonical equations (c.f. Tabachnick and Fidell, 1983) requires establishing 'the relationships between two sets of variables' (op cit. p. 146). These can be understood as multiple regression equations that have a number of criterion variables as well as a number of predictor variables.

The important point for investigative psychologists is that changes in any one predictor variable (the actions) can destabilise the relationship of any other predictor variable with any criterion variable or set of criterion variables (the characteristics). This means that inferences can become invalid. So, for example, it could be established that in rape, a high level of control, a rapid aggressive initial approach, a moderate use of demeaning language and a high level of forensic awareness, predicts an offender age of 26. However, within this, for specific combinations of other characteristics, the most likely age of the offender carrying out an offence in this way may be lower. This may be the case where, for example, the offender has a particularly extensive criminal history.

Where the relationships between the two domains (offending actions and offender characteristics) have this complex form, there are two possible approaches to moving forward to build the scientific body of knowledge that will allow the specific inferences. The first is to build a catalogue, empirically, of what C variables any given action relates to, for every combination of other action variables. This would be an enormous task requiring specification of very single pertinent factor, including aspects of the broader context, the cultural context and even the epoch. The other option, and more widely used method, is to focus on the development of theory that will allow an understanding of the underlying processes so that particular inferences can be drawn on this basis (for example, Canter et al., 2003; Canter and Fritzon, 1998; Canter and Heritage, 1990). For instance, Hakkanen, Lindlof, and Santilla (2004) established that in stranger rapes crime scene actions reflecting Theft, which include actions such as; theft and rummaging through the victims belongings, insulting the victim, attempt at sexual acts, the use of a condom and using multiple acts of violence, predicts an offender with a criminal history of theft and drunk driving. These inferences are specific for the particular actions within the Theft theme and are based on empirical research and an understanding of the structural processes.

## Conclusion

Within the present chapter we have attempted to give a flavour of the conceptual complexities inherent in the 'profiling' process. Issues of a) Criminal Pertinence, b) Contingency Destabilisation, c) Criminal Salience, d) Integrative Modelling, e) Inferential Fluency, and f) the Canonical Form of the A-C relationship, were all touched upon. These issues all highlight the need for investigative psychologists to focus on formal specifications of the problem and in particular to the theoretical and conceptual developments that will allow full solutions to the original Canter Profiling Equations mapped out at the birth of Investigative Psychology.

## References

Alison, L.J. and Stein, K. (2003). Vicious circles: how accounts of stranger sexual assault reflect abusive variants of conventional interactions. *The Journal of Forensic Psychiatry*, 12, 515–538.

Bandura, A. (1986). *Social Foundations of Thought and Action*. Englewood Cliffs, NJ: Prentice Hall.

Canter, D. (1993). Psychology of offender profiling, in *Handbook of Psychology in Legal Contests*, edited by R. Bull and D. Carson. Chichester: Wiley.

Canter, D. (1995). Psychology of offender profiling, in *Handbook of Psychology in Legal Contests*, edited by R. Bull and D. Carson (eds). Chichester: Wiley. Chapter 4.5, pp. 343–335.

Canter, D. (2000). Offender profiling and criminal differentiation. *Legal and Criminological Psychology*, 5, 23–46.

Canter, D. (2005). In the kingdom of the blind. Keynote presentation to 15th Conference of the European Association of Psychology and Law, Vilnius, Lithuania.

Canter, D., Bennell, C., Alison, L., and Reddy, S. (2003). Differentiating sex offences: a behaviourally based thematic classification of stranger rapes. *Behavioural Sciences and the Law*, 21, 157–174.

Canter, D. and Fritzon, K. (1998). Differentiating arsonists: a model of firesetting actions and characteristics. *Legal and Criminal Psychology*, 3, 73–96.

Canter, D. and Youngs, D. (2003). Beyond 'offender profiling': the need for an investigative psychology, in *Handbook of Psychology in Legal Contexts*, Second edition, edited by D. Carson and R. Bull. John Wiley & Sons Ltd. (pp. 171–205).

Canter, D. and Youngs, D. (2009). *Investigative Psychology: Offender Profiling and the Analysis of Criminal Action*. Chichester,UK: Wiley.

Davies, A., Wittebrood, K., and Jackson, J.L. (1998). *Predicting the Criminal Record of a Stranger Rapist* (special interest series paper 12). London: Home Office Policing and Reducing Crime Unit.

Douglas, J., Ressler, R., Burgess, A. and Hartman, C. (1986). Criminal Profiling from crime analysis. *Behavioral Science and the Law*, 4, 401–21.

Farrington, D.P., Snyder, H.N., and Finnegan, T.A. (1988). Specialization in juvenile court careers. *Criminology*, 26, 461–485.

Häkkänen, H. and Pitkäniemi, T. (2003). *Homicide Crime Scene Actions in a Finnish Sample of Mentally Ill Offenders*. Unpublished manuscript.

Hakkanen, H., Puolakka, P., and Santtila, P. (2004). Crime scene actions and offender characteristics in arson. *Legal and Criminological Psychology*, 9, 197–214.

Mokros, A. and Alison, L. (2002). Is offender profiling possible? Testing the predicted homology of crime scene actions and background characteristics in a sample of rapists. *Legal and Criminological Psychology*, 7, 25–43.

Salfati, C.G. (2000). Profiling homicide: a multidimensional approach. *Homicide Studies*, 4, 265–293.

Salfati, G. and Canter, D. (1999). Differentiating stranger murders: profiling offender characteristics from behavioural styles. *Behavioural Sciences and the Law*, 17, 391–406.

Santtila, P., Hakkanen, H., Alison, L., and Whyte, C. (2003). Juvenile firesetters: crime scene actions and offender characteristics. *Legal and Criminological Psychology*, 8, 1–20.

Santtila, P., Hakkanen, H., Canter, D., and Elfgren, T. (2003). Classifying homicide offenders and predicting their characteristics from crime scene behaviour. *Scandinavian Journal of Psychology*, 44, 107–118.

Schutz, W. (1992). Beyond Firo-B -3 new theory derived measures – element B: behaviour, element F: feelings, element S: self. *Psychological Reports*, 70, 915–937.

Shye, S. (1985). Nonmetric mulitvariate models for behavioural action systems, in *Facet Theory: Approaches to Social Research*, edited by D. Canter. New York: Springer-Verlag.

Tabachnick, B.G and Fidell, L.S. (1983). *Using Multivariate Statistics*. London: Harper and Row.

Youngs, D. (2004). Personality correlates of offence style. *Journal of Investigative Psychology and Offender Profiling*, 1, 99–119.

Youngs, D. and Canter, D. *Are Criminals Specialists, Generalists or Both*. Manuscript in Preparation.

Youngs, D. and Canter, D. (in prep). *Specialisation and the Radex Model of Criminal Differentiation*. Manuscript in Preparation.

Zaitsu, W. (2010). Homicidal poisoning in Japan: offender and crime characteristics. *International Journal of Police Sciefnce & Management*, 12, 503–515.

# Chapter 14
# Closing Remarks

David Canter

I have always been impressed by the Talmudic comment which points out that the way to evaluate a teacher is by considering his pupils. This volume, which Donna Youngs has done such an excellent job in putting together, offers for public view the opportunity to consider that powerful interaction. It shows that a professor is only as good as his students. Indeed that the power of any ideas lies in what people do with them. They can be abused, for example in the way racists have abused evolutionary theory, or they can be enhanced, developed and given life as the contributors to this volume have done with the first, halting steps I am taking in developing investigative psychology.

The hypothetico-deductive approach to science, in which I was schooled, emphasises a precise formulation of concepts and their implications that are carefully tested in controlled experiments derived directly from the theory under scrutiny. However, Once I realised how arid and inhibiting of innovation is that approach, as well as its destruction of the psychological phenomena it claims to study, I became more relaxed about offering general frameworks, for considering human activity, or even outlining approaches to solving psychological problems without detailed specification of what those problems are. This book shows how that open approach has provided footholds for people to climb up, plateaus for them to build their careers in and expanses to wander across.

It is this uptake, elaboration and ready exploration by people who have studied and worked with me, of ideas and issues that often started life as thoughts in lectures or asides in conversations that has been the greatest sustenance to me in my academic career. I follow Umberto Eco's answer when asked why he still was involved in teaching late in his career 'I feed on young blood'. But it is the enthusiasm and intelligent engagement that is illustrated throughout this book, which is the real delight and keeps me keen to continue to work in an academic milieu despite the increasingly destructive pressures on its intellectual foundations.

The involvement of people from so many different backgrounds with such a variety of perspectives that are apparent from the chapters in this volume show that Investigative Psychology 'has legs', as they say of ideas for television series. It is going to run and run. As each person brings new ways of thinking and new topics for consideration the field increases in breadth and depth. That is the major excitement for me and what keeps me engaged. Just when I can think of no other direction to move research in a colleague or student raises a question or makes a suggestion that opens up new and challenging vistas.

Inevitably, some people grasp the possibilities and find ways of contributing to the development of theory and practice more than others. Also at any point in time some will be in a better position to contribute to a book like this than others. So although I am impressed and humbled by the contributions to this volume I know that there are many others who have much to offer, whose work in this area will emerge in other ways.

My final word has to be one of gratitude to Donna Youngs who has championed the development of Investigative Psychology and has been tireless in making it such a vibrant field of publication and of practice. This book is as much a tribute to her perspicacity as it is an honour for me.

# SECTION 4
# Selected Works of Professor Canter

**Selected Commentaries by Professor Canter**

# Chapter 15
# Geographical Offender Profiling: Using Insights from Practical Applications to Enhance Theoretical Explorations

David Canter

## Naive Judgments of Criminal Spatial Activity

Since the early Canter and Larkin (1993) and Canter and Gregory (1994) studies showed the empirical validity of determining the area in which a serial offender is likely to live from details of where crimes were committed, the whole area of what has become known as Geographical Offender Profiling (GOP) has generated an increasing amount of research and heated debate around its theoretical basis effectiveness and ways in which it can be applied in a wide variety of police investigations.

In order to demonstrate the ideas behind the emerging principles and findings of GOP research I used to carry out exercises with my students on the MSc in Investigative Psychology at the University of Liverpool from the mid-1990s for about 15 years. In those sessions I gave students details of the crimes committed by serial killers, drawn from published reports, which included information about the victims and dates of the crimes as well as the locations on a map of body disposal sites. The students were asked to guess where the offender lived and provide their reasons. Their decisions were then compared with the results obtained from the existing version of the GOP system, Dragnet (Canter et al., 2000).

This teaching exercise revealed both the distractions and complexities of working with the details of actual cases as well as the limitations of the computer models of offender spatial behaviour available at that time. In some cases students would do better than Dragnet, for example when they took account of useful sequential or land-use information that the computer ignored. In other cases they would do worse, when for instance they made inappropriate inferences about the offender's familiarity with an area or the significance of the body disposal site location.

The exercise thus taught students a lot about the need to defend their assumptions and how easy it was to be misled by irrelevant details. By giving them a number of examples it was also possible to show the variety of spatial distributions of crime site locations and the consequent challenge of developing any simple models that would apply to all criminal spatial activity.

## From Lecture Theatre to Laboratory

Some of my students (Snook et al., 2002, 2004) who took part in those active lectures realised that they could be the basis of some interesting, if somewhat artificial, experiments. They asked their subjects to apply a straightforward set of geometric rules to points drawn on a sheet of paper. These rules amount to asking respondents to mark the spot where they estimate the centre of gravity of the points to be. The dots on the paper reflected locations of offences on a map. So that in so far as the offender's home really is near to the centre of gravity of those locations this task is an analogy for identifying the likely residential location of an offender from where crimes are committed.

What apparently led Snook and his associates to select this as a model for experimental study was that, in general, when students were provided with the broad principles on which computerised geographical profiling systems operate on average their guesses were reasonably close to what the computer would produce, having therefore a similar overall accuracy.

That students can on average be as accurate as GOP software in estimating an offender's location should not be a surprise because the simplified models the students were given that are built into computer systems were derived from empirical studies going back over a decade (Canter and Larkin, 1993; Canter and Gregory, 1993). These studies show that in as many as 80% of cases (and usually in at least 50%) offenders live within an area circumscribed by their known offences and surprisingly often live reasonably close to the centre of gravity of those offence locations. Different algorithms can be applied to give more precision to the predicted base of an offender but the police data on which any calculations are based lack precision and accuracy so as Levine and Associates (2000) have pointed out they all tend to give similar results.

However, the average response of a group of judges looking at dots on a page should not be equated with the workings of a computer. From my experience in workshops using the examples I had used with students, as mentioned earlier, and in discussions with police officers on live enquiries, it is not uncommon for them to be misled by irrelevant crime details that the computer algorithms ignore. They are also typically inconsistent in the criteria that they use for making guesses about an offender's base in a way that a computer is not. The effectiveness of people or computers will depend on the validity and generalisability of the principles being applied to patterns in criminal spatial behaviour not on the whether it is a person or a computer making use of those patterns. As research adds further subtlety to the models of criminal spatial activity so it becomes more difficult for humans to emulate those models as recent studies are showing (Canter et al., 2012)

It is essential to note, though, that no detailed studies of representative samples of cases show that current geographical profiling models are very accurate in more than a small percentage of cases. This small percentage is operationally useful and produces enough impressive case studies to encourage the mass media and police officers to regard geographical profiling as a useful tool. However, the limits to the effectiveness of the systems in use show that there is considerable noise in the data used and many sources of error in the models that further research needs to address.

The errors in the results from current computer algorithms are thus partly a function of how oversimplified are the models of criminal spatial behaviour on which they are built. In essence these models are little more than a set of straightforward geometrical principles. This raises the questions of whether criminals draw, at least implicitly, on such uncomplicated cognitive rules when deciding where to commit their crimes. Initial explorations by Canter and Hodge (2000), in which criminals are asked to draw 'mental maps' of where they commit their crimes, are beginning to show how impoverished are current geometrical models. Therefore the limitations in the effectiveness of geographical profiling systems, whether carried out with or without the aid of computers, are likely to be due to the simple-mindedness of the models of criminal cognition they assume.

As I have commented, the academic experiment of seeing whether people on average can guess where an offender is based as accurately as a computer programme can 'raises some important, but is has to be admitted not especially profound, questions about the judgements people are able to make when faced with a simplified summary of the spatial distribution of crime locations. If the task did simulate an important component of an investigative decision making process it would raise the possibility that the skills the subjects exhibit could replace intensive training sold at considerable expense and requiring a dedicated computer system' (Canter, 2005, p. 664).

These experiments therefore lead to two sets of issues. One is whether the models that have emerged from research require computer systems to put them into practice? In other words are the weaknesses in the predictive power of current models their inherent simplicity? That does seem to be the case raising the further question of what the basis of their limitations are?

The answer to this question can be found in the other challenge to the laboratory simulations/class exercises where people attempt to determine where an offender may have a base. This is about the operational conditions in which the application of geometrical models, and computerised support for those models take place. In other words, should the limitations in predicting a serial offender's base, in academic simulations of GOP, be put down to the fact that these simulations GOP do not take account of other relevant information available to crime analysts and police investigators? If that is the case then this relevant information needs to be incorporated into GOP systems and needs careful definition and the validity of its improvement to GOP needs empirical testing.

## Applying GOP in Practice

Rossmo (2005) disputes the claims that people are as effective as GOP systems by arguing that in actual practice these systems are an adjunct to other information available to the 'geographical profiler'. This can include knowledge of land use and transport routes, guardianship and target attractiveness. But surely is it not more appropriate to think of the lack of these being accounted for in GOP systems as sources for error in current algorithms that need further research?

Furthermore, there is the question of exactly how police investigators do make use of decision support systems? This is important to understand because it has implications for the details of how the system should function and the levels of accuracy required. Such information could therefore indicate that many of the questions about the accuracy of GOP systems are less relevant in practice than other matters such as their robustness and ease of use.

In practice police investigators typically select the series of offences for which they consider geo-behavioural analysis to be appropriate. This, of course, biases the sample on which geographical profiling has been operationally tested. This is quite different from the studies of geographical profiling (for example, Canter et al., 2000), in which a full set of cases, unselected in any way, are subject to study. It is that unbiased sample which reveals the broad findings of offender's geo-behavioural consistencies.

The basis for selecting operational cases to work on is sometimes made to seem sophisticated and experience based. Serial offenders are referred to as predator and an evocatively rich vocabulary is drawn on to imply recognisably distinct styles of predation. This implies that the geographic profiler is not just a behavioural scientist seeking to develop objective models of criminal actions, but a hunter with special skills seeking out a prey. Terms such as 'hunting area', 'troller' and 'poachers' are drawn on as rhetorical devices that can obscure the need to provide detailed definition of concepts and explanations. They suggest that the police officer's decisions are a product of experience rather than being based on established empirical findings.

## When to Use GOP

At present there is no definitive account of the objective processes that can be used to select crimes in order to increase the probability of a geographic profiling analysis being effective, although that is certainly a viable and active area for research. Various police officers, however, have offered up suggestions derived from cases in which they have been involved that do provide interesting hypotheses for further study. Some of the issues they raise are revealed through published case studies (Canter, 2004). These indicate areas in which further understanding of criminal processes would be productive.

One such issue is the question of the minimum number of cases necessary before a geographic profiling analysis can be conducted. A random numbers trial described as a 'Monte Carlo' analysis is sometimes quoted as a way of answering this question, leading to the claim that a minimum of 5 crimes are necessary before geographic profiling can be of value (Rossmo, 2000). This process uses 'a computer program to generate random crime site coordinates based on a fixed-buffer distance decay function' (Rossmo, 2000, p. 206). Clearly, such a trial is artificial in the extreme. It is thus not unexpected that detailed published accounts of studies using Dragnet on a non-artificially selected sample of actual crimes (for example, Canter et al., 2000) have shown that there is no empirical necessity for using five or more crime locations. Indeed there is considerable case study evidence (Canter, 2004) to show that serial offenders often indicate their base location in the first two or three crimes they commit. But even in one-off crimes the likelihood of an offender being local to the offence can be of great value to investigators (cf. Jill Dando murder – Canter, 2004) and just how local can be estimated by using the decay functions at the heart of geographic profiling software.

Another issue is the claim that in order to use geographic profiling the crimes must be 'linked together and the series relatively complete'. Yet consideration of the statistical issues involved make clear that there is no need for the crime series to be complete, as long as it is a representative, unbiased sample of the crimes the offender has committed. Any subset of the offender's crime locations should give the same result if the model is appropriate.

The need for the crimes to be linked is also a consequence of noise in the information available. In a series with a large number of crimes a small number of inappropriately included crimes that do not distort the overall geography of the crime locations will have little effect on the outcome of geo-behavioural analysis. In a smaller series and with crimes that would greatly modify the spatial configuration the problem of errant data is more marked. The issue is thus not a matter of police intuition but one of estimating the consequences of various types of error for the various conclusions that might be reached. The impact of including or omitting various crime locations, which the flexibility of Dragnet, for example, makes possible is one way of determining the sensitivity to possible biases in the data of any inferences drawn. The question of including crimes inappropriately into the series is thus one of error estimation and its consequences.

The same is true for the need to determine if the offender is travelling into an area to commit his crimes, often somewhat erroneously referred to as a 'commuter', or if the offender has moved home during a crime series. As yet there is no published evidence that police officers are able to determine with any accuracy if the offender is based in the area of his crimes or not. Nor are there any objective guidelines that have been empirically supported to determine this.

The lack of guidelines demonstrates the need for research that demonstrates the size and nature of any errors introduced by the complexities of criminal mobility and how they may be reduced. The different patterns of offender mobility introduce errors into current geo-behavioural models. That is part of the reasons why the results of published studies of geographical profiling do not reveal complete accuracy for the process. What is needed is more careful determination of how to reduce errors by specifying the measurable influences on criminal geographical activity.

The most problematic issue is the process of linking crimes to a common offender in the absence of clear forensic or other identifying information. Bennell and Canter (2002) have shown that geo-behavioural information can be remarkably productive in doing this. Such findings rather turn on their head any proposal that crimes should first be linked then geographically profiled. It may be of more operational value to deal with crime locations first and use that as part of the process of linking.

## Is Great Geographical Precision Needed?

Geographic profiling systems provide probabilities across a geographical area rather than a point location. The idea being that the regional probabilities would be used for setting up police searches for possible suspects. However, in the very detailed accounts Canter (2004) gives of a number of police investigations that used geographical searches it transpires that the police do not often set up searches that directly and precisely shaped by the probabilities generated on the geographically profiled map. The search strategies of investigators typically seem to draw on the locations of known offenders and distance from key points on the map, only partly determined by the highest probability indicated by geographical profiling.

This raises some intriguing questions about the cognitive processes underlying police geographical search patterns and how they may be best integrated into geo-behaviourally based decision support systems. Such explorations will improve our currently limited understanding of the mental models on which police draw to make their decisions as well as opening the way for psychologically richer, new generation of geographical profiling systems.

## Conclusions

The exploration of an exercise that started in my lectures as an analogy for police decision making using geographic profiling that Snook et al. (2004) utilised is inevitably limited, being not at all close to operational decision making as Rossmo (2005) argued. Nonetheless, the debate initiated by the confusion of theoretical and operational concerns do help to clarify the ways in which the current simple models built into GOP systems need to be developed to capture more of criminals' geographical behaviour and so be of more practical utility.

The apparent differences between the activity of an experienced police officer and the workings of GOP software help to reveal what limits the effectiveness of geographic profiling computer models. Rather than regarding these limits as merely practical restriction on selecting the offences that can be subjected to computer analysis it is more productive to regard them as areas in which hypotheses need to be developed. In so doing we will understand more about criminals' cognitive processes. We will also open the way to exploring the forms of heuristic that police investigators can actually use when drawing on geometrical representations of criminal spatial activity.

Inappropriate use of geographical profiling can have serious consequences. That is all the more reason why we must develop our understanding of what introduces biases and errors into geo-behavioural decision support systems and into the cognitive processes of those who use those systems. Treating these errors as operational problems that have to remain in the hands of police officers will keep criminal investigation in the dark ages of intuition and hunch.

**References**

Bennell, C. and Canter, D. (2002). Linking commercial burglaries by modus operandi: tests using regression and ROC analysis. *Journal of Science and Justice*, 42(3), 1–12.

Canter, D. (1994). *Criminal Shadows*. London: HarperCollins.

Canter, D. (2004). *Mapping Murder*. London: Virgin Books.

Canter, D. (2005). Confusing operational predicaments and cognitive explorations: comments on Rossmo and Snook et al. *Applied Cognitive Psychology*, 19(5), 663–668.

Canter, D.V., Coffey, T., Huntley, M., and Missen, C. (2000). Predicting serial killers' home base using a decision support system. *Journal of Quantitative Criminology*, 16, 457–478.

Canter, D. and Gregory, A. (1994). Identifying the residential location of rapists, *Journal of the Forensic Science Society*, 34, 169–175.

Canter, D.V and Hodge, S. (2000). Mental mapping. Criminal's mental maps, in *Atlas of Crime: Mapping the Criminal Landscape*, edited by L.S. Turnbull, E.H. Hendrix, and B.D. Dent. Phoenix, AZ: Onyx Press (pp. 186–191).

Canter, D.V. and Larkin, P. (1993). The environmental range of serial rapists. *Journal of Environmental Psychology*, 13, 63–69.

Levine, N. and Associates (2000). *Crimestat: A Spatial Statistics Program for the Analysis of Crime Incident Locations*. Washington, DC: National Institute of Justice.

Rossmo, D.K. (2000). *Geographic Profiling*. Boca Raton, FL: CRC Press.

Rossmo, D.K. (2005). Geographic heuristics or shortcuts to failure? Response to Snook et al. *Applied Cognitive Psychology* (in Press).

Snook, B., Canter, D.V., and Bennell, C. (2002). Predicting the home location of serial offenders: a preliminary comparison of the accuracy of human judges with a geographic profiling system. *Behavioral Sciences and the Law*, 20, 109–118.

Snook, B., Taylor, P.J., and Bennell, C. (2004). Geographic profiling: the fast, frugal, and accurate way. *Applied Cognitive Psychology*, 18, 105–121.

# Chapter 16
# Evaluating Profiling

## A General Response from Professor David Canter

Quite often I am asked by various students doing projects to complete questionnaires or to comment on scenarios of cases as part of an attempt to evaluate the 'effectiveness' of Offender Profiles. The number of such requests is so great that I do not have time to respond separately to each one. I hope therefore that you will forgive me for sending you this general response.

I do not participate in such projects because they are fundamentally flawed and based on a very confused notion of what 'offender profiling' is. Indeed the alacrity with which students are willing to send me e-mails without reading any of my writings that would have made my views clear is very discouraging. The rudeness with which some of them have responded when I have told them their project is a waste of time also saddens me when I think of such students as the academic leaders of the future.

It is not entirely the students fault, of course. These days students often get very little support for their projects and the members of staff who do supervise them are often more ignorant than the students themselves. The blind leading the blind comes to mind.

So let me briefly spell out why any project 'evaluating profiles' is pointless.

These projects typically come in two forms. One is to present one or two accounts of cases and to ask people to guess the characteristics of the perpetrator. The other is to provide a questionnaire that asks questions about success and influence over investigations. Both of these strategies are worthless for the following reasons:

### *Profiling is not a Reliable and Distinct Process*

They assume there is some 'process' of profiling. As if it were some engine or technology that just needed to be turned on. Yet if you read the accounts of people contributing to investigations you will see that there is no such process in existence. It is merely people giving opinions. There is no more point in evaluating this activity than in evaluating astrology columns in newspapers. There is an interesting question about why people believe these charts, but that is a quite different matter.

### *There is no Established Scientific Basis to Profiling*

The reason what astrology columns are not worth evaluating is because there is no reliable system or science behind them. Different astrologers will give quite different recommendations. It is like evaluating a doctor's diagnosis without any idea of the medical background on which it is based.

*Examining the Science of Psychological Contributions*

What needs to be evaluated are the scientific principles and methodologies that are available to contribute to police investigations. I have deliberately coined the term *Investigative Psychology* to cover all the ways in which psychology can contribute to investigations. So the first step is to test out the hypotheses that arise within this discipline. If they are not logical or consistent and if they are not supported by empirical results then there is no point worrying about how 'effective' they are in practice. So far the science is very poorly developed with many challenges to theories, data, modes of analysis and interpretation of results. It is therefore far too early to evaluate how all of this may work in relation to an actual investigation.

All current contributions to investigations are thus little more than informed (or misinformed) opinion. By evaluating this activity you are not evaluating a process but a particular person. It is no more systematic than guessing who is going to win a TV game show.

*The Base Rate Problem*

If the offender is typical of people who commit a certain type of crime then it is relatively easy to characterise that offender. But if he is not typical then there will be no scientific basis to any opinion. So providing summaries of particular cases and asking for opinions on whodunit is daft. The case can be selected to be typical or atypical and the results will be predictable as a consequence. Some crimes will have very heterogeneous offenders so the 'profiles' produced for them will be more likely to be off the mark than crimes that have homogeneous offenders.

*Contributing to Investigations*

The contribution to an investigation is an extremely complicated thing to assess. One small pointer may be crucial, a detailed and intelligent 'profile' may be mishandled and used ineffectively. So counting up the number of hits in the details provided is silly. In fact the notion of a 'profile' as a description of the characteristics of the offender, as being the main form of contribution misses the nature of any expert contribution. In one case the main contribution I made was to tell the police where they could identify the manufacturer of a particular paint. In other cases 'profilers' have advised looking at local shop-lifters without any detailed 'profile' being needed.

Every case is different and the sort of input will be different. Without taking this into account any attempt to evaluate the contribution of an individual will just be confusing. The only way the contribution can really be evaluated is by being part of the investigation right the way through. But even then, as I've said, you are not evaluating a process but a person.

In summary, then, I see the important research as being the development of Investigative Psychology, not following the Hollywood inspired trail of seeing 'how well profiles work'.

Some references for those who are willing to do some real work and read what has already been published.

## Textbooks


Canter, D. and Youngs, D. (2009). *Investigative Psychology: From Offender Profiling to the Analysis of Criminal Action*. Wiley: Chichester.

Canter, D. (2004). A Partial Order Scalogram Analysis of Criminal Network Structures. *Behaviormetrika*, 31(2), pp. 1–21.

Canter, D. (2004). Geographical Profiling of Criminals. *Medico-Legal Journal*, 72(2), pp. 53–66. EMIS.

Canter, D. (2004). Offender Profiling and Investigative Psychology. *Journal of Investigative Psychology and Offender Profiling*, vol. 1, pp. 1–15. Wiley InterScience <http://www3.interscience.wiley.com/cgi-bin/jissue/106558627>.

Canter, D. and Wentink, N. (2004). An Emipirical Test of Holmes and Holmes's Serial Murder Typology. *Criminal Justice and Behavior*, vol. 20, (10), pp. 1–26.

Yokuta, K. and Canter, D. (2004). Burglars' Specialisation: Development of a Thematic Approach in Investigative Psychology. *Behaviormetrika*, 31(2), pp. 1–15.

Youngs, D. (2004). Personality Correlates of Offence Style. *Journal of Investigative Psychology and Offender Profiling*, vol. 1, pp. 99–119. Wiley InterScience <http://www3.interscience.wiley.com/cgi-bin/jissue/108560916>.

Canter, D. and Alison, L.J. (2003). Converting Evidence into Data: The Use of Law Enforcement Archives as Unobtrusive Measurement. *The Qualitative Report*, 8(2), pp. 151–176.

Canter, D., Bennell, C., Alison, L., and Reddy, S. (2003). Differentiating Sex Offences: A Behaviorally Based Thematic Classification of Stranger Rapes. *Behavioral Sciences and the Law*, vol. 21, pp.157–174. Wiley InterScience <http://www3.interscience.wiley.com/cgi-bin/jissue/103527656>.

Canter, D., Kaouri, C., and Ioannou, M. (2003). The Facet Structure of Criminal Narratives, in *Facet Theory: Towards Cumulative Social Science*, edited by S. Levy and D. Elizur (pp. 27–38).

Canter, D., Grieve, N., Nicol, C., and Benneworth, K. (2003). Narrative Plausibility: The Impact of Sequence and Anchoring. *Behavioral Sciences and the Law*, vol. 21, pp. 251–267. Wiley InterScience <http://www3.interscience.wiley.com/cgi-bin/jissue/103527656>.

Canter, D. and Youngs, D. (2003). Beyond 'Offender Profiling': The Need for an Investigative Psychology, in *Handbook of Psychology in Legal Contexts*, Second edition, edited by D. Carson and R. Bull. John Wiley & Sons Ltd. (pp. 171–205).

# Chapter 17
# Narratives of Criminal Action and Forensic Psychology[1]

David Canter and Donna Youngs

## Responding to Ward (2011)

Ward's (2011) commentary on Youngs and Canter's (2011) exploration of the forms of personal narrative revealed in interviews with offenders provides a valuable elaboration of the utility of the narrative approach. Furthermore, by identifying areas for further clarification he shows the fruitfulness of this perspective and the rich research opportunities it provides as well as many practical applications. By opening up the background to the consideration of narratives tracing this back to Plutarch he shows their long-recognised value in providing insights into the human condition. All this is most encouraging and supports our view that the time is now ripe for the careful elaboration of the study and application of personal narratives within forensic and related contexts.

In reviewing the exploration of personal offender narratives Ward raises a number of issues that he sees as crucial. We address these in the current paper and show that the integration of theoretical with methodological considerations helps to resolve them. This integration also provides a basis for incorporating applications of our particular approach to criminal narratives into a wide range of contexts as varied as therapeutic interventions with offenders and investigative interviewing. However, we draw a distinction between the narratives of crimes, which we explore, and the broader life narratives that are Ward's focus. As we show, it is this more limited, focused examination of an offender's account of his experience of a crime that provides the strongest opportunity for developments in theory and method.

Ward identifies three classes of problems in Youngs and Canter (2011) which he says are 'evident within the broader field of narrative theory and research'. He lists these problems as 'definitional vagueness, lack of clarity concerning the nature of the self and its relationship to narrative roles, and methodological problems involving reliability and validity'. We consider these all to be aspects of the methodologies typically used to explore personal narratives. These methodologies have been limited within the 'broader field of narrative theory and research' because, indeed, of the *broadness* of that field. Ward identifies the problems he sees in our paper as typical

1 This chapter was first published in Legal and Criminological Psychology.

of the general narrative approach. This general approach places narrative theory firmly within considerations of identity and emphasises the forms of life-stories that cover many stages in a person's existence. The clearest, often quoted life-time, offender narratives that Ward draws attention to are the scripts that Maruna (2001) explored within the context of desistance from crime; *condemnation* and *redemption*. Such generic conceptualisations of a person's offending history underpin Ward and Marshall's (2007) argument that 'the rehabilitation of offenders depends crucially on the construction of a more adaptive narrative identity' (p. 280). In other words, they see identity as embedded in offenders' overarching, personal narratives. This makes considerable sense when the forms of narrative are lifetime frameworks, dealing with wide-ranging issues of criminality that have some underlying process such as redemption or condemnation at their heart.

However Youngs and Canter (2011) have a more specific objective of understanding what happens in any given crime. They agree with Presser's (2009) argument that a person's narratives can contribute to an understanding of the here and now of a particular set of actions. Youngs and Canter's starting point is the narrative that drives focused criminal action. This recognises that such narratives may differ substantively from narratives that have allowed and seek to explain a criminal lifestyle. In line with this, some of the themes they have identified (Canter, Kaouri and Ioannou, 2003; Youngs and Canter, 2011, 2012) are rather different from the 'victim of circumstance' theme running through the life narrative Maruna (2001) identifies within his persistent offenders. The relationship between the broader issues of lifetime narrative identity and the specific narratives revealed through Youngs and Canter's interviews is an important research question, but to find ways of answering it requires revisiting the origins of Youngs and Canter's model.

## From Offence Actions to Particular Narratives

In essence, Ward (2011) considers the issues Youngs and Canter (2011) raise from the perspective of therapeutic interventions, which is the domain in which the broader narrative perspective has taken root. But although this complements the investigative psychology objectives that were the starting point for our work in this area, the issues he raises are not as problematic in the context of actual crimes especially when quantitative methodologies are used to explore them.

Youngs and Canter's theory emerged directly out of the need to understand offenders' actions in a crime and the aspects of an offender that were salient in his or her criminal activity which could be used to contribute to investigative decision making. The idea here is that making inferences about offenders from their actions required some theoretical modeling. The proposal that this process of inference ('profiling') was more than a matter of deriving statistical relationships from a database was first sketched out by Canter (1994). Subsequently Investigative Psychologists (cf. Canter, 2011) have always been interested in understanding the specific, precise and direct processes that shape criminal actions. Canter made clear that the possibility of making inferences about the characteristics of the offender from his offence actions relies upon making sense of the psychological processes implied by a particular pattern of offending behaviour. In that work he also argued that the coherence that studies identified in criminals' detailed actions implied a narrative. For example, in one of the earliest studies in this domain, Canter and Heritage (1990) indicated that themes may be discerned in the rapist's comments that suggest he thinks he has a relationship with the victim, or in the serial killer's dismemberment of his victims' bodies that shows a distant objectifying of them as part of the killer's own 'adventure' (Canter, 1995). These considerations were the first steps towards identifying what the different narratives might be for different offences.

In subsequent developments, Canter and Youngs (2009) were able to propose particular narratives derived from the groupings or themes of co-occurring actions that investigative psychology studies were observing in the multivariate analyses of detailed offence behaviour. So, for example, they argued that rapes carried out with excessive violence, verbal insults and demeaning language and an extensive range of acts of sexual exploitation could be understood in terms of the vindictive and avenging agenda at the heart of a Tragedy narrative. A rather different narrative was implied by rapes in which the offender apologised to the victim, performed oral sex, asked the victim to participate both physically and verbally and complimented the victim. Canter and Youngs (2009) argue for an underlying storyline of Irony here; a narrative in which the offender seeks to position himself as the victim and does not fully acknowledge the violation he is committing. For Canter and Youngs, the underlying narratives that gave coherence to the empirical patterns of offence actions they were finding had much in common with the literary narrative themes that Frye (1957) had articulated, although clearly in profoundly destructive form. They draw upon his Quest (Romance), Tragedy, Adventure and Irony narratives to make sense of the themes of behavioural coherence emerging across the full range of forms of criminality.

The conceptualisation of criminal narratives in Youngs and Canter (2011) has its roots then in their discovery that the empirical models of the different modus operandi or offending styles seen across a range of offence types, from arson and burglary to rape and robbery, were readily interpreted in terms of 4 narrative themes, each related to a definitive role: The Professional Adventurer, the Victim's Irony, the Revenger's Tragedy and the Hero's Quest. Youngs and Canter's (2011) theoretical paper drew on the same underlying narratives but argued that the Roles the offenders saw themselves playing would be slightly different from those derived from analysis of the actions, advancing a Tragic Hero role from the Tragedy narrative and a Revengeful Mission role from the Quest narrative. As we show though, Youngs and Canter's subsequent empirical examination of the detailed components of each theme showed that the roles described by the offenders themselves could in fact be interpreted in line with the model derived from the offending actions (Youngs and Canter, 2012).

Although the recognition of narratives themes within patterns of offending is not direct evidence that the themes actually generated the actions, the breadth of application of the framework is nonetheless encouraging, particularly the emergence of the same broad themes in the offenders' own descriptions of their narrative offence roles that Youngs and Canter (2012) report.

## Beyond Motive and Personality: Narratives of Criminal Action

The investigative psychology approach to understanding the coherence within offending actions assumes that this requires understanding the meaning of the crime as it makes sense to the offender. This builds upon Canter's (1994) early work drawing on the narrative approach to show how offenders' narratives provide a richer understanding of the meaning of their offending than dispositional or social theories. He argued that as part of a personal story or narrative, motivation and meaning necessarily become the intention to act; the dynamic process that is required to move the drama forward. By understanding the narrative then, we get closer to understanding the action, as Presser (2005) also pointed out. A crucial aspect of this is that, following McAdams (1985), Canter (1994) made a clear distinction between the dynamic aspects inherent in any narrative, because narrative implies an unfolding series of episodes that the central protagonist moves through, and the more static aspects of personality traits that are regarded as enduring characteristics of the individual.

The distinction can be seen as that between the narrative mirroring a functional analysis of a process in which the individual is seen as an agent shaping and being shaped by his own personal story, and the structural components of the personality, on which trait theories and many models of identity focus. Within this framework narratives cannot be equated with a person's self-concept or identity, even if presented in narrative form. Identity is a larger scale concept that can embrace such broad notions as condemnation or redemption and may house many different day-to-day narratives and many sub-identities.

Offence narratives emerge out of specific aspects of a crime. In particular, stories emphasise interactions between the protagonist and others. They thus recognise the fundamentally interpersonal quality of crime; that it is an interactive, implicitly or explicitly social event. Ward (2011) does note that one of the key features of a narrative is that it is told in social relationships, so criminal actions that are lived narratives also imply that crime is an interpersonal transaction. The conception of the self in criminal narratives is necessarily, then, concerned with interpersonal self-awareness rather than introspective issues. In this way, in contrast to the general narratives that have been at the heart of the field of narrative theory and research, the narrative themes that Youngs and Canter illustrate relate to the psychological processes that an offender draws on when committing any given crime.

Although narratives embrace issues that are considered within the realms of personality theory, it is important to emphasise the inherent temporal, processing aspects of offence narratives. This makes their conceptualisation closer to popular ideas of 'motive' than to personality studies and a therapeutic focus on identity. However, the ambiguity of the meaning of criminal 'motives' ranging as it does from explanation, to objective, or even unconscious drive, and the assumption that there is one fixed motive for any crime, make the concept untenable for systematic use. Nonetheless the implications of movement inherent in the root of the term 'motive' is a useful component of this concept that is much more richly encapsulated in the idea of a criminal narrative. The narrative concept, furthermore, adds the implication of intention, whereas motive implies some driving force within the individual that has a less agentic quality than the idea of being hero or a professional, for example.

Legal systems recognise that agency is central to evaluating a person's action. Legal decision-making is based upon understanding what an individual was seeking to do. Yet, as Canter (2008) has argued in some detail, most psychological and social explanations of crime remove agency from the offender. His or her biology, personality or upbringing is seen as the causes of crime rather than the decisions an offender takes. The narrative perspective identifies the person as the agent of his/her own actions. Personal criminal narratives help us to understand the deliberative, defined, criminal activity by drawing attention to the processes that particular actions were part of at particular points in time. In the absence of agency based theories, we cannot explain why those actions are not committed at other points or by other individuals with similar background potentiating factors. Personal narratives, created by individuals in relation to their understanding of their own characteristics and circumstances, provide insight into what leads some people to pursue criminal activities whilst others are able to draw on protective factors that make them able to see their actions in a different light.

Furthermore, the dynamic, unfolding nature of narratives allows for a complex pattern of consistency and development of offending behaviour. Any consideration of personal narratives assumes change over time and therefore predicts that any underlying consistency in an offender's actions will draw on the themes to his personal, crime related narrative, rather than some fixed, unchanging pattern of behaviour.

The challenge of investigative psychology is to understand the underlying coherence to detailed, specific patterns of offending actions. This leads to a focus on the offender's meaning and intention, the unfolding development of the offence event and the interpersonal significance of the victim. These challenges are met by adopting a narrative approach to the offence, with the focus on agency, dynamic process and social roles that this allows.

## Narrative Roles: A Methodological Breakthrough

A particularly important aspect of Ward's commentary is the attention he draws to the definitional vagueness and methodological weaknesses inherent in the 'broader field of narrative theory and research'. Canter (1994) made clear, some time ago, that he was aware of these challenges and considered various ways of resolving them. He realised that by focusing on offence narratives we narrow the area of exploration enough to be able to find a proxy for the actual storyline – roles. Influenced by Goffman (1958) and the considerations of role theory within social psychology (Sarbin and Allen, 1968) Canter argued that the concept of role, drawn as it is from the dramaturgical approach within psychology, carries with it the implications of a storyline. When considering whole life narratives there will be many different roles a person plays, but in the limited 'action scene' of an offence, he argued that the particular role played in the crime is a reasonable summary of the storyline for that particular crime.

The assertion is that people can recognise and identify these roles without the complexity inherent in developing the full storyline. This opens up the possibility of a standard, quantitative measure of narrative themes, using Roles as a proxy for narratives. Pilot work demonstrated that offenders could reliably recognise the roles they played as part of a crime and an initial study (Canter, Kaouri and Ioannou, 2003) gave meaningful results. Development of this approach has produced the Narrative Roles Questionnaire (NRQ) (Youngs and Canter, 2012) which is now in use as part of a multi-national study of criminal narratives. This is a 32 item instrument that provides descriptions of possible roles (as illustrated in Table 17.1) that the offender may have felt s/he was taking on when carrying out a particular crime. The offender is asked to indicate on a five-point scale how much the statement describes the offending experience.

Offence event roles provide a medium through which implicit narrative processes are given tangible form and can be related to a given context through descriptions that capture the quality of the agency that is underpinning the detailed action in that event. Early indications are that such abbreviations work well with offending behaviour perhaps because they capture the egocentric focus at the heart of criminal action. This readily allows exploration of the distorted, self-centered, simple and clichéd perspectives that often characterise offending activity. Furthermore, a measure that focuses on the role experienced within an offending event encourages a non-threatening summary of a criminal narrative theme.

The focus on the direct descriptions of an offender's experience of the event does not require overt justification or even readily allow the respondent social desirability interpretation or conscious positioning across items. Such techniques, rather than an overt life story interview, may be particularly useful in narrative research as they do not require the individual to make explicit the underlying themes within their narrative or to provide a coherent 'life story' account. Indeed the roles technique may help reduce the re-writing of narratives and reveal the presence of narrative themes of which the individual may not be fully aware. In studies of criminals' experience, where those themes may be less socially acceptable or where respondents may be less articulate, such techniques have proven particularly powerful. The NRQ provides a more objective account of the dominant theme in a criminal's actions, when completed to describe the role being played when carrying out a specific crime, than a qualitative analysis of the motifs that emerge from a free-flowing account, even though such qualitative material can enhance theory and enrich understanding as Youngs and Canter (2011) show.

Multivariate analyses of responses from many offenders (Canter et al, 2003; Youngs and Canter, 2012) support the identification of the four dominant narrative themes that were illustrated from the qualitative interviews drawn on in Youngs and Canter (2011). The scales derived from these analyses give a more precise operational definition of the narrative themes to which the roles relate than is possible from qualitative analysis of open-ended interviews. So, for example, the item in the NRQ 'I was trying to get revenge', is not highly correlated with items such as 'it was a mission' but is correlated with 'what was happening was just fate'. This helps to operationalise the idea of a doomed 'Tragedy' narrative as being part of the Revenger role rather than that of a Heroic mission. By contrast the Quest narrative appears to be reflected in items such as 'It was a manly thing to do' that implies the offender sees his/her role as that of a Hero, not someone on a Revengeful Mission as Youngs and Canter (2011) had postulated from the qualitative analysis of interviews. The key statements that define each role are shown in Table 17.1.

The exemplar statements in Table 17.1 illustrate how the NRQ allows a more precise definition of each of the narrative themes that were illustrated with case studies in Canter and Youngs (2011). For instance the feelings of helplessness that are associated with seeing oneself as a 'Victim', the recognition that the 'Revengeful' role is interpreted as being the only action available to the offender and what is called the 'Hero' role being considered as manly and a quest for recognition.

**Table 17.1 Indicative statements that define narrative roles taken from narrative roles questionnaire (Youngs and Canter, 2012)**

| | |
|---|---|
| Professional | 'I was like a professional'<br>'For me, it was like a usual days work'<br>'I was doing a job'<br>'It was routine' |
| Hero | 'I was looking for recognition'<br>'I couldn't stop myself'<br>'It was like I wasn't part of it'<br>'It was a manly thing to do' |
| Victim | 'I was a victim'<br>'I was helpless'<br>'I was confused about what was happening'<br>'I just wanted to get it over with' |
| Revenger | 'I was trying to get revenge'<br>'I didn't care what would happen'<br>'It was my only choice'<br>'I had to do it'. |

A high proportion of the items in the NRQ relate to the general theme of being a 'professional' offender. Given the origins of these items in interviews with offenders this is perhaps to be expected. Yet this large number of items does allow some differentiation within the 'Professional' theme. This differentiation draws attention to a subset of the 'Professional' theme that deals with 'excitement' and 'adventure', the criminal activity being 'fun' and 'interesting'. So for some offenders who see themselves as involved in a routine, professional activity, this is nonetheless an adventure, whereas for others there is more emphasis on being in control.

These refinements illustrate the value of this more quantitative approach, especially when combined with multi-dimensional analysis, in facilitating the elaboration of themes. Such elaboration is more difficult when open-ended qualitative material is the only source, which is part of the reason why Ward sought clarification of the definitions in the original Youngs and Canter (2011) paper. As so often in psychology more precise definitions are tied into more specific data collection methodologies. So, the NRQ provides an increase in clarity as well as offering a methodology that is now in use as part of an international research project.

The multivariate analysis of the NRQ reported in Youngs and Canter (2012) shows that the items are unevenly distributed across the dominant narrative themes. In line with the facet approach (Canter, 1985) from which this methodology is derived, this allows development of the pro forma by adding further items that it is hypothesised will enhance the number of items in any particular theme, allowing a direct test of the central thematic hypotheses with new data sets. Such tests help further to clarify the central concepts and ways of studying them.

## Psychological Aspects of Narrative Themes

The specification of offence narratives also reveals the psychological influences operating during offending. The four narrative themes elaborated using the NRQ help to clarify the range of psychological processes inherent in criminal actions. Youngs and Canter (2011) elaborate these implicit psychological processes. These include criminal thinking styles such as justification and harm minimisation, illustrated for example by the 'Professional' offence being presented as one that underplays the harm to the victim and presents the activity as a routine job. They also incorporate self-concepts and other aspects of identity in relation to a particular crime, clarifying the issue Ward raises about the link between identity and narratives. In the context of a particular crime there is an identity that comes from the dominant narrative theme, such as the offender being a 'manly' Hero, or 'helpless' Victim.

Careful consideration of the structure of offence narratives indicates that they carry affective components as well. This answers the question Ward raises about the links between narratives and emotions. As for any dramatic plot, there are distinct emotions associated with it. In the narratives considered here it is hypothesised, for example, that the Professional, especially one with a strong Adventure component would be associated with positive emotions, but in contrast the Victim would involve negative affect. Preliminary tests of this hypothesis (Canter and Ioannou, 2004) not only reveal the strong emotions experienced by a criminal during their crimes, as Katz (1988) proposed, but also that a methodology similar to the NRQ can be feasibly used with offenders to describe his or her emotions when committing their crimes. This thus provides a clear method for exploring the links between emotions and narratives, which is currently in use.

## Potential Contributions of Offence Narratives

We see the emphasis on offence narratives as providing some distinct, additional content to the understanding of the psychological processes inherent in criminal actions. This draws directly from the literary exploration of major narrative themes, such as those discussed by Frye (1957), Booker (2004) or Herman (2009). The relevance of these considerations to psychological explanations can be shown by reference to one central analytic stance within literary explorations. At its most elementary, literary criticism commonly accepts that the difference between comedy and tragedy is that in comedy the person overcomes circumstances but in tragedy the circumstances overcome the person. In psychological terms, these two poles imply a difference in locus of control running over a set of related episodes, the comic reflecting an internal agency and the tragic an external one. In the criminal context we have argued that the positive, controlling narrative is best described as a professional adventure. The negative, external imposition is reflected in victim narratives.

Narratives also incorporate aspects of justification, cognitive distortion and other criminal thinking styles (Walters, 2003). As Youngs and Canter (2012) show in some detail, when criminal actions are seen as part of a personal narrative then, for example, justifications are given a clear dynamic. An offender who says 'it's a tragedy really, the fates were against me' or 'I just had to make clear I was in charge' is recounting a way of exonerating his behaviour by drawing on implicit narratives intrinsic to his/her culture.

In other words, we are not offering the narrative perspective as some entirely new way of conceptualising criminal actions but as a framework that integrates many of the existing psychological approaches and concerns relating to criminal activity. In particular, the narratives suggest particular ways in which the specific emotions, cognitions and interpersonal tendency that have been implicated in criminality by diverse authorities (Bandura, 1990; Katz, 1998; Sykes and Matza, 1957) may combine. Interestingly, the core distinctions identified in these different criminological domains do appear to map on to the four preliminary narrative themes articulated thus far (Youngs and Canter, 2011, 2012). These narrative themes articulate the quality of the agency that activates these various psychological components of offending. In so doing, they offer an approach to explaining what

Presser (2009) referred to as the 'here and now' of crime that criminological thinking usually lacks. We suggest offence narratives are also the basis for understanding the 'how' of offending; explorations that move us beyond general issues of 'why' or broad causal factors on to considerations of the meaning of the specific unfolding actions for the protagonist.

## Further Contributions of Offence Narrative Framework

This focus on criminal variants of narratives and on narratives as they are revealed in specific events, in other words, the Narrative Role, has a broader potential contribution to thinking in criminology and narrative psychology generally. Youngs and Canter (2012) showed how these narrative themes capture the core psychological distinctions in emotion, offenders' cognitions and aspects of interpersonal self-awareness, that have been established previously. In the cognitive domain, two basic distinctions have been specified as underpinning offenders' justifications: (Maruna and Mann, 2006). Youngs and Canter tie the four combinations of distorted thinking produced by these into their four distinct narrative themes. Within the emotional domain, two core dimensions of Arousal/Non-arousal and Pleasure/Displeasure have been delineated. Arguing that with a few exceptions, that general criminal activity varies from highly dis-pleasurable to neutral or mildly pleasurable, Youngs and Canter show that their four offence narratives capture the four combinations of highly aroused/highly dis-pleasurable, Non-aroused/highly dis-pleasurable, highly aroused/neutral and Non-aroused/neutral.

Youngs and Canter also show how the fundamental distinctions delineated in interpersonal tendency are captured by the different narratives. They use this to differentiate the offender's offence-specific identity implied by the narratives. Based upon the view that offending is a fundamentally interpersonal activity, the victim of which may be implicit or explicit (Canter, 1989), they focus on those aspects of identity that concern the offender's self-awareness relative to the victim. Youngs and Canter show how these are reflected in variations in the offence narratives as perceptions of themselves as strong or weak relative to the victim (whether implicit or explicit) and as variations in the extent to which the victim is significant for the offender. The integration of psychological components implied by the narrative themes is summarised in Table 17.2

## Integrating Different Aetiological Factors

Beyond the rich psychological aspects of the narrative perspective on criminal actions as revealed through the NRQ, the particular combinations of the psychological processes that interact to produce the offence roles provide interesting insights into the potential relationships between distinct constructs that come from

**Table 17.2 Narrative integration of affective, cognitive and offence-specific identity components of offending**

| Narrative role | Offence identity | Cognitive distortions | Emotional state |
|---|---|---|---|
| *Quest Narrative*<br>The proposed *Hero* role that emerges from a *Quest* narrative is hypothesised to be comprised of the following: | Strong;<br>Others Significant | Present Own Alternative Evaluations of Actions; Refocus impact in terms Offender's Own Objectives | Calm;<br>Displeasurable |
| *Tragedy Narrative*<br>The proposed *Revenger* role hypothesised to emerge from the *Tragedy* narrative, is further hypothesised to have the following components: | Weak;<br>Others Not Significant | Responsibility Attributed to Others; Minimise Impact | Aroused;<br>Neutral |
| *Adventure Narrative*<br>The proposed *Professional* role, rooted in an *Adventure* narrative, is hypothesised to emerge out of the following: | Strong;<br>Others Not Significant | Present Own Alternative Evaluations of actions; Minimise Impact | Calm;<br>Neutral |
| *Irony Narrative*<br>The proposed *Victim* role is hypothesised to emerge out of the *Irony* narrative and to comprise following: | Weak;<br>Others Significant | Responsibility Attributed to Others; Refocus impact in terms offender's own objectives | Aroused;<br>Displeasurable |

fundamentally different criminological schools. They draw together aspects of the emotional experience of crime emanating from Katz's (1988) innovative writings on the affective 'seductions of crime', with the cognitive focus of Sykes and Matza's (1957) techniques of neutralisation and Bandura's (1990) theory of moral disengagement, as well as aspects of criminal identity that can be tied into the subcultural perspectives of Cloward and Ohlin (1960) and others.

The roles suggest some specific relationships between the cognitive, affective and identity concepts that have previously been studied in isolation. They suggest, for example, that through the Hero role, a tendency to distort cognitive interpretations of crime by focusing on one's own objectives only and presenting one's own evaluation of events rather than attempting to minimise the harm, will tend to co-occur in criminal activity underpinned by a negative, non-aroused emotional state during which the offender will have a strong sense of self-awareness and where the others involved are significant. Many other refutable hypotheses can be derived from the narratives of criminal actions as summarised at the end of this paper.

## Reaching Out to Therapy

A particularly interesting contribution of Ward's comments is his proposal that the narrative themes we have identified have potential in treatment interventions with offenders. A better understanding of the detailed, substantive nature of the different narratives that underpin offence action opens the way for more refined utilisation of narrative ideas in treatment. Our approach proposes that it is not only the broad lifetime narratives that are relevant when treating offenders, such as the *condemnation* and *redemption* frameworks proffered by Maruna (2001), but the detailed consideration of actual criminal events and whether the offenders see themselves as Victims, Heroes, Professionals or on a Revengeful mission in that crime. The particular nature of the narrative themes carries direct intervention implications. For example, an intervention focus in respect of a Victim Role may be the rewriting of past disappointments, while for the Revenger issues of anger management may be more pertinent. Furthermore, the articulation of the problem (the offence) in a narrative form opens up the possibility of treatment in the form of direct counter-narratives, in much the same way that Ward's Good Lives model focuses on developing positive general life stories.

In preliminary explorations of this approach with actual clinical interventions it has been found fruitful to use the NRQ as a starting point for discussions with offenders. This allows consideration of the many forms of psychological process that are inherent in the narrative themes of particular crimes. However, framing the therapeutic intervention within the narrative perspective is less threatening and invasive for offenders than a direct confrontation over thought patterns and beliefs. It also allows the therapist to embed the intervention in the cultural story-lines with which the offender will be familiar.

## Conclusions and a Research Agenda

The development of the NRQ was aimed specifically at dealing with the sorts of concerns Ward (2011) expressed as 'evident within the broader field of narrative theory and research', namely 'definitional vagueness, lack of clarity concerning the nature of the self and its relationship to narrative roles, and methodological problems involving reliability and validity'. By developing a systematic research instrument that uses groupings of roles as summaries of narrative themes it has been possible to provide more precise definitions as well as reliable measurement that validly captures accounts given in much fuller open-ended interviews.

The nature of the self-revealed within these narrative roles has also been clarified through careful consideration of the complex mixture of psychological processes captured by the NRQ. Youngs and Canter (2012) show that the four narrative themes map readily onto the two axes of Potency and Intimacy that McAdams (1985) argues underpin all personal narratives measures; the Victim, for instance, being Low Potency and High Intimacy, whereas the Hero is High Potency and High Intimacy. Further, each narrative theme also carries implications about a) the cognitive interpretation the offender has of the offence, b) the emotional aspects of the involvement in the offence and c) the interpersonal identity. In other words, narrative roles reflect the relationship the offender sees himself having with others, as shaped by his cognitions and emotions. There is thus no simple relationship between a person's identity in general and the narrative roles that are actualised in a crime. Indeed the presence of narrative roles relating to particular crimes does raise the question of whether general identity or self-concept is always an appropriate focus for considering offenders. Ward opens up what he calls a post-modern view of a person having multiple identities, but it is not necessary to go that far, merely to recognise the different roles a person may play in different situations. How the experience of these episodes gives shape to a self-concept is an interesting and important area for further study.

### *Elaborating Substantive Themes*

The four narrative themes described by Youngs and Canter (2011, 2012) were derived from interviews with offenders followed up by the development of standard questionnaires. However, the analysis and careful consideration of the results does indicate that the Hero, Victim, Professional and Revenger narrative themes are only the essence of crime narratives and many refinements are possible. They provide four cardinal points but research to elaborate and develop them will be of great value.

The dynamic quality of the whole notion of narrative provides a particular challenge for research. The question of what is consistent and what varies in an offender's unfolding crime narratives requires careful research design and analysis to answer. Indeed it may be expected that some narratives may be more consistent across crimes for an offender than others. For example, it is a reasonable hypothesis that the Professional narrative implies a particular pattern of activities that would be repeated from crime to crime. The Revenger on the other hand may see himself as more buffeted by the fates and behave very differently in different circumstances. The tools are now in place to explore such issues.

How exactly do offence actions relate to the Narrative Roles? The models of different patterns of offending style can be interpreted in terms the four narrative themes. But research has not yet been published that establishes clear relationships between the offenders' descriptions of their offence Narrative Role and their offence actions in those crimes. Some quite complex relationships might be expected because of the implications that the narrative role has for interactions with others and the significance of the particular situation.

### *Influences on Narrative Roles*

The Narrative Roles that Youngs and Canter (2011, 2012) posit were identified with incarcerated offenders who had been convicted for the crime they described. It is reasonable to assume that this context may have had an influence on the themes described, although the meaningful differences within this sample do point to a general validity. But research does need to establish the impact of various post offence events, including conviction and treatment on the accounts offenders give of their crime experience.

We see the assertion that offenders' accounts of their Narrative Roles as simply post offence rationalisations as less problematic. In describing the role that was dominant in an offence an individual has to draw upon narratives s/he regards as plausible. So even if they are implicit justifications, respondents are demonstrating which storyline they consider the most relevant to their own understanding of their circumstances. It is that personal account that forensic psychologists have to work with either in investigations or in therapeutic interventions.

*Offence Narrative Roles and Life Narratives*

Any life story consists of many episodes. There may be an overarching theme to it as revealed in Maruna's (2001) explorations of desisters and persisters, or there may be many different aspects to it in a more complex set of distinct incidents. There is thus an interesting research question as to the ways in the four narrative themes operate in relation to larger scale life narratives.

*Correlates of the Narrative Roles*

Offenders' crime narratives, especially as revealed through the NRQ encapsulate many aspects of the psychological processes underpinning criminal actions. They add a strong dynamic to the consideration of illegal behaviour and place the agency for the crime firmly with the criminal. In this way, they give rise to many and varied hypotheses about the psychological characteristics and backgrounds of offenders showing different forms of this agency. Indeed, crime narratives offer a rich framework for considering many aspects of criminality, different forms of agency generating different hypotheses about the emergence of offence forms, their development, maintenance and decline.

One particularly interesting possibility is that distinct narrative roles may relate to different diagnostic categories. Psychopathy and depression would be expected to be expressed in different narrative roles and the forms that other aspects of psychosis take when expressed as narrative accounts of crimes would also be hypothesised to be distinct. Intriguingly, research in its early stages has indicated that psychiatric patients are able to complete the NRQ and produce meaningful answers.

In conclusion, then, the offence narrative framework as encompassed in the NRQ, focuses on what happens in a crime and how the offender makes sense of that. This provides methodological and definitional clarity to the study of criminals' narratives that is difficult to achieve when drawing on the broad life narratives that are central to Ward's critique of the utilisation of the narrative approach. This development opens up many areas for research, spawning many testable hypotheses.

## References


Bandura, A. (1990). Mechanisms of moral disengagement, in *Origins of Terrorism; Psychologies, Ideologies, Theologies, Sates of Mind*, edited by A. Reich. New York, NY: Cambridge University Press (pp. 161–191).

Booker, C. (2004). *The Seven Basic Plots: Why We Tell Stories*. London: Continuum.

Canter, D. (1989). Offender profiles. *The Psychologist*, 2, 12–16.

Canter, D. (1994). *Criminal Shadows*. London: Harper-Collins.

Canter, D. (1995). Psychology of offender profiling, in *Handbook of Psychology in Legal Contexts*, edited by R. Bull and D. Carson. Chichester: Wiley (pp. 343–355).

Canter, D. (2008). In the kingdom of the blind, in *Psychology and Law Bridging the Gap*, edited by D. Canter and R. Zukauskiene. Aldershot, UK: Ashgate.

Canter, D. and Heritage, R. (1990). A multivariate model of sexual offence behaviour: developments in offender profiling. *The Journal of Forensic Psychiatry*, 1, 185–212.

Canter, D. and Ioannou, M. (2004). A multivariate model of stalking behaviour. *Behaviourmetrika*, 31, 113–130.

Canter, D., Kaouri, C., and Ioannou, M. (2003). The facet structure of criminal narratives, in *Facet Theory: Towards Cumulative Social Science*, edited by S. Levy and D. Elizur. Ljubljiana, Slovenia: University of Ljubljana, Faculty of Arts, Centre for Educational Development (pp. 27–38).

Canter, D. and Youngs, D. (2009). *Investigative Psychology: Offender Profiling and the Analysis of Criminal Action*. Chichester: John Wiley & Sons.

Cloward, R. and Ohlin, L. (1960). *Delinquency and Opportunity*. New York, NY: Free Press.

Frye, N. (1957). *Anatomy of Criticism: Four Essays*. Princeton, NJ: Princeton University Press.

Goffman, E. (1958). *The Presentation of Self in Everyday Life*. New York, NY: Double Day.

Herman, D. (2009). *Basic Elements of Narrative*. Chichester: Wiley-Blackwell.

Katz, J. (1988). *Seductions of Crime: Moral and Sensual Attractions in Doing Evil*. New York, NY: Basic Books.

Maruna, S. (2001). *Making Good: How Ex-Convicts Reform and Rebuild Their Lives*. Washingtion D.C.: American Psychological Association.

Maruna, S. and Mann, R. (2006). A fundamental attribution error? Rethinking cognitive distortions. *Legal and Criminological Pschology*, 11, 155–177.

McAdams, D. (1985). *Power, Intimacy and the Life Story: Personological Inquiries into Identity*. New York, NY: The Guilford Press.

Presser, L. (2009). The narratives of offenders. *Theoretical Criminology*, 13, 177–200.

Sarbin, T.R. and Allen, V.L. (1968). Role theory, in *Handbook of Social Psychology* (2nd ed.), edited by G. Lindzey and E. Aronson. Reading, MA: Addison-Wesley (pp. 488–567).

Sykes, G. and Matza, D. (1957). Techniques of neutralization: a theory of delinquency. *American Sociological Review*, 22(6), 664–670.

Walters, G.D. (2003). Changes in criminal thinking and identity in novice and experienced inmates. Prisonization revisited. *Criminal Justice and Behavior*, 30, 399–421.

Ward, T. (2011). Commentry – narrative identity and forensic psychology: a commentary on Youngs and Canter. *Legal and Criminologcal Psychology*, 1–12.

Ward, T. and Marshall, W.L. (2007). Narrative identity and offender rehabilitation. *International Journal of Offender Therapy and Comparative Criminology*, 51, 279–297.

Youngs, D. and Canter, D. (2011). Narrative roles in criminal action: an integrative framework for differentiating offenders. *Legal and Criminological Psychology*, 16(2), 99–119.

Youngs, D. and Canter, D. (2012). Offenders' crime narratives as revealed by the Narrative Roles Questionnaire (NRQ). *International Journal of Offender Therapy and Comparative Criminology*, 1–23.

# Chapter 18
# Selected Writings for UK Newspapers

Professor Canter has written numerous articles for national newspapers in the UK over a ten year period on particular cases as well as broader social issues. The following is a small selection of these commentaries.

I am grateful to Stacey Fitzgibbon for her help in compiling the case summaries that provide background to the small selection of Professor Canter's *Times* articles presented here.

Do we need the Police?

A shorter, edited version of this article was published in *The Times* 6th March 2012 under the title 'Policing is no longer a general-purpose job'.

## Do we need The Police?

*Professor Canter*

Following up a murder enquiry, I was surprised to discover that the Senior Investigating Officer who had managed that case was not available. He was in charge of public order policing at the Notting Hill Carnival. It struck me that very different knowledge and skills were required for these two remarkably dissimilar roles. Yet the assumption that senior police officers can be expected to turn their hand to any of the vastly different areas that the police look after goes unchallenged. Do we still require one monolithic police force? Do we need *The Police*? Or is the range of activities in which they are involved now so varied, each area requiring such specialist knowledge, that the whole organisation and basis for our police services should be reviewed? Perhaps we should be looking for much more highly trained, much more specialist units, than one monolithic Police Force.

In the age before universal car ownership, DNA and CCTV, social networking, hundreds of mother tongues spoken in the homes of our cities, rapid developments in computing capabilities, huge databases available for examination at the click of a mouse, it may have made sense to assume that being a policeman was a general purpose task. That training in police procedures and the relevant law was all that was needed to join the thin blue line. But every aspect of policing now has become a sophisticated speciality. Indeed Google and insurance companies now have more highly developed information on people, and ways of using it, than any police force. Perhaps it is no longer possible for police officers to pick up a few technical details and understand what they are part of without a specialist intellectual basis on which to build their actions.

I suggest that the generalist approach to being a member of the police force, working your way up from being a lowly constable, without any academic training, moving through a variety of roles, is one of the main reasons for the turmoil the police are in now. If you put recent issues together it is clear that they face a very wide gamut of challenges that may not be open to a little tinkering. For example, the Crown Prosecution Service complained recently that rape cases are not being linked effectively, so that serial rapists go free. But the developments currently possible from information technology and behavioural science that would improve detectives' effectiveness are not part of the police response. I worked with the Met, at great expense to the tax payer, to develop a computer system that their own analyses proved could improve detection rates at virtually no extra cost. But this system still languishes on a desk somewhere because there is not the long-term, strategic vision to set in motion its operation. There may be local knowledge about neighbourhood villains, but a deeper understanding of the nature of serial rape and how these offenders leave virtual traces of themselves is not available to police officers who have found their way into the rape squad because they were good at catching neighbourhood burglars.

At the other end of policing, people at the top of the Met are being castigated for having too close a relationship with the barons of the press. Their arguments that it is important to maintain good relations with the press is rather disingenuous given that all police forces have specialist press officers. When a major enquiry is underway that requires help from the public experienced public relations staff give detailed advice on how the press is to be handled. It may be that a detective can have a mutually helpful relationship with journalists in his area that does not break any rules of engagement, but when that experience is translated to the highest levels of policing the question has to be asked of whether habits learned in the lower ranks are being inappropriately translated to the highest levels.

Public order policing is another area that now has a growing academic research base. But as has been shown in a number of recent events, most notably the August 'riots', weaknesses in being able to conceptualise what is going on in any other way than what has happened before limits productive reactions. In other words, the lack of an intellectual as well as a pragmatic perspective to events limits the flexibility and resilience of those in charge.

Top-up courses at the police staff training college rarely go beyond the practicalities of police activity and are dominated by police officers sharing their experiences with those less experienced. This does mean that if, for example, a typical hostage event occurs there is a highly effective process to put in place. But if something unusual happens, like Raul Moat driving around shooting apparently at random, or crowds gathering, urged on by social media, standard procedures are not sufficient. The question then has to be asked of whether senior officers have the strategic and intellectual skills to develop novel rapid responses for new circumstances. Most of the people who move through the staff training college have no university qualifications. So, I once proposed to the head there that he should provide a general introductory course on science and social science. This was pooh-poohed as too academic, but many police forces around the world see it very differently.

In many other countries people are selected from the start to become senior police officers. There is no assumption that you will work your way up from being a bobby on the beat. In India senior officers are selected by stringent examination in which a handful is selected from thousands of applicants all of whom have good university qualifications before they are allowed to sit the entrance examination. In Portugal and Spain some police training covers the equivalent of five years at university. In Sweden police officers have to spend two years in college before they are given any authority. When I gave a course of lectures to police officers in Israel I got questioned on the sorts of technical details I would be happy for my own PhD students to raise, but then many Israeli policemen and women have Masters or Doctorate degrees.

Soldiers who join the army to play in military bands are expected to get rapid training as paramedics if they are needed in a war zone, but they are not expected to work their way up to plan major campaigns. Yet despite the rapid increase in the sophistication of every branch of human knowledge and activity that policing connects with, police constables taking the examination to become a sergeant typically still have to master key aspects of traffic law even though they are hoping to join the squad dealing with domestic violence.

The Labour Party asked Lord Stevens to carry out an enquiry into the future of policing. The good Lord did himself work his way up from a constable catching villains on the street to the highest rank in the police, but the word is he is aware of the limits in that process and is considering something other than people pulling themselves up the ranks by their boot straps. Let's hope, for all our sakes, that he reaches even more radical conclusions.

Professor Canter is Professor of Psychology at The University of Huddersfield. His most recent book is *Forensic Psychology: A Very Short Introduction*.

## On the Unabomber

*Background*

Theodore John 'Ted' Kaczynski was born in Chicago Illinois on May 22nd 1942. He was an American mathematician who was accepted into Harvard University at the age of 16 completing a mathematic degree, and later moving on to complete his PhD. Kaczynski gained employment at the University of California Berkley as an assistant professor but resigned two years later after and isolated himself from the world in a cabin that he built. After watching modern developments destroy the wilderness he decided to start a bombing campaign. Between 1978 and 1995 he sent 16 bombs to Universities and airline resulting in 3 deaths and 23 seriously injured people.

## Fanatic who Nurses Rage Risks Forensic Science Trap

*Professor Canter: Published, in The Times February 8 2007*

The parcel bomb has been the violent gesture of choice for the fanatic or middle-aged criminal demanding money with menaces since the 1800s.

The man (there are no obvious female precedents) who foments a vicious campaign in the mistaken belief that it will make people take notice of his cause has to nurse his rage for months or even years while he focuses his obsession on selecting and preparing to attack his targets.

The explosive device itself will channel his attention, becoming the tool of his anger. It is relatively easy for him to construct; if he logs on to the internet he can go to any number of websites with full details of how to construct parcel bombs. So background technical knowhow is far less important than a single-minded certainty that his cause is the right one and any victims are just pawns to be exploited.

Extreme Scottish and Irish nationalists, as well as animal rights activists, have all used the postal system to send bombs in the past, but so have individuals with a much more personal mission.

Ted Kaczynski, known as the Unabomber, drew attention to his tirade against various forms of technology by sending bombs to university professors and airline companies, which killed three people and injured twenty-eight over a twenty-year period.

When his brother identified him from the almost incomprehensible tirade that he had insisted be published before he would stop sending the bombs it became clear that this strange recluse was suffering from serious mental illness that had gone untreated for a long time.

The common association with motor vehicles in the recent series of parcel bombs does smack of a similar generalised anger, although anger with precisely what is not at all clear yet.

As a device for exerting extortion, the postal bomb allows a person with limited physical strength or courage to plot what he believes will be the perfect crime.

These violent criminals never need to come face to face with the people they maim or kill. For them the whole enterprise may seem some distant abstraction. This helps them to convince themselves that innocent victims are just unlucky; struck down by the fates rather than the consequence of their bombs.

Whether driven by a violent ideology or a vicious extortion, the bomber is trying to draw attention to his mission or demands. Therefore at some point he must express his purpose. He will have to contact the authorities if he wants people to understand the meaning of his acts.

The police will have to filter this out of all the crank and criminal messages they get claiming ownership. If they identify any genuine claims they will be unlikely to make any such messages public because of the help they give their investigations.

There will be plenty of other information the police can glean from all the forensic science material that the bombs provide. Even the way the parcels are addressed can give up helpful psycholinguistic clues to the background and identity of the sender.

The amount of background information not in the public domain that will be drawn from the details of the lethal parcels is one reason why we must be cautious about drawing any rapid inferences about the perpetrator.

Uninformed speculation can generate unnecessary fear and cause misleading messages to fill the vacuum of our public ignorance. As members of the public we try to assuage our anxieties by guessing what the reason for these indiscriminate bombs must be, but it will be the minute examination of the forensic evidence that the bombs carry that will eventually lead the police to the culprit.

## On the 2006 Ipswich Murders

Background: Steve Wright was convicted of the murders of five Ipswich prostitutes in 2006. Steve Wright was born in a quaint town in Norfolk in 1958. His father was a military policeman and they lived nearby at RAF West Beckham. His mother left the family home when Steve was just 8 years old losing contact with her for 25 years. He had a varied work life varying from job to job. His family and friends and prostitutes that he frequently used for sex described the serial killer as kind and gentle with not a malicious bone in his body. The twice divorced killer had a previous criminal record for theft denies his guilt in killing 5 prostitutes from the Ipswich area.

## Find First Crime and You Crack the Case

*David Canter: Analysis Published in The Times December 12 2006*

Contrary to fictional portrayals, serial killers do not suddenly become vicious predators picking on vulnerable women. They frequently have criminal backgrounds that can include burglary and theft, drug dealing or, of course, violence. They evolve through various stages of criminality, but by far the biggest influence on their unfolding violence is getting away with their first murder.

This means that if the police can identify the perpetrator's first violent crime, they will come very close to solving the case. At the time of that first crime, he would not have honed his skills. Vital clues can be gathered.

Crimes like these grow out of a festering anger that is aggravated by a distorted view of women as either paragons or whores. There are fundamentalist cultures that see women as evil seductresses who deny men the virtues that will take them to Heaven. It is not surprising that even within our own society there are men who harbour the same confused perspective.

But these speculations about the killer's inner turmoil add little to the police investigation. Officers no longer believe that magical insights can be had from the poorly informed opinion of some Cracker-like figure.

Things have moved on since I first produced a summary pen picture of a person who committed a series of murders and rapes 20 years ago.

The investigative psychologists who contribute to police investigations do not call themselves profilers any more but behavioural investigative analysts. They see their job as operational guidance rather than psychological profiles.

They help the police to decide how to identify potential suspects. They give guidance on how suspects may be put into some order of priority. Most importantly, they draw on geographical profiling to create a very detailed analysis of where the victims' bodies were found to build a picture of what the offender's "mental map" is of the area, and how it may be influenced by other locations with which he is familiar, such as where he lives or works. That can then be used to focus house-to-house inquiries and other intelligence searches.

Police then need to identify the interpersonal and intellectual consistencies that the offender exhibits by detailed study of how he committed the crimes. For example, leaving the bodies in water will have reduced the forensic evidence but could carry great psychological significance. If there is no obvious sexual activity, as has been reported in this instance, it suggests anger rather than sexual sadism.

One significant problem in this case will be the unwillingness of most potential witnesses – clients of prostitutes – to present themselves for questioning. The complexities are compounded once the police recognise that they have a serial killer. The investigation immediately draws into its remit all the unsolved murders in the area, and beyond. The problem will not be finding suspects, but eliminating all the potential killers.

Fewer than one in twenty murders in Britain goes unsolved. This is partly because of the vast resources put into murder inquiries. But it is also because the police have learnt a great deal since the days of the Yorkshire Ripper.

## Further Commentary for The Times on the 2006 Ispwich (UK) Murders

Steve Wright's denial of any guilt, despite being convicted, closes down any possibility of learning directly from him why he killed. It leaves the field open to speculation about what gave rise to such a concerted outbreak of calculated violence. We have to turn to the crimes themselves, and any earlier analogous cases to glean some insights into why he murdered, then relate what emerges back to what we now know about Wright's unfolding life story.

Each of the five young women, whose naked bodies were found near Ipswich over the space of a few days in December 2006, appears to have been killed by some sort of severe pressure to her throat. There are no other signs of struggle or fighting back. The best estimate is that they were murdered by the force of a forearm or a similar object, probably while the victims were weak or comatose from drugs. The lack of forensic evidence makes it difficult to be sure of anything much more than this. But even these bare facts indicate that they suffered a cold execution rather than a violent explosion of emotion. What are the roots of such calculated violence?

Serial killers usually kill out of anger. Not the sudden anger that flairs up in most of us when we feel frustrated, hurt or insulted. But a steady poisonous drip of anger that comes from feelings of being humiliated and disgraced over a long period of time. The killer feels *he* is the victim and that the women he kills represent the cause of his distress. By the time he comes to murder he thinks of his prey as little more than animate objects that need to be executed and got rid of.

We can get a chilling insight to this mindset from what Gary Ridgeway, known as the Green River Killer, who killed over 40 women working as street prostitutes, told his defence attorney Mark Prothero when asked why he'd killed them:

"I did it because I hated them … because women had control over me and I don't like being controlled. I was not strong enough … to tell people to not take advantage of me, not to use me. I had control when I killed the women. I got my rage out for a time. I did cry but I still killed them and I didn't care anything about 'em".

The chilling parallels to Wright's contacts with prostitutes that he so openly admitted in court are reflected in Ridgeway's confession. He said he had been friends with some of his victims before he killed them. That is something we've seen in other serial killers. They do not always prey on complete strangers, as in the movies. They are able to present an unthreatening face to their victims and keep their rage hidden until they decide to strike.

This is particularly important in the Ipswich murders because the time between the girls going missing and their bodies being found was more than the few hours that a person is likely to be kept in a car. Certainly in the past where prostitutes have been abducted they have been kept in a house or lock-up of some kind, so that the killer could continue to abuse them. But there is no sign of physical or sexual abuse here. This suggests an even more leisurely stay where they did not feel at risk. The confident and controlled way in which Wright answered challenges in court is certainly compatible with a smooth talker who told these women he was there to help them and fed them drugs until he killed them? Perhaps as the police pressure built up the drugs were not working quickly enough so he decided he had to kill them to avoid them being possible witnesses? The way he killed them, though, shows further what a cold-blooded brute he was.

It could possibly have been more than one man, as the prosecution made clear throughout the trial. About one in ten serial killers of prostitutes have an accomplice. These are women who survive on the street so are not easily cowed. Yet as far as can be established there was no obvious wounding from the women struggling. So if two men were not involved one man would have had to be reasonably fit and strong to kill even a defenceless woman. Wright certainly seems to have the build for that.

In only about one in ten murders of prostitutes are the victims strangled and then usually with a rope or some other ligature. To smother a victim as seems to have happened with these women takes quite a lot of effort and would be extremely difficult to do in a car or an open field without the victim struggling. Strangling by hand also is much more difficult than usually portrayed in fiction. The victim has to be unable to wriggle free and the man has to hold on for some time. These modes of killing show a cold determination and total confidence on the part of the killer. He knew he had these women at his mercy and that they would have no chance. He did not mind the physical contact that many of us would shy away from, he wanted to overpower them with his own hands. The task he had, as he saw it was to execute these women. He wants to rid the world of them. The logic of his disposing of their bodies was precise and clinical. He knew he could then strip them and leave their bodies in such a way that the police would have a very difficult time tracing the killing back to his doorstep. However he did not know enough about the cleverness of modern forensic science and left just enough evidence to convince a jury.

But this only gets us a little closer to the killings. Why did he strip the victims and why on two occasions did he leave their arms stretched out in the form of a crucifix? The simplest suggestion is that he destroyed their clothes to get rid of any forensic clues that would link him to the women. The posing of the bodies could similarly be a ruse to try and suggest some religious maniac was the culprit. All of this implies a devious cleverness that is not in accord with some reports of Wright being considerably below average intelligence, having left school with no qualifications.

A much more startling possibility was put forward by Dr Adrian West at the time the bodies were discovered. He is the forensic psychologist called in to advise the British police in most major murder enquiries. He was convinced from the finding of the first naked victim that the bodies had not been stripped solely to hide any forensic evidence. He thought the bodies had been stripped because of some fetish relating to women's clothing. Such a fetish goes beyond the titillation that men may associate with women's lingerie. It is an obsession with many aspects of women's clothing which has its roots in the person's confusion and discomfort about his own gender. This is not the unusual, but not fundamentally unhealthy, transvestism such as that proclaimed by Grayson Perry. Dr West pointed out to the police when they were still searching for the culprit that this 'gender dysphoria' can lead to a desire to wear women's clothing. It is a secret search for sexual gratification whilst dressed as a woman. He advised the police that the investigative implication of this was to look for possible suspects amongst men who were secret cross-dressers. So far no solid evidence has emerged that Steve Wright had any confusions about his gender or ever wore woman's clothing.

Steve Wright was abandoned by his mother when he was 8 years old and seems to have a tempestuous relationship with his father throughout his life. He married a Thai woman who took all his money and left him stranded in Thailand, but was eventually apparently happily settled with a Pamela Goodman who took his surname. Does this provide the basis for the gender dysphoria that Adrian West proposes or even the less profound horror of a man who develops a mission to kill street sex workers? If there is any hint that his actions have the roots in experiences going back many years then another question emerges. Why should this spate of killings have taken place when he was in his late 30's and not a lot earlier in his life? So far there have been no other violent crimes that have been linked to Wright, nor even any indication of violence or aggression against others as a style of interaction.

The police will be searching case records in the UK and Thailand to determine if there are any linked cases, but in their absence we have to look for other mechanisms. Some forensic psychiatrists use the steam engine metaphor of people being 'overcontrolled' as if they are suffering great internal pressure which is usually kept in check until one day it is too great to manage and explodes in violence. Holding his breath until he passed out, as Wright's mother says he did when fearful of punishment from his disciplinarian father, is perhaps an indication of how totally he tended to control his emotions. Wrights frequent association with and use of prostitutes over many years, even to the extent of running the Ferry Boat Inn, in Norwich, known as a haunt for street workers, may have given him a disdain that evolved into hatred for them. He would not the first serial killer who held the confused belief that they tempted him to commit sexual acts he later hated himself for. Perhaps closer than any other serial killers to Harold Shipman, who killed hundreds of the patients he had professional dealings with, Wright might have harboured the arrogant belief that he had to get rid of the women he used and despised.

In Ipswich all the women who were killed were prostitutes, but we know from many other cases that if their murderer had not been caught so quickly his vicious spree would have spilt over to other women innocently walking the streets. The vulnerability of street level prostitutes is therefore a cause for general concern because it so easily becomes a breeding, or training ground for men who want to attack women.

The knee-jerk reaction to the Ipswich killings is to call once again for the legalisation of prostitution in some form or other. This is naïve in the extreme. It is thought that allowing brothels or containment zones, in which prostitution is tolerated, amidst a strong police presence, will somehow remove the possibility of predatory killers picking on these vulnerable young women. But this ignores the dysfunctional, drug-fuelled life style that drives otherwise sensible women on to the streets.

The only way to reduce to an acceptable level the risks to women who sell sex on the street is by a multi-agency approach that gets them off drugs and into a healthier environment. This is not a task the police can tackle on their own, but needs the health and social services, drug rehabilitation agencies and probably the educational authority as well all to work together.

Unless Brothels were to become part of the National Health Service (that some futuristic fiction from Alphaville onwards has predicted) they will always be a magnet for crime. They suck in women as little more than slaves. What is thought of as the Dutch model, which really only applies on any scale to Amsterdam, where the red light district, known locally as the *Rossebuurt*, is as much a tourist feature as a market for sex, is also an illusion. The women who are bussed into these shop windows are not the disturbed and disorganised street prostitutes who can be found in other parts of the city. Violence against sex workers outside of the gaudy lights of *Rossebuurt is still not uncommon.*

There are many ways, these days, for women and men to advertise their sexual services, way beyond postcards in telephone boxes. Great areas of the Internet are devoted to such advertising. The old fashioned Yellow Pages also make access to the quasi-legal escort agencies a phone call away. These allow sex workers to control the time and place of their trade. The women who stand on the streets trying to make eye-contact with passing motorists cannot sort out their lives well enough to get postcards printed or a www presence. They are all the more vulnerable because they are so desperate to make their money on the street.

About one in 20 women who are murdered are prostitutes who work the streets to supply their heroin habit. They need to make over £150 a day just to feed their habit, so they take risks that no-one else would. The figures we have from the US show that serial killers kill about a third of those prostitutes who are killed. Nearly all of these men have used prostitutes for sex. Like Steve Wright and Gary Ridgeway they are not strangers to these women, who mistakenly think they can tell who is a safe punter and who not.

Street level prostitutes have ideas about how they can protect themselves from the risks of their trade. Although our studies show these ideas are often mistaken. They believe that by staying close to other people in well lit areas and by keeping in touch with others through mobile phones they can manage the inherent danger every time they get into a car. The numbers who get killed shows that these attempts to reduce the risk do not always work.

Steve Wright's denial of the murders will lead to many speculations as to his reasons for some time to come. But the predatory abuse of women who work the streets cannot be denied. The strong possibility remains that it is the very presence of these desperate women in the many places he found them, and his ready exploitation of them, that sowed the seeds of his violence. They were killed because they so easily could be.

## E.On Harold Shipman

*Backgound*: Harold Shipman who has been denoted Britain's most prolific serial killer was jailed for life after being found guilty of murdering 15 of his patients whilst working in the Greater Manchester area. The killer who has been estimated to have killed 260 of his patients throughout his career was discovered deceased in his cell by prison service staff on 13th January 2004. Shipman had used his bed sheets to hang himself from the window bars of his cell. He had previously shown no signs of suicidal behaviour, and had given the prison authorities no cause for concern.

## He Knew He Was Just Like the Rest: A Killer

*By David Canter*
*Published in The Times, January 14 2004*

It was not really surprising that Shipman's lack of fellow-feeling was turned on himself

HAROLD SHIPMAN killed himself to avoid ever having to face up to how banal were the reasons for his killings.

As he languished in his cell, he would have been unable to sustain a state of denial. He had steadfastly refused to admit to his crimes and had apparently discussed even making an appeal.

These outward displays of being a misunderstood innocent bolstered his inner denial that he had done anything wrong. As long as he could avoid engaging with explanations for his actions he could stop himself facing what he had done.

But prison gives plenty of time for contemplation: that was the original intention of the Quakers who first proposed private repentance in isolation from the ills of society as a civilised substitute for deportation or capital punishment.

For Shipman this isolation was less likely to be an opportunity to search his conscience than for a growing awareness of the black emptiness that he dragged around with him.

Someone as self-centred and totally immune to the feelings of others as Harold Shipman will have killed himself for egocentric reasons.

The never-ending prison routine stretching in front of him, controlling his every action, will have been anathema to a man so enthralled with holding the power of life and death over others.

As he thought of putting forward an appeal, in which he would once again have had to parry questions about why he murdered so many patients, he will have become more aware of the lack of any heroic or quasi-philosophical mission to his vile acts.

Not for him the spurious posturing of the Moors murderer Ian Brady, who eventually wrote a book implying descent from the near existentialist philosophy of the Marquis de Sade.

As he got to know the other prisoners who shared his world, Shipman will have begun to realise that he had much more in common with them than the magnitude and enormity of his crimes might have suggested. He will have met people who were violent out of annoyance or just because they could get away with it, or even because they enjoyed inflicting pain on others. He would have shared prison with people who committed crimes out of habit, or as an easy way of resolving a personal problem.

None of them will have had the resource or trust of vulnerable victims the way he did. Perhaps he became aware that this was all that distinguished him. He could kill and could get away with it over and over again. Was it this dawning realisation that he could no longer live with? His reasons for murder were those common to all criminals.

Many murderers in Britain kill themselves, often soon after they kill someone else. This is an interesting contrast with American killers, who are more likely to want to sell their stories and bask in their notoriety.

Murder followed by suicide in Britain does tend to be a pattern among those who kill their loved ones in a fit of anger. Outside gangster traditions, our culture, happily, still does not assign kudos to those who are violent or kill.

Once the mundane experiences of prison life bury any excitement that may come from being in the public eye, there is little left to find worth within.

Fred West, who killed many young women over a 20-year period, including his former wife, his daughter and two women, each of whom was pregnant with his child, killed himself in his cell. He was awaiting trial and had spent the previous six months pouring out in police interviews the admissions of his terrible, vicious crimes.

What is revealing about West, and may help us to understand Shipman's suicide, is that West had been writing a sort of memoir of the highlights of his life, leaving it not quite finished when he, like Shipman, hanged himself during the night. West's memoir paints a curiously rose-tinted picture of his earlier life with no mention at all of the atrocities he committed. It seems possible that as the trial approached, he became more aware of just how untenable that image of himself was.

Is this what Shipman also realised? Whatever denial he had managed to maintain in the years since his conviction could not be sustained for ever. No one should be surprised that Shipman killed himself in his prison cell. If anyone knew the ways to death it was this man who probably killed more than 200 people in the most premeditated way possible.

He knew that his victims trusted him as their considerate family doctor, yet he was able to push any flicker of conscience to one side, or any shred of professional concern and, in the coldest of blood, give them a lethal injection. For a doctor, so schooled in keeping those who trust him alive, who trains for years to perfect his skills and manage his compassion, for such a professional to make a private career out of killing his patients must mean that deep down he sees himself and those around him as mere objects that he can dispatch at will.

I am too much of an optimist about human nature to think that a doctor can kill his patients and still have any empathy or sympathy for the harm he is doing. Such a lack of fellow-feeling will inevitably be turned on himself, as he sees the need to cancel out the void that envelops him.

## On a UK Police Foiling of Terrorist Plot

*Background*: Nine men were arrested in February 2007 as part of an alleged plot to kidnap a Muslim soldier, who was believed to have served in Afghanistan but who was back on home leave. The police think terrorists intended to torture and kill their victim before broadcasting their actions on the internet.

## Ex-UK Cleric 'Inspired Plot to Kidnap Soldier'

*Professor Canter wrote the following piece an edited version of which was published in The Times.*

The suspected terrorists recently arrested in Birmingham were apparently not planning to bomb their way into public attention. All the indications are that there was a chilling change in strategy, to kidnap and broadcast the execution of their victim. This is all the more disturbing because experts for some time have been predicting that bombing would be augmented by kidnap. The prediction is based on the simple fact that terrorist groups carefully study what each other have been doing and the impact of their actions.

The London bombings generated outrage across many Islamic communities, who were quick to point out the number of Muslims killed. One primary objective of all terrorist acts is to divide communities against each other and so open the doors to escalating recruitment to their cause. Randomly killing their co-religionists only achieves this objective if the reactions from the authorities are so severe that they alienate more than they support. The British police have learnt this lesson very quickly, so that Muslim communities are not radicalised wholesale by intensive investigations.

Bombings also lose their media appeal once the traumatic events have been dealt with. Kidnappings can be dragged out for weeks or even months and generate a flurry of community wide concern and involvement. They provide an opportunity for the terrorists' to broadcast their cause and intimidate individuals who think they may be the next target. That is why in the desire for attention, that has been the essence of terrorism since the assassins of the Middle Ages, determined groups will seek to use the most recent tactics in which they have seen others be successful.

Although once a kidnapping is in progress it is difficult to foil or resolve, the targeting of an individual and setting up the abduction and holding of the victim, as well as contact with the media, all demand rather more organisation than a suicide bombing. In some places where kidnapping has become endemic whole networks have emerged with different teams managing every aspect of the process from abduction to negotiation to eventual disposal. With an effective, dedicated police force such networks are extremely vulnerable to having their communications intercepted. Which is probably what happened here.

The overlap between military and police intelligence procedures is now essential because it is no longer possible to distinguish between terrorism as a quasi-military, guerrilla activity, and organised crime. Interviews being carried out by Liverpool Universities Centre for Investigative Psychology with incarcerated Islamic terrorists in South East Asia are already showing that some of the prime movers started their violent careers as criminals involved in extortion and robbery. They have made clear to their interviewers that they joined the *jihad* to broaden their reach and gain prestige within their community. Others have moved from wanting revenge against insult to themselves or those close to them into criminal activity to fund more outrageous terrorist acts.

In Britain the revenge may be for acts committed against notional religious 'brothers' rather than for any personally felt insult, fostered by graphic images on the internet, but there will still be personal objectives of wanting to be noticed and responded to by otherwise distant authorities as well as respect and honour from those whom they admire. The interviews with Pakistani terrorists have indicated they are often acting against the wishes of their families and religious leaders. These are young men who are reacting against the authorities in their own communities, not on behalf of them. The distant leaders, who promulgate the need for acts of terror, do not provide any clear indication of what the end result of the violence should be, other than a change in the status quo. The excitement of being part of a group planning to make an impact on the international stage carries the foot-soldiers through with little need for any thoughtful understanding of the consequences. They can see the effects that suicide bombing and then kidnapping has had in other countries then get caught up in copying the violence with little real thought for its implications.

## On the Paula Gilfoyle Case

*Background*: Paula Gilfoyle was eight months pregnant when she was found hanged in the garage of her home in Wirral, in 1992. Her husband Eddie Gilfoyle, was convicted of her murder in 1993. Gilfoyle has always protested his innocence and claimed his wife had actually committed suicide but still carried out an 18 year prison sentence until he was released in December 2010. At the trial the jury was told by the prosecution that Paula would not have committed suicide that in fact her husband forced her to write her own suicide note and tricked her head into the noose. Her friends and family protested that she was a bubbly, outgoing individual that was happy and would never have taken her own life. But new evidence that became available to Gilfoyle's defence team that provides insight into Paula's character that was not available at the original trial.

A shorter, edited version of this article was published in The Times on January 6 2012

## Box Reveals Capacity for Keeping Secrets

*Professor Canter Commentary*

The ability of people to keep their most desperate, innermost thoughts hidden from those around them is surely something that juries ought to be reminded of in cases where a death could be suicide or murder. But in 1993, when Eddie Gilfoyle was convicted of the murder of his wife Paula no such guidance was given to the court. The judge noted that 14 witnesses had seen Paula in the weeks and days before her death and she had seemed her usual bubbly self. She was 8 and half months pregnant when her body was found hanging in her locked garage and all her friends said she was delightedly looking forward to the birth, so would never have killed herself and the baby.

As is so curious in this type of case the person on trial was really the deceased, Paula, rather than the accused, Eddie. Her mental state was the central issue because only circumstantial evidence pointed to Eddie as the culprit. However, the court chose to accept the public face of Paula as seen by friends and relatives rather than try to ascertain whether there was something that she was hiding.

I had been involved in the legal proceedings from Eddie's original trial in 1993. My evidence had not been used in court, but over the years I had always wondered about the likelihood of a very pregnant Paula putting her head in a noose with Eddie standing behind her because she believed she needed to do this to help him with his studies of suicide. That is what the court and jury had to believe if the full scenario of Eddie's cunning were to be accepted. Paula would have to have done this despite a row weeks earlier over Eddie fancying another woman. I have The new evidence that has become available in a locked black metal box provides insight into Paula's character that was not available at the original trial or in Eddie's two appeals.

Paula's family had all insisted she was happy and undisturbed. Any suggestions from Eddie and his family that this was not the whole story was dismissed as being part of an elaborate fiction concocted to exonerate the murderer.

Yet the newly found evidence shows that in a private letter to Paula her partner of ten years, Gordon Gumley, wrote "The only time I see you happy is when your friends are around when they call you're a different person. Smiling joking all that kind of stuff. I think you talk more to your lodger than you do to me". Here is what Eddie's defence team tried to indicate but never had the evidence to support. Paula was very able to present a positive face to the world, hiding her true emotions.

It was known at the trial that her teenage boyfriend had killed a girl after he had had sex with this victim. At the trial it was claimed that Paula had quickly got over this and expunged him from her life. But the tokens in the closed metal box show that she had kept in a relationship with him, even buying him a wedding ring when he was in prison to honour their earlier engagement. This provides further evidence of her ability to keep secrets from even close family members.

The proposal at the trial was that Eddie had dictated the suicide note found in Paula's handwriting that had been found shortly before her hanging body was discovered. There was only gossip and speculation that this had happened, no clear evidence. But the way the note had clearly absolved Eddie from any culpability was taken as an indication of why he had dictated it in that way. However, in Paula's secret box was a suicide note from Gordon Gumley in which he had said "don't blame yourself". Words repeated in Paula's suicide note. Research shows that people who kill themselves learn from other suicides. Was this something Paula had learned to write from the note she had carefully preserved.

In the light of these revelations the suicide note that Paula left takes on a new clarity. It had been read throughout Eddie's trial and subsequent appeals as being dictated by Eddie to imply he was not guilty of Paula's death. This is a remarkably subtle reading of both the note and the inventive authorship skills that Eddie has never displayed in any other situation. A much more direct reading is that Paula did indeed think she had something to hide. She wrote 'I've done thing in my life that I'm not proud of but I got through somehow but this is just too much' she also wrote 'explain things as best as you can'. Reading these phrases carefully at their face value, does suggest a person who could no longer live with a secret. Was this her anxiety that she was not carrying Eddie's baby, but someone else's? The tragic irony was that it was Eddie's.

In some literary traditions, notably the Japanese, the honourable solution to a conflict of loyalties is ritual suicide. It is not an act that comes out of depression but out of a courageous determination to do what is right. Was Paula's act a mistakenly heroic one as she saw it?

When the Wales football manager, Gary Speed, was found to have killed himself surprise and shock reverberated amongst those who knew him. No-one expected this affable public figure, who had appeared on television the day before without any sign of stress, to commit suicide. Yet from my studies and reports from the Samaritans it is known that more than one in ten suicides give no obvious prior warning, suicide notes or obvious explanations that emerge after the event.

There is a mistaken belief that all suicide is a product of chronic depression or inescapable despair that will be evident to most of the people that the person is in contact with. But time and again celebrities who seem to have everything to live for are found dead by their own hands. The list is legion. But people not in the public eye can also surprise those around them by a totally unexpected decision to take their own life.

# Selected Bibliography

## Authored Books

Canter, D. (1974). *Psychology for Architects*. London: Applied Science Publishers.

Canter, D. (1977). *The Psychology of Place*. London: Architectural Press.

Canter, D., Comber, M., and Uzzell, D. (1989). *Football in its Place: An Environmental Psychology of Football Grounds*. London: Routledge.

Canter, D. (1994). *Criminal Shadows*. London: Harper Collins, [Published in 2000 in the US by Authorlink] winner of Golden Dagger award and Anthony Award, for Best True-Crime.

Canter, D. (1996). *Psychology in Action*. Aldershot: Dartmouth.

Canter, D. (2003). *Mapping Murder: The Secrets of Geographical Profiling*. London: Virgin Books.

Canter, D. and Fairbairn, G. (2006). *Becoming an Author: Advice for Academics and Other Professionals*. New York: Open University Press.

Canter, D. and Youngs, D. (2009). *Investigative Psychology: Offender Profiling and the Analysis Criminal Action*. Chichester: Wiley.

Canter, D. (2008). *Criminal Psychology: Topics in Applied Psychology*. London: Hodder Education.

Canter, D. (2010). *Forensic Psychology: A Very Short Introduction*. Oxford: Oxford University Press.

Canter, D. (2012). *Forensic Psychology for Dummies*. Chichester: Wiley.

## Selected Publications

The list here is of academic publications in refereed/learned publications. If all publications were counted there would be over 400 including more than 30 books (authored and edited). Professor Canter has presented well over 50 invited, keynote papers at conferences worldwide. His work have been translated in German, Italian, Spanish, Japanese, Chinese and Arabic.

Many of these papers are available to download from The University of Huddersfield Repository: <http://eprints.hud.ac.uk/cgi/search/simple?q=Canter&_action_search=Search&_action_search=Search&_order=bytitle&basic_srchtype=ALL&_satisfyall=ALL>.

**Social Psychology**

Canter, D.V. and Breakwell, G.M. (1993). Methodological contributions to the theory of social representations, in *Empirical Approaches to Social Representatiuons*, edited by G.M. Breakwell and D.V. Canter. Oxford: Oxford University Press.

Breakwell, G.M. and Canter, D.V. (1993). Aspects of methodology and their implications for the study of social representations, in *Empirical Approaches to Social Representatiuons*, edited by G.M. Breakwell and D.V. Canter. Oxford: Oxford University Press.

Wilson, M. and Canter, D.V. (1992). Shared concepts in group decision making: a model for decisions based on qualitative data. *British Journal of Social Psychology*.

Canter, D. (1985). Intention, meaning, and structure: social action in its physical context, in *Discovery Strategies in the Psychology of Action*, edited by M. Von Cranach, G. Ginsberg, and M. Brenner. London: Academic Press (pp. 171–186).

Canter, D. and Breakwell, G. (1986). Psychologists and the media. *Bulletin of The British Psychological Society*, 39, 281–286.

Canter, D. (1988). Environmental (social) psychology: an emerging synthesis, in *Environmental Social Psychology*, edited by D. Canter, J.C. Jesuino, L. Sokza, and G.M. Stephenson. Dordrecht: Kluwer Academic Press (pp. 1–18).

Canter, D.V. (1990). In search of objectives: an intellectual autobiography, in *Emergence of Intellectual Traditions*, edited by I. Altman and K. Christensen. New York, NY: Plenum (pp. 315–338).

Canter, D. and Monteiro, C. (1993). The lattice of polemic social representations: a comparison of the social representations of occupations in favelas public housing, and middle class neighbourhoods. *Empirical Approaches to Social Representations*. New York: Oxford University Press (pp. 223–247).

Canter, D. (2000). The violated body. *Journal of Popular Science*. Cambridge University Press (pp. 57–74).

**Medical/Clinical Psychology**

Canter, D.V. (1993). Can health be a quantitative criterion? A multi-facet approach to health assessment, in *Towards a New Science of Health*, edited by S. Fulder and R. Lafaille. Routledge.

Canter, D. (1993). The wholistic organic researcher: central issues in clinical research methodology, in *The Wholistic Organic Researcher: Central Issues in Clinical Research Methodology*, edited by G. Powell, R. Young, and S. Frosh (eds) Curriculum in clinical psychology. Leicester: BPS (pp. 40–56).

Canter, D. (1987). A research agenda for holistic therapy. *Complimentary Medical Research*, (2) 1.

Canter, D. and Booker, K. (1987). Multiple consultations as a basis for classifying patients' use of conventional and unconventional medical practice. *Complementary Medical Research*, 2, 141–160.

Canter, D. (1988). How do we know that it works? Therapeutic outcome as negotiation. *Complementary Medical research*, 3(1).

Canter, D.V. and Nanke, L.G. (1989). Emerging priorities in complementary medical research. *Complementary Medical Research*, 3(3), pp. 14–21.

Canter, D. and King, K. (1989). Ward development project, in *Psychology in action*, edited by D. Canter. Hanover, NH: Dartmouth University Press (pp. 157–173).

Canter, D. and Nanke, L. (1989). Individual variation and sympiomatology: a homoepathic perspective. *British Homoepathy ResearchGroup Communications*, 1(19), pp. 43–91.

Canter, D. and Cooper, A. (1998). Design context and nursing roles, in *Stress and Organisational Problems in Hospitals*, edited by D. Wallis and C.J. de Wolff. London: Croom Helm (pp. 157–173).

## Facet Theory and Research Methodology

Canter, D. (1982). Facet approach to applied research. *Perceptual and Motor Skills*, 55, pp.143–154.

Canter, D. (1983). The potential of facet theory for applied social psychology. *Quality and Quantity*, 17, pp. 35–67.

Canter, D. (1983). Phases et roles de la participation des sciences humanines a l'elaboration de projets. *Extrait de Recherches Sociologiques*, 3.

Canter, D., Brown, J., and Groat, L. (1985). A multiple sorting procedure for studying conceptual systems, in *The Research Interview: Uses and Approaches*, edited by M. Brenner, J. Brown, and D. Canter. London: Academic Press (pp. 79–114).

Canter, D. (1992). An evaluation of 'cusum' stylistic analysis of confessions. *Expert Evidence*, 1(2), pp. 93–99.

Canter, D., Rivers, R., and Storrs, G. (1985). Characterizing user navigation through complex data structures. *Behaviour and Information Technology*, 4(2), pp. 93–102.

Canter, D. (1985). How to be a facet researcher, in *Facet Theory: Approaches to Social Research*, edited by D. Canter. New York: Springer (pp. 265–275).

Canter, D., Powell, J., Wishart, J., and Roderick, C. (1986). User navigation in complex database systems. *Behaviour and Information Technology*, 5(3), pp. 249–257.

Canter, D. and Chester, J. (1997). Investigation into the claim of weighted cusum in authorship attribution studies. *Journal of Forensic Linguistics*, 4(2), pp. 252–261.

Canter, D. and Alison, L.J. (2003). Converting evidence into data: the use of law enforcement archives as unobtrusive measurement. *The Qualitative Report*, 8(2), pp. 151–176.

Canter, D. (2004). A partial order scalogram analysis of criminal network structures. *Behaviormetrika*, 31(2), pp. 1–21.
Bache, R., Crestani, F., Canter, D., and Youngs, D.E. (2010). A language modelling approach to linking criminal styles with offender characteristics. *Data & Knowledge Engineering*, 69(3).

## Environmental Psychology

Canter, D. and Larkin, P. (1993). The environmental range of serial rapists. *Journal of Environmental psychology*, 13, pp. 63–69.
Canter, D. and Donald, I. (1987). Environmental psychology in the United Kingdom: origins and current trends, in *The Handbook of Environmental Psychology*, edited by D. Stokols and I. Altman. New York, NY: Wiley.
Canter, D. (1982). Contributing to environmental design, in *Psychology in Practice: Perspectives on Professional Psychology*, edited by S. Canter and D. Canter. New York: Wiley.
Canter, D. (1983). The physical context of work, in *The Physical Environment at Work*, edited by D.J. Oborne and M.M. Gruneberg. New York: Wiley (pp. 11–37).
Canter, D. (1966). On appraising building appraisals. *The Architects' Journal Information Library*.
Canter, D. (1968). Office size: an example of psychological research in architecture. *The Architects' Journal Information Library*, 24 April, pp. 881–888.
Canter, D. (1969). An intergroup comparison of connotative dimensions in architecture. *Environment and Behaviour*, 1(1), pp. 37–48.
Canter, D. and Wools, R. (1970). A technique for the subjective appraisal of buildings. *Building Science*, 5, pp. 186–198.
Canter, D. and Canter, S. (1971). Close together in Tokyo. *Design and Environment*, 2, 2, pp. 60–63.
Canter, D. (1972). Royal hospital for sick children: a psychological analysis. *The Architects' Journal*, 156, pp. 525–564.
Canter, D. and Lee, K.H. (1974). A non-reactive study of room usage in modern Japanese apartments, in *Psychology and the built environment*, edited by D. Canter and T. Lee Tonbridge. Kent: Architectural Press (pp. 48–55).
Canter, D., Sanchez-Robles, J.C., and Watts, N. (1974). A scale for the cross-cultural evaluation of houses, in *Psychology and the Built Environment*, edited by D. Canter and T. Lee. London: Architectural Press.
Canter, D. (1969). Attitudes and perception in architecture. *Architectural Association Quarterly*, 1(2), pp. 24–31.
Canter, D. (1970). Need for a theory of function in architecture. *The Architects' Journal Information Library*, 4(2), pp. 299–302.
Canter, D. and Wools, R. (1970). The effect of the meaning of building design on behaviour. *Applied Ergonomics*, 1(3), pp. 144–150.

Canter, D. (1997). The facets of place. *Advances in Environment, Behaviour and Design*, 4, 109–147.

Canter, D., Gilchrist, J., Miller, J., and Roberts, N. (1974). An empirical study of the focal point in the living room, in *Psychology and the Built Environment*, edited by D. Canter and T. Lee. London: Architectural Press.

Canter, D., West, S., and Wools, R. (1974). Judgements of people and their rooms. *British Journal of Social and Clinical Psychology*, 13, pp. 113–118.

Canter, D. and Tagg, S.K. (1975). Distance estimation in cities. *Environment and Behaviour*, 7(1), pp. 59–80.

Canter, D. (1988). Action and place: an existential dialectic, in *Environmental Perspectives*, edited by D. Canter, M. Krampen, and D. Stea. Etnoscapes, vol. 1, Avebury, pp. 1–17.

Canter, D. (1975). Building in use, in *Environmental Interaction: Psychological Approach to our Physical Surroundings*, edited by D. Canter, P. Stringer, I. Griffiths, P. Boyce, D. Walters, and C. Kenny. London: Surrey University Press/ New York: International University Press.

Canter, D. and Kenny, C. (1975). The spatial environment, in *Environmental Interaction: Psychological Approach to our Physical Surroundings*, edited by D. Canter, P. Stringer, I. Griffiths, P. Boyce, D. Walters, and C. Kenny. London: Surrey University Press/New York: International University Press.

Canter, D. (1975). An introduction to environmental psychology, in *Environmental Interaction: Psychological Approach to our Physical Surroundings*, edited by D. Canter, P. Stringer, I. Griffiths, P. Boyce, D. Walters, and C. Kenny. London: Surrey University Press/New York: International University Press.

Canter, D. (1975). Contributing to environmental decision making, in *Environmental Interaction: Psychological Approach to our Physical Surroundings*, edited by D. Canter, P. Stringer, I. Griffiths, P. Boyce, D. Walters, and C. Kenny. London: Surrey University Press/New York: International University Press.

Canter, D. (1977). Children in hospital: a facet theory approach to person/place synomorhpy. *Journal of Architectural research*, 6(2), pp. 20–32.

Canter, D. (1977). Why architecture is necessary. *RIBA Journal*, 84, pp. 261–262.

Canter, D. and Scott, M. (1993). Designing a research centre, in *Psychology in Action*, edited by D. Canter. Dartmouth (pp. 255–271).

Canter, D. and Craik, K. (1981). Environmental psychology. *Journal of Environmental Psychology*, 1, pp. 1–11.

Canter, D. and Brown, J. (1981). Explanatory roles, in *The Psychology of Ordinary Explanations of Social Behaviour*, edited by C. Antaki. London: Academic Press (pp. 222–242).

Kenny, C. and Canter, D. (1981). A facet structure for nurses' evaluation of ward designs. *Journal of Occupational Psychology*, 54, pp. 93–108.

Canter, D. and Kenny, C. (1981). The multivariate structure of design evaluation: A cylindrex of nurses' conceptualizations. *Multivariate Behavioral Research*, 16(2), pp. 215–236.

Canter, D. (1982). Psychology and environmental design, in *Psychology in Practice: Perspectives on Professional Psychology*, edited by S. Canter and D. Canter. New York: Wiley (pp. 289–310).

Canter, D. and Rees, K. (1982). A multivariate model of housing satisfaction. *International Review of Applied Psychology*, 31, pp. 185–208.

Canter, D. (1983). The purposive evaluation of places – a facet approach. *Environment and Behavior*, 15(6), 659–698.

Canter, D. (1983). The environmental context of nursing: looking beyond the ward, in *Social Psychology and Nursing*, edited by S. Skevington. Chichester: Wiley.

Canter, D. (1983). Putting situations in their place: foundations for a bridge between social and environmental psychology, in *Social Behaviour in Context*, edited by A. Furnham. Boston: Allyn & Bacon.

Canter, D. (1984). Beyond building utilization, in *Designing for Building Utilisation*, edited by J.A. Powell, I. Cooper, and S. Lera. London: E & FN Spon (pp. 41–47).

Canter, D. (1984). Vandalism: overview and prospect, in *Vandalism, Behaviour and Motivations*, edited by C. Lévy-Leboyer. New York: Elsevier Science Publishers (pp. 345–356).

Canter, D. (1984). Way-finding and signposting: penance or prosthesis, in *Information Design*, edited by Easterby and Zwaga. New York: Wiley (pp. 245–264).

Canter, D. (1987). Implications for new generation prisons of existing psychological research into prison design and use, in *Problems of Long-term Imprisonment*, edited by A. Bottoms and R. Light. Aldershot: Gower.

Canter, D. (1991). Understanding, assessing, and acting in places: is an integrative framework possible? in *Environment, Cognition, and Action*, edited by T. Garling and G. Evans. New York: Oxford University Press (pp. 191–209).

Canter, D. (2000). Seven assumptions for an investigative environmental psychology, in *Theoretical Perspectives in Environmental Behaviour Research: Underlying Assumptions, Research Problems and Methodologies*, edited by S. Wapner, J. Dmick, T. Yamamoto, and H. Minami. New York: Plenum (pp. 191–206).

Canter, D. (2008). Do we need a metatheory of the built environment? *Building Research and Information*, 36(6), pp. 663–667.

## Organisational Psychology

Canter, D. and Miles, H. (1976). Motivation, not science, is clue to saving energy. *The Times Higher Education Supplement*, p. 10.

Canter, D. (1984). From knobs and dials to knowledge. *Design*, August, pp. 31–33.

Canter, D. and Cooper, A. (1988). Design context and nursing roles, in *Stress and Organisational Problems in Hospitals*, edited by D. Wallis and C.J. De Wolff. London: Croom Helm (pp. 157–173).

Canter, D.V. and Donald, I. (1990). Temporal and trait facets of personnel assessment. *Applied Psychology: An International Review*, 39(4), pp. 413–429.

Canter, D. (2003). A tale of two cultures: a comparison of the cultures of the police and academia, in *Policing a Safe, Just and Tolerant Society. An International Model*, edited by Villiers, P. and R. Adlam.

### Human Behaviour and Emergencies

Canter, D., Breaux, J., and Sime, J. (1980). Domestic, multiple occupancy and Hospital fires, in *Fires and Human Behaviour*, edited by D. Canter. New York: Wiley (pp. 117–136).

Canter, Professor Canter. (1980). An overview of human behavior in fires, in *Fires and Human Behavior*, edited by D. Canter. New York: Wiley (pp. 205–234).

Canter, D., Donald, I., and Chalk, J. (1992). Pedestrian behaviour during emergencies underground: the psychology of crowd control under life threatening circumstances, in *Safety in Road and Rail Tunnels*, edited by A.E. Vardy. Kempston: ITC (pp. 135–150).

Canter, D. (1980). Fire and human behaviour: emerging issues. *Fire Safety Journal*, 3, pp. 41–46.

Canter, D. and Tagg, S. (1980). The empirical classification of building aspects and their attributes, in *Meaning and Behaviour in the Built Environment*, edited by G. Broadbent, R. Bunt, and T. Llorens. New York: Wiley (pp. 1–19).

Canter, D. and Powell, J. (1986). The management factor technique as an aid to decision-making by industrial safety management, in *Human Decision Making and Manual Control*, edited by H.P. Willumeit. Holland: Elsevier Science Publisher (pp. 289–298).

Canter, D. (1990). An overview of human behavior in fires, in *Fires and Human Behaviour: Second Edition*, edited by D. Canter. Fulton: London. (pp. 205–234).

### Criminal/Forensic/Investigative Psychology

Canter, D. (1988). To catch a rapist. *New Society*, 4 March, pp. 14–15.

Canter, D. (1989). Offender profiles. *The Psychologist*, 2(1), 12–16.

Canter, D. and Heritage, R. (1990). A multivariate model of sexual behaviour: developments in offender profiling 1. *The Journal of Forensic Psychiatry*, 1(2), pp. 185–212.

Canter, D and Larkin, P. (1993). The environmental range of serial rapists. *Journal of Environmental Psychology*, 13(1).

Canter, D.V. and Gregory, A. (1993). Identying the residential location of rapists. To be published in the *Journal of the Forensic Science Society*.

Canter, D. (1992). An evaluation of the 'cusum' stylistic analysis of confessions. *Expert Evidence*, 1(2), pp. 93–99.

Canter, D., Missen, C., and Hodge, S. (1996). Are serial killers special. A case for special agents. *Policing Today*, 2(1).

Canter, D. (1997). Beyond profiling psychology and the investigative process. *Forensic Update*, 48, pp. 29–31.

Canter, D. and Fritzon, K. (1998). Differentiating arsonists: a model of fire setting actions and characteristics. *Legal and Criminal Psychology*, 3, 73–96.

Canter, D. (1998). Profiling as poison. *Inter-alia*, 2(1), pp. 10–11.

Canter, D. and Hodge, S. (1998). Victims and perpetrators of male sexual assault. *Journal of Interpersonal Violence*, 13(2), pp. 222–239.

Canter, D., Hughes, D., and Kirby, S. (1998). Paedophilia: pathology, criminality, or both? The development of a multivariate model of offence behaviour in child sexual abuse. *The Journal of Forensic Psychiatry*, 9(3), pp. 532–555.

Canter, D. (1999). Equivocal death, in *Offender Profiling Series II – Profiling in Policy and Practice*, edited by D. Canter and L. Alison. Aldershot: Ashgate (pp. 123–156).

Canter, D. (2000). Offender profiling and criminal differentiation. *Legal and Criminological Psychology*, 5, pp. 23–46.

Canter, D., Coffey, T., Huntley, M., and Missen, C. (2000). Predicting serial killers' home base using a decision support system. *Journal of Quantitative Criminology*, 16(4), pp. 457–478.

Canter, D. and Hodge, S. (2000). Criminals' mental maps, in *Atlas of Crime: Mapping the Criminal Landscape*, edited by L.S. Turnball, E.H. Hendrix, and B.D. Dent. Phoenix AZ: Oryz Press (pp. 184–191).

Canter, D. and Kremer, M. (2000). Psychological autops, in *The Pathology of Trauma*, edited by K. Mason. London: Arnold.

Canter, D. and Youngs, D. (2002). Offender profiling: the need for an investigative psychology, in *Handbook of Legal Contexts*, edited by R. Bull and D. Carson. Wiley & Sons.

Canter, D. (2002). The violated body, in *The Body*, edited by S.T. Sweeney and I. Hodder. Cambridge University Press.

Canter, D. and Youngs, D. (2003). Beyond 'offender profiling': the need for an investigative psychology, in *Handbook of Psychology in Legal Contexts, Second Edition*, edited by D. Carson and R. Bull. John Wiley & Sons Ltd. (pp. 171–205).

Canter, D., Grieve, N., Nicol, C., and Benneworth, K. (2003). Narrative plausibility: the impact of sequence and anchoring. *Behavioral Sciences and the Law*, 21, pp. 251–267.

Canter, D., Kaouri, C., and Ioannou, M. (2003). The facet structure of criminal narratives, in *Facet Theory: Towards Cumulative Social Science*, edited by S. Levy and D. Elizur (pp. 27–38).

Canter, D., Bennell, C., Alison, L., and Reddy, S. (2003). Differentiating sex offences: a behaviourally based thematic classification of stranger rapes behavioural. *Sciences and the Law*, 21, pp. 157–174.

Canter, D. (2004). Geographical profiling of criminals. *Medico-Legal Journal*, 72(2), pp. 53–66. EMIS.

Canter, D. (2004). Offender profiling and investigative psychology. *Journal of Investigative Psychology and Offender Profiling*, 1, pp. 1–15.

Canter, D.V., Alison, A.J., Alison, E., and Wentink, N. (2004). The organanized/disorganized typologies of serial murder: myth or model? *Psychology, Public Policy and Law*, 10(3), pp. 7–36.

Canter, D., Giles, S., and Nicol, C. (2004). Suicide without explicit precursors: a state of secret despair? *Journal of Investigative Psychology and Offender Profiling*, 1(3), pp. 227–248.

Canter, D. and Ioannou, M. (2004). A multivariate model of Stalking behaviours. *Behaviormetrika*, 31(2), pp. 1–18.

Canter, D.V. and Ioannou, M. (2004). Criminals' emotional experiences during crimes. *International Journal of Forensic Psychology*, 1(2), pp. 71–81.

Canter, D. and Wentink, N. (2004). An empirical test of Holmes and Holmes's serial murder typology. *Criminal Justice and Behavior*, 20(10), pp. 1–26.

Canter, D. (2005). Confusing operational predicaments and cognitive explorations: comments on Rossmo and Snook et al. *Applied Cognitive Psychology*, 19(5), pp. 663–668.

Canter, D. and Hammond, L. (2006). A comparison of the efficacy of different decay functions in geographical profiling for a sample of US serial killers. *Journal of Investigative Psychology and Offender Profiling*, 3, pp. 91–103.

Canter, D. and Hammond, L. (2007). Prioritizing burglars: comparing the effectiveness of geographical profiling methods. *Police Practice and Research*, 8(4), pp. 371–384.

Canter, D. (2009). Developments in geographical offender profiling: commentary on the special issue of JIP-OP dealing with the Bayesian approach to geographical offender profiling. *Journal of Investigative Psychology and Offender Profiling*, 6(3), pp. 161–166.

Canter, Professor Canter V. (2010). The multi-faceted nature of terrorism: an Introduction, in *The Faces of Terrorism: Multidiscplinary Perspectives*, edited by D. Canter. Wiley-Blackwell (pp. 1–19).

Canter, Professor Canter V. and Sarangi, S. (2010). The rhetorical foundation of militant jihad, in *The Faces of Terrorism: Multidiscplinary Perspectives*, edited by D. Canter. Wiley-Blackwell (pp. 35–61).

Youngs, D. and Canter, D. (2011). Narrative roles in criminal action: an integrative framework for differentiating offenders, *Legal and Criminological Psychology*, pp. 1–17.

Youngs, D. and Canter, D. (2011). Offenders' crime narratives as revealed by the narrative roles questionnaire (NRQ). *International Journal of Offender Therapy and Comparative Criminology*, pp. 1–23.

Canter, D. and Youngs, D. (in press).Victim role assignments in violent crime: a general model of offending style. *Journal of Forensic Psychiatry and Psychology*.

Canter, D. and Youngs, D. (2012). Applications of narratives of criminal action to forensic psychology: responding to Ward. *Legal and Criminological Psychology*.

# Index